Slavery and Crime in Missouri, 1773–1865

Slavery and Crime in Missouri, 1773–1865

HARRIET C. FRAZIER

McFarland & Company, Inc., Publishers
Jefferson, North Carolina, and London

Library of Congress Cataloguing-in-Publication Data

Frazier, Harriet C.
  Slavery and crime in Missouri, 1773–1865 / Harriet C. Frazier
    p.   cm.
  Includes bibliographic references and index.
  ISBN 0-7864-0977-0 (library binding : 50# alkaline paper) ∞
    1. Crime — Missouri — History.   2. Slaves — Missouri — Crimes
against — History.   3. African American criminals — Missouri —
History.   4. Criminal justice, Administration of — Missouri —
History.   I. Title.
  HV6793.M8 F738 2001
  364.9762 — dc21   2001030381

British Library Cataloguing data are available

Manufactured in the United States of America

McFarland & Company, Inc., Publishers
  Box 611, Jefferson, North Carolina 28640
    www.mcfarlandpub.com

Acknowledgments

In the mid-1980s I was doing research on the death penalty. In 1989 that research narrowed to Missouri's death penalty. That year, and at my request, Central Missouri State University (CMSU), Warrensburg, Mo., purchased the Missouri files of Watt Espy, Capital Punishment Resource Project, Headland, Ala. From these accounts of many of those lawfully put to death in Missouri, my research for this book began. In 1993, also at my request, the CMSU library purchased a multireeled microfilm edition of *The Register of Inmates, Missouri State Penitentiary, 1836–1931*, allowing my research to progress.

I thank CMSU for two funded leaves, spring 1989 and spring 1996, and a course reduction in my teaching in spring 1993. I used the first leave to learn about Missouri's death penalty and the second to research this book and begin its writing.

I thank the National Endowment for the Humanities for a Travel to Collections Grant, summer 1993, which facilitated several of my many trips to the Missouri State Historical Society in Columbia, Mo.

I gratefully acknowledge the following CMSU librarians for their assistance: Nancy Littlejohn, who, among much else, ordered the Espy files and the prison records; Joyce Larson, who introduced me to the library's microfilm collection of pre–Civil War Missouri newspapers; Pat Downing and Lori Fitterling, who located and ordered extensive material that I obtained through interlibrary loan; Doris Brookshier and Wanda Moore, who managed the library's Special Collection of Missouri materials; and Linda Medaris and Naomi Williamson, for their general assistance. I also thank Ann Garner and Kevin Cooney, graduate students in 1994–95 in my department (Criminal Justice), for their research assistance.

Sue Cunningham, then a librarian working on the Missouri newspaper project at the Missouri State Historical Society, Columbia, Mo., and other staff members deserve thanks for their help with that fabulous newspaper collection. Laurel Boechman and Marie Concannon of this same society are also due thanks for their assistance with Missouri county histories and other relevant holdings.

The Western Missouri Manuscript Collection, Ellis Library, University of Missouri, Columbia, houses court records from Spanish rule of Missouri. I thank those who administer the collection for the use of those records.

Christel Webb traveled with me on several trips to Columbia. She was both a diligent researcher and a fine companion.

Coralee Paul ferreted out the noncapital slave cases from territorial St. Louis, which are housed at the Missouri Historical Society in St. Louis. She located important letters, journal entries, and all reports of coroners' inquests under American rule. Her diligence and knowledge were crucial to this book.

Annette Curtis, a specialist in slave genealogy, Mid-Continent Public Library, Independence, Mo., was a constant source of assistance and insight. Annette's colleagues, Janice Schultz and Darlene Nyhart, also offered their courtesy, assistance, and resourcefulness regarding my project. I am grateful for the contributions of all these women.

At the Kansas City Public Library, Kansas City, Mo., I thank: Brenda Hunnicutt for her interlibrary loan ordering of microfilm of many newspapers; the staff of the Missouri Valley Room, especially Rose Huffman, Stewart Hinds, and Sara Nyman; Heather Davis, who located plaques about Annice I; and Dennis Halbin, Judy Klamm, and Scott Sjolin, all reference librarians, who imaginatively and diligently answered my numerous queries.

My thanks also go to the director of the University of Missouri–Kansas City Law School Library, Patricia Harris O'Connor, for her support, courtesy, and encouragement; and to that library's reference librarian, Lawrence Maclachlan, who provided superb conversation and invaluable aid in whatever form it was needed, from accessing information stored in computers to going through old books with me page by page in a search for whatever I needed to confirm or deny.

Constantly interspersed with my time in libraries were conversations about race relations, including slavery, with my friend Norman Smith as he and I walked my dogs in Loose Park, Kansas City. As a child in Holly

Grove, Monroe County, Ark., Norman knew Calvin Mayo, born in the 1830s, and Calvin's son-in-law, Amos Brown, born in the 1850s. He listened to and remembered what these old men related of their firsthand experiences as bondpersons. Norman told me what former slaves Calvin and Amos told him. Their memories inform this book.

I thank the following for providing me with multipaged copies of their counties' criminal records pertaining to slavery: clerks of the circuit courts Earl Davis, Callaway County; Jerry P. Sampson, Marion County; Charles P. Hutson, Cape Girardeau County, and its local archivist Caroline Beggs; the staffs of the clerks of the circuit courts of Clay and Crawford Counties; and the Arrow Rock State Historic Site, Saline County.

Betty Harvey Williams, Warrensburg, Mo., member and former chair of the Governor's Task Force on Local Records, personally checked records for me at several courthouses, and she generously shared her research with me, including her work on Clay County probate records. She gave me copies of all her reference guides to Missouri newspapers on microfilm, and she put me in touch with Coralee Paul. Betty is acknowledged for all of this and a great deal more.

Shelly J. Croteau and Patricia M. Luebbert, archivists at the Missouri State Archives, Jefferson City, are due my thanks. They provided me copies of a Washington County probate file, the known territorial capital case with a slave defendant, and all extant pardon papers pertaining to slaves. They often knew the answers to my obscure queries, and they always cheerfully, promptly, and accurately found the answers to those they did not know.

The staff of the Family History Center, Church of Jesus Christ of Latter-Day Saints, Independence, Mo., obtained microfilm of difficult-to-locate criminal records pertaining to slavery in Missouri. These volunteers are thanked for their helpfulness, never-failing courtesy, and warmth.

I would also like to thank the staffs of the law school libraries of Indiana University, Bloomington; the University of South Carolina; and the University of Virginia, as well as the Library of the Supreme Court of Arkansas and the Illinois State Historical Library, Springfield, Ill., for providing me with early statutory law.

Other facilities whose materials were important for this book include the Mark Twain Project, University of California, Berkeley; the Kansas University Medical School Library and the Kansas University History of Medicine Library, both in Kansas City, Kans.; the Medical School and the Miller Nichol Libraries, University of Missouri-Kansas City; the University of Missouri-Columbia Law School Library; and Washington University Library, St. Louis, Mo. My thanks to their staffs for their help.

Others who assisted me include Helen Beedle, Cheryl Brugger, Cheryl Burbach, Nancy Cridland, Bill Davilla, Greg Field, Jeannine Gerhardt, Andy Hannas, Ann Justus, Bobbi McConnell, Dorothy McKinley, Annette Morgan, Nancy Morgan, Evelyn Moore, Harry Penner, Willard Rand, Jeanne Williams, and Tim Van Zandt.

Finally, I am especially grateful to Tom Fairclough, Wichita Falls, Texas, for reading anything I wanted read from 1960 until the present, including successive drafts of this book, and always with amazing accuracy, knowledge, good cheer, and friendship.

Contents

List of Illustrations

Missouri Counties in 1860. The Missouri River flows south from extreme northwestern Missouri to northern Jackson and then east to St. Louis. To its north are Clay, Ray, Carroll, Chariton, Howard, Boone, Callaway, Montgomery, Warren, and St. Charles; to its south are Jackson, Lafayette, Saline, Cooper, Moniteau, Cole, Osage, Gasconade, Franklin, and St. Louis. The Mississippi River runs south and immediately east of Clark to Pemiscot. The Missouri River joins the Mississippi in St. Louis County. Based on a map in *A History of Missouri for High Schools*, 1944.

Preface

Though I have lived in Missouri many years, I am not a native. I was born and raised on the east bank of the Ohio River in Wheeling, West Virginia. On the west side of this river was the state of Ohio. My father came from western Pennsylvania, a free state, 20 miles east of Wheeling, and my mother from a place of slavery. Her mother, my maternal grandmother, was born in the same farmhouse, the Casey Place, and all her children, including my mother, on the same farm as Mark Twain's mother, in Adair County, Kentucky. My mother's home was 427 miles southwest of Wheeling. Though there was frequent contact with the Pennsylvania relatives, I spent every summer from my beginnings through my 14th year in Kentucky. That childhood experience on a family farm helped make this book possible.

West Virginia was a segregated state when I lived in it, and Kentucky, like Missouri, was a former border slave state. It was impossible in such settings to avoid the sickness of racism. However, it is not a fatal illness if one can only acknowledge, as a wise friend once remarked, "We are all at best recovering racists." This disease infects Caucasians, Asians, American Indians, African Americans, and every racial mixture.

I taught American and English literature in various universities for 12 years. Afterward, as an attorney licensed in Missouri, I taught law for 22 years in the Criminal Justice Department, Central Missouri State University, Warrensburg, Mo. When I retired in 1997, I devoted my full energies to this book.

The word *slavocracy* occurs throughout my narrative. Although by its construction the word might be construed to mean "rule by slaves," it actually means "rule by slave owners." Its earliest uses were in free-state newspapers in the 1840s.

This book makes only passing reference to runaways. Unlike most slave states, under Missouri law the bondperson did not commit a crime when he fled from the service of his master. As a result, without other charges he or she was neither a defendant in a criminal proceeding nor entitled to an attorney, a trial, or most any other aspect of due process when the master reclaimed his human "property."

All cases discussed herein involve one or more persons of color; these include American Indians, African Americans, and mulattos. A few were free, but most were enslaved. Their stories are told in 14 chapters.

Chapter 1, "Spanish Colonial Administration," traces Spanish rule of Missouri from its start in the 1760s, through the first known criminal records in 1773, involving American Indian slaves, through the transfer of the Purchase from Spain to France. The governor-general and his courts in New Orleans decided all Missouri lawbreaking of any importance, including death penalty crimes.

Chapter 2, "Early American Rule," describes the mix of laws applicable to Missouri's slaves after the United States bought the area from France. During the territorial period, 1804 to 1821, bondpersons were governed by the following: Virginia's slave code, including its death penalty statutes for bondpersons who prepared, exhibited, or administered any medicine, chiefly arsenic; the laws of the Northwest Territory; federal statutes, such as one that allowed the additional punishment of dissection for condemned felons; and the Bill of Rights to the U.S. Constitution.

Chapter 3, "Noncapital Territorial Wrongdoing," looks at a number of court records, principally from St. Louis. Most concern slaves' stealing and burglary with intent to steal. The stolen items range from a goose of unspecified value through beaver pelts worth $1,500 ($150,000 in today's money).

Chapter 4, "Slave Elijah's 1818 Trial on a Charge of Conspiracy," is Missouri's only extant territorial death penalty case with a black defendant. The accused admitted that he put arsenic in his mistress's sausage. The government alleged that other slaves were co-conspirators in the crime. Elijah's defense attorney was David Barton, one of Missouri's most capable lawyers, later president of Missouri's Constitutional Convention and one of its first two U.S. senators.

Chapter 5, "The 1820 Missouri Constitution and Its Background," compares Missouri's law with that of other slave states. In most slave jurisdictions, the state paid the owner the slave's appraised value when it executed his bondperson(s); under American rule of Missouri there was never owner compensation when the sheriff hanged those in bondage. Virginia compensated owners of the condemned, and its laws included 73 death penalty crimes for slaves. After Missouri's first constitutional convention created this state's constitution, it punished only one crime with death: murder. Members of the convention included David Barton and Edward Bates, later a slave woman's attorney and still later Abraham Lincoln's attorney general. They and other convention delegates were influential public figures during territorial days, and they wrote into Missouri's constitution most of the same protections for the accused that federal statutory and constitutional law had required during the earlier territorial period.

Chapter 6, "Costs in Criminal Cases," catalogues the many expenses that slave owners assumed when those in bondage were successfully prosecuted for noncapital offenses. In capital cases the government footed the bill, but one sheriff believed that his fee for the proper hanging of two indigents, including one slave, was inadequate, and he sued the county court.

Chapter 7, "Against Themselves: Black-on-Black Crime," brings together multiple instances of slave suicide and black-on-black violence. Adult male slaves—usually owned by different masters—sometimes beat or murdered one another, and their cases became matters of court record and contemporary newspaper coverage. These documents make clear that the death penalty was rarely used with black-on-black murder. When assaultive bondsmen shared the same owner, his required payment of court costs minimized the intervention of any court: the matter was handled in-house. The victims of slave women were often their own infants and small children. One governor pardoned a 15-year-old who killed her newborn before she either pled guilty or her trial began. Hers is the only known pretrial pardon for murder in Missouri's history.

Chapter 8, "White Perpetrators, Black and Mulatto Victims," examines white brutality against persons of color. Though whites terrorized slave men, the more frequent object of white male sadism was the black female. The batterers were not on the fringes of society; often they were prominent. One, a major in the U.S. Army at the time he beat his slave woman to death because he believed that she had hidden misplaced keys, was subsequently promoted four times and achieved the rank of major general.

Chapter 9, "Noncapital Statehood Crime: White and Black," surveys liquor violations; business dealings with slaves without their owners' permission; slave use of insulting language to white persons; stealing, burglary, mutilation, and death of farm animals; arson; and attempted murder. Principally whites were prosecuted for the sale of alcohol to slaves and additional forbidden commercial transactions with bondpersons; slaves were the alleged perpetrators in this chapter's other offenses.

Chapter 10, "Capital Cases: Girls and Women," gathers together all of Missouri's extant death penalty crimes involving black females during the antebellum period. All were slaves. One was the youngest known person executed in Missouri's history; another, defended by Edward Bates, was wrongfully convicted but given a new trial; and in the most notorious proceeding, the defendant, a 19-year-old victim of longstanding sexual assault, went on trial for her life because she used deadly force against her owner-rapist.

Chapter 11, "Capital Crimes by Coerced Boys and Men," compares the high numbers of capitally punished bondpersons in jurisdictions wherein owners were compensated when the state executed their human property with the much smaller number of Missouri's executed slaves. It discusses every known male slave whom Missouri sentenced to death because he killed a person with power over him. All murdered one of the following: a master, lessee, overseer, slave trader, or master's wife. Most of these killings occurred in the state's interior counties. In counties that bordered places of freedom, namely Illinois and Kansas, it appears likely that slaves ran to freedom rather than taking the lives of those who coerced them.

Chapter 12, "Capital Crimes by Wandering Boys and Men," discusses male slaves tried for the murder of persons without power over them. It includes one slave's murder of another, several killings incident to robbery or to rape, the youngest known person sentenced to death in Missouri's history, the last slave trial for murder in the late–Civil War period, and a case that arose in Mark Twain's home county when he was a boy.

Chapter 13, "Rape: The Crime, Its Punishment, and Its Pardons," distinguishes Missouri from every other place wherein human bondage existed throughout much of the Civil War. In all other slave jurisdictions the black man's rape of a white woman was punished by death. In Missouri all convicted rapists, without regard to race, were punishable by castration, not death, from 1808 until the legislature decreed in 1835 that whites convicted of rape be sent to the newly built state penitentiary. It began receiving inmates in 1836. Colored males, either slave or free, who either raped or attempted to rape a white female continued to be subject to castration throughout Missouri's slavery period. No court record was ever located that documented the carrying out of castration. Probably, owners customarily sold their bondsmen who may have been convicted of a lesser offense, such as assault. The whole slave was a far more valuable property than one who had been dismembered pursuant to court order. Two governors pardoned bondsmen convicted of the rape of a white female, one in 1849 and the other in 1854. The latter pardon took place after the Supreme Court of Missouri upheld the slave's sentence of castration.

Chapter 14, "Antebellum Lynching of Blacks, Slave and Free," challenges the assumption that slavery protected slaves from vigilante violence. In states that compensated owners when the sheriff executed their properties, slave lynchings were probably rare, but in Missouri's antebellum period, mobs put to death a few free black males and at least 17 slave men and two slave women. All were believed guilty of a serious crime. Some were burned to death; one *auto-da-fé* in St. Louis in 1836 was especially well documented. So frequently did the extralegal killing of slaves occur that in 1855 the legislature changed the law to allow the collection of court fees, whether or not the sheriff officially hanged the bondperson. In one county, bills of costs are extant for three slaves charged or convicted in unrelated crimes in 1859; they were lynched on the same day in broad daylight in the county seat.

My primary sources for this book are handwritten court records. A few are surprisingly complete; most are not, and whenever possible, contemporary newspapers are used to flesh out the many stories contained in these court records. When newspapers are not available, the often less accurate county histories may have been the only sources. I use them. In one early case under American rule all that survives of what was probably the hanging of a slave woman is a letter. I cite it. However, there is always some factual basis for any of my speculations. I could never confirm either death sentences for slaves or their lynchings in the Missouri county of which I am a long-term resident, Jackson. Perhaps other researchers will discover them; I did not.

Throughout I emphasize which crimes featured slave men and women. Sexual differences were often important factors in crimes involving those in bondage. Did the crimes concerning bondpersons *always* take place because of slavery? Probably not. At times the criminal act is unimaginable without it. At others the role of bondage in the lawbreaking is less clear. This narrative contains no theory that ascribes *all* criminal acts involving slaves to involuntary servitude.

I never located any court costs that were fees for criminal defense attorneys for their representation of slaves. At times an interested white probably paid them, but it appears that most legal work on behalf of those in bondage was free of charge or pro bono. Most likely, some lawyers who defended Missouri's slaves slept during their trials, were alcohol impaired, or were preoccupied with extraneous matters. However, ineffectual assistance of counsel for slaves accused of major felonies here appears to have been the exception, not the rule. Commonly, those who defended slaves on serious charges were the state's finest lawyers. A hero of the Mexican War, two U.S. senators, a presidential cabinet officer, members of both the Missouri General Assembly and the U.S. Congress, several circuit court judges, and several governors defended slaves accused of murder and rape. Most were lawyers for slaves early in their careers, but not all. One of the most zealous defenses came late in the career of a former speaker of the Missouri House and former three-term member of the U.S. Congress. Further, he represented two, a young woman and a boy, on unrelated charges of murder in different trials. I believe that he helped his death-sentenced clients escape from jail, in one case, to permanent freedom either out of state or out of the country.

Finally, my purpose in writing this book is the same as that of the Polish-born English novelist Joseph Conrad in his work, which he saw as "a single-minded attempt to render the highest kind of justice to the visible universe, by bringing to light the truth." He defined his task as "by the power of the written word to make you hear, to make you feel — it is before all, to make you see." These are my intentions in the pages that follow.

Chapter 1

Spanish Colonial Administration

Missouri differed from most American places of slavery. Excluding Texas, a portion of Missouri jutted farther west than any other slave state. It extended farther north than any other jurisdiction in the United States wherein the law, in effect from its eighteenth-century French settlement until the last year of the Civil War, permitted one human being to own another. Its northern exposure made most of its climate unsuitable for crops such as cotton, rice, and sugar, which lent themselves especially well to cultivation by large numbers of slaves. As Trexler noted, "the great plantation with its white overseer and gangs of driven blacks was comparatively uncommon.... Missouri was a state of small slaveholdings."[1]

As early as 1784, when Missouri belonged to Spain, legislation of the Continental Congress, written by Thomas Jefferson, which would have prohibited slavery after 1800 in *all* the western territories, failed to achieve the necessary votes to become law.[2] If this bill had passed, slavery would have been forbidden in two of Missouri's neighboring states, Kentucky and Tennessee, before Spain in 1803 completed its transfer of the Louisiana Territory to France. In 1787 Congress passed the Northwest Ordinance, and it excluded involuntary servitude, except as punishment for crime, from a vast expanse of land, including the present states of Ohio, Indiana, and Illinois. Had Jefferson's 1784 proposal become law, there would have been no legalized slavery in Missouri after France sold the area to the United States in 1803. As it turned out, Kentucky, Tennessee, and Missouri all joined the Union as slave states. However, there was a major difference between Missouri and Tennessee. Though both were bordered by eight other jurisdictions, only other slaveholding states surrounded Tennessee. In sharp contrast, to Missouri's east was Illinois, to its north Iowa, to its northwest Nebraska, and to its west Kansas, or 75 percent of this state adjoined free territories, which in due course became free states.

The French introduced the institution to Missouri in 1720 when the Frenchman Philip François Renault stopped in San Domingo (Haiti), then a French colony, where he purchased bondpersons to work in the lead mines of the southeastern part of the state.[3] In 1724 the French king, Louis XV, issued an "Edict Concerning the Negro Slaves in Louisiana," usually known as the "Black Code." It was published in New Orleans; contained a number of provisions that guaranteed slaveholders' rights in their property; protected whites from slave conspiracy, rebellion, and insurrection; and regulated the religion of slaves by requiring their instruction and baptism into Catholicism. Spain never repealed this code, and it continued to govern the lives of slaves during the Spanish regime in Missouri.[4]

Because no records of slave crime survive from the French governance of Missouri, this narrative begins after France transferred what is now Missouri to Spain. The start of the transfer occurred when France and Spain were signatories to a secret treaty at Fontainebleau, France, in 1762. Its terms were made public in 1763, when Great Britain, France, and Spain signed the Treaty of Paris, which ended the Seven Years' War in Europe, a conflict known in America as the French and Indian Wars. Under this treaty France lost her North American possessions east of the Mississippi River to England, including Illinois (originally a slave colony and territory, eventually a free state), and west of this river to Spain, including Arkansas, Louisiana, and Missouri (all slave colonies, territories, and states).

With the arrival of the first Spanish governor in New Orleans in 1766, Spain reluctantly assumed control of the Louisiana Territory, then almost entirely an immense wilderness. Most of its residents were French. As March observed, "although Spain controlled the territory for more than thirty years, hardly more than a handful of Spaniards settled there. Even the Spanish soldiers who had been sent up the river from New Orleans, left when their tours of duty were finished."[5] The population of the entire region was approximately 7,500 when Spanish rule began and 50,000 when it ended in 1803.[6] Because colonial Spain neither prohibited nor discouraged human bondage, after the passage of the Northwest Ordinance in 1787, which excluded slavery north of the Ohio River, the migration of American settlers and their slaves to Missouri increased. In 1803 Spain retroceded the territory to France, and in 1804 the United States acquired this land from the French under the terms of the Louisiana Purchase. By the year of the Purchase, Americans made up more than 50 percent of the total population of 10,350, including 1500 slaves, who resided in Upper Louisiana.[7]

The earliest extant criminal cases in Missouri involving slaves as either perpetrators, victims, witnesses, or stolen property occurred under Spain's rule. This country owned and governed Missouri, also known as Upper Louisiana, also known as Spanish Illinois, from 1766 until 1800. By the Treaty of San Ildefonso, signed October 1, 1800, the entire Louisiana Territory was returned to France, then under the stewardship of Napoleon Bonaparte. He postponed occupation of his North American acquisition until, among other matters, he made peace with England, was proclaimed consul for life in France, and resumed war with England. In the interlude Spain continued to govern the Louisiana Territory until the actual transfer of power from the Spanish to the French in New Orleans on November 30, 1803.

The Spanish ruled what was eventually to become 13 states, including three that joined the Union as slave states, by continuing the 1720 or 1721 French division of Louisiana Territory into immense districts. The original nine that France created included the Illinois, an area both east and west of the Mississippi River between the Ohio River and the Great Lakes. Spain eventually created five additional districts from that portion of the Illinois that it acquired under the terms of the Treaty of Paris, the land west of the Mississippi, or Missouri. Its earliest settlements, later Spanish districts, were founded in the following order: Ste. Genevieve (1750), St. Louis (1764), St. Charles (1765), New Madrid (the winter of 1786–87), and Cape Girardeau (1793). So vast were these Spanish divisions of Missouri that New Madrid District included most of the present state of Arkansas. Spain governed all parts of its enormous domain by combining civil, military, and judicial affairs. In Missouri its highest ranking resident was a lieutenant governor who lived in St. Louis. In each of the larger villages, such as Ste. Genevieve, St. Charles, New Madrid, and Cape Girardeau, the Spanish continued the French arrangement, which dated from 1731, of combining civil and military authority in a commandant.[8] As Davis explains Spanish rule, "District government was in charge of a *Commandant,* a combination military, administrative, and judicial official who also acted as Indian agent. He registered titles to land, witnessed contracts, performed marriage ceremonies, took inventories of property, acted as sheriff of his district, and judged all cases involving not more than $20."[9]

During the Spanish ownership of Louisiana Territory, all its officials were appointed. There were neither elections nor jury trials. It was only under authority headquartered in New Orleans that civil suits that exceeded $20 in damages could be decided. In criminal matters the commandant could decide the matter, as Arnold notes, "only if the criminal cause was quite light."[10] Specifically, there was no authority in any one of Upper Louisiana's five districts either to try a capital case or to sentence any person to death. The few potentially capital cases that have survived from Spanish control of Missouri were sent to New Orleans for disposition. The governor-general of the entire Louisiana Territory was headquartered there. He received the written statements from his commandants and referred cases to various courts. In serious criminal cases the commandant's duties were to investigate by taking depositions of witnesses, keep the potential defendant(s) under guard, inventory his possessions, send a report to the governor-general in New Orleans, and await his instructions.[11] In capital cases, the governor-general secured the permission of the captain-general in Cuba before pronouncing any death sentence(s). In Spain's highly centralized organization of her colonies, Spanish Louisiana was subordinate in both military and political matters to the command of the captain-general in Cuba.

However, as Kerr observes, the power of the governor-general in New Orleans "was practically supreme. He represented the person of the King."[12] To assist him Spanish authorities established seven courts, only three of which received cases involving slaves from post commandants in remote areas such as Missouri: the governor's civil and criminal court, the mayor's court (*alcaldes ordinarios*), and the governor's military court. The first of these, the governor's civil and criminal court, was the appellate court for criminal appeals from the alcaldes' courts and the majority of cases that post commandants investigated and the trial court for any criminal case the governor deemed worthy of his attention. The second category, the *alcaldes ordinarios*, were criminal trial courts for offenses that ranged from petty through capital, and they also functioned as appellate courts for minor cases decided by post commandants. Clearly, the governor's civil and criminal court and the *alcaldes ordinarios* court heard similar cases, and whether a case was heard by one court or another, or both, was chiefly the decision of the governor. As Kerr notes, "Much of the division of cases depended on the governor's desire to make an example of an offender or his availability to handle the court."[13] Finally, the governor's military court heard court martials of military persons as well as nonmilitary cases for all entitled to a military privilege or trial. Because the records of the governor's military court were returned to Spain, little evidence of crimes committed by Spanish military personnel remains in the United States other than the names of offenders, their victims, and their crimes.[14]

One important legal and theological institution never gained a foothold during Spain's tenure as a North American colonial power. There was no Inquisition. In April 1790 Governor-General Miro had a zealous Capuchin, who was attempting to bring the Inquisition to Louisiana Territory, arrested and returned to Spain. Miro gave his reason in his official dispatch to the Spanish government: "His Majesty has ordered that I should foster an increase of population.... The mere name of the Inquisition uttered in New Orleans ... would not only suffice to restrain the emigration, which is already beginning to take place, but might also cause those who have recently arrived to retire."[15] Despite its absence, the official religion under the Spanish throughout colonial Louisiana was Catholicism, and Jews were excluded.[16]

The implementation of Spanish law began in 1769, shortly after the arrival of Governor-General Alejandro O'Reilly, an Irishman in the employ of the Spanish government. He promulgated a number of substantive and procedural ordinances and instructions for the governance of the Louisiana Territory. These included crimes for which slaves were prosecuted: (1) "insurrection against the King or the state ... shall be punished with death"; (2) "whoever shall outrage another either by wounds, cuffs, or blows ... shall be punished as the judge may think suitable"; (3) "robberies ... shall be punished corporally according to the nature of the same, and the rank of the person"; (4) "he who shall ravish [rape] a girl, a married woman, or a widow of reputable character, shall suffer death"; and (5) "he who shall commit wilful murder ... shall suffer death."[17] Insofar as there are preserved records involving slaves and crime from Spanish rule of this state, they derive from Ste. Genevieve and St. Louis Districts. New Madrid District was the scene of the first known execution in what is now Missouri, and although neither the victim nor the perpetrator(s) were slaves, its importance lies in the fact it was carried out under Spanish authority.

The definition of persons who might be slaves was broader in this state's earliest recorded past than during most of its statehood years. Though white persons were never enslaved in Missouri, Indians were, and their enslavement was surprisingly well documented. Despite earlier French ownership of Indians, Governor O'Reilly declared in 1769 that throughout Louisiana Territory all Indian slaves in being were free at the deaths of their masters and all afterborn free after the publication of his emancipating ordinance. Nonetheless, their owners could retain them until the pleasure of the king could be known, and this event apparently never occurred. However, enslaving Indians, said O'Reilly, "was contrary to the wise and pious laws of Spain."[18] The reason for Spain's two-part abolition of Indian slavery appears to have been its eagerness to leave undisturbed the French residents' property rights in their Indian chattel and simultaneously to maintain untroubled diplomatic relations with the Indian tribes that peopled its new colonial possession. A 1769 Spanish document listed 27 separate tribes accustomed to receiving presents in the district of Illinois at St. Louis Post,[19] a French practice that the Spanish continued. As late as 1802 the King of Spain continued to approve the list of presents that his lieutenant governor in St. Louis ordered.[20]

Further evidence of Governor O'Reilly's policies regarding the eradication of Indian slavery is preserved in his requirement that Spanish officials in all of Missouri's posts enumerate their resident Indian slaves. These Spanish censuses are preserved from Ste. Genevieve and St. Louis Districts, dated May 28 and July 12, 1770, respectively. They contain the names of all Indian slaves, their sexes, ages, nations, values, and the names of their owners. The influence of the official religion, Catholicism, can be seen in these censuses in the question of whether each slave had been baptized. There were 28 Indian slaves in Ste. Genevieve and 66 in St. Louis. For the most part women, children, and infants constituted the Indian slave population of both settlements. Clearly, enslaving Indian males in their prime was not common. The few who were listed were owned by influential persons such as François Vallé, captain of the militia in Ste. Genevieve. Likewise, the maximum number any individual Indian slaveholder owned was six, and the average number of Indian slaves per household was less than two in both districts.[21]

Further direct evidence of Indian slavery in Missouri is contained in court records such as one from Ste. Genevieve in which Louis De Noyon executed a civil document giving his slave Jeanette her liberty. She was an Indian woman known for her high moral qualities, this record asserted, and for this reason her owner emancipated her.[22] However, Jeanette's freedom appears to have been pseudo-emancipation because her owner required that she stay with him until his death, perhaps in concubinage without marriage. Spanish law in Missouri would not have afforded a slave, of whatever ancestry, any greater right to refuse sex with her owner than she later experienced on the same soil under American territorial or state law. Though Spanish law required a death sentence for any male who raped a woman of "reputable character," that status was largely determined by the social position of her male family members. Were the victim of unwelcome and unwanted sexual advances not of "reputable character," the judge was free to punish as "he may think suitable to the case."[23] No slave had the legal right to refuse her owner sex, no matter how advanced her high moral qualities were.

The courtroom battles regarding the last vestiges of Indian slavery in Missouri were protracted skirmishes. They originated in Governor O'Reilly's declaration that all Indian slaves born after his emancipating ordinance of 1769 were free. Descendants of Marie Jean Scypion, a woman with an Indian mother and a Negro father, presented their petitions for freedom to various Missouri courts over a 30-year period, beginning in 1806 and finally ending with their successful civil suit for freedom in 1838. In the course of these multiple proceedings the Supreme Court of Missouri ruled in 1834, by a divided vote, that Indian persons could not be held as slaves.[24] Foley's research regarding Marie Jean Scypion's descendants demonstrates the difficulties of proving Indian heritage after Missouri law in 1804 classified any person with 25 percent or more Negro blood as mulatto.[25] The first Spanish censuses that listed *all* slaves held in both Ste. Genevieve and St. Louis were compiled in 1772, and for Ste. Genevieve 287 were enumerated and for St. Louis 198.[26] They did not indicate heritage, only white and slave, male and female. In the general Spanish census in Missouri of 1796, Indian slaves were no longer enumerated. Instead, mulatto and Negro slaves were separately counted, and of the 638 persons held in bondage throughout Missouri, 458 or 72 percent were listed as Negro.[27] Of the 28 percent that the Spanish classified as mulatto in 1796, a significant but largely undocumented number must have been of partial Indian ancestry. After the Missouri Supreme Court ruled in 1834 that Indians were not proper subjects of slavery, at least in theory, all persons held in bondage in Missouri were of either African or African American heritage.

The earliest surviving records in this state of slavery and criminal charges derive from Ste. Genevieve District and involve Indian slave women as stolen property if not, in one case, as the victim of a homicide. Céledon, a white part-time Ste. Genevieve boarder and a trapper who plied his trade in the Missouri wilderness, was suspected of the theft of an unnamed female Indian slave owned in English Kaskaskia, then a village near Ste. Genevieve on the eastern side of the Mississippi River. Captain Hugh Lord of Kaskaskia contacted Louis Villars, commandant of Ste. Genevieve Post, and at Villars's request, François Vallé, captain of the militia, sent a scout after the trapper, who had recently left town. Shortly, the scout found the exposed dead body of a "sauvagesse" [Indian slave woman] near Ste. Genevieve on March 28, 1773. When the scout reported his findings, François Vallé led a detachment of men to retrieve the body, and Jean Baptiste Laffont, a surgeon from English Kaskaskia, examined it. The resulting inquest, signed by Laffont; Joseph Morancy, a member of the Ste. Genevieve militia; and Vallé, confirmed that the dead woman, disguised in men's clothing, was killed by a bullet shot through both her breasts. The entrance wound was in the right breast and the exit wound in the lateral part of her left breast. These findings made Céledon a suspect in both the theft of the Kaskaskian female Indian slave and her murder. The angle of the mortal wound, however, suggested that her death was accidental.

In keeping with the commandant's instructions, the documents contained, in addition to matters directly relating to the inquest or cause of the woman's death, an extensive inventory of Céledon's possessions. Included in his property were two horses, saddles, bridles, a dress made of equal parts cloth and animal skin, a cloak, card games, and wooden shoes. Officials also inventoried multiple tools of the suspect's trapping profession. A gourd containing three pounds of gunpowder, a knife to scrape skins, beaver traps, bludgeoning instruments, bullets, firearms, a hatchet, a small hammer, eating utensils, and miscellaneous other items were listed in this March 1773 record as Céledon's property. His possessions were to be sequestered until he was apprehended and tried for the theft of the Indian female slave from Kaskaskia and perhaps for her murder.

As Ekberg relates the matter, in April 1773 Céledon returned to Ste. Genevieve village to entice another Indian woman, Slave Marianne, property of Widow Aubuchon, to become his companion and trapping partner in the wilderness. He found her chained in a barred room, sleeping with one of her sons, nine-year-old Baptiste, the night of April 21–22. She left without her two sons because the younger child, six-year-old Louis, would slow her flight, but she hoped to return with Indian braves for them. With Céledon's help Marianne removed her chains and cut the window bars of the room in which she was confined, and on ponyback they fled the Aubuchon residence. A detachment of militia failed to capture them. In October 1773 Céledon's possessions, confiscated from his Ste. Genevieve boardinghouse, were auctioned at the Ste. Genevieve church door, and most likely Widow Aubuchon received the proceeds from this auction to compensate her for her loss of Slave Marianne. From the 1770 Spanish census of Indian slaves at Ste. Genevieve we know that the total value of Marianne and her two children was 2,000 livres ($400), that all three were baptized, and that she was approximately 28 years old when she left the home of her mistress.

From March 1773 through March 1774 Captain Vallé collected facts regarding Céledon, a fugitive from Spanish justice in the theft of both the unnamed Indian slave woman from English Kaskaskia and of Slave Marianne. Though neither Vallé nor his superior, Commandant Louis Villars of Ste. Genevieve Post, had any authority to try him, their clear duty was to investigate his case, inventory his possessions, take him into custody, and refer the matter to the governor-general headquartered 700 miles south. They were the local authorities to find sufficient cause to believe that he was guilty of a serious offense such as murder. Had he been captured, he might have been tried in New Orleans in either the governor's civil and criminal court or the mayor's court.

Vallé took a number of depositions from men who knew Céledon, slave Marianne, and their life together on Missouri's frontier as the deponents returned from trapping trips to Ste. Genevieve village. Ekberg pieces together this explanation of the unnamed slave woman's death. Céledon told other men whom Vallé deposed that she shot herself accidentally when, unaccustomed to firearms, she seized a weapon that easily discharged. The angle of the mortal wound, which entered the right breast and exited the left, does not suggest an intentional death. Likewise, Vallé never established any motive for Céledon's murder of the Indian slave, whom he stole in English Kaskaskia and with whom he made his way west to Ste. Genevieve. At the time Vallé took depositions from these men who had contact with Céledon and Marianne, these trappers did not believe that he had ever committed murder. Throughout Vallé's investigation of this matter, Céledon remained a fugitive from Spanish justice. He and Marianne lived together in the Missouri wilderness as hunters and trappers, and he understood Widow Aubuchon's property rights in his companion. Were he not a fugitive, he would work in order to purchase her. Despite the ambiguity of O'Reilly's 1769 decree concerning Indian slaves, their purchase and sale would have been an illegal contract and forbidden by the time the trapper and his Indian slave companion appeared in preserved records from Ste. Genevieve District in 1773.

The men whom Vallé deposed related Marianne's sadness that she was permanently separated from her boys, one of whom Widow Aubuchon retained and one of whom she sold to her brother. Their mother never attempted to reunite with her children. After a year of investigating, Vallé ostensibly concluded that the stolen and deceased Indian slave woman who had been taken from English Kaskaskia had died accidentally, and he discontinued his queries, apparently never referring the case to New Orleans. Thus ended the first known criminal investigation involving slaves in Missouri.[28]

The earliest extant record of any slave as the certain victim of a homicide in Spanish Illinois is a fragment. His killing took place in Ste. Genevieve, and most likely the soldier-perpetrator, Pedro Armand Riault, artillery gunner, was drunk when he stabbed Slave Quierry after his victim, who had been offered a puff of the soldier's pipe, happened to break it. The slave's death occurred, as Kerr explains, "at a seemingly friendly riverside gathering."[29] The meager account of the incident, unearthed by Kerr, dated January 21, 1779, is a part of the Spanish Judicial Records in New Orleans. Nothing more is known of the incident, including the perpetrator's punishment, if any. Since he was a soldier, his case would have been tried in the governor's military court, and these records were returned to Spain.

Records that remained in America illustrate several major distinctions between Spanish colonial and English common law. The latter formed the basis of American territorial and later state law in Missouri. First, Governor O'Reilly's instructions of 1769 made clear the lengthy minority of children. Men were minors until age 25 and women until age 20.[30] Any judge examining a delinquent was required to ascertain, among other matters, his age, and if the accused was under 25 years of age, the law required that "he shall be enjoined to choose a guardian; and upon his refusal to do so, the judge shall appoint someone for him, by reason that the said examination cannot proceed without the presence and authority of the said guardian."[31] Since the criminally accused in colonial Louisiana were entitled to a defense attorney without charge, any juvenile defendant's guardian had legal training. Most extant court records do not contain the ages of the accused, especially not from posts as removed from New Orleans as Spanish Illinois. However, Kerr's tables of the disposition of criminal cases in New Orleans contain the ages of two young slaves. In 1781, 13-year-old Slave Carlota was sentenced to 50 lashes after her conviction for the attempted arson of her master's house, and in 1799, 10-year-old Slave Eduardo, convicted of the murder of a four-year-old slave, was adjudged "too young for execution, left in prison."[32] In contrast, the English saw no impediment to capital punishment in the youthful age of the criminally convicted. Both Carlota and Eduardo would have been death-eligible under British law, and Missouri's state law regarding the execution of children, especially slave children, followed British, not Spanish, law.

Another important difference between Spanish colonial law and its English-American counterpart in Missouri concerned the vast reach of centralized Spanish colonial law as opposed to the limited jurisdiction of American government. Under American rule county officials arrested, indicted, tried, sentenced, and punished, among many other persons, slaves convicted of crimes. Likewise, excluding capital cases, county taxpayers and slaveholders bore the costs of most proceedings in slave criminal cases. During Spain's administration of the Louisiana Territory bondpersons were imprisoned as punishment for crime and their masters fined. Under American law in Missouri no slave was sentenced to either a jail or prison term as punishment for crime, and after 1816 the statute expressly prohibited the fining of slave owners because of their bondpersons' criminal conduct.

Just how remarkably different from the American was the Spanish colonial system of slave crime and punishment can be seen in the part Ste. Genevieve slaveholders played in helping to finance Spain's biggest slave criminal case in North America. An ordinance in French is preserved that required all inhabitants of Ste. Genevieve Post who owned slaves, of whatever age and sex, to pay six escalins (75 cents) within eight days for each in order to defray the expense of the executions in New Orleans of those who were guilty of sedition. It is dated September 2, 1795, and is signed Don François Vallé, captain of the militia and commandant of the Post of Ste. Genevieve, Illinois.[33]

The collection from Ste. Genevieve (700 miles north of New Orleans) and other districts remote from New Orleans for hangings in the capital city was undertaken in order to distribute the costs of punishing the April 1795 Pointe Coupée, Louisiana, slave seditionaries. Their plot called for an uprising the first Friday after Easter 1795. The conspirators planned to murder the white men, older white women, and small children. The white girls' and young women's lives were to be spared because they were desirable sexual objects, and they were to be used accordingly. Some Tunica Indians first reported what they had heard of the plot to two brothers, who in turn relayed the information to the authorities on April 10. Two slave witnesses supported the Indians' account that the uprising was set for the night of April 12–13, 1795.

Pointe Coupée was about 150 miles north of New Orleans on the west bank of the Mississippi River, and its plantations were spread for more than 20 miles. Its slave population of 7,000 greatly outnumbered its white settlers of 2,000. The great advantage in sheer numbers obviously encouraged this extensive preparation for revolt. By the time the would-be crimes, criminals, and their punishments had run their course, many more slaves were imprisoned and executed for this abortive rebellion than for any other criminal act in Louisiana Territory during the 1766–1803 Spanish administration of this vast domain.

By mid-April Captain Du Parc and his men had arrested five ringleaders. By May 15 Governor-General Carondelet was advised that the number of prisoners at Pointe Coupée had reached 60. Because the settlement's small jail was inadequate for such numbers, the commandant's house, as well as a riverboat, was used to confine the jail's overflow of prisoners. Carondelet sent an official, Manuel Serrano, who spoke French, the language of the settlers and their slaves, to conduct the investigation and trial. Defendants who wished were permitted to testify, and some spoke only various African languages. All witnesses who needed interpreters were supplied them. The hearings began May 2 and ended May 19, and on their conclusion Serrano sent Governor Carondelet in New Orleans the accumulated testimony, confessions, and recommended punishments. After Carondelet secured the approval of the captain-general in Cuba, customarily sought in capital cases, he began his extensive sentencing in this case.

Unlike any American criminal cases involving bondpersons in Missouri, 22 Pointe Coupée slaves received 10 years at hard labor, and 9 received 5 years. They were shipped from New Orleans to prisons (*presidios*) at Havana, Cuba; Pensacola, Florida; San Juan, Puerto Rico; and San Juan de Ulua in Veracruz, Mexico. Carondelet ordered the executions of at least 23 slave conspirators. The hangings began May 29 and concluded June 2. Fifteen were hanged at Pointe Coupée, and 12 of their heads were strategically placed at intervals to dissuade other potential slave conspirators. Some hangings took place on shipboard as the *Victoria* was piloted downriver to New Orleans. Others were hanged in New Orleans, and the city's public hangman officiated at these mass hangings.

Kerr explains that the duties of this full-time executioner included lashings as punishment and torture to extract confessions. He also received bonus pay for each execution. Despite its providing a small salary and free room and board at the New Orleans jail, the job was not a coveted one, and black prisoners on probation were often recruited for the difficult-to-fill position of executioner. As with later professional hangmen, the nature of the work led to heavy drinking. Though the precise number of Pointe Coupée slave conspirators hanged in New Orleans is not available, Kerr's research shows that Antonio Sousa, New Orleans public hangman, received 430 pesos for his execution of the Pointe Coupée seditionaries. The slave owners in Ste. Genevieve, Missouri, and probably those from other far-flung posts of Spanish Illinois contributed to Sousa's bonuses, as well as to the cost of building the gallows, the ropes used for the hangings, the digging of the pit that became the mass grave of the executed, and other necessities associated with hangman Sousa's extensive and gruesome duties of early June 1795.[34]

At the time, the trip from New Orleans to various posts in Spanish Illinois took three to four months upriver and between 12 and 20 days downriver by boat.[35] Most likely Ste. Genevieve commandant Vallé wrote his executions-expense ordinance almost immediately upon receiving his instructions. Since 292 slaves are listed in the 1794–95 Ste. Genevieve census,[36] at six escalins (75 cents) per slave, if all slaveholders paid in full, the proceeds would have totaled 1752 escalins ($219). Presumably, Spanish Illinois commandants in Cape Girardeau, New Madrid, St. Charles, and St. Louis received similar instructions from Governor Carondelet in New Orleans, and they also collected from their resident slaveholders moneys to defray the costs of the Pointe Coupée hangings. A general Spanish census of 1794–95 listed six different villages in the western settlements of Illinois and a total slave population of 604. How much the authorities in New Orleans collected from slaveholders in Missouri to hang slaves in the capital city is unknown.

It is certain that Governor Carondelet issued a decree fixing the compensation for each slave lost in the Pointe Coupée matter. Shortly he updated a royal decree of May 1777, which indemnified owners for slaves taken from them by Spanish government action. In June 1795 the governor-general ordered compensation for the owners whose slaves were in the future "killed in flight [as runaways], executed, or condemned to the public works."[37] As early as 1773 Spanish authorities agreed to a plan whereby any bondperson sentenced to death was appraised, and owners were taxed to cover the expenses of such reimbursements.[38] Whether Spain ever indemnified any slaveholders in Upper Louisiana for their economic loss because their human properties were killed as runaways, hanged as condemned felons, or taken as public workers as punishment for crime is unknown. In theory, under Spanish compensation decrees the owner of any slave who lost him or her as a result of government action would have been entitled to compensation, but there are no known records of payment in Missouri.

The criminal records that are preserved include regulations that the Spanish published in Ste. Genevieve in 1794 for the governance of African slaves. The law's intent was to restrict their movement, assembly, and ability to work without their owners' permission. The enslaved were not masters of their own labor, and the punishment for breach of these rules involved fines for whites and whippings for blacks. Just how ineffectual these regulations were is shown by a 1796 case from Ste. Genevieve involving Slave Sem. Englishmen were giving him whiskey in return for his playing the violin for them as he neglected his owner's work of planting crops. Though it is not known how Sem fared, there are no extant records of a fine being either assessed against or collected from the white men for whom he fiddled in return for liquor.[39]

The first known detailed account of a white man killing an African slave in Missouri occurred in Ste. Genevieve District in an area known as the Saline in 1783. Slave Tacouä was at work at the salt furnaces of his owner, Jean Datchurut (one of the wealthiest slaveholders in Spanish

Illinois), when his master's overseer, Jean-Baptiste Lacroix, struck him in the head with a pickax. The preserved inquest of Tacouä's death is of interest because the only eyewitness whom officials interrogated was a 50-year-old named Jacob. Unlike later American law, unless the slave was testifying against his master, Spanish colonial law permitted Negroes to testify against whites if white witnesses were unavailable.[40] Before giving his evidence Slave Jacob said that he professed the Roman Catholic religion; then he swore on the Bible and promised God, the king, and justice to tell the truth about what he had witnessed the previous day, November 15, 1783. He related to the commandant with hatred but without intimidation, as the record noted, that the overseer struck Tacouä at the work site after the slave continued to answer a question that the overseer had asked him about the salt furnace not already being lit. When the perpetrator told the victim to keep silent and the victim resumed his explanation, the white man felled him with a single blow to his head. Apart from a cry that the mortally wounded Tacouä uttered as he was lifted from the ground and taken to a hut where he expired 18 hours later, he died without speaking a word.[41] Probably because the town surgeon's inspection of Tacouä's head injury corroborated Jacob's account of this killing, the town surgeon ruled that the slave came to his death as a result of Lacroix's blow to his head. Though Spanish law made the murder of a slave a criminal offense, there is no record of any punishment. The overseer who struck and killed him was still a member of the owner's household four years later.[42]

The frequency with which law officially protected those in bondage from criminal acts at the hands of their owners, overseers, and others is a well-established aspect of the history of slavery, including Missouri's. Less well documented, but very much a part of the total picture, is the stunning lack of conviction and punishment of white owners, lessees, and overseers who perpetrated crimes, including murder, against their human property. The first extant record of what appears to have been official inaction in a Missouri case involving a white perpetrator's killing of a slave took place in Ste. Genevieve in 1783.

A black-on-black incident of slavery and crime arose in Ste. Genevieve District in the 1790s. Slave Philippe, owned by one prominent resident, murdered a slave belonging to another prominent resident, Jean-Baptiste Vallé. The lieutenant governor of Upper Louisiana, Don Zenon Trudeau, conducted the investigation of this killing, and the evidence of Philippe's guilt was strong. His owner testified against him, his only slave and his valuable possession, and the perpetrator admitted his guilt. Early in 1795 both the prisoner, Slave Philippe, and a detailed record of the evidence against him were sent to Governor-General Carondelet in New Orleans for trial and sentencing. In contrast to the speed and severity with which the Spanish tried, sentenced, and punished the Pointe Coupée conspirators that same year, the handling of this case indicated the general laxity with which adult slaves who killed other adult slaves were punished throughout slavery in Missouri. Reports began reaching Ste. Genevieve that Philippe was conducting himself as a free man in New Orleans. In the spring of 1798 Louis Caron, Philippe's owner, received a bill from the New Orleans jailer asking that he remit the cost of living expenses for his supposedly imprisoned slave criminal. On behalf of the slaveholder the post commandant and other prominent persons wrote an indignant letter to the governor-general of Louisiana, explaining that the miscarriage of justice in Philippe's case would, in the future, discourage owners from reporting any criminal violations by their slaves.[43]

Though the outcome of this case is unknown, Kerr's meticulous research of Spanish Louisiana judicial records allows him to conclude that "slaves convicted of murdering their masters always received the death penalty, but the murder of another slave often secured a milder sentence."[44] Had Philippe been hanged in New Orleans, his owner would have been compensated for his death, not billed for his keep. Because Spain's financial management of its North American colony was poor, the governor-general and his advisers in New Orleans were eager to cut government disbursements. For example, by 1785 Great Britain was spending about 15 cents per capita in North Carolina, and Spain $16.55 per capita in Louisiana Territory. The Spaniards never met expenses.[45] Therefore, without any requirement of a speedy resolution to any slave-on-slave murder case, especially one sent from remote Spanish Illinois, by careful management of it the authorities could raise revenue, not expend it. Kerr lists an Avoyelles Parish, Louisiana, killing in 1793 that ultimately resulted in the defendant slave's release from custody in 1800.[46] Had the victim been his owner, almost certainly the Avoyelles Parish slave would have been swiftly tried and swiftly hanged, and Spanish colonial authorities would have indemnified his owner's estate for the loss of its slave's labor.

There are no extant murder prosecutions from Spanish rule of St. Louis District. However, there was great dread of such crime. Though the only successful slave revolt in the Western Hemisphere occurred in 1791 in Santo Domingo (Haiti), where at least 500,000 Africans vastly outnumbered the French colonists, there was considerable anxiety among North American slaveholders about a similar action among their bondpersons. Well before the plantation destruction in Santo Domingo in 1791 or the abortive revolt at Pointe Coupée, Louisiana, in 1795, the Spanish took legislative precautions to ward off any intimations of slave independence in

Louisiana Territory. A 1781 ordinance given at St. Louis of the Illinois by Lieutenant-Governor Cruzat "strictly forbid all ... to leave their cabins at night, ... to receive in their cabins other slaves, except those who belong to their own masters.... We enjoin [their] masters ... to watch over their conduct ... as concerns the nocturnal assemblies which these colored people are accustomed to hold."[47] As this law demonstrated, the fear of insurrection was well established when Spain governed Missouri.

The preserved records of crime in St. Louis District during Spanish rule are slender. The first known slave criminal case took place in January 1779 near the village of St. Louis, when Slave Lorine assaulted Slave Marianne. (The victim's owner was Fernando De Leyba, lieutenant-governor of Upper Louisiana.) The offensive touching arose from a dispute between these separately owned women over washing rights in a hole in the ice. The perpetrator threw the victim in the water, and but for the intervention of another slave woman, Franchon, who rescued Marianne, the victim would have drowned. Lorine continued her attack on Marianne with blows that knocked her into a fire. Franchon again rescued Marianne, who survived with her clothes partially burned. At Lorine's trial, held three days later, both Franchon, owned by the Widow Dodier, and Melanie, owned by the curate, the Reverend Father Bernard, were prosecution witnesses against Lorine, who was found guilty of assaulting Marianne. The records indicate that the punishment meted out to her was 100 lashes. She was to receive the first 50 on January 23 and the remaining 50 on January 24, 1779. In addition the owners of the offending slave, M. and Mme. Roublieu, were held responsible for another court appearance of Lorine in the event her victim died as a result of her injuries. They were also ordered to pay the surgeon's fee for his attendance on the victim, as well as the costs of Lorine's prosecution.[48]

Other known details involving slavery and crime from St. Louis District mention various massacres of white settlers in which Indians killed all members of the household. In May 1780 and a short distance from the village of St. Louis, Indians killed seven settlers in a surprise attack, including a slave known only as "Joseph Chancellier's Negro," who along with three white persons were buried within St. Louis village on the same day they were murdered.[49]

The only other violent slave death from St. Louis District that we know about from the Spanish governance of Missouri occurred in December 1785, when ten regular soldiers and some militia stormed the barn in which Slave Batiste was present in order to capture two former Indian slaves. In the confusion of the capture of two of eight marauding Indians who had robbed, stolen Negro slaves, set fires, and murdered as they pillaged the countryside, the faithful servant, Batiste, was accidentally shot. Mrs. Chouteau, one of the most prominent early settlers of St. Louis, owned the man, who died at the hands of the Spanish government, and documentation concerning the disposition of this matter survives.

Against the background of the two Indian criminals secured in the St. Louis jail, Lieutenant Governor Cruzat sent a surgeon to conduct an inquest. Batiste "had been killed by a shot from a gun, which had gone through his body and lungs."[50] The widow, Mrs. Chouteau, wrote Lieutenant Governor Cruzat, requesting $1,000 compensation from Joseph M. Papin, Mrs. Chouteau's son-in-law, at whose command Mrs. Chouteau's slave had attempted to detain the pillaging Indians with rum. Her request for this sum was based on Spanish law, which, as Sem's case illustrated, prohibited the employment of any bondperson without the consent of his or her owner. Of Batiste, his owner wrote Spain's highest official in Missouri: "His services were invaluable...; his good qualities, ability, his attachment to the family, the care he continually took of my interests ... so that I could safely trust him with the management of all my slaves, in the flower of his age, no money can remunerate me for his loss."[51]

Joseph M. Papin informed Cruzat in a lengthy account of the circumstances of the death of his mother-in-law's Negro man. His defense was that he was acting on government orders in a public matter and that it would be unjust for the entire burden of compensation to fall on him when the Negro was a volunteer whom Papin had a right to command. It was agreed that Batiste had died in a dark place in the confusion attendant on capturing two criminal Indians, one of whom was wounded at the same time an unknown person or persons shot him dead.

Ultimately, and in conformity with Spanish administration of such matters, Señor Miró, the governor-general of Louisiana in New Orleans, settled both the liability and damages to be awarded to Mrs. Chouteau. At his behest the former owners of the eight freed Indians, whose crimes led to the incident in Mrs. Chouteau's barn in which Batiste was killed, paid the government an aggregate of $600. On the personal order of Miró Mrs. Chouteau received this sum in May 1787 as compensation for the accidental death of her Negro man 18 months earlier.[52]

From Spanish control of St. Louis District another aspect of slavery and crime survives: legislation passed in September 1782 for the governance of the village of St. Louis. The owners of persons who transgressed a number of laws, dealing largely with livestock and fence repairs, were held liable for damages caused by their chattel, both animal and human. The offending humans, the legislation specified, were to be whipped. Similarly, ordinances effective January 1798, pertaining to St. Louis, St. Charles, and

other municipalities, authorized fines and imprisonment for free whites
who sold slaves items such as gunpowder and liquor without permission
from their masters. No records survive regarding any punishment under
these St. Louis ordinances.

The remaining racial mixture of crime and punishment under Spanish rule is preserved from New Madrid District. The murder in this case
is a well-known event, and several histories of Missouri mention it.[53] The
most complete account is a compilation of documents by a descendant of
the victim, David Trotter, a white man born in Augusta County, Virginia,
c. 1755 and a soldier in the American Revolutionary War. In 1790 he was
listed in the census of Bourbon County, Kentucky, and by 1801 he, his wife,
about eight children, and five or six slaves had migrated to the New Madrid
District of Upper Louisiana, where he was listed as filing for a Spanish land
grant. By 1802 Trotter was living in Grand Prairie (New Madrid District),
and he was permitted to sell liquor to Indians. He died in January 1802 at
the hands of at least five Mascouten Indians, to whom he refused to supply intoxicants. Two of the victim's slaves, a man and a woman, attempted
to defend the homestead, but they were no match for the Indians, armed
with guns and tomahawks. The perpetrators shot, hacked, scalped, and
stabbed Trotter and burned his house and its contents.

Unlike the known murders in Ste. Genevieve District, wherein all the
victims were slaves, in the Trotter case the perpetrators were Indians and
the victim a white man. Probably his move with his wife, children, and
slaves was precisely the sort of immigration the Spanish wished to encour-
age. The former commandant of New Madrid District, Charles Delassus,
had been appointed lieutenant governor of Upper Louisiana in 1799, and
he occupied the position throughout the remainder of Spanish control of
Missouri. Delassus ordered a large number of militia, the main group of
which came from New Orleans, to search for the perpetrators of this crime.
In all, the militia's expedition to New Madrid took approximately six
weeks. Once in this district, the troops captured five of the Indian suspects, and the defendants were sent to New Orleans for trial and sentencing. There the governor-general found Tewanaye, the prime culprit, guilty
of David Trotter's murder and condemned him to death by firing squad
in New Madrid. Spanish troops returned him from New Orleans by boat,
and he attacked the man in charge of transporting him in an escape
attempt. Thereafter, he was placed in irons for the remainder of his journey. In preparation for his execution the Spanish assembled a formidable
show of force in the event of an Indian uprising. Lieutenant Governor
Delassus's troops were joined in New Madrid by 184 trained militia from
Cape Girardeau District. These men had been promised grants of land if

they agreed to act as guards during Tewanaye's execution. Amid this impressive assemblage of Spanish military might, the first known execution in Missouri under the authority of white men took place on January 3, 1803, in New Madrid District when a firing squad shot to death the Mascouten Indian Tewanaye. In keeping with the general lenience of Spanish rule and its desire to keep peace with various Indian tribes, the other four Indian prisoners were released to their chiefs who, along with many others, witnessed the execution ritual of the death of Tewanaye. Cavalry, drum beating, and coffin bearing were all a part of the pageantry of the Spanish military's dispatch of an Indian who had murdered a white man.

There would be no further use of the firing squad in any execution in Missouri until the Union army employed it during the Civil War. Because Spain relinquished control of the Louisiana Territory to France on November 30, 1803, the pursuit, capture, trial, sentencing, and execution of David Trotter's murderer, the Indian Tewanaye, is the last known Spanish disposition of any case in Upper Louisiana.

Spain sounded the death knell of Indian slavery, but it otherwise left the institution of African and mulatto slavery the same as it inherited it from the French. With the exception of reducing the use of poison as a murder weapon, Spanish influence on the future course of slavery in Missouri was insignificant. Its language, religion, law, monetary policies, and politics were never successfully transplanted there.

After a 20-day interlude of French control of Louisiana, or from November 30, 1803, until December 20, 1803, France began the transfer of Louisiana Territory to the United States. The French officially ended their claim to Upper Louisiana on March 9, 1804. For the next seven months most Spanish district commandants remained at their posts to administer their country's colonial law, which remained in effect during the brief French rule and the early American ownership of the transferred land. On October 1, 1804, Spain officially ceased to govern throughout the Louisiana Purchase. Thereafter until statehood all laws operative in Missouri, including those concerning both slavery and crime, were ordinances of towns such as St. Louis, American territorial law specifically fashioned for the district of Louisiana (1804), the territory of Louisiana (1805), and the territory of Missouri (1812), or U.S. law applicable in any district or territory.

Chapter 2

Early American Rule

The United States Constitution, which went into effect in 1789, gave Congress exclusive power to "make all needful Rules and Regulations respecting the Territory belonging to the United States,"[1] and under American law a territory was properly defined as any portion of the country not yet admitted to the Union as a state. The legal precedent for this federal right of territorial control was the Ordinance of 1787, which set up the Northwest Territory. Under this act of the Continental Congress, the four states with colonies in the Northwest Territory (Virginia, New York, Massachusetts, and Connecticut) ceded all their colonial lands to the U.S. government. The ordinance also established a form of territorial government by which subsequent western territories, including Missouri, were created and later admitted to the Union as states. March aptly describes the process: "As the population of the territory grew, the degree of self-government allowed would be increased through successive grades from a temporary form of government in which no popular participation was provided to a second grade in which representative government was permitted, and ultimately to statehood and admission to the Union."[2] The formation of the Arkansas Territory from Missouri Territory in 1819 illustrated another aspect of the 1787 ordinance; from a portion of one territory another could be established and later admitted to the Union.

In the "Treaty Ceding Louisiana to the United States," the United States and the French Republic agreed that the inhabitants of the ceded area shall enjoy "all the rights, advantages, and immunities of citizens of the United States; and in the meantime they shall be maintained and

26

protected in the free enjoyment of their liberty, property, and the religion which they profess."[3] The religion of the French residents was Catholicism, and the liberty and property these new white American citizens continued to enjoy included their freedom to own slaves.

Though the Jefferson administration bought Louisiana Territory from Napoleon under a treaty concluded in Paris on April 30, 1803, Congress allowed the Purchase to become a part of the United States and drew the blueprint for its early government. In October 1803, the Eighth U.S. Congress passed an act that enabled the president to take possession of the territories ceded by France to America.[4] In separate ceremonies— one in New Orleans on December 20, 1803, and the other in St. Louis on March 9–10, 1804 — the Louisiana Purchase was officially transferred to the United States. President Jefferson appointed W. C. C. Claiborne (1775–1817), an American lawyer and governor of the Mississippi Territory, and General James Wilkinson (1757–1825), an American Revolutionary War officer and adventurer, as commissioners to receive it in New Orleans from the French on December 20, 1803. After its receipt Claiborne assumed the civil duties of the Spanish governor-general and Wilkinson his military responsibilities.

To spare the French government the expense of sending a French official to the remote St. Louis Post, the commissioner in New Orleans, M. de Laussat, designated an American attorney and Revolutionary War veteran, Amos Stoddard (1762–1813), as the French government's agent in the transfer of Upper Louisiana from the Spanish to the French. Captain Stoddard took possession of Upper Louisiana in the name of the French republic on March 9, 1804. He was also the American representative at these same transfer events, and on March 10, 1804, he assumed the territory and government of Upper Louisiana in the name of the United States.[5] Claiborne appointed him the first American governor of Upper Louisiana, and on his civil superior's authority Captain and First Civil Commandant Stoddard, Upper Louisiana, made no important changes in either the applicable Spanish laws or their administration. He reappointed many Spanish officials, including most of the former commandants of each district. The Spaniards who had possessed both civil and military authority under their own nation's control of this territory retained only civil authority under early American rule.

Congress gave the president a free hand to appoint one or more persons to exercise "all the military, civil, and judicial powers"[6] of Spain's governor-general. However, in keeping with the U.S. Constitution's separation of powers into legislative, executive, and judicial, as well as this document's requirement of civilian control of the military, Stoddard's specific instructions from Claiborne and Wilkinson insisted that the civil and military functions that, under the Spanish government "were confounded & blended together ... must be kept carefully separate & distinct."[7] In conformity with these orders Stoddard reorganized the militia and commanded companies formed at St. Louis, Ste. Genevieve, Cape Girardeau, and New Madrid from March 10, 1804, until July 1, 1804, when Major James Bruff, Stoddard's superior officer, assumed military command of Upper Louisiana.

Stoddard's letters help to clarify his governance of the former Spanish colony. He wrote Claiborne and Wilkinson in New Orleans of the Spanish law and procedure he was required to administer: "The criminal code is very defective. All capital offenders must be sent to New Orleans for trial — but what is and what is not capital, depends more on the *aggravation* than on the *description*."[8] By *aggravation* Stoddard, an attorney trained in both England and Massachusetts, meant that circumstances extrinsic to the crime such as the reputation of the a victim, either increased the crime to a capital offense or diminished it to noncapital. By *description* he meant the definition or elements of the crime that under English common law and American statutory law existed independent of the rank or reputation of the victim. Stoddard had read the English legal commentator William Blackstone, who described rape as unlawful carnal knowledge of a woman forcibly and against her will.[9] At least in theory the relative social positions of the perpetrator and victim did not enhance a minor crime to a capital offense in the late-eighteenth-century law that Amos Stoddard, the New Englander, had studied and practiced. Clearly, the 1804 Spanish colonial law of Upper Louisiana was a quagmire of subjectivity for him.

His letters to various correspondents reveal another aspect of Stoddard's governance of Upper Louisiana for which his New England background did not prepare him: slavery. In 1784 he had lived in the home of Charles Cushing and clerked for his older brother, William Cushing, chief justice of the Supreme Court of Massachusetts (1777–89), and President Washington's first associate justice appointment to the U.S. Supreme Court in 1789.[10] In 1783 Justice Cushing wrote *Commonwealth* v. *Jennison,* a decision that abolished slavery in Massachusetts because the institution was inconsistent with the 1780 Massachusetts Bill of Rights. *Jennison* declared that "all men are born free and equal, ... every subject is entitled to liberty, ... and ... the idea of slavery is inconsistent with our own conduct and Constitution."[11]

Twenty-one years later Amos Stoddard, Cushing's former clerk, among other duties, counted the number of free persons and slaves in each of Upper Louisiana's five districts. His enumerations included this language:

160 whites and 12 slaves, Arkansas settlement; 800 whites and 100 slaves, New Madrid District; 1200 whites and 200 blacks, Cape Girardeau District; 1978 whites and 520 blacks, Ste. Genevieve District; and 3738 whites and 667 blacks, St. Louis District, which included the villages of both St. Louis and St. Charles, for a total of 7876 whites and 1497 blacks in Upper Louisiana, a combined total of 9,373.[12]

Shortly, and by letter, August Chouteau, president of the Committee of the Town of St. Louis, advised Captain Stoddard, "There exist among the Blacks a fermentation — which may become dangerous ... increased by the report spread by some Whites, that they will be free before long. In all Countries where slavery exists there is a Code that establishes ... the Rights of the Masters and the Duties of the slaves." The Committee's communication also referred to earlier St. Louis Spanish ordinances that restricted slave gatherings, especially at night: "There is also a watchful policy which prevents their nocturnal Assemblies, subjects them to Labor, provides for their Subsistence, and prevents as much as possible their Communication with the Whites." The letter concluded, "Under the old French Government and Spanish, the Black Code was our guide. Be so kind Sir as to have it put in Force, keep the Slaves in their Duty ... in the Respect they owe generally to all Whites and more especially to their Masters; put them again under the subordination which they were heretofore."[13]

The writer was colonial and territorial Missouri's most influential French citizen, and the military man promptly advised this important St. Louis resident that he was "unacquainted with the usual police [civil administration] adopted in slave Countries," and it would be his great pleasure if "the Committee would suggest such rules and regulations as appear necessary to restrain the licentiousness [excessive liberty] of the slaves and keep them more steadily to their duty."[14] Except for August Chouteau, neither the names of the members of the committee nor any of their suggested rules and regulations are extant, but most likely the committee was composed of the same influential residents of the town of St. Louis (mostly French who owned the slaves whose names appeared in territorial St. Louis criminal records). As for their proposed rules, they were probably similar to the French and later the Spanish slave codes with which these prominent persons were both familiar and comfortable. What these wealthy men most feared was the emancipation of their bondpersons.

As early as March 1804, the U.S. Congress had passed and President Jefferson had signed well-publicized legislation that took effect October 1, 1804, concerning the Purchase. On this date, provided the law, Captain Stoddard's duties as the first American civil commandant of Upper Louisiana were to cease; the area was to attach temporarily to Indiana

Territory, a place where, under the terms of the 1787 Northwest Ordinance, slavery was forbidden. This law divided the Purchase into two territories: Orleans and the District of Louisiana. In keeping with precedent established by the Continental Congress for the governance of the Northwest Territory, which a governor, three judges, and a secretary administered, the Eighth Congress also provided that the same men who officiated in Indiana Territory should temporarily govern Upper Louisiana, the portion of the Purchase north of the thirty-third parallel.[15] It was a vast expanse, but its actual machinery of government was limited to areas along the Mississippi River in what are now Missouri and Arkansas.[16]

Despite explicit congressional protection of slavery in the Territory of Orleans, Congress was mute about slavery in the District of Louisiana. As March comments, congressional silence about slavery in Upper Louisiana "had created the presumption that congress intended to abolish [it], especially since the area was attached to the free Territory of Indiana."[17] The region's slaveholders were eager to assure the continuation of their human property rights, which they had enjoyed under Spanish rule and still earlier under French ownership of their country. When the Eighth Congress provided on March 26 that effective October 1, 1804, "the governor and judges of the Indiana Territory shall have power to make all laws which they may deem conducive to the good government" of the District of Louisiana,[18] Upper Louisiana's slaveholders were firm in their belief that American laws protecting slavery were essential elements of good government for their district.

The same governor, William Henry Harrison, and two surviving judges, John Griffin and Henry Vanderberg, whom President John Adams appointed to oversee Indiana Territory when it was created in 1800, President Jefferson reappointed to continue their Indiana Territory responsibilities, as well as the additional duties federal law gave them concerning the District of Louisiana. Jefferson filled the vacancy made by the death of Judge William Clark (Adams's remaining Indiana Territory judicial appointee) when the president named Thomas Terry Davis, a man well acquainted with slaveholders' wishes in Upper Louisiana because Davis had visited the area before the Purchase. These four men, the governor and three judges who formed the legislative council for the District of Louisiana, all arrived in St. Louis on October 12, 1804.[19] By the date of their arrival the prior Spanish administrators and their Spanish colonial law were superseded by these American officials and the statutes they had earlier adopted at Vincennes, Indiana Territory, for the District of Louisiana effective October 1, 1804.

"The Law Respecting Slaves for the District of Louisiana," which

Governor Harrison and Judges Davis, Griffin, and Vanderberg signed into law, comprehensively addressed the concerns of Upper Louisiana's slave owners. Its 35 separate sections demonstrated that the civil rights of slaves were no more advanced under American than under the French and later the Spanish governance of Missouri. Obviously powerful proslavery voices had made their views known to the governor and three judges to whom the Eighth Congress delegated responsibility to write the laws for Upper Louisiana.

Violette summarized the similarities between the 1804 slave code and the earlier French and Spanish codes: "In each of the codes ... there were provisions against slaves leaving the plantation of their masters without passes, against them carrying arms, making riots, gathering in unlawful assemblies, making assaults upon their masters, plotting conspiracy, offering of resistance to arrest, and engaging in trade."[20] The almost verbatim source of the 1804 Law Respecting Slaves was Virginia. Still earlier, when Kentucky became a state in 1792, Virginia law was the model for Kentucky's slave code. When it is remembered that two native Virginians, Governor Harrison and Judge Griffin, as well as the Kentuckian Judge Davis, occupied three of the four seats on the District of Louisiana's legislative council, its adoption of Virginia's repressive slave code as the law of Upper Louisiana is not a surprising choice.

Among its features that had no counterpart in Spanish colonial law was the broad definition of a mulatto as a person with only one Negro grandparent.[21] Virginia adopted this definition in 1787, and its law made no provision for the issue of a Negro and an Indian.[22] Missouri law followed Virginia's in its silence about Indian slaves, as well as in its presumption that mulattoes were proper subjects of slavery. The classification of persons as mulattoes, with as many as three Indian grandparents, immensely increased the difficulties anyone of color encountered when seeking his or her freedom because of Indian heritage. Equally important, Missouri law declared the bloodline adequate for perpetual servitude.

Unlike the Spanish law which generally permitted slave testimony against whites, another new feature of the Virginia-inspired 1804 slave code for the District of Louisiana was its prohibition against either Negroes or mulattoes testifying against whites. Excluding a handful of cases, the record of persons of color testifying against whites in Missouri courts is virtually nonexistent throughout slavery. In keeping with most, if not all, slave states, Negro and mulatto testimony was essentially used only against other Negroes and mulattoes.

Three other entire sections of the 1804 slave code had no French or Spanish counterpart in earlier law that regulated slave life in Louisiana.

These new statutes concerned slaves preparing, exhibiting, or administering any medicine. The gravity of even the first offense was indicated by its proscribed punishment: "He or she so offending shall be judged guilty of felony and suffer death."[23] This strange law's intent was not to prohibit slaves from practicing the druggist or pharmaceutical profession. Other sections of the 1804 slave code punished the master or owner of the slave permitted to either "go at large and trade as a free man" or "go at large or hire him or herself out."[24]

The language of the 1804 slave code's three sections concerning slaves administering medicine was lifted word for word from 1748 House of Burgesses' laws. Its intent when enacting these statutes was to deter slaves from poisoning their owners under the guise of giving them medicine. The law's purpose was stated in the Virginia statute itself: "Many Negroes, under pretense of practicing physic, have prepared and exhibited poisonous medicines, by which many persons have been murdered, and others have languished under long and tedious indispositions."[25] The operative word in this prefatory material was *physic*, meaning a cathartic or purge. Eighteenth-century American medicine, as Duffy explains its theory and practice, consisted primarily of "bleeding, blistering, purging, vomiting, and sweating — all designed to restore the proper balance of body humors or to rid the body of putrid or peccant humors."[26]

In sharp contrast the physicians of Louisiana Territory, under French leadership, rejected excessive purging and vomiting. They preferred to assist nature in their patients' cures and were cautious in their use of potent and perilous drugs.[27] Shortly after Governor O'Reilly began his duties in New Orleans, he gave pharmacy its first legal recognition in America as a separate branch of the healing arts. By his decree of 1770 apothecaries were required to conform to seven different regulations concerning drugs, and among them were laws relating to poisons. The pharmacist was obligated to keep a register of the purchasers of all remedies "which may be abused" and "to compound exactly the prescriptions as ordered by the doctor without ever adding anything."[28] Sellers of poisonous drugs were held personally responsible for the resulting harm and were liable as accomplices.[29]

From the beginning of the Spanish regime, French physicians remained in the majority throughout colonial Louisiana, and the Spanish continued the French practice of attempting to provide a doctor for every sizable settlement. The first seven physicians to practice in Missouri for whom any records exist were army surgeons assigned to military posts. They arrived between 1765 and 1800. All were foreign born; most were French and had been educated in Paris. The first American-born doctor to reside in Missouri did not arrive until the fall of 1806.[30] By this time medical practice in Missouri had been under French influence many years. The differing practices in the healing arts in the Purchase and the English colonies in eighteenth-century America help to explain the paucity of slave prosecutions for poisoning whites or any other persons in colonial Louisiana. Unlike the great volume of poisoning cases in eighteenth-century Virginia, of the more than 300 criminal cases that Kerr uncovered in colonial Louisiana between 1770 and 1804, only three, none from Upper Louisiana, all with slave defendants, concerned poisoning or attempted poisoning: one in 1773, another in 1774, and the third in 1785.

When Missouri was under Spanish rule and its dominant culture was French, there was no pervasive fear among slaveholders that their bond-persons would poison them under the pretense of giving them medicine. The reason was straightforward: their pharmacists were heavily regulated, their physicians were licensed, and slaveholders were not constant ingestors of drugs, dangerous or otherwise. As Duffy explains colonial Spanish medicine, "In Louisiana, and other sections of the Spanish empire, the free and easy atmosphere of the English colonies, which permitted anyone to establish himself in medical practice simply did not exist."[31] As a result, there was no criminal law concerning slaves and medicine when Missouri was governed by French and later by Spanish colonial law.

It was otherwise in mid-eighteenth-century Virginia. Its large slave population (approximately one-half of its inhabitants throughout most of the eighteenth century) and the belief of its influential citizenry in the efficacy of dangerous medicines to cure most diseases contributed to slave owners' fear of being poisoned by their slaves. Other factors that increased American slaveholders' dread of being subtly murdered by their medicine-bearing chattel were the absence of any uniformity in drug dosages; the absence of licensing requirements for physician-apothecaries, pharmacists, or other mixers of drugs; and the ready availability of home medicine chests, either for those unable to afford a physician or for pioneer families remote from any town. With the chest of many medicines came a manual of common diseases, their symptoms, and the recommended doses to effect the necessary purging, vomiting, blistering, and bleeding of the purported cure. One of its staples was arsenic. In Missouri the use of this poison remained both common and unregulated throughout slavery and into the twentieth century.

If no other medication had been widely prescribed and easily acquired, its ready availability made the administration of medicine a potentially lethal endeavor. Long before a Frenchman introduced the first slaves to Missouri, a Swiss physician and prescriber of arsenic, Paracelsus (1493–1541), knew that "all substances are poisons; there is none which is not a poison. The right dose differentiates a poison and a remedy."[32] By colonial American times arsenic was used for a wide spectrum of complaints. It is no mystery that slaves, especially otherwise powerless women, seized on the simple expedient of doubling their owners' arsenic dosages to settle many and varied grievances. It was considered efficacious to combat paralysis, epilepsy, rickets, heart disease, cancer, parasites, headaches, colds, influenza, and general debility. It was a health aid for those who suffered from neurasthenia, a female malady characterized by fatigue, depression, and various localized physical pains without precise diagnosis. Men afflicted with impotence ingested it; women who wished to improve their complexions took it; and both sexes used it as a tonic.[33] One home-medicine-chest manual that went through at least five editions between 1821 and 1833, including one published in St. Louis, recommended it as an "excellent remedy in fevers."[34] The theory of its use was that the human body and its pathogen(s) were poisoned together; the arsenic killed the disease-causing agent(s), and the larger and strong host survived unharmed.

There was no easier way for the slave to debilitate or kill her owner than to increase the dose of arsenic that either the physician-apothecary prescribed or the self-medicating slaveholder used for many maladies. Unlike lye, whose caustic taste immediately alerted the ingestor to its toxicity, the consumption of arsenic was far more insidious. The eminent authority on poisoning, Alfred Swaine Taylor, observed, "Most of those persons who have been criminally or accidentally destroyed by arsenic, have not been aware of any taste in taking the poisoned substance."[35]

Though the autopsy was sufficiently perfected in America by the mid-eighteenth century to determine that the cause of death was arsenical poisoning, autopsies did not become routine practice of the coroner or medical examiner in deaths of questionable cause until the end of the nineteenth century, that is, long after slavery had run its course.[36] In the absence of an autopsy, pinpointing the cause of death as arsenic poisoning was very difficult.

Though the skills of the general practitioner were available to the ill, the dying, and the prosecutors of antebellum America, those of the pathologist, the toxicologist, and the biochemist were not. Even had such specialists existed, they could only detect and treat poisonings when they suspected them.

The symptoms of arsenic poisoning, such as severe stomach cramps, vomiting, and diarrhea, were often mistaken for food poisoning, acute indigestion, or cholera, or these maladies were wrongly diagnosed as poisonings. The link between drinking contaminated water and the frequently fatal disease of cholera was not confirmed until the 1880s.[37] During American slave times those who drank unclean water were unaware of its lethality. Were the confusion of cholera, acute indigestion, and common food poisoning with arsenic poisoning not a sufficiently vexing problem for the sleuth, additional features of arsenic further obfuscated both its use and the identity of the perpetrator.

No arsenic poison worked its malignity until it was absorbed into the blood, and the action of the poison was slower if taken when the stomach was full because absorption was delayed. The age, physical condition, habits, tolerance, and general health of the victim all affected the appearance of any symptoms. Whether the poison was administered in one massive dose or in a number of small ones influenced the speed and severity of the victim's discomfort. The onset of symptoms ranged from a few minutes to 16 hours, and death might result any time between a few hours and three months. Webster stated the cumulative effect of chronic poisoning with arsenic as one that "may not prove fatal for some time, but sooner or later the system will be so undermined by the constant action of these small doses that death will result."[38] A study of homicide investigation noted of this substance, "It is rather rare that poisoning by arsenic ... is suspected at the time of the victim's death."[39] Given the great variability in symptoms and their occurrence, as Taylor wryly observed, "It is easy for the artful person to ... poison ... and to accuse another of having administered it."[40] To what extent the suicides, accidental deaths, and homicides (husband, wife, and child murder) among slaveholding Americans were blamed on their slaves was another imponderable.

Finally, additional uses of arsenic confounded the investigator. During the antebellum period, the substance was a common household item. It was used to control vermin, as an insecticide, a preservative, and a tanning agent. Hence its presence in the manor or on the farm or plantation provided no cause for alarm. Equally intriguing, the substance was regularly used in the nineteenth century in embalming fluids, and from this use it leaked into the soil of cemeteries. Postmortem examination of exhumed remains ran the risk of confusing the arsenic added to the body in order to preserve it with the deceased's cause of death.[41]

No doubt because of the immense difficulties of proving arsenic poisoning, Virginia slaves used this means to destroy some of their owners and their owners' families. The 1748 Virginia law acknowledged the problems inherent in proving any intentional poisoning: "It will be difficult to detect such pernicious and dangerous practices if they [any Negro or other slave] should be permitted to exhibit any sort of medicine."[42] Hence the House of Burgesses aided the county prosecutor by criminalizing behavior that *was* susceptible to proof, namely that a slave had prepared, exhibited, or administered any medicine.

However, the realistic concern about slave poisonings under the guise of administering medicine could only exist in a society wherein purging, vomiting, sweating, and bleeding were standard medical care and where caustic medicines were readily available and frequently used to rid the body of its many maladies. The last illnesses and deaths of the prominent Virginians George Washington (1732–99) and his wife, Martha (1732–1802), illustrate the medicating practices of eighteenth-century America. On the last day of his life, December 14, 1799, the former president awoke with an acutely sore throat, probably a strep throat caused by a bacterial infection, and he requested that his overseer bleed him. Next he sent for his physician, and his doctor applied leeches to his throat and behind his ears, ordered an enema for him, and twice more bled his famous patient. Two more physicians arrived at Mount Vernon, and its owner was bled a fourth time; he expired that evening. Duffy observes that though Washington might not have survived the infection, "the debilitating and dehydrating measures taken by his medical attendants could only have hastened his death."[43]

A revealing note survives from the last month of Martha Washington's life: "Mrs. Washington desires [the druggist] to send by bearer one quart bottle of his best castor oil."[44] Clearly, she too believed in physic or violent purging. At her husband's death she had become mistress for life of 150 slaves. An old friend, Abigail Adams, visited the widow at Mount Vernon and wrote her abolitionist sister of her distinguished hostess's uneasiness as the owner of this multitude of human property: "She did not feel as though her life was safe in their hands."[45] Because her demise would free 150 slaves and she shared her partner's belief in violent purging, she may have chiefly feared that her slaves would administer her medicine with ill intent. She wisely emancipated all of her inherited human property approximately 18 months before she fell ill of a fever May 5, lingered 17 days, and passed May 22, 1802. Presumably, her death was natural, not arsenic induced.

Both George and Martha Washington were adolescents when the House of Burgesses in 1748 eased the prosecutor's burden of proving any slave-perpetrated poisonings by making the slave's administration of medicine a crime. They passed from youth to old age to death, and accusations of slave poisonings in Virginia continued. Likewise, purging, vomiting, bleeding, and sweating remained the standard American medical cure for most maladies during their lifetimes. Excluding the crime of stealing, between 1706 and 1784 the Commonwealth of Virginia tried more slaves for poisoning than for any offense. No fewer than 179 were charged with one variation or another of this crime. Between 1748 and 1784, 95 of the 119 slaves were charged under the slave-administration-of-medicine statute. Of those so charged 35 were sentenced to hang. Among major felonies in Virginia between 1785 and 1831, more women (27.3 percent) were convicted of poisoning crimes than any other offense, and of those accused of poisoning, most were slaves.[46] Who was guilty and of precisely what offense will never be known.

Besides sidestepping those aspects of slave poisoning of whites that were basically not susceptible to proof, Virginia's mid-eighteenth-century House of Burgesses also addressed white Virginians' fears of African medicine or slave voodooism by enacting statutes in 1748 regarding the slave preparing, administering, or exhibiting medicine. Those fearful of slave medicine were not limited to the early-nineteenth-century boundaries of Virginia. What became Missouri's neighboring state of Illinois was a county of Virginia between 1778 and 1784, and at least two slaves were put to death in Illinois during this time for Negro witchcraft and slave voodooism.

The 1748 Virginia law excused slave administration of medicine that had neither ill intent nor bad consequences, and the 1804 Missouri slave code was identical to Virginia's statutes. During Missouri's Spanish regime, the regulation of pharmacy and French medical practice with its avoidance of dangerous drugs saved lives, both directly and indirectly, among patients and their care-providing slaves. However, as Americans arrived in the territory, they brought their slaves and their medicating beliefs and practices with them. They also patronized newly opened drug and medicine shops, which sold arsenic and other dangerous potions. Consequently, one poisoning case survives from Missouri's territorial period, and the Christian and surnames of the slave's owner and his victim, John and Elizabeth Noyes Smith, suggest that this couple's place of birth and rearing was an English colony, perhaps Virginia. In 1825 the Missouri General Assembly passed a noncapital version of the slave-administration-of-medicine statute. Its later, less severe punishment was put in place to accommodate changes in the law that the 1820 Missouri Constitution mandated. Several known poisoning cases with slave perpetrators exist from statehood years.

When the governor and judges of Indiana Territory adopted statutes for Upper Louisiana in 1804, they borrowed most of Virginia's slave laws in their entirety in order to regulate both civil and criminal aspects of slavery in Missouri. Likewise, they adopted nearly word for word the "Crimes and Punishments" section of the laws of the Northwest Territory for the governance of the general population, including slaves, within their newly assigned domain. Multiple offenses, including murder, manslaughter, burglary, assault, robbery, and larceny, appeared in the same order with the same punishments in both codes. What was initially enacted for the "Territory of the United States northwest of the river Ohio" in 1788 was put in force for the District of Louisiana effective October 1, 1804.[47]

The governor and judges of Indiana Territory also established courts in the District of Louisiana for hearing cases arising under the new American law. Like the statutes themselves these courts began functioning October 1, 1804. In their fact-finding aspects the most important difference between American and Spanish law was the right to trial by jury "of twelve good and lawful men of the vicinage."[48] Such a jury was one of the neighborhood in which the crime was committed. Under earlier Spanish law in Missouri, when criminally accused persons were taken into custody, they were hauled hundreds of miles to New Orleans for disposition without juries before courts in which the most important judge was the governor-general of Louisiana Territory. In contrast, under American law the powers of government were separated, and the governor of Indiana Territory/District of Louisiana never exercised the office of judge. For the first time in Missouri's history all criminal cases were offenses against the United States, and they were to be filed in the name of the new government.

The courts in which criminal defendants were to be tried under the 1804 laws were organized as follows: the governor appointed a competent number of justices of the peace, none of whom were attorneys, for each of Missouri's five districts. These men were authorized to hear petty criminal cases individually. Three of these justices of the peace when meeting together became the court of quarter sessions, and the law specified that it hold four terms in Missouri each year in each district. Though the court of quarter sessions had jurisdiction in criminal cases, between 1804 and 1807 and after 1810 until statehood capital cases were heard only by the Superior Court, also known as the General Court.

As Upper Louisiana grew, its officials, including those of its criminal justice system, increased. The governor appointed a sheriff, coroner, and clerk of courts for each district, and the governor and judges created the office of attorney general and defined his duties. The governor was empowered to appoint "a suitable person learned in the law" to prosecute all civil and criminal cases on behalf of either the United States or the Territory.[49]

Louisiana Territory's first governor, James Wilkinson, a Maryland native, named the Irish-born James Lowry Donaldson (1781–1814), a distinguished Baltimore lawyer, as the Territory's first attorney general. Early undated American court records contain L. Donaldson's signature as attorney general of Louisiana. One alleges a crime occurred on May 30, 1805, and the other specifies illegal acts involving slaves from December 20, 1805, until March 17, 1806. John Scott, a Virginia native and a member of the U.S. Congress from Missouri, was another early attorney general. A court of quarter sessions slave case from 1809 bears his name as prosecutor and the name of Edward Hempstead as defense attorney. Hempstead (1780–1817), a Connecticut attorney who moved to St. Louis in 1806, emerged as another of the territory's chief law enforcement officers. He was first appointed deputy attorney general for the districts of St. Louis and St. Charles in 1806. In 1809 Governor Meriwether Lewis named him attorney general for the territory, and he held this office until 1812. He prosecuted several slave criminal cases for which some records survive. In 1813 Governor Frederick Bates appointed David Barton, of Tennessee, attorney general for Missouri Territory. Barton also served as judge of the northern circuit between 1815 and 1817, and in 1818 he was the lead defense counsel in a territorial poisoning case. It heard the only extant death penalty case from Missouri's territorial period in which the accused was a slave.

In 1805 the same Congress, the Eighth, which created the District of Louisiana, disentangled its administration from Indiana Territory, renamed it the Louisiana Territory and legislated the specifics of its government. In 1812 the Twelfth Congress admitted the Territory of Orleans to the Union as the state of Louisiana, and to avoid confusion between it and Louisiana Territory, Congress substituted the name *Missouri* for *Louisiana* and provided Upper Louisiana with a second class of territorial government. That same year, and pursuant to authority vested in him by the U.S. Congress, the territorial governor issued a proclamation that changed the name of the area's chief unit of government from *district* to *county*. These were basically the former Spanish districts of St. Charles, St. Louis, Ste. Genevieve, Cape Girardeau, and New Madrid. Subsequent territorial law allowed the division of the county into as many as six townships and a constable's appointment for each such subdivision of the county.

For its first eight years the legislative power of the territory was continued in the governor and the three judges of the General Court, but in 1812 Congress created a bicameral general assembly that consisted of a governor, a legislative council, and a house of representatives. Until 1816, when the Fourteenth Congress allowed qualified voters to elect one member to the legislative council from each county in Missouri Territory, the president appointed both the governor and all members of the legislative council. He chose its nine congressionally authorized members from a list

St. Charles County had neither western nor northern limits within the United States. St. Louis, Ste. Genevieve, and Cape Girardeau extended more than 200 miles west. St. Louis County included eastern Jackson; Ste. Genevieve, eastern Vernon; and Cape Girardeau, eastern Jasper. New Madrid County included most of the present state of Arkansas.

of 28 nominees, all resident-owners of at least 200 acres of land, submitted by the territorial house of representatives. The Twelfth Congress fixed the membership of the Missouri Territorial House of Representatives at one for every 500 free white male inhabitants and provided for the immediate election of 13 and the ultimate election of no more than 25 members. By federal law any person elected to this body was a free white male of at least 21 years of age, a resident of the territory for at least one year prior to his election, a landowner in the county from which he was elected, and a county or territorial tax payer. His term of office was two years.[50]

In 1815 the territorial legislature divided Missouri Territory into two judicial divisions and commissioned the governor to appoint a circuit judge and a circuit or prosecuting attorney for both. The circuits were termed the northern and the southern, and the older counties of St. Charles, St. Louis, and the newly created county of Washington made up the northern, and the counties of Ste. Genevieve, Cape Girardeau, and New Madrid the southern. As the population of the territory increased, the governor appointed additional judges and circuit attorneys for the new circuits that the General Assembly created. The courts of these circuits replaced those of quarter sessions whose membership was composed of non-attorney justices of the peace. The original circuit court jurisdiction included all criminal cases except those involving capital punishment. Death penalty cases continued to be heard only by the three presidentially appointed members of the Superior Court. Any two of them constituted a quorum.

In 1807 the legislative authority established the mechanism for a court of oyer and terminer, a common term in the United States for a higher court that hears criminal cases, in each of the five districts of Louisiana Territory. Its membership consisted of one judge of the General Court who, when a capital case arose in any district, was authorized to appoint two judges of the Court of Common Pleas, a civil court, to preside as a three-judge panel at the death penalty trial. Until this court's abolition in 1810 and the restoration of its trial jurisdiction to the General Court, whose members were *all* presidential appointees, the court of oyer and terminer heard all potentially capital cases in the territory, including *U.S. v. Long,* which is discussed in chapter 6.

In 1808 lawmakers expanded the crimes and punishments that the governor and three judges of Indiana Territory had borrowed in 1804 from the laws of the Northwest Territory and adopted as the criminal code of the District of Louisiana. Excepting murder, arson, and rape, for which penalties for slave offenders were specified, the designated punishments of the 1808 act extended only to free persons; slaves were to be punished at the discretion of the court.[51] In 1816 territorial legislation indicated how courts were to exercise their discretion concerning the punishment of bondpersons for most crimes: "no part of the punishment of such slave shall be fine or imprisonment, but the court before whom the conviction is had, may punish such slave with stripes."[52]

The 1808 legislation continued the 1804 offense of larceny (stealing), but it also added the separate crimes of horse stealing and hog stealing. Hog theft was a criminal act expected of both free and slave defendants. Though its $100 fine was unsuitable for those in bondage, its designated whipping of no less than 25 and no more than 39 lashes was tailored for slave offenders. In addition it carried no enhanced punishment for a second conviction. Horse stealing, on the other hand, was wrongdoing expected of free persons. From its first appearance in 1808 it was a more serious crime than hog stealing. First offenders were required to pay the owner double the value and receive no less than 50 and no more than 100 stripes. For a second conviction the offender could be imprisoned for up to seven years and fined $1,000. The primary use of stolen swine was food, but equines were means of swift, and often enough for slaves, forbidden transportation.

Crimes for which the 1808 laws specified the punishment for slaves included arson and murder. In 1804 the law had provided that any person convicted of arson receive a death sentence. In 1808 and for the first time under American law in Missouri, only slave arsonists were sentenced to death. Free persons guilty of this crime were eligible for imprisonment of up to seven years and a fine of up to $10,000. The reason for the discrepancy between the punishments of slaves and free whites for this offense against the habitation most likely was the fear of arson as a weapon of slave sedition. The 1835 Missouri laws listed, among other capital crimes, the commission of arson in furtherance of slave insurrection. The possibility of their chattels' revolt was always uppermost among slaveholders' concerns, and in Missouri and all other slave states legislation reflected these fears.

The punishment for murder, which carried a death sentence for both slaves and free persons, was refined when the territory's legislative authority adopted certain features of the federal death penalty. In 1790 the First U.S. Congress enacted and President Washington signed major legislation dealing with crime and punishment. Among other features, congressional law specified, "The manner of inflicting the punishment of death shall be by hanging the person convicted by the neck until dead."[53] In 1808 the territorial legislature adopted this statute verbatim when providing for the execution of all offenders, both slave and free.[54]

This uniform method of executing both slave and free criminals for all offenses distinguished American territorial government from the older slave states, such as Delaware, Georgia, Maryland, North Carolina, South Carolina, and Virginia, which formed the Union and were guided only by their own state constitutions and the laws enacted pursuant to them regarding, among other matters, the punishment of slaves. No territorial legislature could adopt a more severe law for the punishment of crime than the federal. Unlike the original 13 states, wherein the 1791 federal Bill of Rights did not apply, its multiple provisions were applicable in the territories. Since hanging was considered the most humane method of executing the condemned in the 1790s, it did not violate the Eighth Amendment's prohibition against cruel and unusual punishments. It remained the exclusive manner of carrying out death sentences under the authority of Missouri until 1938, when the gas chamber replaced the noose.

In 1808 the territorial legislature borrowed another remarkable feature from the First Congress's 1790 major crimes bill: the judge was permitted to add an additional sentence of dissection after death as punishment for condemned murderers. This enhanced form of capital punishment became English law in 1752. As its British preamble explained: "For the better preventing the horrid crime of Murder ... it is ... become necessary that some further Terror and peculiar mark of Infamy be added to the Punishment of Death."[55] Dissection, or cutting up the deceased into minute pieces in the interest of science, had existed in England since the sixteenth century, when Henry VIII granted surgeons four bodies of hanged felons each year. Though that number was increased by two in the seventeenth century, by the eighteenth, heightened interest in human anatomy, physiology, and the more accurate practice of medicine led to a greater demand for more cadavers than six a year.

Cadavers for dissection were readily obtainable in Paris as early as the 1700s at the French capital's four major hospitals, especially those receiving indigent patients who expired in these facilities. The Parisian hospitals' access to cadavers helps explain the French preeminence in medicine, especially surgery. It logically followed that Spain obtained the service of doctors trained in Paris for military posts in areas such as Missouri during the eighteenth century. Such physicians were skilled in the treatment of likely medical problems of soldiers. For example, at least one master surgeon in Paris fired bullets into cadavers to study their trajectories and the resulting damage to the human body for his course on gunshot wounds.[56]

By contrast, no such instruction was available in England, where the demand for dead bodies greatly exceeded their availability. Body snatchers bent on a quick sale to anatomists emptied graves to the great grief and rage of the English citizenry. Parliament's reaction was the 1752 act that allowed the judge to impose the additional sentence of dissection on condemned murderers. English law changed in 1832 when the Anatomy Act allowed the government to supply anatomists with the bodies of paupers, too poor to pay for their own funerals and burials, who died in public institutions such as hospitals, almshouses, and workhouses.[57] Until 1832 the exclusive legal source of cadavers in England was the gallows.

In America dissection as an additional sentence for crime was first made law in New York in 1789. The next year the First Congress made it federal law, and in 1796 New Jersey adopted dissection as punishment for crime.[58] When Arkansas Territory was carved out of Missouri Territory in 1819, it adopted the law of the territory from which it was formed, and when Arkansas was admitted to the Union as a slave state in 1835, its law permitted the sentencing judge to condemn the convicted murderer to the additional sentence of dissection, provided as under federal and Missouri law "that such surgeon, or some other person by him appointed for that purpose, shall attend to receive and take away the dead body at the time of the execution of such offender."[59]

Massachusetts was the first state to provide for the anatomical needs of its doctors and medical schools in legislation similar to the English anatomy Act of 1832. In January 1831, or 15 months before the English Anatomy law took effect, it passed "An Act more effectively to Protect the Sepulchres of the Dead and to Legalize the Study of Anatomy in Certain Cases." Massachusetts permitted the authorities to donate for dissection the bodies of persons who would otherwise be buried at public expense. The law provided that preference in the distribution of cadavers be given to faculty in the state's two medical schools, Harvard and the Berkshire Medical Institution.[60]

Harvard Medical School was founded in 1782, and by 1823 there were eight medical schools in New England.[61] By the 1830s prisons, lunatic asylums, almshouses, and other houses of refuge dotted the New England landscape.[62] The laws of the region provided either dead bodies of destitute inmates of these states' multiple institutions and/or those of executed felons be made available for dissection. Between the remains of the poor and the capitally punished, the medical schools and medical practitioners in the Northeast received, if not an adequate supply of cadavers, far greater numbers than could be legally obtained in frontier Missouri.

In early statehood years the corpses of Missouri's hanged criminals, first made available under the 1808 law, provided only a tiny trickle of dead bodies. Unlike New England, Missouri of the early 1830s had no state prisons, lunatic asylums, or other public almshouses whose deceased residents could provide a steady source of cadavers. Grave robbers of the era apparently supplied most corpses that were made available to the state's anatomists. The work of body snatchers horrified the surviving relatives of the dead whose graves were opened.

In 1835, and under the leadership of the St. Louisan, Speaker of the House Henry Geyer, the Missouri legislature reacted. It criminalized both opening of graves for the purpose of selling their contents to anatomists and the act of receiving dead bodies for dissection purposes. The law provided three circumstances in which the sale and removal of the body for dissection or anatomical experiment was not a crime. The near relations of the deceased might give permission for dissection; those donors were few! Otherwise, the only legal source of cadavers was "the body of any criminal executed for crime, or the body of a slave with the consent of his owner."[63]

How many Missouri slaves were dissected, how many of those were guilty of crime, and exactly when the practice of using their dead bodies for scientific purposes began will never be known. However, bondpersons in this state met the same anatomical needs as paupers who died in prestigious Paris hospitals, English poorhouses, and New England almshouses.

Their dissection was probably most common in the eastern part of the state. In central and western Missouri some executed slaves were not dissected; they were buried. The law always required that the surgeon or persons appointed by him attend the hanging(s) and remove the corpse(s).

When the General Assembly in 1835 increased the legal supply of cadavers by adding the dead bodies of slaves to those of executed criminals, it began permitting dissection for educational purposes. However, as late as the 1830s there was no formal medical education in Missouri. Transylvania University in Lexington, Kentucky, which began offering medical courses in 1817, was the only medical school west of the Allegheny Mountains. Its first regional rival was the Ohio Medical College of Cincinnati, which graduated its first class in 1821. Prior to 1840 approximately 75 percent of physicians in the Midwest received their medical education through the apprentice system.[64] Because there were insufficient executions in settled areas such as St. Louis to meet the doctors' demands for dead bodies, probably by 1835 professor-physicians from this city persuaded the legislature that it should legalize an already existing practice when it officially permitted slave dissection. After this enactment Missouri's first medical association was organized in St. Louis in 1836, and this city became the site of the state's first medical schools: McDowell Medical College in 1840, the Medical Department of St. Louis University in 1840, and Humboldt Medical College in 1859.[65] Until slavery's demise, the remains of the executed and those in bondage legally supplied the anatomical needs of these institutions and physicians who taught apprentices. Only after the Civil War did the corpses of the afflicted who died as paupers in Missouri's penitentiary, insane asylum, hospitals, and poorhouses replace deceased slaves as anatomical specimens.

Among much else, such treatment of African-Americans took place because the Jefferson administration wished to accommodate influential slave-owning French residents and numerous slave-owning Americans on this land at the time of the Purchase. "The Law Respecting Slaves," which the governor and judges of Indiana Territory adopted for the District of Louisiana in 1804, became and basically remained the law of Missouri throughout slavery. Persons with 25 percent Negro blood were fit subjects of human bondage throughout its Missouri tenure. Slave testimonial incapacity against whites endured throughout slavery, and the statute forbidding slave preparation, exhibition, or administration of any medicine continued as Missouri law well into statehood years. The crimes and punishments that the governor and judges adopted in 1808 for the fledgling territory clearly revealed both an agrarian society concerned with hog and horse theft and the influence of the latest federal methods of treating condemned prisoners. Dissection of slaves (with their masters' permission), which was first adopted in 1835, remained Missouri law until slavery perished.

Just how the criminal law affected slaves during territorial times is best shown in the surviving criminal cases concerning them from that time period. These stories are the subject of the next two chapters.

Chapter 3

Noncapital Territorial Wrongdoing

With few exceptions, the examined territorial cases and newspaper advertisements concerning slavery and crime originated in St. Louis District/County. Three cases survive from St. Charles County; in 1818 the circuit attorney obtained indictments against one slave for separate offenses and a third indictment against another. No matter how trivial the crime, all territorial cases were offenses against the United States and were prosecuted on behalf of the federal government. All court records were at best summaries because any method of obtaining word-for-word transcripts was first employed long after slavery ended. No inspected case from St. Louis County during 1820 and 1821 contained the names of the owners of accused and convicted slaves.

In 1818 Jesse, a slave and the property of Jacob Coil, pled guilty to two separate offenses in St. Charles County Circuit Court. One was an indictment for stealing a goose and the other for stealing a knife. Though the records do not connect these crimes, Jesse probably stole the knife either to kill the fowl, or if he killed or planned to kill the stolen goose by wringing its neck, he intended to use the knife to remove the guts before cooking his stolen food. The judge sentenced him to 15 lashes for stealing the goose and 15 for the knife. Jesse's separate whippings were both to be administered "on his bare back well laid on." The flaying of Jesse and any other slave convicted of a similar crime was usually a duty of the sheriff, but in the event this official was unavailable, the task fell to the county coroner or his hiree.

The several officials who participated in Jesse's arrest, indictment, guilty plea, and punishment were compensated. In January 1816 the territorial legislature required that slave owners pay all costs in noncapital slave criminal cases. Afterward, noncapital convictions recited potential indebtedness such as "if ... the owner of said Jesse shall neglect or refuse to pay the costs of this prosecution that the said Jesse be sold for the payment of the same according to the statute in such cases made and provided."[1] The expenses associated with due process for slaves, the particulars of which are discussed in chapter 6, partially explain the small number of court records in rural areas for offenses such as stealing geese and knives. The legal process's many costs encouraged Missouri's owners or their overseers to handle in-house, and without the intervention of a court, most petty offenses involving slaves.

Another case from St. Charles County arose in 1818 when Slave Bill was tried before the St. Charles Circuit Court and found guilty of burglary. His court-imposed punishment was 100 lashes.[2] The case did not indicate whether his entire punishment was to be administered seriatim, one lash through 100. This record contained neither the proceeds, if any, of his burglary, its structure(s), nor the name(s) of his victim(s). Bill's case contained his owner's name, Dr. Antoine Reynal (1741–1821). The attorney-historian Houck considered Reynal among the richest, most influential, and most intelligent Frenchmen in Missouri Territory.[3] He was the third physician to arrive in Upper Louisiana. He began practicing medicine during the Spanish regime at St. Louis Post in 1776, and for approximately 20 years he remained a St. Louis doctor. When Dr. Reynal moved to St. Charles at the beginning of the nineteenth century, the first proceedings of the court of quarter sessions for St. Charles District met in his home in January 1805, and the St. Charles Courthouse was erected on the site of his residence.[4] He died in St. Charles in December 1821 at 80 years of age.[5] When Slave Bill was found guilty of burglary in 1818, his owner was a financially comfortable septuagenarian who surely paid with ease all costs associated with the case. Because the physician could well afford the costs of due process for his slave, neither he nor one of his employees personally punished the burglar. Instead the United States prosecuted Slave Bill.

A fragment of a territorial case survives from Howard County. Slave Phil was charged with larceny (stealing), and his owner, Daniel Muncie, had earlier posted a recognizance bond in which he guaranteed that his accused slave would attend court on the appointed day. On July 13, 1819, Phil, a black man, appeared in Howard County Circuit Court to answer the stealing accusation against him. His owner was discharged from his obligation to pay the United States in the event of the nonappearance of Phil, and the charges against the slave were also dismissed.[6]

The remainder of the discovered territorial cases from Upper Louisiana derive from St. Louis. With few exceptions they arose in the town of St. Louis, whose population then ranged from a low of 1,000 to an approximate high of 3,500. Scharf described the best society in it as "people like the Gratiots, Soulards, Chouteaus ... Chenies, and so many more like them, gentle, easy, bright men, lively charming, beautiful, and accomplished women."[7] These fashionable persons owned the slaves whose names appeared, and probably reappeared, in criminal records. Most likely, such owners did not hire overseers to supervise the few whom any individual owned.

The earliest American court records about bondpersons were fragments of civil suits that Sarah Pickens, widow executrix of the estate of her deceased husband, John Pickens, filed in St. Louis Superior Court against Pascal Cerré and Antonio Soulard in 1804. Under English law a married woman as young as 17 could serve as executrix of a last will and testament.[8] American territorial law in Missouri permitted married women aged at least 21 years to serve as executrixes. In one writ or court order Chief Justice Thomas T. Davis commanded James Rankin, the first sheriff of St. Louis District, to deliver to Sarah Pickens a Negro girl named Lucie and a Negro boy named Charles, whom Pascal Cerré had unjustly detained. In another writ of this same date Judge Davis ordered the sheriff to deliver to the Widow Pickens a Negro man named Peter, a Negro boy named Peter, a Negro boy named Paul, a Negro boy named Justen, a Negro woman named Lucy, and a Negro girl named Claris, all of whom, Pickens's complaint presumably alleged, Antonio Soulard unjustly detained. In returns of service Rankin confirmed that he had redelivered the Negroes to Sarah Pickens and summoned Cerré and Soulard to appear in the Superior Court at St. Louis in and for the District of Louisiana on May 6, 1805.[9]

On December 18, 1804, the first grand jury for the Territory of Louisiana, St. Louis District, met in St. Louis and continued to meet periodically until September 17, 1805. Because the U.S. Constitution was in force in the territories, the majority vote of this body was required before the prosecutor could file any formal criminal charge against the accused. Charles Gratiot served as the foreman of the territory's first grand jury, and among its 24 members was Antonio Soulard.[10] Sometime prior to the May 1805 term of the Superior Court, it indicted John Pickens, yeoman, on charges that he "did ... feloniously steal" the slaves of Antonio Soulard and Pascal Cerré to their owners' damage and "against the peace, government & dignity of the United States."[11] The six named were Peter, Luce,

Charles, Peter, Paul, and Justine. These are duplications with alternate spellings of the slaves named in Sarah Pickens's civil suits against Soulard and Cerré.

The indictment was signed by the prosecutor, J. L. Donaldson, attorney general of Louisiana Territory, and Charles Gratiot, foreman of the grand jury that returned a true bill against John Pickens, "late of the territory." Gratiot (1752–1817), a French Huguenot born in Switzerland, was a prominent resident of St. Louis. As noted in chapter 2, Captain Amos Stoddard received Upper Louisiana in behalf of the United States from the French government on Charles Gratiot's portico. Houck considered him "about the only man in St. Louis who took a personal interest in the transfer of [the Louisiana Purchase] to the United States."[12] Gratiot served as foreman of several early grand juries.[13]

In 1805 the only territorial law applicable in *U.S.* v. *John Pickens* came from Virginia's slave code, which the governor and judges of Indiana Territory adopted for the District of Louisiana effective October 1, 1804: "If any person ... shall steal any negro ... from ... the owner ... of such slave, the person ... shall suffer death."[14] Further, the theft of slaves was one of the few property crimes in territorial Missouri that upon conviction mandated the death penalty. Today any American criminal case is mooted by the death of the defendant, but under the law of Louisiana Territory, restoration of the stolen property to the rightful owner was a part of the penalty for the crime, and Soulard and Cerré stood to benefit financially if John Pickens, alive or dead, was found guilty of the theft of the six slaves.

Nothing further is known of either Widow Pickens's complaint against Soulard and Cerré or the government's charges against her late husband, John Pickens. Sarah and John Pickens were not prominent persons. No trace of them appears to exist independent of these court records that bear their names. On the other hand, Houck identified Pascal Cerré as the owner of several slaves.[15] Don Antonio Soulard, a surveyor of Upper Louisiana, captain of the militia, was assistant mayor (*ayudante mayor*) of St. Louis under Spanish colonial rule.[16] Whether John Pickens's indictment on charges of stealing Soulard's and Cerré's slaves was a direct result of Soulard's presence on the grand jury that voted a true bill against this dead man is unknown. Perhaps these influential men used the law to harass Widow Pickens and deprive her of her rightful ownership of the slaves named in the surviving documents.

Other early court records from St. Louis District, Louisiana Territory, include two that contained the signature of L. Donaldson, attorney general. One indicted Frederick Connor, for keeping and maintaining a "disorderly house" by permitting and encouraging Negro slaves to meet and drink and selling liquor to them to the "evil example of others" from December 1 through December 15, 1805. Another document alleged that Frederick Connor, from December 20, 1805, through March 17, 1806, "did to the common nuisance of the District, and against the peace, dignity, and government of the United States, keep and maintain a disorderly house by encouraging negroes slave and free to frequent the same for unlawful purposes."[17] Both the congregating of slaves for any purpose and the sale of alcoholic beverages to them without their owners' consent were violations of the 1804 slave code. Frederick Connor probably permitted other undesirable behaviors on his property between December 1, 1805, and March 17, 1806.

A "disorderly house" had a precise American definition during the early nineteenth century; "a house of ill fame, a bawdy house" were both the only 1809 meanings and the earliest located for the phrase.[18] Frederick Connor was probably the proprietor of a St. Louis whorehouse during early American governance of Missouri. However, there were no statutes, criminal or other, concerning prostitution under American rule in territorial Missouri, and the accused could not be convicted for the violation of a nonexistent law. Therefore, Attorney General Donaldson's available remedy against this disorderly housekeeper was nuisance law. A common nuisance annoyed and disturbed an indefinite number of persons, and under both English and American law the attorney general was authorized to abate or remove what offended the community in a continuing, not a single or momentary, disturbance.

On July 9, 1806, and possibly in response to the Connor case, the territorial legislature enacted a statute concerning taverns. It provided a number of conditions for the annual renewal of any proprietor's required license. Among them were prohibiting "any disorder, fighting or drunkenness," providing "good entertainment," and refusing to sell "rum, brandy, whiskey, beer, or other spirits" to bond servant[s] or slave[s] ... without first obtaining permission of their masters."[19] Gambling per se would not have been subject to nuisance law because prior to 1814 games of chance among free persons were prevalent amusements in territorial times and were basically unregulated.[20] Probably, slaves and free blacks had sex, fought, got drunk, gambled, and otherwise misbehaved on Frederick Connor's premises. Bondmen paid for their gambling losses, drinking, and whoring, if no other way, with their own labor, and doing so without their owners' permission was always a violation of slave law under French, Spanish, and American governance of Missouri. No record of any license for Connor to operate a tavern could be located. Nothing further is known of his legal problems.

Many of these court records clarified how landowners guaranteed the

court appearance of slaves, usually their own, at the same time their owners continued to benefit from their bondpersons' labor. Because the U.S.
Constitution was in force in the territories, in noncapital cases the Eighth
Amendment, which prohibited excessive bail, applied to slaves as well as
free whites. Almost certainly, at the time of arrest the accused spent at
least a few hours in confinement. Jails and jailers were the subject of early
territorial legislation, and the 1808 statute mentioned already existing "jails
of the respective districts," probably a reference to the use of a military
guardhouse for St. Louis District prisoners.[21] However, slaves in noncapital cases usually did not languish in detention awaiting their trials, which
typically took place no sooner than six weeks after the offense. Instead,
and at times on the same day as the occurrence of the charged crime, a
man of property signed a pledge for a stated amount in which he acknowledged his indebtedness to the United States. Afterward, the prisoner was
quickly released from jail, and he continued to labor for his owner before
and after his arrest, trial, and punishment.

In these extant territorial slave cases, the sums that the surety guaranteed the government ranged from a low of $100 to a high of $500, and
the amounts reflected the seriousness of the charge(s). In cases involving
multiple slave defendants, a separate guaranty was posted for each to insure
the court appearance of all accused persons to answer criminal charges
against them on a designated date. The phrase *recognizance bond* also
referred to the amount of pledged money that was forfeited to the government if the defendant failed to appear. All these pledges were entered
into and recorded before a court or magistrate. Though some later slave
criminal cases recorded the forfeit of recognizance bonds, in all known
during the territorial period, there was no forfeiture of the stated amount
because the bondperson appeared for trial. No money actually changed
hands because the amount of the pledge was to be taken from the pled-
gor's real and personal property.

Of the nine separate recognizance bonds examined, the slave's owner
posted six of them, and in three a friend or a business associate pledged
a specified amount of his property that another's slave would appear for
trial. With one exception men were the designated owners of all slaves in
these territorial criminal records. A man posted the recognizance bond for
the one examined case involving an accused slave owned by a female.
Women appear never to have posted any sureties for the court appearance
of their slaves in criminal cases. Though they served as executrixes of
estates, the only role girls and women played in all known slave criminal
cases in Missouri were as witnesses or as the accused.

The surviving records show that Charles Sanguinet appeared before a justice of the peace on July 14, 1809, and acknowledged himself indebted to the United States in the amount of $100. The document recited that this sum "shall be made and levied of his body, goods, chattels, lands and tenements to ... the use of the said United States" in the event that Helene, a slave and his property, should fail to appear at the November term of the court of quarter sessions and abide its judgment. Slave Helene was charged with larceny in stealing two blankets from Louis Cailloux.[22]

Her victim was probably a member of a family by the surname *Cailloux* who moved from Kaskaskia to St. Louis in 1780.[23] Her owner was far more important. Charles Sanguinet, the son of a French physician posted to Canada, was born in Montreal and moved to St. Louis District during the Spanish regime. He owned property near St. Louis and engaged in the fur trade. His wife, Marie, was the daughter of Dr. Andrew August Conde, a Frenchman and the first physician to arrive at St. Louis Post in 1776. She and her husband reared many children. In 1810 one of their daughters, Constance, married the oldest son of August Chouteau. In 1818 their youngest daughter, 18-year-old Caroline Anne, married Horatio Cozens soon after the groom completed his work as one of the defense attorneys in the slave poisoning case. Sanguinet, a businessman, died in 1818 in St. Louis at an advanced age.[24] Most likely included among Helene's work as a house slave of Charles and Marie Sanguinet was a great deal of laundering, kitchen duties, and child care. Perhaps she slept in a very cold place, and she was making provisions for winter when she stole two blankets in or near July. Equally likely may have been her intention to barter these items to an unscrupulous peddler in return for other items or for money. The blankets she took could not have been of any great value; otherwise, her bond would have been much larger than $100.

A record survives from 1811 similar to Slave Lorine's 1779 attack on Lieutenant Governor De Leyba's Slave Marianne during the Spanish regime. In the American case Marie Philip LeDuc acknowledged himself indebted to the United States in the sum of $200 to be levied of his goods and chattels, lands and tenements as a guarantor of the appearance of Catherine, a black woman and the slave of Antoine Chenie, on November 4, 1811, at the court of quarter sessions for St. Louis District "to answer to an indictment of the United States for assaulting, beating, wounding, and ill treating Catiche, a Black Woman, the slave of Manuel Lisa."[25]

The men who owned these slaves and the one who posted Catherine's recognizance bond were all outstanding members of St. Louis society when the incident involving the women occurred. Marie Philip LeDuc (1773–1843) was a Frenchman who arrived in New Madrid District in 1792 and became secretary to the commandant of New Madrid Post, Charles

DeLassus. When DeLassus was promoted to lieutenant governor of Spanish Illinois in 1799, he moved to St. Louis, and his secretary came with
him. In 1804 LeDuc was appointed clerk for both the court of common
pleas (a civil court) and the court of quarter sessions. In 1805 he became
the official interpreter for the board of land commissioners. In this same
year he witnessed a bond for $4,000 to Governor William Henry Harri-
son in which James Rankin, Antonio Soulard, and August Chouteau guaranteed the performance of James Rankin as the first sheriff of St. Louis
District. Marie Philip LeDuc also served two terms in the legislature: in
1818 he was a territorial representative from St Louis, and in 1820 he represented St. Louis County in the first General Assembly of statehood years.
At his death he was aged 70 years.[26]

Catherine's owner, Antoine Chenie (1768–1840), was born in Montreal and first appeared as a St. Louis resident in 1795. He moved there from
St. Ferdinand, the largest settlement in St. Louis District outside the town
of St. Louis. In St. Louis, he began employment as a clerk in the fur trade;
in 1805 he left this business and established a bakery. In 1811 he and Manuel
Lisa were among the signers of a petition to Congress concerning the government of Louisiana Territory. At his death this long-term resident of St.
Louis was described as "an old and highly respectable Frenchman."[27]

Manuel Lisa (1772–1820), a fur trader, explorer, and successful St.
Louis businessman, was born of Spanish parents in Cuba and came to St.
Louis in 1807 after a probable residence in New Orleans. He owned real
estate in the town of St. Louis, and he was a business partner in the fur
trade with men such as William Clark, later a territorial governor of Missouri. Among his other ventures he was one of the founders of the Bank
of St. Louis. By July 17, 1811, the date of the recognizance bond, Manuel
and his first wife, Mary, were St. Louis residents and the parents of several young children, including Raymond and Manuel Lisa Jr.[28] Probably
Catiche, among other responsibilities, cared for the Lisa children. When
Catherine assaulted her, the law was available to punish the alleged aggressor because her victim's owner, Manuel Lisa, was one of the most powerful men in Louisiana Territory. After the death of his first wife in 1818, he
married a widowed sister of Edward Hempstead, attorney general of
Louisiana Territory at the time Slave Catherine allegedly assaulted Lisa's
Slave Catiche. Had Catherine attacked a free black, and the 1810 census
for Missouri enumerated 607 free blacks,[29] most likely no criminal charges
would have been filed against her.

On May 8, 1817, Henry Geyer, circuit attorney for the northern circuit, tried a larceny case before a jury of twelve good and lawful men that
involved the theft of a watch valued at $60. The jury might have found

the slave defendant not guilty, and its verdict would have ended any additional court proceedings. As it turned out, the jury found the mulatto boy guilty as charged. The record noted that the watch had not been restored to its unnamed owner. The convicted slave was committed to the custody of the sheriff of St. Louis County. On May 12, or four days after the jury found him guilty of larceny, his attorney made a successful motion for a new trial. Usually a slave convicted of any noncapital offense was whipped as punishment within 24 hours of the conviction. Setting aside a jury verdict and granting a new trial in any criminal case is not and has never been common. It meant that the judge determined that the jury verdict was unsupported by fact and contrary to law.

Four days later on May 16, 1817, John W. Thompson and Robert Wash jointly posted a recognizance bond of $300 to be levied of their respective goods and chattels, lands and tenements to guarantee the October 16, 1817, court appearance of the mulatto boy for retrial on the larceny charge. In the interval between bail being made for him and his pending second trial, at the October St. Louis term of the northern circuit court, the slave defendant was not in jail and remained unconfined and unpunished by any court order. On October 14, 1817, circuit attorney Henry Geyer exercised his discretion as prosecutor by electing to "no further prosecute the said indictment," and the judge ordered the accused discharged. In *U. S. v. Slave Don Quixote* all charges were dropped against the defendant.[30]

Though Don Quixote's recognizance bond did not identify Thompson and Wash, the men who posted it, as his masters, since it did not identify any other person as his owner, it is reasonable to infer that he was the property of one or both of them. The name *Don Quixote* suggests that Robert Wash (1790–1856), a Virginia-reared and-educated attorney, named him after hearing about or reading Cervantes' novel in one of several easily available English-language versions.[31] The word *quixotic* derives from the novel, and it means "striving with lofty enthusiasm for visionary ideals."[32] *Don* is a Spanish title for a lord or gentleman of high rank, and *Quixote* is Cervantes' invention. Whatever else can be said of an appropriate name for a slave, when his owner named him or continued to call him *Don Quixote*, he did so as one now names a pet. That Slave Don Quixote's very name was a piece of fiction reflected the total power his owner had over him. His purpose for life was slavery.

His owner never intended harm to his mulatto boy over the theft of a watch, which almost certainly would have been restored to the rightful owner between a recognizance bond being posted for him and the dismissal of all charges. The intertwined lives of Don Quixote's judge, prosecutor, and owner(s) help to explain the favorable outcome of his case. His judge,

Nathaniel Beverly Tucker (1784–1851), was a Virginian by birth, rearing, and education. He graduated from William and Mary College in 1801, where he studied law. He practiced in Virginia until he came to St. Louis in 1815. Soon after his arrival, the governor appointed him judge of the northern circuit. Tucker remained on the bench for approximately 11 years, including several of early statehood service. In 1833–34 he returned to Virginia and became a law professor at his alma mater, William and Mary.[33]

Don Quixote's prosecutor, Henry Geyer (1790–1859), like Don Quixote's owners, served in the War of 1812, where he rose to the rank of captain. He first came to St. Louis the same year Judge Tucker arrived, 1815, and like the judge, Geyer was already an educated and practicing attorney in Maryland before he moved to territorial Missouri. Within a year or so the governor appointed him circuit attorney for the northern circuit upon the resignation of Robert Wash.

Geyer's career was distinguished as a publisher in 1817 of the statutes of Missouri, member in 1818 of the Fourth Territorial Legislature, and repeatedly elected member of the Missouri General Assembly. He served four terms in this body between 1820 and 1840, and he was Speaker of the House during three of them. He was a major reviser of the Missouri statutes of both 1825 and 1835. In 1850 President Fillmore offered him the position of Secretary of War, which he declined. He was elected a U.S. senator in 1851 and served from 1851 until 1857. He argued several cases before the U.S. Supreme Court, the best known of which is *Scott* v. *Sandford* or the Dred Scott case (1857). Geyer represented the slave owner's right to retain his property, and Chief Justice Taney, who adopted Geyer's arguments, wrote a convoluted decision for the majority that Scott's residence in Illinois had not freed him, and he was still a slave. Sandford's victory was not for posterity because this infamous decision is best remembered as a precipitating factor in the Civil War. Despite Scott's later notoriety, Henry Geyer was one of Missouri's most distinguished, influential, and capable attorneys.[34]

The men who posted a recognizance bond for Don Quixote were, like his prosecutor, veterans of the War of 1812. John W. Thompson rose to the rank of lieutenant colonel and commanded the First Regiment from St. Louis County. Governor Clark appointed Robert Wash, a second lieutenant in this war, and he served on the staff of General Howard, a former governor of the territory. The odds favor the U.S. Army friendship of Geyer, Thompson, and Wash. By the time of Don Quixote's legal difficulties Thompson was in his third year as sheriff of St. Louis County; Governor Clark appointed him in April 1815 and reappointed him for two more years in April 1817.[35] Other sheriffs may have posted recognizance bonds for their prisoners, but Sheriff Thompson's doing so was the only discovered incident of such pledging in these slave cases.

Robert Wash had recently vacated the position of circuit attorney for the northern circuit when his slave was prosecuted for theft of the watch, and Geyer succeeded him as circuit attorney. Like Geyer, in 1818 Wash was elected a representative from St. Louis County to the Fourth Territorial Legislature. His primary importance in Missouri history was as a judge on the Supreme Court of Missouri. He was appointed early in 1824, and he served until 1837.[36] In addition to participating in most death penalty decisions involving slave defendants that this court decided, he also cast a minority vote in this body's decision that held that Indians were not suitable subjects of slavery. In his dissent Wash wrote: "Slaves have been always esteemed, and are at this day esteemed, the proper goods or property of their masters or owners; and to be sold, exchanged, or bartered, as merchandise or property.... It is out and out, from beginning to end, a pure question of power."[37] Nothing more is known of Slave Don Quixote's brush with the law other than the likelihood that he escaped a whipping for stealing a watch because his owner, Robert Wash, wished to avoid an official punishment for him. Marie Jean Scypion, the issue of an Indian and a Negro, owed her and her progeny's freedom to the other Supreme Court of Missouri judges.

On June 9, 1818, in St. Louis Circuit Court, a jury of 12 good and lawful men found Maria, a black woman and the slave of Thomas Peebles, guilty of larceny in the theft of property valued at $75. Of that total, $24.50 had already been restored to the owner, Thomas Brown, by the date of Maria's trial. This record contained no description of the stolen property, and the victim of the theft cannot be identified. Her owner opened a "house of entertainment" in St. Louis at the sign of the Union Hall, formerly known as the Missouri Hotel in January 1816.[38] Most likely, such a business provided lodging, food, and other incidentals to its customers. Maria was probably a slave worker in her owner's business. The judge sentenced her to "20 lashes on her bare back well laid on" and ordered the sheriff of St. Louis County to execute her punishment that same evening, a Tuesday, between 7:00 and 9:00. In Missouri, like all other American places of slavery, no viewer of a judicially imposed punishment was excluded. Those who watched such scenes might be slave or free, old or young, men, women, and children, whoever wished or was ordered to observe it. The court required that Maria's owner, the entertainment-house owner, Thomas Peebles, make restitution to Thomas Brown in the amount of $50.75, pay the costs of the prosecution, and be notified of his slave's sentence. The record also contained standard language regarding her sale should her owner not pay court costs.[39]

Other slave criminal cases that arose in St. Louis County in 1820 were equally sketchy. For example, in August 1820 the grand jury indicted Slaves Ned and Simon on larceny charges. Simon was found guilty and sentenced to 25 lashes, but the court records contained no description of the stolen property, its value, or the names of either Simon's victim or his owner.[40]

Pieces of four 1809 slave criminal records survive from the District of St. Louis, Louisiana Territory. Only one, Slave Helene's case, has already been discussed. The others are considered with later cases because some proof, however slight, exists that a defendant from an 1809 proceeding may have been a repeat offender in a later case.

The evidence was especially strong that a slave charged with larceny in 1809, a mulatto woman named Lilise, whom Madame Lammé then owned, was the same Slave Lilise charged with larceny in 1817, whom Madame Lammé also owned that same year. The charges against her involved items of little worth. The surviving records indicate that on May 30, 1809, Henry Delouers appeared before a justice of the peace to post a recognizance bond of $100 to guarantee the appearance of Slave Lilise at the next court of quarter sessions on July 3, 1809. As these cases demonstrated, often the slaveholder posted a bond for his own slave or that of a friend or business associate, but in this case Lilise was the property of a woman, and a man handled her recognizance bond. In the earlier proceeding Lilise was charged with stealing from Louison LaRoche two silver dollars, one and one-half yards of white muslin valued at 25 cents, and a bunch of thread valued at 50 cents. Perhaps she wished to make a dress from the fine and delicately woven cotton cloth she appropriated, and she needed the thread to sew it. She may have intended any number of purchases with the two dollars she stole. At the July 1809 term of the District of St. Louis Court of Quarter Sessions, Edward Hempstead, attorney general of Louisiana Territory, prosecuted the accused slave, and the jurors found her guilty of stealing in the daytime on May 30, 1809, from M. LaRoche.[41] No record of Lilise's punishment for the theft of the two dollars, muslin, and thread exists. Since she was found guilty, the sheriff or the coroner was probably assigned the task of lashing her.

Lilise reappeared in St. Louis court records in 1817. The grand jury returned a true bill against her for larceny, and her arrest was ordered October 17. Circuit attorney Henry Geyer prosecuted her on October 21, 1817, for stealing property in the amount of $10 from Charles W. Hueter, and the jury found her guilty. The record noted that the property had been restored to its owner by the time of Lilise's trial. The judge sentenced her to 24 lashes on her bare back well laid on the next day, October 22, between the hours of 7:00 and 9:00 A.M. The sheriff was sworn that he would apply the designated lashes "openly and publicly" and "without any favor or affection." The court also ordered that if Madame Lammé, mistress of Lilise, neglected or refused to pay the costs of the prosecution, the sheriff of St. Louis County should sell her slave at a public auction within 30 days.[42]

Her owner was not prominent. She was a widow; otherwise, M. Lammé, not his wife, would have appeared as the slave's owner. Scharf identified "Madame Lami" as the resident in 1811 at 118 S. Second Street, St. Louis, a building that was both a dwelling and a tavern, and she was also the proprietor of "Madame Lami's tavern."[43] Probably, Lilise was a house and a tavern servant, and her labor included hauling water, making fires and soap, washing and ironing clothes, preparing and cooking food, and cleaning her owner's residence and tavern. Neither of her victims was traceable; both were probably peddlers or small shopkeepers. The 1817 court records did not identify the accused as a repeat offender, nor did any of the inspected records. Likewise, the 1817 record contained no description of the stolen property other than assessing its value at $10.

In another criminal case from 1809, Attorney General Edward Hempstead obtained an indictment against two slaves, George and Joe, on November 30, 1809. It recited that "the jurors of the United States for the body of the District of Saint Louis upon their oaths present that one George, a Negro man, the slave of Clement B. Penrose, and Joe, a Negro man ... the slave of Rufus Easton" about 9:00 P.M. on November 30, 1809, burglarized the dwelling of Joseph Philliberth and stole the proper goods and chattels of Antoine Artibuse "to the evil example of all others, ... against the statute of this territory in such cases made and provided and against the peace and dignity of the United States."[44]

The stolen goods listed in George's and Joe's indictment included two cloth coats valued at $20, three shirts at $10, two vests at $3, and three neck handkerchiefs at $1. Another document inventoried Joe's alleged theft of the following: a trunk that contained "$18.50 in specie [coins, not paper money], one cloth coat, one coatée [vest], three pair of breeches, four shirts, eight cravats [scarves or neckties], two pocket handkerchiefs, three pair of stockings, two waistcoats, one jacket, one pair knee buckles, one umbrella, four towels, one hat, one pair of shoes, and one uniform coat."[45] Penrose's bond in behalf of his slave, George, basically recited the same articles. Both their quantity and place in the wardrobes of gentlemen suggest that neither George nor Joe was stealing for his own need or use; rather, both were part of a burglary ring when they happened to be apprehended. These items may have been fenced by a third party, perhaps a white receiver of stolen goods whom his slave partners in crime could not testify against because they were black and he was white.

The owners of the accused burglars were among the most eminent Americans whose slaves were charged with criminal acts in these surviving territorial records. Both Clement B. Penrose, owner of George, and Rufus Easton, owner of Joe, received appointments in the territory from President Jefferson. He appointed Penrose (1771–1829) as one of three members of the Board of Commissioners to adjust land titles in the Purchase. Missouri's first governor, James Wilkinson, married Penrose's aunt. After receiving a liberal education, in part in Europe, Penrose arrived in St. Louis from Philadelphia as a man of considerable wealth. He invested in real estate in the town of St. Louis, but his investments were not profitable, and at his death, he occupied no higher office than that of justice of the peace.[46] Perhaps, sometime after 1810, his circumstances required that he sell George.

Rufus Easton, owner of Slave Joe, was even more prominent. In 1805 Jefferson named Easton (1774–1834) as one of the three judges on the territorial Superior Court. In 1806 another appointee replaced him as a judge, but Easton was St. Louis's first postmaster and attorney general of the state of Missouri between 1821 and 1826. In addition, in 1814 he was elected a territorial delegate to the U.S. Congress. He died of cholera in St. Charles, Missouri.[47]

Easton and Penrose appeared separately before a justice of the peace. They acknowledged themselves indebted to the United States and to be levied of their goods and lands should their accused slaves fail to appear on March 5, 1810, before the court of quarter sessions to answer to a prosecution against them for breaking open the shop of one Antoine Artibuse. Easton posted a $300 bond for Joe on December 7 and Penrose one in the same amount for George on December 9, 1809.[48] Unlike Helene, Maria, and Lilise, who almost certainly acted alone and whose stealing would now be classified as shoplifting, George and Joe were charged with burglary, or breaking and entering the dwelling, shop, or store of another at night with the intent to commit a crime, and in this case larceny was the crime they committed. The records are incomplete, and nothing more is known regarding this 1809–10 case.

In keeping with most of these territorial slave criminal cases from St. Louis, much more information survives about the owners of the accused in *U.S.* v. *George and Joe* than their victims. In 1811 Joseph Philliberth was the proprietor of a St. Louis tavern, and in 1815 he was granted a license to trade on the Platte and Arkansas Rivers.[49] Antoine Artibuse, whose goods were stolen, cannot be located. Perhaps he was both a small shopkeeper and a part-time peddler who stored his wares in places, common in St. Louis at the time, such as the tavern-homes of men such as Philliberth.

An 1819 proceeding in which the United States charged Slave George, Carlos, and Dick with larceny in St. Louis Circuit Court may or may not be connected to the 1809–10 case. On April 7, a St. Louis County grand jury returned a true bill against them, and all three were indicted for larceny. The government experienced difficulty in assembling its witnesses against these defendants. On April 10 and on motion of the circuit attorney, the court issued an order of attachment to compel the attendance of George Gibson. Such a writ commanded the sheriff to bring before the court anyone guilty of contempt of court, for example, in refusing to testify. Similarly, on July 31 additional prosecution witnesses, Louis Lasource [?] and John P. B. Gratiot, failed to appear and bear witness against the slave defendants, and the court issued attachments to compel their appearance.[50] Detail concerning these government witnesses was sketchy. Nothing could be gleaned regarding George Gibson; John P. B. Gratiot (1799–1876) was the third son of Charles Gratiot Sr.[51] and a small child when the territory was transferred to the United States on the porch of his parents. The name of Louis *Lasource, Lasous, Lasour* appeared as a subscriber in an 1812 petition to Congress regarding territorial government.[52] However, given the uncertainty of the spelling of his surname, the witness and the subscriber may not be the same person. The prosecutor believed that all three were material witnesses to the thievery.

Although the record did not specify any particulars of the stolen property, the amount of the surviving recognizance bonds suggests that it, whatever its components, was of considerable value. On April 10 Manuel Lisa posted a $500 bond in which he guaranteed the court appearance of his slave, George; and on April 16 Gregorie Sarpy separately pledged $500 that Carlos, a slave of August Chouteau, would appear at the next term of court to answer a charge of larceny.[53] No posted bond was located for Slave Dick, and his owner is unknown. George's owner, Manuel Lisa, who owned Catiche, the victim of Catherine's anger, has already been described as a St. Louis fur merchant of considerable prominence. Perhaps he bought George from Clement B. Penrose when the latter began experiencing financial difficulty.

Because the 1804 slave code classified slaves as personal property as opposed to real property or real estate, it is difficult to prove the change in ownership of any given slave. Unlike real estate, wherein the sale of land was recorded at the courthouse and could be traced through the office of the recorder of deeds, no such documentation existed for the sale of slaves. Proof is usually wanting that any particular owner sold a bond servant or any particular buyer purchased that same slave. However, effective August 21, 1813, when the territorial legislature incorporated the territory's first bank, the Bank of St. Louis, of the 13 commissioners whom the legislature appointed for this bank, no fewer than seven owned slaves whose names occurred and reoccurred in these St. Louis territorial criminal records. These included Clement B. Penrose and Manuel Lisa.[54] In any town of approximately 3,000 residents, any person probably knew any other person, but Penrose and Lisa met a number of times as St. Louis bank commissioners, and Penrose's sale of George to the more prosperous Lisa during their service as commissioners is a distinct possibility. Gregorie Sarpy (17??–1824), the surety for Carlos, was a well-to-do person in territorial times. He and August Chouteau were French residents of St. Louis; both served as captains in the militia during the War of 1812. Sarpy was a fur merchant during the Spanish regime and a friend and business associate of the owner of the slave for whom he posted a recognizance bond in 1819.

August Chouteau (1750–1829) was the most distinguished French resident of St. Louis. His mother, Marie Therese Chouteau, owned Slave Batiste, and following Batiste's accidental death in 1785 in an incident discussed in chapter 1, the Spanish governor general in New Orleans awarded her $600 to compensate her for the loss of Batiste. Her son's obituary described August Chouteau as the "patriarch of St. Louis." He was the wealthiest man in St. Louis, owned more land than any other resident, lived in the largest house, and controlled the fur trade during the Spanish regime. He remained equally prominent when the United States bought Missouri. He was a judge of both the court of common pleas and the court of quarter sessions, an appointee of President Madison to the territory's legislative council, chairman of the Board of Trustees for the town of St. Louis, one of the commissioners of the Bank of St. Louis, president of the Bank of Missouri, a colonel in the militia, U.S. pension agent, U.S. commissioner to deal with Indians, and husband of Marie Therese Cerré, daughter of Gabriel Cerré, owner of large numbers of slaves and tracts of land in both St. Louis and Cape Girardeau Districts.[55] There was no more influential resident of Missouri Territory than the owner of Carlos at the time the slave was indicted for larceny in 1819.

Between the difficulty of the government in compelling the attendance of witnesses against George, Carlos, and Dick and the enormous prestige and importance of the known owners of two of them, it was no surprise that all three slaves were found not guilty on all charges in a jury trial on August 4, 1819. The judge ordered that George, Carlos, and Dick be "discharged from the said prosecution and go ... without delay."[56] Perhaps this jury verdict reflected the same political considerations as the outcome in Slave Don Quixote's case.

Was August Chouteau's Slave Carlos, who was tried for larceny in August 1819, also known as Slave Charles? Among Chouteau's papers is a bill he paid on May 23, 1820, from Joseph C. Brown, sheriff of St. Louis County, for Slave Charles's imprisonment. *Carlos* is Spanish for the English and French name *Charles,* and perhaps the Carlos acquitted on theft charges in August 1819 was the Charles of his owner's continuing concern during the spring and summer of 1820. Though the bill did not explain Charles's detention, he may have been incarcerated because of additional legal problems, an unsuccessful attempt to run away, failure to conceal his uppity attitude toward his enslavement, or some combination of these factors. The sheriff's bill for him totaled $29.50.

Of this sum $15 was for "provisions for 30 days at 50 cents per day." One dollar and fifty cents was for committing Charles to the St. Louis jail, and because he broke jail the same day, there was a charge of 25 cents for his jail-breaking and an additional charge of $1.50 for committing him a second time. The remaining portion of $1 was a fee for his discharge.[57] This bill made clear that August Chouteau boarded a difficult slave in late April 1820 or eight months after his Slave Carlos of court records was acquitted on larceny charges. This bill is also of interest because a fee of 50 cents per day for provisions, which would have included food, water, straw, and the like, provided a convenient method of calculating current equivalent prices. In 2000 the cost of keeping a prisoner in the Jackson County jail in Kansas City, Missouri, was $50 per day or 100 times greater than in the St. Louis jail in 1820.[58] On Charles's release from jail, his keeper became Francois Menard, a Frenchman whom Houck identified as a resident of St. Ferdinand in 1794.[59] Chouteau commissioned Menard as his agent in the sale of this bothersome slave, and on the steamboat *Frankfort* they traveled to New Orleans together. Chouteau insisted that Charles be sold because he misused kindness and made it difficult for him to maintain his other slaves in "the proper subjection." As an expressed condition of his sale of Charles, Chouteau required "that this Negro may never be sent back into our territory.... It is necessary [as an] example for my other slaves."[60] The eventual whereabouts of Charles are unknown. He may have become a member of a slave gang in one of Louisiana's parishes, which were ideal for the growth of sugar cane, a far harsher existence than he had experienced in St. Louis.

As for his likely 1819 codefendant, George, a year later, on August 4, 1820, the government once more prosecuted Slave George for larceny in

St. Louis Circuit Court. This time he was found guilty of stealing five packs of beaver furs valued at $300 per pack or $1,500 worth. At the time of his trial three of these packs had been located and presumably restored to the rightful owner, and two had not been found. The court assessed Slave George's punishment at 39 lashes.[61] It is tempting to speculate that Clement B. Penrose's Slave George of the 1809–10 burglary who perhaps became Manuel Lisa's Slave George, acquitted on larceny charges in 1819, continued his thieving ways and in due course was apprehended, tried, and convicted on fresh stealing charges involving valuable beaver furs.

The modus operandi in all three cases involving a Slave George was organized criminal activity. In two of them he had at least one co-defendant. The subject of the theft in all three court proceedings could not be for the personal use or need of any individual slave. Most likely, the human property of Manuel Lisa, a fur merchant, would have known how to obtain entrance to warehouses where beaver pelts were stored. What seems a certainty is that no solitary slave, acting wholly alone, could successfully complete the theft of $1,500 worth of beaver pelts in 1820 without the assistance of at least one free person. Using the hundredfold increase in the boarding costs of jail inmates in urban Missouri between 1820 and 2000 as a benchmark, the beaver furs would be worth $150,000 today. Their conversion into commodities of value to a slave would require considerable assistance.

This 1820 record omitted both the name of Slave George's owner and his victim, but by this time and for a number of years the St. Louis fur trade was controlled by two men and their respective family members, associates, and companies: August Chouteau and Manuel Lisa. These fur barons were never partners. As Foley and Rice note, an intense rivalry existed between the Frenchman and the Spaniard for both the control of the fur trade and the provisioning of various garrisons under the Spanish regime. Once the area passed to American control and it became clear to both men that the new government would grant neither a monopoly in trading privileges, as these authorities on early Missouri describe the matter, "Lisa moved to patch up his differences with the powerful merchant family.... The Chouteau-Lisa feud, and particularly its tranquil termination suggests that on the Upper Louisiana trading frontier ... commercial alliances and rivalries were conditional and influenced by the shifting tides of market forces."[62]

What of shifting liaisons among the slaves of these powerful men? Did they steal from their owners, their owners' rivals, or both? These questions must remain unanswered. However, most bondpersons in the town of St. Louis prior to statehood had neither the knowledge nor the opportunity to pilfer $1,500 worth of beaver pelts. Only great fur merchants such as Chouteau or Lisa seem plausible owners of such a spectacular thief. Given August Chouteau's insistence in June 1820 that Slave Charles be sold and remain outside Missouri Territory, nothing suggests that he purchased George from Manuel Lisa after their separately owned slaves, Carlos and George, were acquitted on larceny charges in 1819. As a result, Manuel Lisa is the most likely owner of the Slave George who stole $1,500 worth of beaver furs in 1820.

However, the court records omitted his owner's name in the 1820 proceeding, and, perhaps in ironic honor of President Washington, *George* was a common slave name. Therefore, definitive proof that *U.S.* v. *George* (1810), *U.S.* v. *George* (1819), and *U.S.* v. *George* (1820) involved the same slave is lacking. Nonetheless, all Slave George cases arose in the town of territorial St. Louis and concerned the theft of a considerable quantity and quality of property. Perhaps Clement B. Penrose sold George to Manuel Lisa after 1810. If Lisa continued to own George on August 4, 1820, the date of his conviction for the theft of five packs of beaver furs, he soon became an asset of Lisa's estate because the fur merchant died unexpectedly eight days later near St. Louis on August 12, 1820.

These territorial slave cases suggest that farms and plantations provided a far better environment in which to enforce perpetual servitude than did any urban area. Punishment for petty slave crime appeared to be far more harsh in the country than in the town, as Slave Jesse's 30 lashes for the insignificant offense of stealing a goose and a knife indicate. Cities were places of far more lax behavior than the countryside. In rural places of the time there were few or no disorderly houses to frequent or attractive wares to steal, and the life of the typical country slave must have been far more labor intensive than that of a slave in the town of St. Louis. These cases illustrated how very whimsical was the application of the law concerning slaves. Jane Pickens probably lost her slave property because powerful men coveted that property, and Don Quixote, George, and Carlos escaped without any punishment because one or more powerful men protected them. Slave women such as Maria and Lilise were not owned by great persons, and these bondwomen felt the full rigor of the law and their owners its costs. When the slave's owner was of modest means, as was Madame Lammé, owner of Lilise, the more petty her slave's crime. Unlike most male slaves discussed in this chapter, Lilise stole items such as a bunch of thread and one and one-half yards of muslin. She acted alone, and she stole articles for her own use.

On the other hand, the more powerful and prosperous the master of the thieving slave, the larger the booty of his pilfering. Joe, George, and

Carlos were all owned by members of St. Louis's highest society, and their stealing was organized. It almost certainly depended on white partners in crime who would arouse less suspicion that commodities such as beaver pelts were stolen than black peddlers of such valuable properties. The 1804 slave code, which prohibited a black or a mulatto from testifying against a white facilitated widespread larceny in territorial St. Louis. This town was strategically located at the confluence of two great waterways, the Missouri and Mississippi Rivers, among much else conveyers of commerce, legally and illegally acquired.

The surviving court records discussed in this chapter include only those cases in which a slave was arrested and never those who were undetected. Since the clearance rate (i.e., offenses known to police and considered solved by arrest) for both larceny and burglary remained under 20 percent in the 1990's,[63] it was surely no higher in the early nineteenth century. Then no fingerprinting, photography, video camera surveillance, burglary detection devices, and a multitude of other security measures were in use. The testimonial competence, without regard to race, of some members of thieving gangs against others was also in the future. Crimes such as stealing and burglary no doubt thrived in Missouri's territorial capital under such circumstances.

The next chapter concerns another slave who was probably a repeat offender. Unlike the bondpersons retried for crimes against property, such as larceny, the second time a Slave Elijah stood trial, it was on charges that he conspired to murder his mistress, a capital offense.

Chapter 4

Slave Elijah's 1818 Trial on a Charge of Conspiracy

Throughout its existence the United States has much more frequently indicted persons for conspiracy than have the various states, including the state of Missouri. The earliest known case involving this crime under American rule in Missouri Territory occurred in 1818. It may involve a slave who nine years earlier was charged with larceny. In the 1809 case Risdon H. Price posted a recognizance bond on February 18 in the amount of $400 that his slave, Elijah, would appear at the March term of the Court of Quarter sessions in Louisiana Territory, St. Louis District, to answer a charge of stealing $100 on February 9, the property of Jeremiah Connor "against the statute in such cases made and provided and against the peace and dignity of the United States."[1] Attorney General John Scott obtained the indictment against Elijah, and on March 8 Scott tried him before a jury, which found him guilty.

Though Edward Hempstead as defense attorney filed a motion for a new trial for Elijah on grounds that the verdict was contrary to the evidence and the law, it did not succeed. The judge of the court of quarter sessions, before whom Elijah was tried, sentenced him to three successive days of 25 lashes. The slave was to remain confined until the entire sentence was completed and the costs of the prosecution paid.[2] An undated document addressed to Thomas F. Riddick, clerk of the court, from John Coany, coroner of St. Louis District, redundantly stated, "Sir You will please to send me the order of the Court respecting the whipping of Elijah,

67

sentenced to be whipped; as I have engaged a person to do that duty."[3] Obviously, the flaying of a slave 25 times per day for three successive days was an assignment for which the sheriff was unavailable, and the coroner readily delegated the unpleasant task to an unnamed individual.

Unlike most of these slave territorial records involving larceny, in *U.S.* v. *Negro Elijah* (1809) the victim, Jeremiah Connor, can be identified. He was the third sheriff of St. Louis District/County; Governor Wilkinson appointed him in September 1806, and he served until November 1810. He was also an auctioneer; notices appeared in the town of St. Louis's only newspaper, the *Louisiana Gazette,* in both 1808 and 1809 regarding his auction of various goods.[4] Though the record contained no description of the stolen property, most likely Elijah pilfered merchandise that Sheriff Connor intended to sell to the highest bidders. Elijah's owner, Risdon H. Price, was an equally well-known business man. Among other activities he was one of the founders of the Episcopal Church in St. Louis in 1819. He died at age 65 in December 1845 after a lengthy residence in Missouri.[5]

The remaining case was the most serious crime for which any territorial court records were discovered, and it also concerned Slave Elijah. Because the government sought a death sentence in *U.S.* v. *Elijah and Gabriel, Slaves of John B. N. Smith and others not known,* it was not tried in St. Louis County Circuit Court. Rather, its trial took place, as federal law required, in the Superior Court. An act of the Twelfth Congress, which created Missouri Territory, specifically mandated the trial of any case in which the prosecutor sought a death sentence be held in the Superior Court, the only one in the territory whose three judges were appointed by the president of the United States.[6]

Elijah was prosecuted under a portion of the Virginia slave code that the governor and judges of Indiana Territory adopted for the District of Louisiana in 1804. It read: "If any negro or other slave shall ... conspire to rebel or make insurrection or shall plot or conspire the murder of any person ... the slave or slaves convicted thereof shall suffer death."[7] Though the language of this law came from Virginia, its substance and intent were almost as old as the white man's enslavement of Indians, Africans, mulattoes, and African Americans in Missouri. Within four years of the first known introduction of slaves to Missouri in 1720, the French king, Louis XV, issued an "Edict Concerning the Negro Slaves in Louisiana." Among other proscriptions, it criminalized slave rebellion, insurrection, and conspiracy. When control of Louisiana passed to Spain in 1766, the Spanish colonists continued the French slave code, including its provisions concerning slave conspiracy and insurrection. The most extensive and severely punished slave criminal case during the 37-year Spanish rule of its North American domain, the 1795 Pointe Coupée conspiracy, was prosecuted under statutes similar to those the French had adopted in New Orleans more than 70 years earlier. Though none of the intended white victims were physically harmed, the Spanish arrested 60 slave conspirators and executed at least 23, sentencing another 22 to prison terms as public workers, all as a part of punishing slave conspirators who planned to rebel.

Unlike any substantive crime of which slaves were convicted wherein the corpus delicti or body of the crime required, for example, a death for murder and missing property for larceny, there was no such requirement for the crime of conspiracy. The word *conspire* has Latin roots that mean "to breathe together."[8]

The essence of conspiracy law in England as early as the sixteenth century was "to combine privily to do something criminal, illegal, or reprehensible."[9] The Crown used this crime to prosecute perceived enemies of the state such as Mary Queen of Scots and her supporters. As her biographer, Fraser, observes of a statute the British Parliament formally enacted in 1585 and termed the Act of Association, "If it could be proved that a particular conspiracy had been aimed at the elimination of [Queen] Elizabeth and the placing of Mary on the throne, Mary herself was as much eligible for execution as any of the plotters, even if she had been in complete ignorance of what was afoot."[10] The next year, 1586, Mary was tried, found guilty, and beheaded under the Act of Association. By 1611 the "notorious Court of the Star Chamber," as Mitford notes of this English court, "declared that the essence of the crime of conspiracy lies in the agreement — not in a crime committed, but in the planning of a crime."[11]

Under both English statutes and the American adaptations of them, the law required two or more conspirators. No one could be indicted and found guilty of conspiracy if he or she acted alone. Its essence was in the consent of the parties to commit one or more overt act(s) in furtherance of the criminal stratagem. The English used this law to prosecute the minority Catholic queen, Mary Queen of Scots, and to maintain the Protestant queen, Elizabeth, on the throne, and the English colonists transplanted it to keep their slaves in proper subjection.

Missouri's 1804 slave code did not extend conspiracy law to all crimes slaves might commit. For example, in the 1809 larceny case involving Elijah, had he been tried with a co-defendant (and he was not), the government could not charge them with conspiracy to commit larceny because the slave conspiracy statute was limited to murder and insurrection. The latter was an English crime dating from at least as early as the fifteenth century and involved the use of arms in open rebellion against established authority. In 1450 the English captured and executed the rebel Jack Cade for this crime. When the English colonists imported the crime of insurrection to North America, they linked conspiracy statutes to it, and slaves tried and found guilty of conspiring to commit insurrection were executed.

On the other hand, the governor and judges for the Northwest Territory, a region wherein slavery was prohibited, enacted neither insurrection nor conspiracy laws in 1788; nor did the District of Louisiana's legislative council adopt any such statutes for the general population in 1804. At the time of Elijah's and Gabriel's indictment in 1818, there were no territorial statutes in Missouri applicable to white defendants who admittedly committed the kinds of acts that led to the capital charges against two of John B. N. Smith's slaves. Crimes such as attempt, solicitation, and conspiracy were later additions to Missouri's criminal code, and once the state of Missouri came into being and prosecuted those in bondage, it did so for substantive crimes such as murder, not conspiracy to commit murder.

The story regarding the conspiracy charges against Smith's slave probably began on February 11, 1818, when ten directors of the Bank of St. Louis met and by a six-to-four vote agreed to terminate the employment of the bank's cashier Mr. John B. N. Smith. As cashier, he was an officer and in charge of the day-to-day operations of the first bank in Missouri Territory, one destined to survive only three years. Among the commissioners whom the legislature appointed for this bank was Risdon H. Price, owner of Slave Elijah in 1809. On September 2, 1816, Price became one of the bank's directors, and he was serving in this capacity when it opened for business on December 2, 1816, with John B. N. Smith as cashier.[12] Despite the absence of any locatable bill of sale for him, the change in Elijah's ownership from Price to Smith might have occurred any time after 1809, but if it did take place, the chances of Smith's purchasing Elijah from Price seem most likely after he began his employment as cashier in 1816. Though there may be no connection between Smith's dismissal and the events in his home four days later that led to capital charges against his slave Elijah, the likelihood is that Smith's dismissal from his bank employment on February 11 considerably influenced what happened in the former cashier's home on February 15, 1818.

Smith's firing from his job was not a private matter. On both February 6 and 13, 1818, a front-page notice concerning the bank appeared in the *St. Louis Missouri Gazette*. The advertisement denied the apparent rumor that the Kentucky Insurance Company planned to redeem its notes at the bank.[13] This notice's appearance in the newspaper suggested that its board feared the public loss of confidence in its directorship. When ten of the board members met and terminated Smith, the newspaper carried a two-column story about the tumultuous week at the bank, including Cashier Smith's dismissal on Wednesday, February 11, 1818.[14]

He was surely agitated and unhappy when he returned home on this day. As a married man, the owner of at least three slaves, the father of as many as five children, all under 16 years of age, he was the wage earner for his large household. Any fired or downsized person might behave with uncharacteristic irrationality in the aftermath of dismissal. By February 15 Smith could not have busied himself by going out and about because it was Sunday, and all shops in St. Louis were closed pursuant to a city ordinance. Elijah may have been inventing from whole cloth, or he may have told the truth, when after his trial he related to his attorney that at the time of his crime he was "cut with knives, ... thrust in his flesh with forks, ... that he acted from the heat of passion, ... and acted alone from the tortured feelings of that moment & not in conspiracy with anyone else."[15]

Though the documents may be missing, the surviving file in this case contained almost no mention of Gabriel, the slave boy with whom Elijah was charged of conspiring to murder Mary Noyes Smith. The grand jury returned a true bill against both. Likewise the indictment handed up against them stated:

> Elijah, a negro man ... not having the fear of God before his eyes, but being moved and seduced by the instigation of the devil [on February 15, 1818] ... together with one Gabriel a negro boy ... and others whose names are to the jurors unknown did plot and conspire feloniously, wilfully and of their malice aforethought to kill and murder one Mary N. Smith.

What proof, if any, the prosecutor provided regarding Gabriel cannot be determined. No subpoena for him is extant; there is no evidence that he was tried, and the jury did not return a verdict in his case. The file contained no information about the other co-conspirators whose names were unknown and who very likely did not exist.

Because of the absence of any factual summary of the chronology of events that led to Elijah's trial on capital charges, some guesswork is involved in piecing together its basic outline. Though none stated the witnesses' testimony, more than 20 separate subpoenas, many of them summoning two or more witnesses, survive in *U.S. v. Elijah*. Most indicated which party called the witness: the prosecutor, the United States of America, or the defendant, Slave Elijah. It is from these multiple subpoenas, the indictment, the jury's verdict, the motions for a new trial, and other items that any coherent explanation of the events of February 15, 1818, begins, insofar as what transpired on this date in the John B. N. Smith home can be recreated.

The court record did not disclose who allegedly attacked Slave Elijah, but his master because of his greater physical size and strength could cause the object of his displaced wrath greater injury than Mrs. Smith. Perhaps Elijah raised his hand in opposition to his master in self-defense, and his enraged owner ordered his slave's arrest because he fought back. Though the Negro or mulatto who was "wantonly assaulted" could defend his otherwise criminal behavior on grounds of self-defense,[16] the slave's testimonial incapacity against any white person made the assertion of this defense difficult if not impossible.

What cannot be ascertained from the surviving records is precisely when and by what means any member of the Smith household discovered the existence of a large quantity of arsenic in the sausage prepared on February 15, 1818, for Mary Noyes Smith's consumption. Under conspiracy law, if two slaves planning together put poison in food intended for their mistress's diet, such an act would be sufficient to convict one or both of them on capital charges. The surviving documents clarified neither exactly what happened nor when it occurred.

Elijah was charged with conspiracy to commit murder because on February 15 he admittedly put a large quantity of arsenic in the sausage that most probably Rebecca, a slave woman, prepared for her mistress, Mrs. Smith. Among other unknowns is whether Mrs. Smith ate any of it. If she ingested the arsenic-laced sausage, doing so surely made her ill. However, it did not kill her because she appeared as a prosecution witness against Elijah both before the grand jury that indicted him and at his trial in August 1818.

He was not formally charged until nearly six months after his crime. We can infer from this delay that the authorities were uncertain what had transpired on February 15, and the prosecutor only convened a grand jury when he had amassed sufficient evidence to convince it to return a true bill against the slave for conspiring to murder his mistress. The prosecutor built the grand jury aspect of his case by calling at least nine witnesses to testify on August 3 through August 5, 1818. Among them were Mary Noyes Smith; John Smith, son of John B. N. Smith; Rebecca, a black woman and the slave of John B. N. Smith (all members of the Smith household); and Lt. James J. Wilkinson, Lt. Edward Brown, and Maj. Thompson

Douglas (all officers in the U.S. Army). They were probably stationed at Post of Bellefontaine, which General Wilkinson established in 1807 in or near the town of St. Louis.[17] In territorial St. Louis respectable citizens frequently invited army officers to their homes. Scharf wrote of these military visits, "to an educated, ... well-born, well-bred, and intensely pleasure-loving class such as the officers of the army, the society they found in St. Louis was a perpetual source of delight and cause for Thanksgiving."[18] Probably, these men were Sunday dinner guests at the home of John B. N. Smith; they had been invited prior to his dismissal, and despite it the invitation stood. Another government witness who testified before the grand jury was David V. Walker, a physician, who almost certainly explained to this body the harmful effects of arsenic when ingested. Perhaps Mrs. Smith became Dr. Walker's patient if she actually ate the poisoned sausage.

The first six witnesses presumably testified before the grand jury regarding relevant events and their aftermath in the Smith home on February 15, 1818. The grand jury heard two other witnesses regarding important incidents after Elijah's arrest and his incarceration in the St. Louis County jail. Though John B. N. Smith's subpoena may be lost, perhaps the prosecutor avoided calling him as a witness because of his aberrant behavior in stabbing Elijah with knives and forks on the day of his slave's crime.

The file in this case contained nothing pertaining to costs, including any sheriff's bill. Probably no one posted a recognizance bond for Elijah's release. It is possible that he was originally arrested on noncapital charges and that John B. N. Smith left in jail his slave who raised his hand against his owner. Equally likely was Elijah's arrest on suspicion that he conspired to murder Mary Noyes Smith, a capital offense. Under both English law and its American adaptation, bail could be denied in death penalty cases. Almost certainly, Elijah remained a prisoner in the jail from his arrest on or shortly after February 15, 1818, until his trial and its aftermath seven months later.

While an inmate in the St. Louis County jail and awaiting a hearing on what may have been lesser charges, Elijah had at least two visitors, and the prosecutor subpoenaed both of them. Their purpose was to obtain a confession regarding the slave's use of arsenic on February 15. Their testimony before the grand jury helped to indict Elijah on capital charges, and their evidence at trial helped to convict him. It was from his attorneys' motions for a new trial that details concerning these men's earlier trips to the slave's jail cell survive. One of them, Arthur McGinnis, cannot be identified. Perhaps he was a deputy sheriff. He visited Elijah in jail twice, and on the second visit told him that "it would be best to disclose," and "he promised the slave that his statements would be represented to his mistress."[19] Instead McGinnis, as far as can be ascertained, repeated Elijah's statements to the grand jury that indicted him and the trial jury that convicted him.

The prosecutor subpoenaed Salmon Giddings on three separate dates: August 5, as a witness before the grand jury; August 21, for Elijah's trial; and September 7 at a hearing on Elijah's request for a new trial. Giddings was a well-known minister who organized the first Presbyterian church west of the Mississippi River in Bellevue Valley, 10 miles south of Potosi, Missouri, in 1816. Houck quoted an authority on Rev. Giddings who described the minister as "one of the most quiet, patient, plodding, self-denying and faithful missionaries the Presbyterians or Congregationalists ever sent to this country."[20] In 1816 he opened a school that provided education for boys and girls in St. Louis and began preaching there.[21] In addition to his preaching, teaching, and church-founding activities, the Reverend Giddings was also Slave Elijah's "spiritual confessor," and he visited the slave in jail in order to obtain his confession. Giddings apparently testified that the slave had "confessed conspiracy."[22]

Independent of what a slave might understand of a recondite subject such as conspiracy, one may wonder why a court would permit a prisoner's spiritual confessor to testify against him. The priest-penitent privilege was the weakest of those imported from England, perhaps because of its association with the late-sixteenth- and early-seventeenth-century minority religion, Catholicism. When Father Henry Garnett, superior of the Jesuits in England, attempted to assert it when tried as a co-conspirator in the 1606 Gunpowder Plot, the object of which was to remove King James and all of Parliament, the privilege was rejected, and Father Garnett was convicted and executed for conspiring to commit treason.[23] The eminent authority on evidence, John Henry Wigmore, wrote of this privilege: "Since the Restoration, for more than two centuries of English practice, the almost unanimous expression of judicial opinion ... has denied the existence of a privilege."[24] Likewise, the judges of the Superior Court received the testimony of the Reverend Salmon Giddings concerning Slave Elijah's confession as a conspirator, whatever form the slave's admission might have taken. Most likely, the prosecutor needed the testimony of both Arthur McGinnis and the Reverend Giddings, among the other witnesses he presented to the grand jury, in order to obtain Elijah's indictment on or shortly after August 5, 1818.

Though the surviving records did not contain the name of Henry Geyer as prosecutor, they contained several references to the circuit attorney, and Geyer had been in office as circuit attorney for at least a year as of April 1818.[25] Almost certainly the prosecutor of Helene for the theft of property worth $10 and Don Quixote for theft of a watch also prosecuted Elijah for conspiring to murder Mary Noyes Smith.

No guesswork is involved regarding the identity of the judges who tried this slave on capital charges. A different president selected each of the attorneys who served as a judge on the Superior Court of Missouri Territory in 1818. Jefferson appointed the Frenchman John B. C. Lucas; Madison, Judge Silas Bent, born in Massachusetts; and Monroe, Judge Alexander Stuart, born in Virginia. Though the law required that two of them constituted a quorum, the surviving documents clarify that all three presided during Elijah's August trial and September motion for a new trial.

Almost certainly Elijah made his admission to both Arthur McGinnis and Salmon Giddings without the advice of counsel. Though the Sixth Amendment to the U.S. Constitution, which became law in 1791, guaranteed a slave accused of any criminal act in the territories the right to the assistance of counsel, the Constitution is silent regarding the payment of counsel. If Smith's slave languished in the St. Louis County jail on noncapital charges such as raising his hand against his master, neither territorial nor federal law required that the government provide him a lawyer. Slaves were always unable to retain their own counsel; since they owned no property and they were forbidden to labor without their owners' consent, they had no means of paying any legal fees.

However, at the point the government indicted Elijah on capital charges, several provisions of the First Congress's 1790 major crimes bill came into play. Under this important act the federal law allowed every person accused of a capital offense to make a "full defense by counsel learned in the law"; the court before whom such persons were tried or some judge thereof was "authorized and required immediately upon his request to assign such person counsel, not exceeding two ... to whom such counsel shall have free access at all seasonable hours." The federal law also allowed the accused "to compel his witnesses to appear at his trial, as is usually granted to compel witnesses to appear for the prosecution against him."[26]

The judges of the Superior Court appointed Elijah's attorneys, and throughout Missouri's antebellum period those appointed to act as lawyers for slaves customarily served without compensation.[27] They were Horatio Cozens and David Barton; these qualified men admirably represented their slave client. Cozens (1795–1826) was the lesser known; he arrived in St. Louis in 1817, and he died on July 14, 1826. At the time he was co-counsel for Elijah, he was a 23-year-old bachelor. In November 1818 and shortly after the conclusion of Elijah's case, Cozens married Anne Caroline San-guinet, the 18-year-old daughter of Slave Helene's owners, Charles and Marie Sanguinet.[28] The surviving court documents indicate that Cozens and Barton shared the defense of their client, but the more experienced attorney was Barton (1793–1837).

He was born in Tennessee, the oldest of six brothers, and he came to Missouri early enough to serve in the War of 1812 as a mounted ranger. By 1812 he was in practice as a St. Louis attorney with Edward Hempstead, Elijah's defense attorney in 1809. In March 1813 Governor Bates appointed Barton attorney general of Missouri Territory, and in April 1815, Gover-nor Clark appointed this capable attorney the first judge of the Northern Circuit, and he served in this capacity until he resigned in order to resume the practice of law. Nathaniel Beverly Tucker, Don Quixote's judge, replaced Barton. In 1820 Barton was elected president of the convention that wrote Missouri's first constitution. That same year, and by a unani-mous vote of the territorial legislature, he was elected one of Missouri's first two United States senators, and he served until 1830.[29] As a former prosecutor, former judge, and popular and experienced attorney, there was no better lawyer available for Slave Elijah's defense than the 34-year-old bachelor, the Honorable David Barton.

Among the surviving documents that Barton helped to generate in this case is a list of potential jurors dated August 24, 1818. It contained 64 names and was signed by Sheriff Thompson. Of this number, only 12 heard the evidence. Some names were scratched through; many contained var-ious symbols such as x, -, and +. Most were American, both Christian and surnames, but a significant number were French. All were white males.

After jury selection had been completed, Elijah's trial began on August 24, a Monday, and the defense subpoenaed at least one witness as late as August 29, a Saturday. All subpoenas were signed by the presiding judge of the Superior Court, John B. C. Lucas. Most specified that the witnesses were required "to testify and the truth to tell ... on the part of the said United States." Because the government always has the burden of proof beyond a reasonable doubt in a criminal trial, almost invariably it sum-mons and puts on more witnesses than the defense.

Elijah's attorneys subpoenaed and presumably put on the testimony of at least three persons at trial, perhaps four or more if subpoenas are missing and Elijah testified in his own behalf. Probably Elijah did not take the stand because, with the assistance of his lawyers, he asserted his priv-ilege against self-incrimination under the Fifth Amendment to the U.S. Constitution. The known witnesses who appeared for the defense at trial were Ephraim, a black man, the slave of Eli B. Clemson; Bernard G. Farrar; and Risdon H. Price. Ephraim's owner and the other two can be identified.

Eli B. Clemson was another director of the Bank of St. Louis.[30] Perhaps he bought Ephraim from Risdon H. Price at approximately the same time that Price sold Elijah to John B. N. Smith. As such, Ephraim and Elijah at one time served the same master, Risdon H. Price. Since slave assembly was restricted under French, Spanish, and American control of Missouri Territory, Barton's calling Clemson's slave as a defense witness virtually assured that Ephraim's association with his client was legal. Probably this slave testified to the peaceful reputation of his fellow bondman, Elijah. The 1790 act of the U.S. Congress gave the defendant the right to summon witnesses on his behalf, and

David Barton (1793–1837) who in 1818 was Slave Elijah's lead defense attorney in Missouri Territory's only known slave death penalty case. Earlier Barton was the territory's attorney general and then a judge. Later he served as president of Missouri's first Constitutional Convention and one of the state's first two U.S. senators. Used by permission, State Historical Society of Missouri, Columbia, all rights reserved.

this federal law potentially conflicted with the 1804 slave code that prohibited a black or mulatto from testifying against a white. Most likely, Ephraim spoke no ill of anyone, only good of his former fellow slave, Elijah.

No fewer than three separate subpoenas exist for Risdon H. Price. Always the defense summoned him as a witness. Since the government never called him, it is unlikely that Price was in the Smith home on February 15, the date of the crime. Unlike free persons, especially whites, slaves did not officially have white business associates, white acquaintances, or white friends. The only relationship a reputable white had with a slave was as his trader, his overseer, his leasor, his owner, or as a member of the family who leased or owned him. That the defense repeatedly subpoenaed

Risdon H. Price as a defense witness is the strongest evidence that Elijah was a repeat offender, that he was the Elijah convicted of stealing $100 of the goods of the sheriff-auctioneer in 1809. However, there is a great difference between stealing and conspiring to murder, and Price presumably also testified to the peaceful character of his former slave.

The third witness the defense subpoenaed for trial was Dr. Bernard G. Farrar, the first American doctor to practice medicine in the territory. He arrived in the town of St. Louis in the fall of 1806 after studying medicine in Cincinnati, Ohio, and Lexington, Kentucky. His brother-in-law was John Coburn, whom President Jefferson appointed a judge on the Superior Court in 1806, and Dr. Farrar followed Judge Coburn to Missouri. The physician quickly rose to a position of prominence in the town of St. Louis, and when Dr. David Walker arrived in 1812, these men formed a partnership. They practiced medicine, surgery, and midwifery together and owned a drug and medicine store. They also married sisters and remained partners until Dr. Walker's death in 1824.[31]

In *U.S.* v. *Elijah* these men testified for different parties, Dr. Walker for the United States and Dr. Farrar for Slave Elijah. The defendant probably purchased the poison used in the crime from the drug and medicine store these physicians owned. After his trial the prisoner told his attorneys that Mrs. Smith "sent him" for the arsenic, and as the record made by his defense attorneys noted, this fact was not brought out when she took the stand. Perhaps she felt ill and needed a dose of arsenic after learning that her husband had been dismissed as cashier on February 11, 1818.

The physicians probably both testified to their knowledge of this poison. One or both may have attended Mrs. Smith on or shortly after February 15. Dr. Farrar likely believed that the amount of arsenic Elijah put in Mrs. Smith's sausage was not enough to kill her; otherwise, the defense would not have subpoenaed him. Had the slave put the poison in his mistress's medicine, the amount would have been irrelevant because the prosecutor could argue that the accused slave administered medicine with ill intent. If so, Elijah would have been death-eligible. However, the statute under which he was prosecuted required proof that he *conspired* to *murder* his victim, not to make her ill. Perhaps the slave never intended the death of his mistress, only her indisposition, to insure that in the aftermath of his owner's firing, Elijah would be needed, not sold.

The United States called the same witnesses for trial that it put on to secure the indictment from the early August convening of the grand jury. John B. N. Smith may have testified against Elijah at trial, but no subpoena for him is extant for any aspect of the proceedings. If we knew exactly what happened at the Smith household on February 15, the evidence of the prosecution could be summarized. All that can be concluded of the testimony of the prosecutor's witnesses and whatever exhibits, if any, he presented was that the United States convinced the jury beyond a reasonable doubt that Elijah conspired to murder Mary Noyes Smith by putting a large quantity of arsenic in her sausage. An undated verdict survives that reads, "We the jury do find the prisoner Elijah, a Black man, Guilty as in the manner and form stated in this indictment."

On September 7, 1818, the Superior Court heard Barton's and Cozens's motion for a new trial and in arrest of judgment and presumably the prosecutor's motion opposing both. Since juries only decide questions of fact, such as whether or not Elijah put arsenic in his mistress's sausage, and they never decide questions of law, such as whether there was a conspiracy to murder the victim, much remained for the judges to decide after the jury returned its verdict. The defense argued at this postconviction hearing that the court should refuse to uphold the jury's verdict because, among other defects at trial, there were errors in the instructions, no longer extant, which the judges gave the jury.

Each side subpoenaed witnesses on September 7. The prosecutor requested all of the same who testified before the grand jury and at trial except Lt. Edward Brown, who may have been transferred to another military post by this date. These were Mary Noyes Smith, John Smith (son of John B. N. Smith), Slave Rebecca, Lt. James Wilkinson, Maj. Thompson Douglas, Dr. David Walker, and Rev. Salmon Giddings. Once more, no subpoena is extant for John B. N. Smith; he probably never testified against his slave in this capital case.

The defense subpoenaed three witnesses: Risdon H. Price, Dr. Bernard Farrar, and John Bobb Sr. The last was a St. Louis bricklayer, and most likely he both saw persons interrogating the slave prisoner and overheard their conversation with Elijah as this workman laid bricks during construction of the St. Louis County jail. The work began in 1817, but because of insufficient funds, it was not completed until the winter of 1819–20.[32] Though no subpoena is extant for Bobb during the trial, David Barton described Bobb's testimony in his September 10, 1818, motion for a new trial. Barton wrote that Bobb attempted to testify that the slave's confessions were not "obtained voluntarily from a sense of guilt in the prisoner, ... rather through the influence of hope or fear," and the convicted slave's attorney argued that as such the confessions were improperly gotten and not good evidence against the prisoner.

At trial the prosecutor had caused the court to reject Bobb's testimony on the allegation of witnesses that "they had heard said [that Bobb said] he did not believe in God." As McCormick explains, "Belief in a divine being who, in this life or hereafter, will punish false swearing was a prerequisite at common law to the capacity to take the oath."[33] The theory of rejecting the testimony of atheists was the widespread belief that if they lied under oath they had no fear of divine punishment, and as a result they were far more likely to perjure themselves than were God-fearing witnesses. The defense argued that evidence of what Bobb was alleged to have been heard to say when not under oath was illegal and should not have been admitted into evidence. To what extent the defense attorneys' arguments regarding the inadmissibility of Elijah's confessions influenced the outcome in this case is unknown. What is remarkable is that counsel for the accused made any argument regarding the voluntariness of his slave client's confession.

Whether any of the prosecutor's or the defense's witnesses took the stand and gave additional testimony at the September 7, 1818, session of the Superior Court cannot be ascertained from surviving documents. The main thrust of the defense's arguments for a new trial and in arrest of judgment concerned not the arsenic in the sausage but the conspiracy charge. Had Mary Noyes Smith died as a result of ingesting it, Elijah would have been charged with murder, and the prosecution's case would have been far easier than proving that the slave *conspired* to murder his mistress.

Among other arguments the defense advanced on September 7 before the judges to stay the jury's guilty verdict and in support of a new trial for Elijah were the following: (1) Slave Gabriel was neither tried for nor convicted of conspiracy; (2) no warrant or subpoena had been issued to force Slave Gabriel to answer the indictment; (3) the court erred in deciding that the statement of the prisoner that others conspired with him was evidence of a conspiracy against the prisoner; (4) the verdict was founded on the enormity of the crime and not on the evidence; and (5) a plurality of persons was necessary for the commission of conspiracy, and Elijah acted alone.

The defense's arguments prevailed. The Superior Court awarded Elijah a new trial, and because the circuit attorney stated that he would not further prosecute the case, Elijah was released from the St. Louis County jail on or after September 7, 1818. Though he was not a free man because he remained the slave of John B. N. Smith, neither was he hanged. His defense attorneys, especially the more experienced David Barton, zealously advocated their client's cause. The result might have been very different without the many safeguards that federal law imposed in the territories when the government sought a death sentence. Elijah's judges were presidential appointees, and they assigned him talented defense attorneys pursuant to a 1790 act of the First Congress. This federal law also permitted him to call witnesses in his behalf, as did the Bill of Rights, which, with its multiple provisions, was applicable in the territorial poisoning case because the federal government prosecuted the accused.

Nothing further is known of Elijah after his release from jail in September 1818. Perhaps he was sold to pay a small portion of his owner's mounting debts. John B. N. Smith never regained his position as cashier. He was repeatedly sued for sums as large as $8,000 by entities such as the Bank of St. Louis,[34] and the St. Louis Circuit Court in which the suits that were heard found for the plaintiffs, not the defendant. The former cashier died August 20, 1822, and his wife, Mary Noyes Smith, expired September 8, 1822, leaving John B., Samuel, Henry, Sarah, and Charles L. Smith, all less than 21 years of age, without parents.[35] It would appear that neither his life nor the lives of his family and slaves were ever harmonious after his February 11, 1818, loss of his bank employment.

The legacy of *U.S.* v. *Elijah* lived on in the influence this case, and perhaps others that are not extant, had on Elijah's defense attorney, David Barton, president of the 1820 Missouri Constitutional Convention.

Chapter 5

The 1820 Missouri Constitution and Its Background

As early as 1817 a petition circulated in Missouri Territory in which its multiple signers requested that the U.S. Congress allow the state of Missouri to join the Union. In January 1818 John Scott, the territorial delegate, presented this "Memorial of the Citizens of Missouri Territory" to the U.S. Senate and House of Representatives. Among other arguments in favor of statehood it emphasized that the population of Missouri Territory was 40,000 and the territories of Tennessee, Ohio, and Mississippi (respectively admitted to the Union in 1796, 1803, and 1817) all became states with fewer inhabitants than Missouri. Further, it was argued, after eight years in the first grade of territorial government (1804–1812) and five years in the second grade (1812–1817) "they with deference urge[d] their right to become a member of the great republic."[1]

After considerable congressional debate, which extended over several years, much of it acrimonious because it concerned slavery, in March 1820 the Sixteenth Congress passed important legislation affecting the Missouri Territory. According to Houck, "at this time the total population was 70,168 of which 11,234 were slaves, the largest slave-owning county being St. Louis with 1,603, Howard with 1,409, and Cape Girardeau with 1,082."[2] This congressional enactment is best known as the Missouri Compromise. It forever barred slavery within the Louisiana Purchase north of Missouri's southern border (36 degrees and 30 minutes north latitude) for future states except in Missouri.

This act of Congress also "authorize[d] the people of Missouri Territory to form a constitution and state government and for the admission of such state into the Union on an equal footing with the original states."[3] Among other provisions, Congress determined that free white male citizens of the United States, at least 21 years of age and residents of the territory three months, who were qualified to vote for representatives to the territorial general assembly could choose representatives to form a convention. It also apportioned the 41 representatives among the 15 counties of the territory, set May election dates for them, and decreed that the elected representatives to the convention meet at the seat of government on the second Monday of June "and shall then form for the people of said territory ... a constitution and state government."[4]

Accordingly, in the city of St. Louis 41 delegates from 15 counties met in convention from June 12 until July 19, 1820, and they wrote Missouri's first constitution. St. Louis County was represented by eight delegates; Howard and Cape Girardeau Counties had five each, Ste. Genevieve four, and the remaining 11 counties three or fewer delegates. It is generally agreed that David Barton, Slave Elijah's attorney, a former attorney general in Missouri Territory, judge of the Northern Circuit, later one of the state's first two U.S. senators, was the guiding light of the convention. As Floyd Shoemaker wrote of Barton, "his vote on a constitutional measure was practically identical with the adoption or rejection of that measure."[5] Barton was not only one of St. Louis County's eight delegates, he was also chosen president of the convention.

In addition to Barton (1783–1837), other influential members of the convention, according to Shoemaker, were Edward Bates (1793–1869), St. Louis County; Henry Dodge (1782–1867), Ste. Genevieve County; Duff Green (1791–1875), Howard County; and John Rice Jones (1759–1824), Washington County. Excluding Dodge, who was both a lead miner and a farmer, all of these named delegates were attorneys. They were born and reared in diverse places: Barton came from Tennessee; Bates from Virginia; Dodge from Indiana, Kentucky, and Missouri; Green from Kentucky; and Jones from Wales and England, where he graduated from Oxford University. As early as 1789 Jones moved to what is now the state of Illinois, and he became the first practicing lawyer who resided in Illinois Territory. Obviously these delegates were men of intelligence, ability, and knowledge of the U.S. Constitution, federal and territorial statutes, the laws of various states, and those of other nations. After 38 days of meeting, these capable men and their fellow delegates had written Missouri's first constitution, and it survived slavery in Missouri.[6]

In keeping with the other slave state constitutions, this document prohibited the legislature from emancipating slaves without the consent of their owners. Slave ownership was an integral part of life in Missouri, and the abolition of slavery could never be achieved by any act of the legislature, no matter how many votes might exist in the General Assembly for the emancipation of Missouri's slaves. Excluding the abolition of slavery, under Article 12 the delegates gave the legislature the authority to amend the Constitution by a two-thirds vote of each house. As Swindler notes of the rarity of this provision, among state constitutions only Georgia's of 1798 and Connecticut's of 1818 provided likely precedents.[7] The men who met in St. Louis vested Missouri's legislative power in its General Assembly, which consisted of a senate and a house of representatives. Each county was allocated at least one representative, with the entire lower house never to exceed one hundred. Its members were to be chosen every second year. The senate was to be made up of no fewer than 14 and no more than 33 members, and the state was divided into convenient districts for the election of senators, who were to be chosen every fourth year. From the start the enumeration of residents gave no special consideration to Missouri's slave-rich counties.

Unlike the federal Constitution of 1789, which permitted slave states to add three-fifths of their slaves or 60 percent of them to their free populations for purposes of determining the number of each state's representatives to the U.S. Congress, in Missouri's General Assembly neither the number of representatives per county nor the shape and size of senatorial districts was based on the numbers of Missouri slaves or their locations. No slave-rich county necessarily received more representatives in the state legislature than one that was slave-poor. Of Missouri's many counties in 1848 wherein the slave population was less than 20 percent (83 to be exact), the slave percentage of the county ranged from 19 percent down to .005 percent or enslaved populations in the single digits.[8] What mattered for purposes of representation in Missouri's General Assembly was the number of free white male inhabitants, and St. Louis County had more state representatives and state senators than any other Missouri county because its population was the largest in the state.

As early as 1821 the population of St. Louis County had reached 9,733.[9] Its growth accelerated at such speed that no other Missouri county rivaled its influence during the antebellum period. Unlike plantations and farms, where unskilled and uneducated slave laborers were efficiently employed, cities did not lend themselves to the profitable use of large numbers of bondpersons. As the territorial cases demonstrate, the town of St. Louis was the scene of mischievous, rowdy, and larcenous behavior on the part of some of its slaves.

By 1820 there were 196 free persons of color in St. Louis County,[10] and in 1830 the slave percentage of St. Louis County peaked at 20 percent.[11] More than 400 free persons of color were enumerated there in the 1836 Missouri census.[12] By 1848, among Missouri's counties with a small percentage of its population slave was St. Louis County, with 6 percent.[13] By 1858 St. Louis's slave percentage had dropped to one, and approximately 70 percent of that 1 percent were women.[14] No doubt the female slaves of St. Louis County were largely employed, as had been Helene, Lilise, Catherine, and Maria, as maids, housekeepers, child-care providers, and other domestics in the wealthiest homes of Missouri's greatest city, St. Louis. By 1860 only 1,542 persons were enumerated as slaves in the city of St. Louis or less than 1 percent. In effect, there were fewer in this city than in any other major southern city in the United States.[15]

The delegates decreed that for apportionment purposes the number of white males solely determined representation in Missouri's General Assembly. The members of this demographic group were to be counted in 1822, 1824, and every fourth year thereafter, and the number of representatives per county and the geographical size of each senatorial district was to be based on these state censuses. In 1820 the franchise everywhere in the United States was, at best, limited to white males. Excluding members of the military, all white males who were citizens of the United States, aged 21 years or older, residents of Missouri one year before an election, and residents of the county or senatorial district three months prior to an election were deemed qualified electors of all elective offices. Among slave states, only Arkansas's constitution of 1836 and Texas's of 1845 were less limiting of the franchise than Missouri's of 1820 because neither required wealth nor tax payment of its voters. Both states permitted free white males aged 21 or older to vote after a state residence of six months.

The majority of slave-state constitutions were more restrictive of the franchise than Missouri's. Several of them, such as Delaware, Florida, Kentucky, and South Carolina, required a two-or-three-year residence of their voters prior to considering them qualified electors. Others limited their electorate to those possessed of minimum wealth or occupational skills. Georgia's electors were either worth ten pounds or members of any mechanic trade. Maryland, North Carolina, and South Carolina limited their franchise to those who owned a minimum of 50 acres. Tennessee required that its voters own at least 200 acres. Other slave states placed wealth restrictions on those elected to their legislatures. Delaware, Georgia, Louisiana, Maryland, Mississippi, and Virginia required some combination of real, personal, or taxable property worth a certain number of pounds or dollars for eligibility to stand for election to either the lower or upper houses of their legislatures. South Carolina went even further in confining election to its legislature to the affluent. Under its 1790 constitution all members of its lower house were required to own either a minimum of 500 acres and 10 slaves or real estate valued at 150 pounds. Its senate comprised only members whose estates were valued at a minimum of 300 pounds sterling that was debt free. The wealth requirements for election to these various slave-state legislatures, embedded in their constitutions, remained unchanged until all slave states were required to rewrite their constitutions in the aftermath of the Civil War.[16]

In sharp contrast, there were neither occupation, slave, land nor any other property ownership requirements for election to Missouri's General Assembly. White males elected to either house were required only to have paid a state or county tax. As of 1820 the only state constitutions, according to Shoemaker, with the same qualifications for their state legislators were Ohio, Indiana, and Illinois.[17] Two influential delegates to Missouri's constitutional convention, Dodge and Jones, had resided in Indiana and Illinois respectively. Equally important, that Missouri chose the free states to her east as opposed to the slave states to her south and southeast in determining the qualifications of her legislators was a feature of the importance of geography, or the proximity of Illinois to eastern Missouri. By severing eligibility to serve in Missouri's legislature from any form of wealth, in yet another way aristocratic slaveholding interests here were not given the advantages in Missouri that they enjoyed in so many other slave states. Missouri required only that members of its General Assembly had met their state or county tax obligations. What these might have been in late territorial and early statehood Missouri, we know in considerable detail. As for their numbers, out of a population of 60,000 white persons, there were approximately 14,000 enumerated taxpayers in Missouri between 1819 and 1826. They paid or were delinquent in paying taxes on land, slaves, licenses to sell goods, run a ferry, sell groceries or spirits, practice medicine, law, and auctioneering, keep pleasure carriages, own watches, and other personal property.[18] If free white males did not qualify for taxation under at least one of these many categories of state or county taxes, there was always the tax on bachelors. As a lifelong bachelor, David Barton, the president of the 1820 Missouri Constitutional Convention, was well acquainted with this aspect of territorial and early Missouri statehood revenue-raising legislation. He would have known that if the bachelor failed in the payment of his tax obligations, he was committed to jail until he or another paid his bachelor tax.

In 1822 this tax was repealed and replaced by a poll tax on every free white male inhabitant. This tax varied from a low of 25 cents to a high of

1 dollar in 1861 as the Civil War neared.[19] Since it was almost impossible in Missouri to avoid all taxes, from early statehood the electorate included a far more socially and economically varied group of eligible voters than did the older slave states of the Southeast. The greater variety, both economic and geographic, of her voters would naturally be reflected in the greater diversity of legislators who represented her many citizens. To be certain, slave interests would be protected in Missouri's legislature, but not at any cost. Had protection of slaveholders been of the same importance in Missouri as, for example, in South Carolina, the Missouri Constitutional Convention of 1820 would have limited those eligible for election to the Missouri legislature to slave and/or land owners. From the start of Missouri's state government affluence was never required of those who wrote its laws.

Because the 1820 constitution endured until Missouri's 1865 constitution abolished slavery, it is useful to examine closely the many ways the earlier document affected its slaves. Federal law was in place in the territory from October 1, 1804, until President Monroe officially proclaimed Missouri a state on August 10, 1821. As a result, both provisions of the 1790 congressional statute and the 1791 Bill of Rights to the U.S. Constitution, which played such significant roles in slave criminal cases in territorial times, greatly influenced the writing of Missouri's first constitution.

Though most slave-state constitutions were silent on the subject of slave rights, Missouri's contained a detailed enumeration of them in criminal cases. In keeping with all slave states and the federal government, Missouri assigned counsel to any slave charged with a capital offense.[20] Only by the exercise of this right could an illiterate and ignorant person, such as the typical slave charged with a crime, assert any other rights the state might grant him or her. The 1820 Missouri constitution went further than most slave states and required courts of justice before which slaves were to be tried to appoint them counsel in "prosecutions for crime." In other words, in Missouri the state need not seek a death sentence before a bondperson was assigned an attorney.

The first Missouri constitution also granted the slave charged with a crime the right to trial by an impartial jury. In every instance in Missouri, the slave's "impartial jurors" were, as has been shown in many territorial cases, white men, though not necessarily slave owners. No African American male sat on a jury in a criminal case in any slave state during slavery. The first known summons of a black male in Missouri for jury duty was in Kansas City in 1893.[21] It was in Spokane, Washington, that the first Negro woman called for jury duty anywhere in the United States can be identified as late as 1912.[22] Missouri women were not permitted to serve on juries until guaranteed that right in Missouri's fourth constitution in 1945.

That only free white males served on juries was an integral part of the unexamined racism and sexism of pre–Civil War America. No one questioned the all-white-male jury of the slave in any Missouri documents that have survived. What the framers of Missouri's 1820 constitution saw as a great advancement in the protection of slaves, and rightfully so, was their right to a jury trial. For example, no slave in colonial Virginia charged with a capital crime was permitted one. Its justices of the peace acted under the authority of the governor to try and sentence the defendant "without the solemnitie of the jury."[23] Eventually all slave states permitted jury trials in slave capital cases, and only in North Carolina was the jury pool limited to white-male slave owners.[24] Though many a Missouri judge accepted a guilty plea from a slave in a non-capital case, in all Missouri death penalty cases for which there are extant court records, all bondpersons sentenced to death in Missouri courtrooms were found guilty of their crimes by juries. There are no records of any judge in pre–Civil War Missouri accepting a guilty plea from a slave and summarily sentencing him or her to death. That feature of Missouri jurisprudence came long after slave days.

In addition to the Missouri slave's right to counsel and to a jury trial in a criminal case, the delegates to Missouri's 1820 Convention also decreed that "a slave convicted of a capital offence shall suffer the same degree of punishment, and no other, that would be inflicted on a free White person for a like offence."[25] This provision distinguished the state of Missouri in 1820 from any other slaveholding jurisdiction in the United States, and it guaranteed several important protections for Missouri slaves. Just as the 1790 federal law and the 1808 adoption of it in Missouri restricted all executions, slave and free, to death by hanging during territorial times, the 1820 state constitution assured the continuance of uniform methods of capitally punishing slave and free under state law.

The framers of Missouri's first governing document, among many other desirable attributes, brought diversity of geographic origin to writing this state's 1820 constitution. Delegates such as David Barton, a territorial attorney general, judge, and criminal defense attorney in Missouri, well understood the necessity of an explicit constitutional prohibition against different degrees of capital punishment for slave and free whites. These men knew that their state constitution best continued the basic protections that federal law in Missouri between 1804 and 1821 accorded the accused and the convicted, slave and free. Based on their varied places of origin and education, the majority of these intelligent, educated, and sophisticated delegates knew the revolting truth about the executions of slaves elsewhere. Their occurrence had stained other American colonies and states wherein court orders had authorized and officials had carried out barbaric judicial decrees of torture, mutilation, and death.

In 1709 a woman was burned alive on charges that she set fire to her master's house in the colony of South Carolina.[26] In Orange County, Virginia, Slave Eve was convicted of petit treason in 1745 in the poisoning murder of her owner, and her death sentence required that she be carried "upon a hurdle to the place of execution and there to be burnt."[27] In 1780 in Augusta County, Virginia, Violet was convicted of burning her master's home. She was hanged and her head publicly displayed on a pole.[28] In 1786 in Rockridge County, Virginia, one slave, executed for the murder of another, was hanged and decapitated and his head was impaled on a stick at the fork of the road.[29]

Much nearer to Missouri, according to one nineteenth-century Illinois county history, the sheriff of the District of Kaskaskia, Illinois (then a town across the river from Ste. Genevieve), was instructed to burn Slave Manuel to death for witchcraft on June 19, 1781.[30] At this time Illinois was a county in Virginia, and perhaps Manuel's witchcraft was a variation of his perceived preparation, exhibition, or administration of some medicine with ill intent. Another early Illinois history related that in Cahokia, Illinois (near East St. Louis), several other slaves were burned at the stake for Negro voodooism about 1790.[31] This date must be in error because by September 1788 the laws of the Northwest Territory, wherein slavery was prohibited, governed what is now the state of Illinois, and under its statutes neither witchcraft nor voodooism were crimes. Though the laws of Virginia from the beginnings of legislation in 1619 through their compilation in 1809 contain no witchcraft statutes,[32] it seems unlikely that two Illinois histories are complete fabrications of the state's past. Something dreadful must have happened to slaves in both Cahokia and Kaskaskia under the authority of Virginia law when Illinois was a Virginia county between 1778 and 1784.

Both these towns (which no longer exist) were within 75 miles or less of these Missouri counties: Cape Girardeau, Franklin, Jefferson, New Madrid, Ste. Genevieve, St. Charles, and St. Louis, or the home counties of 24 of the 41 delegates to Missouri's Constitutional Convention. The great majority of the delegates who met in convention in St. Louis during the summer of 1820 had surely heard about the slave burnings that had occurred in the neighboring state of Illinois during their or their parents' lifetimes. The influential delegate John Rice Jones had been Illinois Territory's first resident attorney. He must have known the worst features of slave capital punishment in Kaskaskia because he was practicing law in this town by about 1795.[33] Word of mouth, if no other source, insured that slave deaths by burning in Illinois were not forgotten.

It is frequently assumed that the 1791 Eighth Amendment's prohibition against cruel and unusual punishments must have ended all cruel and unusual death sentences in the United States. It did not. The Bill of Rights was applicable in Missouri between 1804 and 1821 because Missouri was a territory, and the only governing authority was the United States. If any *state* sentenced a slave to death, the federal Constitution did not apply. The evil of cruel and unusual slave executions under state law continued after the First Congress in 1790 restricted all capital punishment to death by hanging. As late as 1830, under state law in Abbeville, South Carolina, a young male slave was burned to death for the attempted murder of his mistress.[34] An authority on slavery correctly stated the matter in 1856: "Slavery is a positive and peculiar institution of each of the states in which it subsists, over which the other states, neither separately nor collectively, nor the Federal Government itself, can rightfully exercise any power."[35]

Just two months before Missouri's 41 delegates met in St. Louis to write Missouri's first constitution, at least two Missouri newspapers, one in St. Louis County and the other in Cape Girardeau County, carried front-page reprints of an out-of-state news item about the execution of Slave Ephraim and Slave Sam for the murder of their master in Edgefield District, South Carolina. As the account made clear, these slaves' separate death warrants required Sam's death by fire and Ephraim's hanging and decapitation so that his head could be publicly displayed. The account of the matter that these Missouri newspapers ran contained, "It must be a horrid ... sight to see a human being in the flames.... From some of the spectators we learn that it was a scene which transfixed in breathless horror almost everyone who witnessed it."[36] The delegates read these newspapers; they knew about this then recent slave burning. They had all lived under the civility of federal statutory and constitutional law during Missouri's territorial period, and they showed their disdain for cruel slave capital punishment when they prohibited any distinction in the method of executing slave and free white.

Of equal protection to Missouri's slaves was the enumeration of the particular crimes the framers of Missouri's 1820 constitution permitted future legislators to punish with death. If state law permitted David Barton's slave client to hang for conspiring to murder, it must also require the execution of white persons convicted of such acts. The language of the prohibition was clear. There could be no distinction between slave and free white in capital cases. Only those crimes for which free whites might die on a county seat gallows could also send slaves to their death under the authority of Missouri.

Missouri's constitutional evenhandedness and consequential limiting of slave capital offenses was a radical departure from the laws of the Southeast. The model for the older slave states' proliferation of death penalty crimes was English. Though England never experienced slavery, Blackstone wrote of English law in the 1760s: "It is a melancholy truth, that among the variety of actions which men are daily liable to commit, no less than a hundred and sixty have been declared by act of Parliament to be felonies ... worthy of instant death."[37] By the end of the eighteenth century the number of capital offenses under English law had climbed to more than 200.[38] When the early settlers came from England to America, they brought a great deal of English law with them, including many of the mother country's capital offenses and methods of carrying out various capital punishments. That female slaves in America, convicted of petit treason, suffered death by burning is directly traceable to English law.

Blackstone clarified the law on the subject of treason, both high, as in the murder of a king, and petit or small. The latter was the crime an inferior committed when he or she murdered a superior. He wrote, "for a wife to kill her lord or husband, a servant his lord or master, and an ecclesiastic his lord or ordinary is denominated petit treason."[39] The punishment for this offense, he continued, "in a man is to be drawn and hanged and in a woman to be drawn and burned."[40]

As the law developed in colonial America, the punishment reserved in England for servants who killed their mistresses or masters was easily and logically transferred to African slaves who killed their white owners. The aspects of English law that required cruel death sentences for wives who murdered their husbands or clerics who murdered their bishops never took root in America. By the nineteenth century, any executions by fire for either of these categories of condemned felons was in America's dim past. Apart from the excesses against white women in New England's witch trials of the late seventeenth and early eighteenth centuries, they and members of the clergy so infrequently suffered death upon conviction of crime in this country, especially in the slave states of the Southeast, that neither group required constitutional protection. It was otherwise with slaves; the full rigor of imported English law dealing with crime and punishment was applied to them.

In the older slave states of the Southeast, considerable disparity developed between capital offenses for slaves and for free whites. If there was any discrepancy between capital crimes for these groups, always the law provided a lesser punishment for the white convicted of the same offense. In an excellent comparative study of statutory law, first published in 1856, that pertained to slavery where it still existed in mid-nineteenth-century

America, George M. Stroud illustrated those distinctions between crimes punishable by death for free whites and for slaves. The most egregious disparity in punishment was in the Commonwealth of Virginia. Its code listed no fewer than 73 capital offenses for slaves, and only one of them, first-degree murder, was also a capital offense for a convicted free white. Typically the white was punished by a term of years, either one to five or three to ten, and the slave, in 25 crimes for the second offense, was punished by death. For the first offense of "attempting by force or fraud, to have carnal knowledge of a white female," Virginia provided no punishment for whites, but punished slaves convicted of the same with death.[41]

Stroud also surveyed the unequal punishments between slaves and free whites in Mississippi based on its then current revised code and discovered therein 37 crimes punishable by death for slaves that for whites were either not crimes or were punishable by a whipping, fine, or imprisonment for one year or less. For example, under Mississippi law the offense of attempting to burn a cotton-house adjoining a store was not a crime either at common law or by statute for a white person but punishable by death for the convicted slave.

Stroud surveyed other slave states and found the following discrepancies based on the most recent revision of those states' laws that would have been available to him in 1856. In Georgia there were 13 capital offenses for whites and 25 for slaves; in Kentucky, 4 capital offenses for whites and 11 for slaves; in North Carolina 34 capital offenses for whites and 40 for slaves; in South Carolina 27 capital offenses for whites and 36 for slaves; and in Tennessee, 2 capital offenses for whites and 8 for slaves. Among the slave states whose statutory law Stroud examined, only one had an equal number of capital offenses for slave and free white: Missouri.

The 1820 constitution required that within five years after its adoption "all the statute laws of a general nature, both civil and criminal, shall be revised, digested, and promulgated, in such manner as the general assembly shall direct, and a like revision, digest, and promulgation, shall be made at the expiration of every subsequent period of ten years."[42] In both 1825 and 1835 and under the leadership of Speaker of the House Henry Geyer, the legislature systematically eliminated capital offense distinctions between slave and free, largely by phrasing the various laws as prohibitions affecting "every person."

The 1820 constitution also created the Supreme Court of Missouri. It replaced the territorial Superior Court, to which petitioners to Congress as early as 1817 objected on grounds that it was "constructed on principles unheard of in any other system of jurisprudence, having primary cognizance of almost every controversy, civil and criminal, and subject to correction by no other tribunal."[43] These petitioners overstated the matter because under the Spanish regime Missouri's cases were sent to New Orleans for trial in the governor's civil and criminal court, which had both original and appellate jurisdiction. It was of course thanks to the Superior Court judges that Slave Elijah was not hanged. Had he been tried after statehood, his trial would have taken place in St. Louis County Circuit Court.

The 1820 constitution limited the Supreme Court of Missouri to appellate jurisdiction, and it borrowed several features of the territorial Superior Court when the delegates continued the membership of the Supreme Court of Missouri at three judges, any two of whom should be a quorum, and required it to hear appeals in convenient districts, not to exceed four, throughout the state. Just as the president of the United States, with the advice and consent of the U.S. Senate, appointed judges to the territorial Superior Court, so too under the 1820 constitution, the governor, with the advice and consent of the senate, nominated and appointed all judges, including those of the Supreme Court of Missouri and the circuit courts of each county.[44] Among amendments to the 1820 constitution that the General Assembly later proposed were those concerning the power of the governor to appoint judges. The legislature wished to introduce elective principles regarding the state's judicial officers. Until 1851 the governor continued to appoint the judges of the Missouri Supreme Court, but earlier the qualified voters of each county elected circuit court judges.[45]

Though the 1820 Missouri constitution established the appellate jurisdiction of the Supreme Court of Missouri, it did not guarantee the slave the right to an appeal in a capital case. However, neither did it guarantee appellate review for the free white sentenced to death. There were slave appeals in capital cases, and there were free-white appeals in capital cases. By the 1840s the white criminal defendant clearly enjoyed a greater measure of due process than the slave, but nothing in extant records suggests that Missouri courts were initially more careful of the free person's rights than they were of the slave's.

After statehood, no pre–Civil War Missouri criminal case was ever decided with reference to the U.S. Constitution. Not until the twentieth century did a federal court render a decision in a criminal case arising in state court in Missouri. In antebellum Missouri, for both slave and free white, the criminal defendant's only appeal was to the Supreme Court of Missouri. In Missouri, as probably in all other American pre–Civil War jurisdictions, the great majority of persons convicted of crime, both slave and free white, were punished pursuant to court order without an appeal being taken from their conviction.

In contrast to the slave, free whites in Missouri had more punishment options. As during the territorial period, under statehood judges could sentence white persons to fines, forfeitures of property, imprisonment, or death on the public gallows. Only the last of these punishments was also available for slaves. However, both slave and free persons could be the subject of a pardon. The governor granted at least one to a slave before her trial and the others after their convictions, including one wherein the Supreme Court of Missouri upheld the conviction and punishment. The governor exercised his pardoning power under Article 4, "Of the Executive Power," of the 1820 constitution.

Missouri was in a minority of slave jurisdictions, but not alone, in a now scarcely remembered aspect of slave capital cases. When Spain owned Louisiana Territory, it compensated owners when their human properties were executed, killed as escaping runaways, or condemned to the public works. It is unknown whether any slaveholder in Missouri received money from the Spanish under these circumstances. Once the Purchase was transferred to the United States, Congress decided all legislative matters of any importance pertaining to Missouri. It never passed statutes to compensate owners of slaves taken from them as punishment for crime. From the start of the United States, any matter pertaining to slavery was a highly divisive issue within Congress, and had any such law been proposed, the votes would have been insufficient for its passage.

The compensation statutes were primarily passed by the older slave states of the Southeast to remunerate slaveholders when their bondpersons were put to death. The state treasurer or the state auditor reimbursed the slave-deprived owner varying percentages of the executed slave's worth, and the percentages varied from 50 to 100 percent of the value of the condemned slave. The particular percentage depended entirely on the statute that the colonial and later the state legislatures passed or did not pass into law. This legislation, so beneficial to the planter class, did not derive from the Fifth Amendment to the U.S. Constitution, which prohibited the government's taking private property for public use without just compensation.

First, these slave-owner reimbursement statutes existed well before the Bill of Rights became a part of federal law in 1791. The earliest of these statutes in several jurisdictions, including Virginia, can be found in seventeenth-century codifications of colonial law.[46] Equally, if not more important, the U.S. Supreme Court ruled unanimously in 1833 that the U.S. Constitution's Just Compensation Clause of the Fifth Amendment applied only to the federal or central government's taking private property for public use; the High Court held that the Bill of Rights or the first

10 amendments to the U.S. Constitution did not apply to the states.[47] To be exact, the U.S. Constitution had no application to any feature of *state* criminal law, including all aspects of slavery. Moreover, Chief Justice of the United States Taney specifically disavowed any connection between the Fifth Amendment's Just Compensation Clause and punishment for crime in a federal case that upheld a slave's conviction for the theft of a letter from the mails. He wrote, "A person, whether free or slave, is not taken for public use when he is punished for an offence against the law.... Society has a right to punish for its own safety, although the punishment may render the property of the master of little or no value."[48]

Bills that compensated owners of slaves when their slaves were put to death were exclusively within the prerogative of the colonial and later the state legislatures to pass or not to pass into law. Among the original 13 colonies, according to Kay and Cary, all but those in New England provided compensation to slave owners when the colony executed their slaves.[49] The first 10 slave jurisdictions that formed or joined the Union, wherein slavery continued until the Civil War, enacted slave-owner compensation statutes. These were Delaware (1787), Georgia (1788), Maryland (1788), South Carolina (1788), Virginia (1788), North Carolina (1789), the District of Columbia (1790–91), Kentucky (1792), Louisiana (1812), and Alabama (1819). For the most part, these were states whose constitutions required lengthy residence of their voters and some combination of land, slave, or other property ownership of their legislators. The oligarchic nature of those elected to their legislatures splendidly served slaveholding interests.

As the residence and wealth requirements for state lawmakers declined in the newer slave states, so did the owner-compensation-for-executed-slave statutes become more uncertain. Mississippi joined the Union in 1817, and it reimbursed owners of executed slaves at half value.[50] Among the remaining slave states only Texas, which joined the Union in 1845, remunerated owners of executed slaves. However, if the owner attempted to evade the law, as in a situation wherein the murdered victim was only the slave's wife, then the owner was not entitled to any money from the public treasury upon his slave being put to death.[51] The remaining slave states, Tennessee (1796), Arkansas (1836), and Florida (1845), appear never to have passed owner-compensation statutes.

The majority of slave jurisdictions compensated the owners of slaves when the state hanged or burned their human property as punishment for crime. Missouri did not. The majority of slave jurisdictions capitally punished bondpersons for offenses for which it never capitally punished free whites. Missouri did not. The majority of slave jurisdictions had lengthy residence requirements for their voters and wealth requirements for their state legislators. Missouri did not. On average, between 1810 and 1860 the slave percentage of Missouri population was the smallest of all 16 slave jurisdictions in the United States. In 1821 the first state census in Missouri showed 16 percent of the state population was in bondage.[52] By 1860 only 10 percent of its population remained slave.[53] From the start of state government until the demise of slavery, Missouri's General Assembly always represented both slave and nonslave interests. This mixture of constituents prevented the passage of any legislation, if ever introduced, that compensated Missouri's slaveholders when their slaves were hanged.

Among other beneficent factors in the punishment of bondpersons was the 17-year period of Missouri's territorial status with the constant influence of federal statutory and federal constitutional law. Probably, some slaves were hanged during Missouri's territorial period; a letter discussed in chapter 10 implies that one was. However, the many federal safeguards for the trial of any capital crime suggest that slave executions prior to statehood were few. In the one extant case from territorial Missouri in which the government sought a death sentence, thanks to the dedication, knowledge, and intelligence of the accused's attorneys, the bondman was granted a new trial, and the circuit attorney did not retry him.

It was a measure of the esteem in which Slave Elijah's attorney, David Barton, was held within the territory that two territorial governors appointed him to offices such as attorney general of Missouri Territory and judge of the Northern Circuit. When Congress allowed the residents of the territory to elect delegates, they chose David Barton as one of eight from St. Louis County; when the 41 constitutional delegates elected a president of the 1820 Constitutional Convention, they chose David Barton. Shoemaker believed that Barton's vote on any measure before the delegates determined its outcome. The most important protections for any slave who faced criminal charges were the assignment of counsel in prosecutions for crime; in capital cases the same degree of punishment, and no other, that would be inflicted on a free white person; and the absence of any offense distinctions in capital cases between slave and free. These were all enlightened guarantees under Missouri's first constitution of 1820, and they lasted throughout slavery. The people of Missouri, including slaves, were fortunate that a person of 36-year-old David Barton's experience in the prosecution, judging, and defense of criminal cases was chosen president of the 1820 Constitutional Convention.

However, despite the many protections of this document, it also enshrined human bondage. It continued the basic rights of the slaveholder to buy, sell, lease, give away, inherit, and own bondpersons. Since slaves owned no property, someone else had to pay all bills that arose because of the peculiar institution. The next chapter examines how costs in criminal cases affected slaves.

Chapter 6

Costs in Criminal Cases

The ownership of slaves was never one of pure profit. In addition to the slaveholder's legal duty to house, feed, clothe, and provide some semblance of health care for his human chattel, as early as 1806 the territory of Louisiana taxed all slaves between the ages of 16 and 45. Though their owners could obtain exemptions for blind, insane, or otherwise disabled bondpersons, masters who neglected or refused to pay taxes on their property, human or other, found after a number of days set by statute that it was seized and sold to the highest bidder. The proceeds from the sale were used to pay taxes and the expense of collecting them.[1] The requirement that taxes be paid on slaves and the legality of their forced sale in the event of their owners' tax delinquency were both prominent features of slavery throughout its time in Missouri. Slave lists for tax purposes by Missouri County that included the owner's name and the numbers, ages, sexes, colors, and disabilities, if any, of his bondpersons are extant for the years 1850 and 1860.[2] These documents, which reveal much about the mind-set of those times, omit the names of the slaves, much as the enumeration of horses, mules, and cattle for revenue-raising purposes left out the names of the taxpayers' livestock. Though the owner of a lame mule could legally end the animal's life, the owner of a slave incapable of work could not because doing so was murder; nor could he emancipate her because she was likely to become a public charge. The peculiar institution cost both the owner and the owned.

The payment of court fees was yet another feature of slavery that potentially affected both slaves and their masters. In the earliest of

Louisiana Territory's monetary statutes, the clerk in whose court the costs accrued was ordered to make out a duplicate bill, which one of the judges of the court examined and signed. This bill, according to the 1806 law, specified the items and officers of the court (i.e., clerks, sheriffs, and prosecuting attorneys) to whom various sums were due. The sheriff collected and delivered them to the clerk of the court, and the clerk in turn paid the other officers and himself. This first American territorial enactment did not distinguish between charges in civil and criminal cases, nor did it indicate the specifics of any court fees.[3] However, this early statute set the pattern for Missouri's fee-for-service system, which compensated court officers in criminal cases until the state's 1945 constitution mandated that they be salaried, not reimbursed, for the performance of their duties on the basis of moneys collected.[4]

Just as bondpersons could be sold to pay their owners' taxes, they could also be sold to pay court costs without any criminal charges being filed against them or any wrongdoing on their parts. In 1807 the governor and judges passed a detailed enumeration of fees in all court cases. This list of potentially billable items was lengthy, approximately seven printed pages, and its application in a known capital case involving a white perpetrator (John Long Jr.) and a white victim (George Gordon) resulted in the perpetrator's slaves being sold to pay for, among other charges, the expense of hanging the white murderer.

The costs in *U.S.* v. *Long* began accruing on June 5, 1809, when his stepfather, George Gordon, gave testimony under oath before a Justice of the Peace for Bonhomme Township, St. Louis District, "that from threats and menaces ... he the said deponent is afraid that John Long will take his life or do him other injury."[5] That same day, Andrew Kinhead, justice of the peace, signed an order that commanded the constable of Bonhomme Township to bring the stepson before his court to answer Gordon's charges. On June 8 the accused menacer appeared before Justice of the Peace Kinhead, but the outcome is unknown.

Slightly over two weeks later on June 26, 1809, John Long Jr. shot and killed his stepfather on the victim's doorstep after lying in wait for him. Among other motives for the murder, the stepson resented the transfer of his father's property after his father's death to his mother's second husband, George Gordon. Under then existing English and American law, husbands controlled the property of their wives, and Widow Long's property included both Long's mill and a number of slaves.[6] However, not all in the Long/Gordon home became Gordon's after he married this widow; at least three slaves remained assets of her son John's estate.

On August 14 the grand jury indicted Long for murder, and on August

21 he was tried before a jury at a special term of the court of oyer and terminer, the exclusive territorial court for such prosecutions in 1809 Missouri. The statute required that the sheriff of each district notify the presiding judge of the General Court of any potentially capital cases, and he in turn assigned himself and justices of the court of common pleas to sit on the court of oyer and terminer. In Long's case Chief Judge John B. C. Lucas appointed himself, Silas Bent, and August Chouteau.[7] The jury found the accused guilty, and the judges sentenced him to death by hanging. Though his attorneys filed an extant motion "Why Judgement Should be Arrested," which dealt with alleged improprieties in jury selection and imprecision in the description of the victim's wound, it did not succeed. The stepson was hanged for the murder of his stepfather in the town of St. Louis on September 16, 1809. Because little documentation regarding John Long's court costs is extant, some speculation is involved in estimating the many fees generated by his legal difficulties, including his early June court appearance and his August arrest, jailing, indictment, trial, conviction, motion for a new trial, sentencing, and September hanging.

Among the officials in the trial of *U.S.* v. *Long,* the only salaried person was the chief judge of the General Court John B. C. Lucas, who presided. From the start of the United States the U.S. Congress set the salaries of all presidentially appointed territorial judges. Those in the District of Louisiana received the same salaries as their counterparts in Indiana Territory. By 1807 those in both Indiana and Missouri Territories received $1,200 per year to be paid quarterly. In 1822 the Missouri General Assembly set the salaries of the judges of the Supreme Court of Missouri at $1,100 and those of the circuit courts at $1,000.[8] Throughout Missouri's history the proper role of the judiciary was always one of impartiality, and these officeholders, empowered either to sentence offenders to death or to uphold such penalties, were never compensated on the basis of fee-for-service.

On the other hand, justices of the peace were not salaried. In criminal cases, their jurisdiction was limited to such matters as accepting recognizance bonds, issuing arrest warrants, administering oaths, subpoenaing witnesses, and deciding petty cases. In addition, they were required to make up a bill of costs in every action brought before them, and their fees set by the 1807 statute and allowable to Justice Kinhead in Long's case were 20¢ for every warrant in a criminal case and 10¢ for administering an oath for a total of 30¢ in June 1809.

Constable fees in Long's case were specified in an extant court document at 85¢: 25¢ for serving a warrant and 3¢ per mile for the "circular mileage" of his travel in bringing Long from his residence in Bonhomme

Township before Justice of the Peace Kinhead for an estimated one-way distance of 15 miles.[9] In addition, Constable Dechez summoned the 18 householders whose assemblage the law required after any suspicious death so that 12 of them were available as jurymen for the coroner's inquest. Dechez received 10¢ per householder or $1.80, and 10¢ per witness or 80¢ for the estimated eight who probably testified at the initial inquiry into the cause and circumstances of Gordon's death. Had slaves been competent witnesses against whites, most likely several would have testified both before the coroner's jury and at Long's trial. Despite the law, which barred all blacks and mulattoes from testifying against whites, the constable's fees in the Long case were at least $3.45.

As soon as Gordon's death was discovered, the law required that the coroner for the District of St. Louis view the corpse. The coroner received $3 for looking at Gordon's dead body; 5¢ per mile for his travel from the town of St. Louis to Bonhomme Township and return, or $1.50; 50¢ per juror, or $6 for the 12 who sat on his inquest to determine the cause of Gordon's death; and 20¢ per witness for the likely eight who testified at his inquiry, or $1.60.

After the coroner summoned his witnesses, he put them under oath, committed their testimony to writing, and required them to appear at the next term of the appropriate court to give their evidence. His jurors viewed Gordon's body, listened to the evidence of the witnesses, and delivered their verdict to the coroner who signed it. He in turn informed one or more judges of the General Court, and either at the behest of the coroner or the sheriff, a judge issued an arrest warrant for, in George Gordon's murder, his stepson, John Long Jr. For services rendered in *U.S.* v. *Long* the coroner of St. Louis District received approximately $12.10. In addition, the coroner's 12 jurymen received 25¢ per juror or $3.

The 1807 statute specified that "the fees of the coroner's inquest shall be paid out of the lands ... or chattel of the slayer in case of murder." When the perpetrator lay in wait for his victim as Long did for Gordon, the killing was always *with* malice aforethought, that is, murder. The slayer in such circumstances never acted *without* malice aforethought; hence he was never guilty of manslaughter. Sheriff Jeremiah Connor probably took Long into custody pursuant to an arrest warrant of the General Court after the coroner informed one or more of its members of his findings regarding George Gordon's death. Connor received $1 for arresting Long as well as 5¢ per mile or $1.50 for his circular mileage this arrest required.

The sheriff's fees also included 50¢ for committing Long to the common jail and an additional 50¢ for his turnkey's fee (the sheriff's subordinate at the jail). Since murder was usually not a bailable offense, John

Long Jr. was a resident of the St. Louis jail from or shortly after June 26, a Monday and the date he shot and killed his stepfather, until September 16, 1809, a Saturday and the date of his hanging. In all he remained an inmate at least 80 days. The exact charge for incarcerating him is not available, but an 1808 law allowed the sheriff 25¢ per day for providing food for prisoners unable to buy or procure their own. It seems a reasonable estimate that his stay in jail cost Long's estate 40¢ per day. In all, jail costs in *U.S.* v. *Long* were at least $33.

In addition, the sheriff received 75¢ for summoning Long's trial jury; $4.29 or 13 × 33¢ for serving subpoenas on each witness who testified for and against the defendant; 3¢ per mile for serving each subpoenaed witness, probably $3. If Long confessed, and one of the surviving newspaper accounts of the case suggested that he did, Connor received $1.33 for taking his prisoner's confession, and he recovered $10 for executing Long's death warrant, that is, hanging him by the neck until he was dead. Most likely, Sheriff Connor and his subordinate jailer were entitled to at least $55 in Long's case.

Edward Hempstead, as attorney general, probably prosecuted Long for Gordon's murder. An 1808 statute allowed to this court officer, "for every indictment returned 'a True Bill' by the Grand Jury, in a capital case, to be paid out of the defendant's estate if convicted ... $30."[10] That a French member of the trial jury that convicted Long later admitted to not understanding one word of English suggests the court proceedings were brief.[11] Hence the prosecutor's fee was adequate compensation for his services in obtaining Long's indictment and conviction. Judges of the court of common pleas Silas Bent and August Chouteau each received $3 for every day of Long's trial.[12] As such, court costs for their services as members of the court of oyer and terminer were $6, because the jury in the Long case appears to have heard all the evidence in one day. Each trial juror received 50¢ per day or $6 for the entire panel, and each of the trial witnesses for and against the accused received 50¢ per day as well as 50¢ for every 20 miles of travel from their residences to court and return. Assuming that 13 persons testified in Long's case and one-half of them were residents of Bonhomme Township, witness fees in Long's case were at least $16.25. The territory did not compensate a defendant's attorneys because the 1807 statute provided that only the attorney in whose favor the suit was decided was entitled to a fee to be taxed with the bill of costs. Just as the two appointed lawyers in Slave Elijah's capital case served without pay, so does it appear that Long's attorneys either were paid by Long himself, his family members such as his mother, or did their trial work pro bono.

Still other costs remained in *U.S.* v. *Long*. The 1807 statute listed in excess of 40 different fees allowable to the clerk of the various territorial courts in which his services were needed. Thomas Riddick as clerk of the St. Louis District Court of Oyer and Terminer most likely recovered the following: $1 for preparing Long's arrest warrant; $1 for copying it at 1¢ per word × 100 words for the defendant; 50¢ for recording his indictment; 50¢ for swearing the trial jury; $1 for filing the various motions and other court papers; $1.30, or 6¢ per witness, for swearing the likely 13 witnesses who testified for and against the accused; 25¢ for entering the jury verdict on the record; 25¢ for filing the jailer's receipt for Long's incarceration between his arrest and death; 25¢ for entering the court order to hang Long, and most likely, other charges now unrecoverable without extant court documents. At a minimum, Thomas Riddick, clerk of the court, billed Long's estate at least $9 for his services. Finally, one more functionary received fees for his services in this case, the crier, a court officer who, among other duties, announced the opening and closing of court. For calling the trial jury in this case, he received 25¢; for calling each of the probable 13 witnesses who testified for and against the defendant, 6¢, or 78¢; and 10¢ for calling Long's verdict for a total of $1.13.

In all, the bill that Riddick prepared and Sheriff Jeremiah Connor collected in whole or in part in *U.S.* v. *Long* was approximately $133 or in today's equivalencies $13,000. Out of this sum, the justice of the peace, constable, coroner, coroner's jurors, sheriff, turnkey, attorney general, two judges of the court of common pleas, trial witnesses, trial jurors, clerk of the court, and crier all received for the performance of their various duties the fees that the 1807 statute and its 1808 modifications allowed.

The actual collection of them was a lengthy process because the sale of the hanged murderer's slaves did not take place until March 15, 1811. Two weeks earlier the town newspaper carried this advertisement: "a Negro Man of about 28 years of age, accustomed to plantation business; also a Negro woman and child, the woman being about 35 years of age, being part of the estate of John Long Jr. Dec[eased]" would be sold to the highest bidder.[13] Whether the public sale of Long's slaves and other chattel actually covered the multiple court costs his case generated is unknown. Any fees that exceeded the worth of his estate were paid either by the District of St. Louis or Louisiana Territory.

What of court costs when the convicted criminal was a slave and by definition indigent? Until 1816 territorial law is silent, and this gap in the statutes came about because the model for court costs in Louisiana Territory was not the slave state of Virginia; its source was the law of Indiana Territory, where slavery was forbidden. Hence the enumeration of fees made no mention of slaves because there were none in any territory north of the Ohio River.[14]

In the absence of any specifics regarding the responsible party for court fees in slave criminal cases, very likely the government paid most if not all the charges that arose in territorial Missouri prior to 1816, and the 1807 statute provided the legal basis for them. Fragments of at least six slave criminal cases— Helene's, Lilise's, Catherine's, Elijah's, George's, and Joe's— survive from the years 1809 to 1811. All were prosecutions either for stealing, assault, or burglary with intent to steal. Unlike Long's capital case, wherein no bail was allowed, the owners or their agents posted recognizance bonds in each of these noncapital slave cases, and included among court costs in each of these six were justice of the peace fees of 20¢ per bond.

Though apart from Slave Maria's court-ordered whipping and Slave Helene's guilty plea, little evidence survives regarding the disposition of their cases; presumably juries found most of them guilty as charged. As a result, the judge sentenced each to a designated number of lashes as punishment for their criminal acts, and the sheriff or the coroner or a hiree of either administered the court-authorized whipping in each conviction. The court costs in any of these pre–1816 cases involved many of the same fees already discussed in *U.S.* v. *Long,* including constable's fees for arresting the accused and mileage incident to the arrest; justice of the peace fees for recognizance bonds; attorney general's charges for his prosecution of the slave(s) or $8 per noncapital case; witnesses' and jurors' fees for the trials; sheriff's fees for carrying out punishments; crier's charges for announcing the verdicts; and clerk of the court fees for the multiple aspects of copying and filing the various stages of these slave criminal cases. Though there were no recovered bills of fees with any of these territorial slave criminal cases, an estimate of $20 to $25 per case seems conservative. It may well have been a higher average. The due process that the U.S. Constitution mandated in the territories for both slave and free did not come cheap.

Among other essentials, this document required that both the prosecution and the defense be permitted to summon witnesses in their favor, and in many of these early slave criminal cases, the witnesses spoke languages other than English. In Helene's, Lilise's, and Catherine's cases probably an interpreter was paid at least 50¢ per case because these slave women most likely spoke French, the native language of their owners and most of their victims. Perhaps Catherine's alleged victim, Catiche, spoke Spanish because it may have been the at-home language of her owner, Manuel Lisa and his family, and different interpreters were needed for his slave victim, Antoine Chenie's slave perpetrator, and other government witnesses who saw Catherine's attack on Catiche. Probably Louis Cailloux, the owner of the blankets Helene was charged with stealing; Louison LaRoche, owner of the thread, muslin, and $2 Lilise appropriated; and Antoine Artibuse, victim of Joe's and George's burglary, gave their testimony in French, and the extensive use of interpreters in all these cases increased court costs.

When the territorial government paid them in all slave criminal cases, the benefit it extended to the owners of slaves convicted of crimes became burdens in the form of increased taxes to persons who owned none or owners of law-abiding slaves who stayed out of the criminal justice system. Nothing in surviving records suggests that bondpersons stole, burglarized, or assaulted at a higher rate than the general population.

Prior to 1812 the passage of any legislation was largely a function of presidential appointees eager to please influential slaveholders in the territory. However, in 1812 Missouri achieved a second grade of territorial government and elected its first territorial legislature. Those who stood for election were at least 21 years of age, territorial residents for a minimum of one year prior to their election, landowners, and county or territorial taxpayers, but they were not necessarily slaveholders. Though the earliest sessions of the legislature produced no new laws regarding slavery and crime, change was inherent in the election, as opposed to the appointment, of members of the legislative authority.

Four years after the citizenry began choosing their lawmakers, the second territorial legislature passed a bill that governed the method of financing most slave criminal cases. Its passage of the law occurred at its second session, when 21 elected representatives from seven counties—St. Charles, St. Louis, Washington, Ste. Genevieve, Cape Girardeau, New Madrid, and Arkansas—met at the Dubreuil residence on Second Street in the town of St. Louis from December 4, 1815 through January 25, 1816.[15] The day before it adjourned, this body passed the statute that made the owners of slaves the payers of all court costs in noncapital slave criminal cases, as well as the responsible financial parties for any court-ordered restitution of stolen items that their slaves were found guilty of stealing.

Apparently the meeting of the legislative session in the town of St. Louis gave members ample evidence of the need to fix financial responsibility for the criminal acts of slaves on the owners of offending bondpersons. Once enacted, the new law encouraged slaveholders either to curb the delinquent conduct of their human property or to handle their slaves' petty crime without resort to the legal process. If the owner was unable to pay all costs in noncapital cases wherein his slave was found guilty, the slave convicted of any crime was to be sold to cover restitution, if ordered, as well as all court expenses.[16]

Nonetheless, in 1817, when Don Quixote was granted a new trial after his conviction for the theft of a watch and the prosecutor elected not to retry him, his owner, Robert Wash, was not presented any bill for his slave's arrest and trial. Likewise, when the jury found Carlos, George, and Dick not guilty of stealing in 1819, their owners, August Chouteau, Manuel Lisa, and the unidentified owner of Dick were not assessed any costs. In these cases and in all others in which the accused slaves were not convicted, the territorial government continued to pay the court bills. However, beginning in 1816, if the accused slave was convicted, as were Bill, Jesse, Lilise, Maria, George, Ned, and Simon, their owners, not the public treasury, either paid court fees or sold the offending slaves to cover these charges.

From the beginning of American ownership of Missouri in 1804, the government probably financed all charges in any slave capital case, whatever its outcome. If the slave was granted a new trial and the prosecutor elected not to retry him, as did Elijah's prosecutor, the government footed the bill. After all, his owner had been deprived of his slave's labor over a period of many months, and the government was the losing party. If the slave was convicted on capital charges, the territory's taking of the owner's valuable property was permanent, so, the logic ran, the least it could do for the owner or his estate was finance the costs for the many aspects of federal law that governed capital cases in the territories for both slave and free. Likewise, after statehood the Missouri Constitution essentially decreed the same rights in capital cases for all persons as had earlier applicable federal law.

During the territorial period, no statute specifically addressed the payment of court fees in cases wherein the slave was sentenced to death. By 1825 the legislature required that the state pay the costs when the capitally convicted person had insufficient property to cover these expenses, and indigent hanged felons included slaves. However from 1835 until the end of slavery in Missouri, the law explicitly required that the state pay all costs in slave death penalty cases, including the sheriff's fee for the slave's hanging.[17]

Was the $10 that the state paid the sheriff for his carrying out any slave death sentence sufficient to cover all the incidental costs associated with his hanging the condemned by the neck until dead? These expenses included erecting a gallows, conducting the prisoner to execution and furnishing the rope, and should no physician or his assistant be present to carry away the cadaver for dissection purposes, the sheriff was required to obtain a coffin and bury the body.

The sheriff of Howard County believed the fee wholly inadequate when after carrying out several death sentences of indigent persons, one of whom was a slave, he presented the circuit court of his county with a bill for the extra expenses of two proper executions. From an earlier newspaper advertisement that announced that Slave Hampton had run away from his Howard County master, we know that the condemned slave, Hampton, was a "six feet high" blacksmith.[18] As a result, his burial box was necessarily wider, longer, and more expensive than the average and the preparation of his grave more labor-intensive than would have been the case had the executed slave been of slighter stature. Despite the obvious expense of the sheriff's doing his job correctly, he lost at trial; in 1834 the Missouri Supreme Court upheld the circuit court's refusal to allow payment of his hanging bill.[19] However, and in partial reaction to his case, in 1835 the General Assembly increased the sheriff's fee for executing death warrants from $10 to $15, and there it remained for the next 30 years. The sum was finally increased to $25 after the Civil War.

In 1835 the General Assembly enacted a statute similar to the 1816 territorial law that required owners pay all court fees for the noncapital conviction of their slaves. After a detailed enumeration of the costs of prosecuting free persons, the 1835 legislation stated, "If a slave shall be convicted of any offence … where, if the convict was a free person, he would be liable to pay costs, such slave shall be sold to satisfy such costs, unless the owner or master … pay the same."[20] If the sheriff did not hang the bondpersons, the owner shouldered financial responsibility for all phases of his slave's passage through the criminal justice system. Excluding convictions for murder and after 1835 excluding only slaves found guilty of first-degree murder, owners paid the costs for all other offenses for which their bondpersons were convicted. These other offenses made up the great majority of cases wherein the criminal act(s) of those in bondage came to the attention of a court.

In 1843 the legislature passed a distribution of costs in criminal cases between the state of Missouri and its multiple counties. As under earlier legislation, in capital cases the state continued to pay all fees involving indigents and those unable to afford the cost of their arrests, trials, sentencings, and hangings, including slaves. When the lynching of bondpersons, whom mobs took from county jails, interfered with such payments, lawmakers changed the statute. The new legislation required the state, in cases of the lynching of slaves under death sentences, and the county for all other crimes for which jailed slaves were lynched, to continue to pay court costs. These changes are discussed in Chapter 14.

After the 1843 legislation became effective, in any noncapital cases involving slaves, the county assumed the costs of prosecuting and punishing them. If the offending slave was incarcerated prior to his court-ordered punishment, his owner was required to pay "all necessary expenses incurred by any jailer for clothing and ironing [for] any prisoner, and for medical attendance, fuel, bedding, and menial attendance."[21] Often the offending slave was arrested, tried, convicted, sentenced, and whipped in a single day. After 1831 such was customary in any prosecution for the slave's theft of property; the legislature allowed slaves to be tried without juries for the theft of property worth less than $20. Nonetheless, the owner's financial responsibility remained Missouri law throughout slavery.

As the Civil War neared, the following account of slave misconduct appeared in a Missouri newspaper:

> City Laws Enforced — Two negro wenches, one belonging to H. Laughery, and the other to John Kent, were arrested Tuesday night, and lodged in the calaboose [jail] for being found roving the streets after eleven o'clock. Their masters each had to pay a fine. Mr. Laughery's negro was sailing under false colors having donned the male attire. We think the law should be changed so as to make the punishment fall on the negroes. It looks hard that masters should pay for what they cannot well prevent, and which all guard against.[22]

Though the abolition of slavery and its discriminatory laws was the only realistic remedy for any owner's financial responsibility for the criminal acts of his slaves, this reporter/editor had limited understanding of such matters.

Beginning in 1816 and lasting throughout slavery in Missouri, the legislature always comprehended that bondpersons who lacked both liberty and property could not be the designated financiers of court costs involving them. When slaves paid such fees, they did so, as far as we know, only through their owners' forced sale of them. The payment of court costs always lurked as an extra expense of the ownership of slaves. The only time the government paid them was when it hanged a human property or when a mob took the offender from a county jail and ended his life, and surely there was no slaveholder's enrichment in any violent death(s) of his bondpersons(s).

Chapter 7

Against Themselves: Black-on-Black Crime

From the beginning of slavery in Missouri and elsewhere, the owner's prerogatives included purchase and sale of bondperson(s). Surely some owned persons welcomed new masters, quickly adjusted to their surroundings, and were happy in their servitude. Those slaves were rarely newsworthy, and we know little about their lives. Our knowledge of trafficking in human beings derives from those who were not content to be bought and sold. Because Missouri remained the northernmost place of slavery in the United States, often the sale of its bondpersons was downriver, a destination, both en route and once arrived, in which there was little for the merchandised slave to enjoy and much to dread and endure. However, unless there was an untoward incident, the only mention of these sales in any newspaper was advertisements for them.

Occasionally, all did not go smoothly in these commercial transactions in human beings. Though slaves had little control over life, at times they used that little to end it; doing so was a complex matter. Despite the fact that the psychiatrist Karl Menninger made only passing reference to slavery in his book about self-destruction, *Man Against Himself,* it is useful in understanding slave suicide. Menninger believed that the person who ends his or her own life has three wishes: to kill, to be killed, and to die. First, the slave's wish to kill was often directed against his or her owner. When a slave neither attempted to murder nor murdered his master, as the psychiatrist explained, "perhaps he feared him too much; perhaps he feared the consequences; at any rate he couldn't do it." As Menninger noted of the second element, the wish to be killed "is the extreme form of *submission,* just as killing is the extreme form of *aggression."* The tractable bondperson was the valued slave, and the uppity the undesirable. Insofar as the slave realized his wish to die massa owned a wholly subdued darky. As for the bondpersons' wish to die, Menninger explained that most suicidal persons see life as "hard, bitter, futile, and hopeless."[1] Slaves who ended their own lives also revenged themselves on their owners by permanently depriving them of both the slave's labor and the slave's material worth. Through self-murder, the slave finally achieved a small measure of power. In the words of the old Negro spiritual, he or she could say, "Free at last, free at last, thank God a'mighty, I'm free at last."

Surviving mention of Missouri bondpersons' self-destruction begins before statehood years. Scipio, the slave of Missouri's last territorial governor, William Clark (1813–1821), shot and killed himself in April 1819 because he feared being transported to New Orleans.[2] Overwhelmingly, slaves were shipped there for one purpose: their sale. A more prolonged and painful death of a slave in an eastern Missouri county, Ralls, is found in this April 1835 journal entry: "Suicide — A Negro man of Mr. Elies, having been sold to go down the river, attempted first to cut off both of his legs, failing to do that, cut his throat, did not entirely take his life, went a short distance and drowned himself." The journal keeper, Aaron S. Fry, privately recommended reading "Isaiah, 58:6–7 if you should ever have a notion of dealing in human flesh."[3] These biblical verses concern undoing heavy burdens, letting the oppressed go free, and bringing the poor that are cast out to one's own house. Clearly, not all white Missourians approved of buying and selling human beings, but they said so privately, not publicly.

Newspaper accounts of five slave suicides during statehood years survive, four from central and one from eastern Missouri. In April 1835, Michael, recently sold by a Howard County owner to one from Boone, was immediately shipped south. The bondman escaped en route near Cairo, Illinois, where the Ohio River joins the Mississippi. He returned to Howard County, where his wife resided, and he refused to be sent south unless she accompanied him. He was jailed, and when he learned that he would be sent away without her, he hanged himself. As the newspaper noted of his death, "He resolved to end both his life and his servitude."[4]

In April 1844 a Cooper County slave, a paper recorded, "was found suspended by the neck on the premises of his owner." The coroner's inquest found that "the Negro hanged himself and thereby caused his own death." The known precipitating event in this instance was not the bondman's sale; rather, a short time earlier, his master had whipped him, and the coroner's jury supposed that this "was the cause of his committing suicide."[5] Perhaps his master also threatened to sell him. In June 1845 a Boone County slave who belonged to the estate of a deceased judge tried first to kill his slave wife by cutting her throat. He did not succeed, but he hanged himself from the limb of a tree near his former owner's house, and as the paper noted, his "life [was] entirely extinct."[6] Often, once their owner died, his slaves were sold. Their sale was the only means to divide equally the material value of, for example, four bondpersons among three heirs or the reverse.

In March 1857 a Cole County bondman, about 19 years of age, hanged himself in the barn while his owner and family were at breakfast. The young slave had gone there to harness a team and feed the livestock. He attached one end of a rope to a piece of timber and tied the other end around his neck. The hanging broke his neck, and he died instantly.[7] The newspaper account assigned no reason for the suicide, but whatever the motivation of the unnamed teenager's self-destruction, one fact is certain: he permanently ended his bondage to another. In July 1860 a slave, aged 22 or 23 years, deliberately leaped overboard from the steamboat *Packet Louisiana* on the Mississippi River on its downward trip a short distance below Hannibal, Missouri. He managed to get 30 or 40 feet in front of the wheel paddle, and when it struck him, it killed him instantly. His owner, another passenger, was taking him south for sale.[8] Once more, the young man's suicide deprived his owner of any profit concerning him. In *Beloved* (p. 148) Toni Morrison accurately stated of any slave's demise either by his own hand or anyone else's, "Unlike a snake or a bear, a dead nigger could not be skinned for profit and was not worth his own dead weight in coin."

At times, the slave killed a significant other before ending his or her own life. When the murder-suicide was slave-on-slave, the crime was less sensational than when the suicidal slave killed a white person before he ended his own life. In February 1858 a Howard County slave, owned by a judge, killed a fellow servant by stabbing her twice and then, as the paper noted of his self-murder, "he both cut his own throat and gave himself a severe cut across the abdomen." He thought that his victim had poisoned or tricked him, persisted in his delusional thinking some time, and made a number of unheeded threats.[9] The culture of slavery increased the likelihood that slave women might poison others, and the mental balance of the aggressor slave tipped in a way it might not have had he been free.

In June 1857 George, owned by Mr. and Mrs. John Davis of Monroe County, for the first time refused to obey his mistress. As one paper noted, "he had always been a faithful, obedient and trusty servant — and had been allowed privileges denied to other servants, and bore an excellent character in the neighborhood." On a Monday, June 29, Mrs. Davis asked him to assist her in chastising another male slave; George refused, and according to the paper he did so "in a very insulting manner." She either asked him to tie the other slave, whip him, or attend to both these duties. Unable to accept even one instance of his contrariness, she told him that as soon as her husband returned, and he was then in St. Louis on business, "she would have him removed from the place"; that is, he believed his mistress intended to sell him.

Early Wednesday morning, July 1, and after setting out sweet potato plants at her request, he followed her to the well, 120 yards from the house; there he took her by surprise and wielded an ax with such dexterity that he felled her with one blow of it to her head. Once she was down, he used it to kill her by either severing or nearly severing her head from her body. He approached the house quite bloody, took his master's gun, and left the premises before his victim's daughter discovered her mother's body and raised the alarm. Two days later, Friday, July 3, and approximately 200 yards from where he murdered his mistress, George's own body was found with Mr. Davis's gun beside it. The slave had put his master's rifle under his chin, pulled the trigger, and, as the news account explained "the load entered at the mouth, ranging upwards, blowing off nearly the entire upper part of his head." The paper contained this detail about George's remains: "When found, the crows and buzzards were feasting upon his body. It is said, also that the negroes of the neighborhood, who were greatly exasperated at his hellish conduct, got possession of the body, built a fire, and burnt it to ashes."[10] At least seven news stories are extant concerning George's murder of his mistress and his own suicide. From them, we know that he was about 40 years old, 5'7", "of a pleasant countenance, especially when conversing," and a reward was offered for his apprehension "so that he may be brought to justice." Some 200 persons were in pursuit of him before his body was discovered.[11] Had he been captured alive, he might not have survived to stand trial; an angry mob might have burned him to death.

Clearly, George's was not the usual sort of killing, that is, one slave's bumping off another. His murder of Mrs. Davis threatened the proper order of things. Until he defied his mistress when he refused to help her punish another slave, he had been a hard-working and faithful servant. However, he never had the privilege of telling her, "I prefer not to tie or whip a fellow slave" and voluntarily leaving her employment for work more to his liking. Because she owned him, she had the right, among other prerogatives, to sell him. When she threatened to have him removed from his home, he reacted with a wholly uncharacteristic stealth and violence. The result was her murder and his suicide. If good and obedient slaves were not trustworthy, who was? The newspapers spoke to the fears of all owners who were at risk of a similar fate at the hands of their bondpersons.[12]

Even more frequent than murder-suicide was the violence that one bondman inflicted on another. Usually, news coverage of these crimes was limited to the offense(s) the slave of one master committed against the slave of another. Occasionally, a paper carried a serious fight between those of the same owner. One reported that in Monroe County "two negro men belonging to Mr. Boone ... got into a difficulty about some matter." The result was that one man seized a club and beat the other; the victim recovered and beat the perpetrator's "head fairly into a jelly, causing immediate death. The wounded negro ... was lying in a critical situation from the effects of his wounds."[13] That they may have succeeded in killing each other on a public road was probably the reason a fight between slaves of the same owner was newsworthy. The most frequently documented slave-on-slave crime involved a male of one master who either seriously injured or killed another male owned by a different master. The known particulars are detailed in appendix 1; court records concerning them begin in the territorial period.

In April 1820, in St. Louis County Circuit Court, Murphy was convicted of assault and battery and punished with five lashes.[14] Though the record named neither his owner nor victim, most likely whomever Slave Murphy attacked was the male slave of another owner. The jury may not have assessed any punishment were his victim a free black, but had he been white, Murphy would have received many more than five lashes. In February 1821, in Ste. Genevieve County, south of St. Louis on the Mississippi River, George, a slave of James H. Relfe, and Jim, a slave of Thomas Madden Jr., were indicted for an affray, that is a fight of at least two persons in a public place which disturbs others. By June of that year charges against both were dismissed.[15] Almost certainly, their owners settled the matter of their quarreling slaves privately and thereby avoided court costs of their bondmen's trial and punishment.

At least 28 black-male-on-black-male injuries and killings can be documented in Missouri during statehood years. Drunkenness was a factor in at least three of these altercations. All perpetrators of these assaults and murders were slaves, and excluding at most four free blacks, all victims were slaves. In only two known cases did the homicide result in a death sentence and public hanging, and in only one in a manslaughter conviction.

Prior to 1835 the perpetrator of any unexcused killing committed either murder or manslaughter; in 1835 the legislature divided murder into first and second degrees. Slaves who killed whites were convicted of first-degree murder and executed. Slaves who killed other slaves were convicted of second-degree murder and whipped. However, in 1836 the General Assembly provided an additional remedy for disposing of bondpersons convicted of violent felonies. The law required that the owner post a bond of $500 to insure that his convicted-felon slave was taken from the state within 60 days and not returned to Missouri for at least 20 years "if [the felony] be of such a nature, in the opinion of the court, that it is not safe that such slave should stay in the State."[16] Most likely, such bondpersons were sold down the river, and as the male slave suicide cases illustrate, their forced sale was a far more dreaded punishment than any court-ordered whipping. This statute was used for offenses other than one slave's violence toward another, but it was the primary law applied in these cases.

The earliest known Missouri case involving the sentence of slave transportation occurred in the late 1830s. It arose when Mat, a St. Louis bondman, stabbed Haburn, a slave of Joseph C. Brown. Material concerning this matter is among the pardon papers of Governor Lilburn W. Boggs (1836–40). The difficulty between them took place in Brown's kitchen when Mat claimed Jane as his wife; she was a slave whom Brown probably leased. As the pardon papers explained, Mat told Jane to "hush! She, however, persevered in her discourse until Mat undertook to enforce his authority with a slap." She threatened to cut Mat with a knife if he did not leave her alone. A scuffle ensued between them; he seized a knife from her; Haburn interfered and pushed Mat against the table. The victim struck Mat with a chair, and Mat stabbed him several times.

In St. Louis County Circuit Court, the perpetrator was found guilty of stabbing with intent to kill, ordered whipped 39 lashes, and transported out of state within 60 days for 20 years. At the time the petitioners, Thomas Latimer and some of his friends, requested that Governor Boggs remit the transportation portion of the penalty. Mat had already received his 39-lash punishment. The petition explained that "the circumstances of the case do not warrant so severe a sentence [as transportation] particularly when it is remembered that the boy is yet young and has never committed any similar act, or shown himself vicious or insubordinate or otherwise manifested a disposition which argued danger to the community." Latimer, the owner of Mat's family, had raised him from infancy, was attached to him because of his "honest nature and faithful service," and had a "strong repugnance to parting him from his master and family." If he was permitted to remain with his owner, Mat's one departure from his otherwise good conduct would not again become a problem, the 24 petitioners assured the governor.

This file also contains a letter to the governor from the attorney who represented Mat at trial. In addition to most of the arguments that the friends of Latimer advanced, Mat's lawyer advised the governor, "the verdict operates very hard upon old Mr. Latimer as it will compel him to sell a slave whom he assures me he has been offered $1,200 dollars for perhaps one half the sum." The lawyer alerted the governor that his early action was required because the time for transporting Mat was running out. On February 16, 1839, Boggs acted on the "Petition of Thomas Latimer and others," when he decreed, "Let a writ issue suspending the execution of the sentence for the term of twelve months."[17] Eventually, Mat was permanently parted from his family and his owner, but his sale was leisurely, not forced. Most likely, his flogging was inflicted with a whip similar to one Trexler described as the official Lafayette County "flagellum.... It would cause a very painful blow without leaving a scar. If scarred the Negro would be less valuable, as a prospective buyer would consider him vicious or liable to absconding if bearing the marks of punishment."[18] As a result, Latimer probably disguised the fact that his slave was sold for a fault, and he obtained top, not bottom, dollar for his bondperson whose temper flared when he took possession of a knife from the hand of a young woman whom he claimed as his wife.

A Clay County slave who killed another in August 1848 was convicted of second-degree murder, sentenced to 39 lashes, and transported out of state in October 1848.[19] Afterward, the owner of the murdered slave sued the perpetrator's owner, and at trial the plaintiff prevailed because the aggressor was in the habit of assaulting other bondmen when intoxicated. As in an 1837 decision concerning one slave's murder of another, wherein the court decided the perpetrator's owner was blameless, in 1850 the Missouri Supreme Court ruled that the owner is not liable for the criminal acts of his human property. It held, "The slave [is] a responsible moral agent, amenable, like his master to the laws of God and man for his own transgressions." The master is not liable for "such remote consequences as the murder of another slave."[20] That Missouri's highest court decided this matter twice indicates the frequency with which slaves of different masters attacked one another.

In November 1822, in St. Louis County, an inquest was held on the view of Sam, a black man, the property of Mr. Hartshorn. The coroner's jurors concluded that Jepe, owned by Priscilla Gordon, a widow, killed Sam with a rock in self defense. Nicholas and James Long posted a $2,000 recognizance bond for the court appearance of Jepe, and Nicholas Long posted a $300 bond to insure that his Negro woman, Mariah, "a yellow girl," appear and give her evidence concerning the dispute between Sam and Jepe.[21] This case probably involves some of the same persons discussed in the last chapter. Like John Long Jr.'s, it arose in Bonhomme Township, and almost certainly Widow Gordon's former husband was George Gordon and Nicholas and James Long her surviving sons and brothers of John Long Jr., hanged in 1809 for the murder of his stepfather, George Gordon. Like many court records, these concerning Widow Gordon's Jepe are incomplete.

In February 1824, in Howard County, north of the Missouri River in central Missouri, Slave Cato, a black man, was indicted for murder, pled not guilty, was tried by a jury and found guilty of voluntary manslaughter. The prosecutor requested that Cato receive 100 lashes.[22] Though the extant records contain no mention of Cato's victim, he or she was another person of color, probably another slave. No matter what the circumstances, slaves who killed whites were never found guilty of manslaughter.

Several coroners' inquests from the 1830s exist from St. Louis in which a slave killed another slave or a free black. One asserted that Sandy, probably owned by Mrs. Fugate because the inquest was held at her home, "came to his death by a stab in the breast inflicted with a knife by the hand of Clifford, a slave the property of the estate of John Knight deceased."[23] Another found that John Steele died as a result of blows from Slave Alfred and Slave Peter.[24] This record did not name the owners of the slaves, and since no known capital charges arose concerning John Steele's death, most likely the victim was a free black. A third coroner's inquest concerned the death of Slave William, found with his skull fractured by a brickbat that Sam, who belonged to Mr. Fletcher, threw at him. Since the leasing of slaves was common and the record specified that Fletcher owned Sam and "William was in his service,"[25] Fletcher probably leased William from another owner.

Some news stories about slave-on-slave killings contained their names; others did not. The antebellum Missouri press usually emphasized the injury or demise of the victim, especially if he was a valuable property. In Randolph County, in the north central section of the state, an accidental shooting occurred "when a drunken negro belonging to B. R. Williams was carelessly handling a loaded pistol which went off, the ball striking the shin of another, belonging to N. B. Christian."[26] In Pike County, north of St. Louis on the Mississippi River, one intoxicated slave, belonging to Thomas Stanford, used a butcher knife to kill another drunken slave, belonging to H. H. Yeager.[27] A Howard County case concerned "two slaves, one belong[ing] to Mr. Watts and the other to Dr. Scott

... [who] had a fight last Friday, in which Watts' boy received a blow from the effect of which he died on Sunday. Upon an investigation of the matter, Scott's boy was held to bail in the sum of $500."[28] In western Missouri, in Jackson County, "George, a negro man belonging to Matthew Currant, was stabbed and instantly killed by a negro named Dan, belonging to Mr. Joseph Redmon" at Mr. Redmon's brickyard.[29] A Clay County case arose when "a difficulty occurred ... between two negroes belonging to T. C. Gordon and John Ecton ... which resulted in the death of Mr. E.'s negro, and the wounding of Mr. Gordon's. They fought with knives."[30] Additional news coverage concerned a killing that occurred in Fulton, Callaway County, south of the Missouri River in central Missouri. Slave Isam stabbed and killed Al Barnes, a free black, and the paper noted, "Isam was arraigned before the Grand Jury last week, and they failed to find a bill of indictment."[31] Its failure to vote a true bill against Isam suggests the low level of protection the law afforded free blacks during slavery. Likewise, in Jefferson County, south of St. Louis, when Slave John clubbed and killed a free black, Free Jack, the perpetrator pled guilty and was sentenced to 39 lashes. A county history noted of the crime, "In this case a peculiar characteristic of slavery is observable. Jack, the free negro, represented no value, while John, the slave, did represent value, and his execution ... would have been the destruction of so much property — hence the apparent reason for his being allowed to ... escape with a whipping, which, it is presumed, did not materially injure the property."[32]

The last slave-on-slave homicide that we know about is preserved in court records, Saline County's, north of the Missouri River in the central section of the state. The crime took place the evening of June 4, 1862, when Martin knifed Godfrey in his left side in the Negro cabin of David B. Wood. The victim died within three minutes. Counting the witnesses, the perpetrator, and the victim, the crime involved the slaves of four different masters. David Wood owned Mary, Clay, and Hudson; his brother, William Wood, owned Jim. George Murrell owned Jack and the victim, Godfrey; Charles Lewis owned the perpetrator, Martin.

According to Mary's testimony before Justice of the Peace John Hood, Godfrey came to her master's cabin "once or twice a week." She referred to Martin as her husband and testified that he "stays with me every night." The various owners knew and approved of the sexual relationship between Mary and Martin and the social contact among all of their slaves. However, hard feelings, probably involving Mary, had existed for some time between Martin and Godfrey. She stated that she heard Martin say to Godfrey "that if he did not stay away, it would not be good for him." She testified that she saw Martin get his knife from a sack in the kitchen. She was aware that he obtained it "last spring before corn planting." Tempers flared between the men, and they scuffled for control of a stick. According to Clay, "Martin drew his knife & cut at [Godfrey] twice or three times to make him let the stick loose." Following his victim's death, Martin was arrested in his owner's barn the next day.

It is difficult to find a higher level of homicide in these facts than murder in the second degree, and a verdict of either it or manslaughter carried no greater punishment for a slave than a whipping, sale, and transportation out of state. Moreover, travel to the usual southern slave markets may have been almost impossible during the war years. On June 9 the testimony of the witnesses was taken before Justice Wood, and he issued a warrant for Martin's arrest on murder charges. The order specified that the defendant was to be delivered to the custody of the keeper of the Saline County jail. In June 1862 George Murrell and David Wood posted recognizance bonds to guarantee their own and the various slave witnesses' appearance before the circuit court at its next term. In November 1863, or almost one and one-half years later, the grand jury indicted Martin on first-degree murder charges, and his trial was scheduled to begin in May 1864.[33] This long delay between his crime and his trial surely had two causes: an ongoing Civil War and the authorities' reluctance to prosecute with any speed or vigor one slave's killing another. The record breaks off, and nothing more is known regarding this case.

Yet another feature of adult black-on-black crime during slave times was the frequency with which men injured and killed other men. With few exceptions, all known victims were male. Because the owner of slave girls and women kept them in a highly controlled environment, they were not out and about on the roads and byways, at brickyards, and in the towns where at times deadly quarrels developed between bondmen of different owners. For the most part female slaves remained in the home, the yard, and the fields, out of harm's way at the hands of the slaves of other masters. Her owner desired that his newborns be the fittest slave babies, and he decided whom she could "marry." Usually, farms and plantations were not places of promiscuous sex between slave men and women. Men slept in one group of cabins, women in others, unless they were "married," as Martin and Mary were; and these "marriages" were not possible without their owners' permission. The owner regulated the breeding of his slave women much as a bull watches his cows, and he severely punished any male slave who raped a slave woman. The white man, not the black, was in charge.

The balance of power could be changed occasionally by means such as 92-year-old Lucinda Patterson remembered that she had employed in

1860 when she was 15-year-old Slave Delicia. She was taken to the Cooper County Courthouse in Boonville and put on the auction block. There she saw a Judge Miller, notoriously well-known for cruelty to his slaves. She expected that he would bid on her because she had the reputation of being a good worker, but when he did, she told him, "Old Judge Miller don't you bid for me, 'cause if you do, I would not live on your plantation. I will take a knife and cut my own throat from ear to ear before I will be owned by you." Her threat worked; the despicable master stepped back and allowed someone else to bid on that "sassy niggah."[34]

Delicia's threat of violence was against herself, not a fellow slave. Bondwomen infrequently assaulted and battered other slave women. Insofar as they did, their white owners punished them in-house. To be sure, in the town of St. Louis one court record from Spanish rule of Missouri and another from territorial days dealt with one female slave assaulting another. Probably, there are some undiscovered Missouri records of slave women exchanging blows with other slave women during statehood years; nonetheless, slave-woman-on-slave-woman crime was uncommon. For example, there are no known adult-female-on-adult-female-slave killings in Missouri's history. Black and mulatto victims whom we know about were overwhelmingly the state's own children.

The earliest of these Missouri cases, Annice's, occurred in Clay County in 1828. Because her drowning of five children, two of them her own and all five her owner's, resulted in a capital case, it is discussed in chapter 10. Mention is made of it here to illustrate the varied means these women used to destroy their children and their master's property. In all, 13 known cases of slave mothers attempting to murder or murdering their offspring survive from Missouri's antebellum period.

In Callaway County Slave Jane used two methods to end the life of her daughter, Angeline. On December 8 she gave her child laudanum, an opium derivative, and depending on the size of the ingestor and the amount ingested, a poison. Though it made her infant ill, it did not kill her. On December 11, 1830, Jane smothered her daughter with bed clothes. She was tried for murder, found guilty, and sentenced to death by hanging. An appeal was taken to the Supreme Court of Missouri, and it reversed the verdict because it found error in the indictment.[35] Jane's fate is unknown.

In this same county, Callaway, a slave mother used arsenic to murder four of her own children and a white child of her owner's. On March 3, 1845, three of her children died, on March 4 another, and on March 5, her master's youngster. Physicians examined their remains and found that they were all poisoned with arsenic. The mother of the four black children was arrested and jailed, and she confessed her crimes. Within 30 minutes of her confession, she was also dead by self-administered arsenic poisoning. One newspaper account of "this diabolical act" concluded that "no motive [could be] assigned for the conduct of the woman."[36] There was a motive; she, not her owner, was in charge in these life-and-death matters.

A case of slave infanticide survives in the pardon papers of Governor John Edwards (1844–48). In Warren County, west of St. Louis, in August or September 1846, Slave Nelly, aged about 15 years, killed her newborn, of unspecified sex. On the date of the earlier extant petition, September 24, 1846, she had been arrested, was being held in the county jail in Warrenton, and was indicted for murder but not yet tried. Among other unusual aspects of the request for her pardon was the large number of white male citizens who signed it, more than 110, most of them from Warren County. The unknown length of Nelly's pregnancy suggests an attempt to conceal the date of her child's conception. The petition stated, "It will be difficult to ascertain whether the infant was the production of a mature or premature birth. But … if it were living at its birth, there is little doubt that the mother killed it." The first petition explained that Nelly might not be "held morally accountable for the act charged. We believe she is ignorant even for a slave of her youth & that there is reason to doubt whether at the time of the act the little mind that she has was in a state to make her responsible to the law." One petition in the fall of 1846 requested a pretrial pardon to spare the court appearance of "very respectable ladies who will have to be examined as to the facts." Another mentioned, "The trial will be troublesome & expensive & exceedingly unpleasant to the sensibilities & delicate feelings of the whole community."

The request for Nelly's pretrial pardon begins to make sense when we learn that her owner, Henry Edwards, was deceased and that she had become the property of his widow and their 10 children. Though the extant probate records from this period in Warren County do not reveal the death date of Nelly's owner, the likelihood is great that at some point Nelly became Mrs. Henry Edwards's contraception. Most probably, the accused girl's defense attorneys intended to put in evidence that Nelly's owner raped and impregnated her. These facts would have become a part of the trial record if there were a trial.

Clearly, Mrs. Henry Edwards had no particular success with birth control. Most likely, all she would have known about preventing yet another pregnancy in rural Missouri in the 1830s and 1840s, was "coitus interruptus," "the pullback," "the drawback," and "the way,"[37] and it was not an especially satisfying way for the husband. During or after 10 of Mrs. Edwards's pregnancies, perhaps a few additional if there were miscarriages,

Nelly probably became a far safer means for Mrs. Edwards to prevent her own future confinements and a much more satisfying sexual experience for Mr. Edwards because it did not involve "coitus interruptus."

As Nelly's trial approached, the petitioners reminded Governor Edwards that she was the property of a widow and ten children "with small means for their raising, education & the support of the family." Nelly's hanging would extinguish any value in the young slave girl that would otherwise inure to the benefit of Mrs. Edwards and her many children. Of equal importance, her trial for murder would cause considerable embarrassment in her community. However, Nelly's case was never heard in open court; on October 15, 1846, Edwards pardoned her *before* she was tried.[38] As a result, the length of her pregnancy, the sex of her child, its paternity, the circumstances of its conception, and its age at its untimely death are now obscured. Of the more than 100 known instances in Missouri's history of gubernatorial commutation and pardon for murder, Nelly's case is the only known pretrial pardon in this state's history.

We know about two other slave mothers' murder of their young. In Marion County in 1834 a slave trader purchased three young children. Their mother became so violent that she was tied up, but during the night, she broke loose and used an ax to kill her sold sons and herself. In 1845 in Cole County, Margaret was arrested for murder after her master found a blood-stained knife and a part of her newborn's body, which had been eaten by hogs. A physician testified at her trial that she had used the knife to sever the infant's umbilical cord. She was found guilty, but as in most slave infanticide cases, the record is silent regarding her punishment.[39]

Missouri newspapers confirm the murders and attempted murders of black children at the hands of their suicidal mothers during the 1850s. In October 1853 a woman recently purchased by the sheriff of Montgomery County cut off the head of one of her children and attempted to murder another by striking it five times with the edge of an ax.[40] In April 1857 in Randolph County, a slave mother belonging to Mr. Elias Lay hanged both her son, aged four or five years, and herself. Neither was discovered until both were dead. The article concluded, "No cause is known why she committed the act."[41] When the newspaper supplied a reason for such aberrant behavior, the cause was never the conditions of involuntary servitude. In Monroe County in September 1857, an unnamed slave woman belonging to Daniel Eubanks attempted to drown her children and herself. She threw them in a well and jumped in herself; they all survived because they were quickly pulled out. She gave as her reason for her attempted murder and suicide that her "husband" mistreated her. Though he was temporarily jailed in Paris, Missouri,[42] most likely her status as a slave increased her desire to die and take her babies with her. In April 1862 in Bowling Green, Pike County, the body of a Negro infant was found in a well, and it was presumed to have been thrown there by its mother several months earlier.[43] Though the newspaper did not, indeed could not, identify the victim as a bondbaby, the odds are that it was.

Court records confirm that Emily, property of the estate of Thomas Lakin, was indicted for the December 10, 1855, burning and suffocating death of her infant in Audrain County in April 1856. Her case was continued as late as November 1857.[44] Since the circuit court in its county seat, Mexico, had still not disposed of her case nearly two years after her crime, the likelihood is great that her punishment, if any, was minimal.

Two additional Missouri circuit court records of slave infanticide survive. One arose in the town of Miami, Saline County, on October 27, 1858, when the body of an infant girl less than 60 hours old was discovered. French S. Johnson, then the employer of Mariah, found the dead baby approximately 50 yards from his house. When the authorities examined Mariah, she confessed that she was the mother of the dead child and had destroyed her by both slitting her throat with a knife and suffocating her. At this time, Mariah was owned by the estate of George D. Duvall. At the November term of the grand jury of Saline County she was indicted for first-degree murder, and by November 11 she had applied for and received a change of venue to Lafayette County. As in Emily's case, documents dealing with court costs in Mariah's case are extant from May 1859 or 17 months after her crime was discovered and confessed.[45] During the 1850s the typical time lapse between crime and punishment in slave cases, including those that were capital, was at most six months; frequently, the interval was much shorter. Changes of venue were always rare in bondpersons' cases. Though the record is incomplete, most likely Slave Mariah's punishment, like Emily's, was mild.

The remaining known slave infanticide case arose in Cape Girardeau County in the middle of the Civil War. President Lincoln had abolished slavery in most other American places when he issued the Emancipation Proclamation on January 1, 1863, or shortly before Slave Evaline, the property of Rachael and Jacob Higby, conceived the twins whose skeletal remains were discovered on August 20, 1863. Mr. Higby testified before the coroner's jury that some eight or nine days before the skeletons were found that Evaline "from appearance was pregnant." Then he noticed a change in her appearance, "as if she had been delivered." His testimony concluded that she attended to her work as usual. Mrs. Higby testified that she was aware of Evaline's pregnancy and noticed no change in it until after the tiny skeletons were found. Then she noticed that her slave woman put on more clothing than she customarily wore. About this same time and while Mrs. Higby was gone, Evaline took her own clothing and bedding to a pond some distance from the house and washed them. Her mistress further testified that the dress in which the skeletons were wrapped was one in which Evaline had clothed her older children. Equally intriguing testimony at the inquest came from Cora C. Howard, who at the time was residing with the Jacob Higby family. The morning of August 11 she saw Evaline digging a hole in the garden with a spade. The witness asked the slave woman why she was digging, and Evaline replied that she was collecting dirt to plant flower beans, and upon Cora C. Howard's telling her that it was too late to plant them, she returned to the house and brought the spade with her. Another witness, Lindarenda C. Cotner, testified to Evaline's pregnant appearance, her later nonpregnant appearance, her wearing of additional clothing, and the rolled-up blanket and quilt that the slave did not open when washing other items at the pond in the Cotner woman's presence.

On August 24, 1863, the six-member coroner's jury concluded that the two infant Negro children "came to their deaths by violence at the hands of their mother, Evaline, a Negro woman belonging to Jacob N. Higby." That same day, the four witnesses who testified at the coroner's inquest together posted a $50 recognizance bond that they would personally appear at the next term of the circuit court to give their evidence. The slave was taken to the county jail in Jackson to await her trial on murder charges at the next term of the circuit court.[46] There the records pertaining to her break off.

Probably, she, like other slave mothers who killed their children, was punished lightly. If records of all the intentional deaths of the offspring of Missouri slaves survived, the frequency with which their mothers killed or attempted to kill them would be epidemic. That slave infanticide occurred as often as it did was largely forgotten after slavery perished. Trexler's *Slavery in Missouri, 1804–1865* (1914) made no mention if it, and Greene et al.'s *Missouri's Black Heritage* (1980) described such killings in two paragraphs. A 1981 article never suggested that any criminal act(s) might explain that, as its historian-author discovered, "In 1860 the slave states accounted for 94 percent of the nation's 2,129 reported deaths by suffocation. Most of these victims were probably the children of slaves." The blame for the infants' deaths was fixed on their mothers' poor prenatal and postnatal diet, their drudgery, their sleeping with their children and accidentally rolling over on them and suffocating them as they slept, but mostly on what is now known as sudden infant death syndrome. The author naively observed, "None of the smothering deaths in Georgia, Mississippi, South Carolina, and Virginia in 1860 produced even a hint of infanticide. There was simply no motive."[47] Nearly 150 years earlier, the abolitionist William Lloyd Garrison knew there was a compelling motive for slave women to kill their young. He published other newspapers' accounts of their crimes in his Boston newspaper, *The Liberator,* such as one from the *Indiana Messenger*: "A female slave [in Boone County, Kentucky] ... destroyed her two children to relieve them from the curse of involuntary servitude — she threw one into a well and smothered the other in a ditch. Another woman, in the same neighborhood, about the same time, for the same object destroyed her only child."[48]

Garrison's knowledge regarding these matters was seemingly forgotten until Toni Morrison explored the mind of the slave mother in her novel *Beloved* (1987). It is loosely based on an actual incident that took place in her home state of Ohio in the 1850s. A Missouri newspaper carried a story, headlined "A Shocking Affair," about a runaway from Kentucky, who, pursued by slave-catchers and while in Cincinnati, "to prevent her children from returning to Kentucky ... deliberately cut the throats of two of them, one fatally and the other dangerously."[49] Morrison describes Sethe's, her slave mother's, view of the world: "Men and women were moved around like checkers. They ran off, were hanged, rented out, loaned out, bought up, brought back, mortgaged, won, stole[n], seized, and nobody stopped playing checkers just because the pieces included her children" (p. 23). Sethe escapes from Kentucky to Ohio, and there she slits the throat of and kills her infant daughter, Beloved. By this act she spares her child the intolerable burden of growing up slave.

Morrison's heroine and many similarly situated slave women avenged themselves on their owners by denying them the much-valued product of their pregnancies and childbearing. In a world where white men made most important decisions, slave women decided their children's fate when they ended their lives.

Missouri slaves against themselves was a far more widespread and complex phenomenon than modern scholars have described. It took lives by drowning, throat slitting, shooting, stabbing, poisoning, burning, hanging, smothering, ax wielding, and combinations of these methods. It caused serious injuries and immense heartbreak. With three known exceptions bondpersons who killed other slaves were not punished to the full extent of the law. Instead, in case after case the perpetrator was not found guilty of a capital offense. The next chapter concerns the crimes of whites against blacks and mulattoes, and though their owners at times killed their male slaves, much more frequently the object of the white man's wrath was a woman of color.

Chapter 8

White Perpetrators, Black and Mulatto Victims

In the states, including Missouri, where human bondage was tolerated, color was prima facie evidence of slavery. This rule of law guided justices of the peace, circuit and appellate court judges, and the justices of the Supreme Court of the United States.[1] It meant that in proceedings before any legal tribunal, in the operation of a county jail, and in everyday affairs, any person of color was presumed a slave. She had to prove that she was free; the person or persons who asserted that she was a bondwoman need not come forward with any evidence. The burden of proof was always on colored persons to prove that they had rights that whites were bound to respect. The testimonial incompetence of blacks and mulattoes against whites increased their already great difficulty of asserting any legal rights against white persons. Though the free black had an advantage over the bondperson because she was not a slave, surviving records document that, when she was a victim of crime, courts often treated her as a thing of nought.

These minorities were principally the victims of whites who owned, leased, employed, or otherwise associated with them. The criminal acts of strangers against free blacks and slaves were infrequent; almost always, the victims and perpetrators knew each other. The accounts that survive of black male victims of whites all involve slaves, and aggressors were usually not prosecuted for the harm they inflicted on their own or another person's property.

125

The earliest contested slave beating in Missouri that survives in court records took place in Cape Girardeau District before the Purchase. The signature of Louis Lorimier, the Spanish commandant, appeared in three places in a civil suit that the owner of Slave Ned, Jonathan Foreman, brought against his slave's lessee, William Deakins. The plaintiff charged the defendant with excessively punishing and hence damaging his human property. The matter arose in June 1799, and the issue, which two arbitrators heard under Spanish authority in September 1799, was the alleged wrongfulness of Deakins's chastising a slave who did not labor at full capacity over the course of the summer. Testimony made clear that Ned complained very much of a pain in his side; one witness certified that he "did not earn his diet" because he did not attend to his work. Another testified that she saw "the Negro hold his hands to his side. With that Deakins took a whip & whipt him till he could not whip no more with it. I witnessed it. Deakins confessed afterwards that he threw the club at the Negro" and said to him "'I thought to knock your damm brains out.'" Both arbitrators heard the witnesses and examined Ned's wound. One recommended that the lessee, Deakins, pay court costs and Foreman $20, the maximum that commandants could award without sending the case to New Orleans. The other advised against any fine for Deakins and Foreman's payment of costs. The resolution of this case, preserved in court records written in English with a few notations in French, which Commandant Lorimier signed, was not clarified in the surviving documents.[2] However, no known criminal charges arose when William Deakins whipped and clubbed Ned under Spanish rule of Missouri in 1799.

Likewise, there were few *criminal* cases involving whites' severely injuring and/or murdering male slaves under American rule in Missouri. The excessive punishments, which surely occurred throughout slave times, were probably handled either in-house or under the direction of an owner, his hiree, an overseer, or a lessee. Their terrible treatments of bondpersons are preserved in some civil suits that were appealed to the Missouri Supreme Court. One arose in St. Charles County in early statehood years. The defendant shot and killed the plaintiff's Negro slave, was criminally tried for murder, and acquitted. Nonetheless, the plaintiff-owner of the dead slave recovered damages because the private injury was not merged in the public wrong. In other words, the defendant's acquittal on criminal charges did not protect him from a successful civil suit for the destruction of another man's property.[3]

A Howard County case concerned lost wages, and it demonstrates the cruelty Missouri's criminal law tolerated in the treatment of bondpersons. The slave's owner, Dabney Garth, hired Bird Posey as an overseer for $175 for one year, beginning January 1, 1838. In April of that year, Garth dismissed him because, as the court noted, he "had maltreated and injured [Garth's] negroes." Specifically Posey, when failing in his attempt to whip a male slave for refusing to obey his order, struck him with a handspike, a heavy bar used as a lever for shifting heavy objects. Once the slave was down, Posey beat him with it, as the appeals court observed, "in such a manner that in four days thereafter he died from the effect of the blows." Expectedly Missouri's highest court upheld the circuit court's judgment that Posey was entitled to only $61, not the full year's wages of $175.[4] However, this brutal man had no apparent fear of criminal prosecution for murder when he sued his victim's owner for breach of an employment contract. As late as 1866 Missouri's highest court decided a Clay County civil suit that upheld the plaintiff-owner's award of damages against the man who hired his slave, cruelly and inhumanly beat him, and thereby reduced his value.[5] In this case, as in other earlier civil suits, there was no known criminal conviction of the abusive lessee.

To be sure, the law under which whites could be prosecuted for crimes against blacks was on the books. The 1820 Missouri constitution required that "Any person who shall maliciously deprive of life or dismember a slave, shall suffer such punishment as would be inflicted for the like offense if it were committed on a free white person." This same document also required the General Assembly to pass the necessary laws "to oblige the owners of slaves to treat them with humanity and to abstain from all injuries to them extending to life and limb."[6] Trexler drew attention to these provisions when praising the state for its intended equal punishment of persons whose victims were bondpersons. However, any defendant in a criminal proceeding had a right to a jury trial, and all members of that jury were white males. They never imposed any known felony conviction on any white person accused of any crime, no matter how heinous, against any African American, slave or free.

After several county prosecutors were unsuccessful in their attempts to secure felony convictions against white men who abused and killed slaves, in 1835 the legislature passed a misdemeanor statute that imposed a fine of up to $1,000, or one year in the county jail, or both, on any person who cruelly or inhumanly tortured, beat, wounded, or abused "any slave in his employment or under his ... control, whether belonging to himself or another."[7] Two cases under it survive in Supreme Court of Missouri decisions. In one the court upheld an indictment that arose in Chariton County, north of the Missouri River in central Missouri, for inhumanly beating a bondman. It rejected the defendant's claim that the absence of the owner's name in the indictment prohibited criminal proceedings against him.[8] The appellate decision identified neither the slave's owner nor clarified whether the accused was convicted. In the other case the court reversed a St. Louis County conviction on grounds that the defendants did not bear to the abused slave "the relationship of master or quasi master, [and] such offenses stand on the same ground as when white persons cruelly use each other."[9] Because the defendants were indicted under the wrong law, the double jeopardy provision of the Missouri Constitution barred their retrial for the abuse of a slave whom they neither owned, supervised, nor employed.

In one of these misdemeanor cases the slave was identified as male, and in the other the slave's sex was not specified. In both, we know that the slaves survived their oppressors' cruel treatment because the state brought charges against these defendants for inhumanly beating, not murdering, bondpersons. Trexler cited a murder prosecution from the territorial period that was tried in St. Louis County's General Court in 1820. In it Prinne was found not guilty of murdering his slave, Walter, "by confining him in a dungeon or cell dangerous to his health."[10] Likewise, in the St. Charles County prosecution the defendant was acquitted of murder when he shot and killed another man's slave. There were few criminal charges in Missouri throughout slave times for any white person's murder of a bondman and none located under American rule for the beating death of a male slave. Nor are there visible traces of such prosecutions in extant Missouri newspapers. All that survives is an occasional hearsay account of the master causing the death of his male slave. An instance of cruelty in Saline County occurred when one angered his master. According to the son of a former slave who heard the tale, the victim was "chained to a hemp-brake on a cold night and left to freeze to death which he did."[11] However, there is no known court record nor newspaper story about this matter.

Often, the victimized were not considered harmed; the law permitted the owner's or his overseer's intimidation, beating, and confinement of them because they were slaves. Suits for freedom, including those of Dred and Harriet Scott, were filed as civil actions, alleging that their owners assaulted, battered, and falsely imprisoned them and that the blacks were already or should be freed. Most likely, some owners, overseers, lessees, or their employees whipped bondmen for a variety of petty matters, including, as in Slave Ned's 1799 punishment, not working with sufficient speed or thoroughness, or in Garth's unnamed slave's case, for not obeying an overseer's order. However, many bondmen were large, powerful, and agile, and it was difficult for a man with a lesser physique to single-handedly whip his physical superior to the point of criminal charges, if not to death. Instead, slaveholders sold their insubordinate or otherwise troublesome male slaves because owners had no desire to destroy such valuable properties.

Mostly, the newspaper accounts that survive of the death of bondmen at the hands of whites in the late antebellum period explain the slave's death as either an accident or self-defense on the part of the perpetrator. The exception occurred when a stranger killed a slave, especially one known to be obedient and well behaved. Then the aggressor was taken into custody, as in an incident from St. Charles County in 1856 in which the perpetrator was lodged in the St. Louis jail for safe-keeping when he was unable to make bail in the amount of $3,000. In this instance the perpetrator's account, that the slave was the aggressor in an encounter between them at night when no one was present, was not believed.[12] Nonetheless, John T. Ball, the perpetrator in the St. Charles case, was neither executed nor sent to the Missouri State Penitentiary.

Other Missouri newspaper accounts of the killing of male slaves exonerated the perpetrators. One from Lafayette County concerned a bondman's raising an ax to attack his overseer who ran into the house, got his gun, and when the slave dared him to fire, he shot him above the knee joint, shattering the bone. When it became necessary to amputate the slave's leg, as the paper noted, he died "of nervous shock." Mr. Corder, the overseer, "gave himself up to a magistrate; had the case fairly tried, and was honorably acquitted."[13] In Randolph County a recently sold slave got loose on the streets of Huntsville. He tried to shoot several men with a pistol, and he was gunned down with a shot in the thigh and another through his lungs. Several weapons, including the pistol he drew, were found on his body. The paper explained that the unnamed slave "was a negro of a desperate character, and had successfully resisted two attempts to take him prior to this."[14] In Jackson County a slave purchased from an estate became rebellious when, as the paper noted, his new "master attempted to correct him," euphemistic language during slave times for a whipping. The bondman armed himself with an ax and threatened to kill anyone who approached him. Neighbors joined the new owner, who tried to capture the rebellious slave, but as the paper noted, "His master was forced to shoot him. Several shots took effect, and the negro died almost instantly."[15] A Saline County owner accidentally shot and killed his slave, worth $1,500, when the owner sought to punish his slave for "daring and open rebellion before the rest of the negroes."[16]

Other news stories and some court records that concern the serious injury or death of male slaves at the hands of white men certainly existed, but such potentially criminal behavior appears to have been uncommon.

In most of Missouri's extant court records and contemporary newspaper accounts that concern white men injuring and killing blacks and mulattoes, the victims were girls and women. Apparently female persons of color were Missouri's and probably other slave states' nineteenth-century equivalent of today's battered women. The particulars of 14 known cases of black and mulatto females as the victims of White males during Missouri's slave days are listed in appendix 2.

One of the earliest known records pertaining to any black victim in Missouri under American rule concerned a woman known in court records as "Negress Sylvia." The psychologist Gordon Allport called attention to the use of such labeling: "Sex differentiations are objectionable, since they seem doubly to emphasize ethnic difference: why speak of Jewess and not of Protestantess, or of Negress and not of Whitess?"[17] The person identified is stigmatized as both a member of an ethnic minority and as a female. Despite any mention of her surname, almost certainly, Sylvia was a free woman of color. The 1810 federal census of Missouri listed 607 free Blacks and 3,011 slaves;[18] in other words, 20 percent of the colored population of the territory was free, and "Negress Sylvia" was among them. We know this because the records pertaining to her never mention her owner. In contrast, court records and newspaper accounts of slaves, discussed throughout this book, either term a person a slave or they specify a person or an estate as owning whoever was someone else's human property.

This woman became matter of public record because her body was found at the St. Louis home of Joseph Leblond sometime shortly before November 16, 1813. The coroner conducted an inquest concerning the cause and circumstances of her death. His jurors determined that "the said Sylvia came to her death from mortification caused by irons placed on her legs by said Joseph Leblond." On November 16, one of the judges of the court of common pleas issued a warrant in the name of the United States to the sheriff or jailer of St. Louis County for the arrest and confinement of Leblond because the coroner's jurors had found him "guilty of the death of the said Sylvia." He was arrested and held in the St. Louis jail.

On November 20, 1813, four of his friends, relatives, or business associates posted a $4,000 recognizance bond to guarantee his court appearance, and on the order of John B. C. Lucas, an appointee of President Jefferson as a judge of the General Court, Leblond was discharged from jail on that same day.[19] Had the defendant been treated as was John Long in 1809, Leblond's crime would not have been a bailable offense. Death by gangrene of the legs that results from another's chaining could never arise without the chainer's immense malice aforethought toward his helpless victim. A court record of a white-on-white-male indictment for murder in St. Louis survives from this same year, and it contains the allegation that the accused "feloniously, wilfully, and of his malice aforethought did ... kill and murder to the great displeasure of Almighty God, to the evil example of others, ... and against the peace and dignity of the United States."[20] Perhaps had Sylvia been white, the man who put chains on her legs and thereby eventually caused her death would have been found guilty of murder and hanged. However, there is no certainty of this either because she would have been Leblond's white companion, not his companion of color.[21]

Clearly, this perpetrator was properly chargeable with a major felony in causing the death of another. However, Trexler examined the records of the St. Louis General Court, and he found that Leblond was fined $500 and costs and imprisoned two months for killing Sylvia. This early-twentieth-century historian mistakenly assumed that she was Leblond's slave and wrote that his "provocation is not stated."[22] Most likely, Trexler looked at a record in this case that omitted the manner of her death, and he never saw the coroner's report.

There may be another explanation for her demise, but it looks like kinky sex gone awry. Though she was not Leblond's slave, apparently, she was his sexual plaything. As a result of her liaison with him, she died a prolonged, agonizing, and smelly death over a period of weeks, if not of months. Leblond wanted her to suffer and to suffer greatly. Perhaps he enjoyed watching her rot. Surely, the purpose of her presence in his house was not confined to washing, cooking, cleaning, and other ordinary domestic duties.

Not only was his punishment for his killing almost nominal, but there is no indication that his horrendous act damaged his reputation among his friends and associates. Within a year or so after he served his two-month sentence, he was the executor of the estate of Jacque Comorgan in St. Louis in April 1815.[23] On October 20, 1819, he put his mark on a document in St. Louis that approved the building of a house for the Catholic clergy and the keeping of a school therein for the education of youth. All who signed it were inhabitants and property holders of the town of St. Louis and were either Catholics or allied to Catholic families.[24] We also know that he later married a reputable woman because their three-year-old son, Louis Adolph Leblond, died in St. Louis in September 1840, and notice of the child's death appeared in the newspaper.[25] Despite the bizarre events in Joseph Leblond's St. Louis home in the fall of 1813, he died a seemingly peaceful death in Carondelet, Missouri, in December 1846.[26] He survived to die as he did because he was white, male, and esteemed, and his victim, "Negress Sylvia," was black, female, and disesteemed.

Court records of another case involving a white male perpetrator and his mulatto female victim survive from St. Louis during Missouri's territorial period. William Gordon, identified in these documents as a surveyor, was probably the same William Gordon who accompanied Zebulon Pike on two expeditions from St. Louis: the first in 1805–06 to the headwaters of the Mississippi River and the second in 1806–07 to the Arkansas and Red Rivers.[27] On November 6, 1818, Michael Fouche appeared before Justice of the Peace Fell Guyol to swear on his oath that he was "present when on the evening of [November 5] at the house of Julie Labaddie, a mulatto woman, in the town of St. Louis … a certain William Gordon … did threaten, menace, assault, and beat the said Julie Labaddie and wound her by striking [her] upon the head with a stick." Because this assault had been "without any provocation whatever," Justice Guyol ordered any constable in St. Louis County to arrest Gordon. On November 6 William Gordon, surveyor, and Isaac N. Henry, printer, together posted a $300 recognizance bond that Gordon would appear at the next term of the circuit court for the county of St. Louis to answer these criminal charges. (Perhaps Gordon was a Mason and later served as a pallbearer for his partial surety. When Isaac N. Henry died after a short illness on January 1, 1821, his Masonic brethren conducted him to the grave.)[28] On November 9 Fouche, a material witness, was required to post a $100 recognizance bond that he would appear to give evidence against Gordon. In April 1819, and at the request of Edward Bates, acting circuit attorney, the grand jury indicted Gordon for beating, wounding, ill-treating, and perpetrating other wrongs against the said Julie.[29] Regrettably, the records are incomplete, and there is no way to ascertain whether Gordon was convicted. Certain it is that the perpetrator was white, and his victim was a free woman of color. She was identified in court records as "mulatto"; as Allport noted, it was a term of "condescension"[30] *and* of her inability to testify against Gordon.

Apart from these St. Louis territorial cases and one during statehood years from the city of St. Louis discussed in chapter 14, few extant Missouri cases concerned free blacks as the victims of whites during Missouri's antebellum period. Most surviving records of blacks as the acknowledged victims of whites arose because the black was the white's slave.

As the cases concerning male slaves amply demonstrate, the law gave masters, overseers, and lessees considerable leeway in their allowable punishments. It came from England, a country where there was never slavery, but there were children, apprentices, students, servants, and criminals. English parents, masters, teachers, and law enforcement officers were all authorized to use corporal punishment to discipline those in their custody.

Blackstone clarified its application: "Where a parent is moderately correcting his child, a master his servant or scholar, or an officer punishing a criminal, and happens to occasion his death, it is only misadventure; for the act of correction was lawful." He further explained that if the chastiser exceeds "the bounds of moderation, either in the manner, the instrument, or the quantity of punishment, and death ensues, it is manslaughter at least, and in some cases … murder for the act of immoderate correction is unlawful."[31] Such was the common law that America borrowed from the mother country and applied to apprentices, children, students, and criminals, but above all to slaves.

Because so much of the lawful disciplining of bondpersons was a private matter, there are not now and never were criminal records. They were compiled when the authorities believed that the chastiser had exceeded the bounds of moderation in punishing his slave. This usually occurred because she either came near death or died as a result of her punishment for her real or imagined misdeeds— misdeeds of, at times, astonishing triviality.

A chilling account from the mid–1820s can be pieced together from Cape Girardeau County. The event that probably set the stage for Obadiah Malone's violence toward his bondgirl, Slave Louese, was the natural death from causes now unknown of his wife, 24-year-old Eliza Malone, in July 1824.[32] Eliza was also the daughter of Polly and John Johnson and the mother of Obadiah's five young daughters. Nothing in subsequent court records suggests that the widowed father of these small children had remarried by the spring of 1826. Their caregiver and partial disciplinarian became Louese. The court records contain no age for her, but she was probably not old enough to be called Aunt Louese. Had she been a revered raiser of several generations of children, it is unlikely that the father of the four-year-old, named for her maternal grandmother, Polly, would have become enraged when he discovered on April 22, 1826, that Louese had whipped young Polly on her legs and buttocks with sufficient severity to leave bruise marks. Had the child's mother and Obadiah's wife been alive, in good health, and in the home, she would have been free to delegate the physical punishment of her youngsters to her slave girl. However, Eliza Malone died when her daughter, Polly, was aged two years, and someone had to care for these motherless children while their bereaved father, a farmer, earned a living for his family.

Malone's retaliatory beating of his slave girl may have begun on Saturday, April 22, the same day he discovered that she had whipped young Polly. By Sunday, April 23, Louese appeared at the residence of Polly and John Johnson, the parents of Eliza Malone, Obadiah's dead wife, and the grandparents of his five young daughters. Mrs. Johnson testified at the coroner's inquest that she heard her screams before she saw her: "when she came in my sight she appeared very bloody." Louese immediately entered the Johnson residence on that day and did so with a rope tied around her upper leg. She pled with Captain John Johnson to save her life because her master, Obe, was coming with a gun to kill her. According to the testimony of his son, John M. Johnson, Captain Johnson told Louese that he could not hinder her master from killing her, but he thought he would not. The Johnson family members testified that Master Obe came after her with a loaded gun, called her a "damm bitch," and ordered her out of his former in-laws' home. She asked him to spare her life and assured him that she would not disobey him by running away. Malone drank whiskey at the Johnsons' and afterward continued to beat his slave with a hickory stick, a stool, and a club. A neighbor of his, Malinda Jenkins, testified that on Sunday, April 23, as she was returning from church, she heard Louese cry out that if her master whipped her any more that she would put an end to her existence. Someone did.

The inquest regarding her death was held on Monday, April 24, at the Malone residence when 12 householders of the township of Apple Creek, who made up the coroner's jury, assembled to view her hanging body. These jurors found at least 40 bruises on it from her neck to her ankles, 9 visible bruises on her head, and her skull dented. From the numerous marks of violence on her body and the testimony of at least four witnesses— Polly Johnson; her husband, John Johnson; their son, John M. Johnson; and Malinda Jenkins— the coroner's jury concluded that Malone beat his slave to death, that she had been put in the hanging position by some person, and that Obadiah Malone was the "instigation of her death."[33] A newspaper account made clear that her "body was partly hanging by the neck to a tree and partly resting on the feet upon the ground, covered with much blood and many bruises."[34]

The same day the coroner's jury met, the judge of the fourth judicial circuit, John D. Cook, signed a warrant for Malone's arrest. He was indicted and jailed on a charge of murder. His trial in the town of Jackson, in Cape Girardeau County Circuit Court, began on Friday, May 6, 1826, and his jurors received his case on Saturday, May 7, at 10:00 P.M. By Tuesday, May 10, they were discharged because they were unable to agree on their verdict.[35] After Malone's first trial his attorney obtained a change of venue to Scott, the county immediately south of Cape Girardeau. His retrial in the town of Benton began on June 14, a Wednesday, and it concluded June 16, 1826, when the jury brought in a verdict of not guilty.[36]

That a slave owner was acquitted on homicide charges in the death of his slave is not a surprise. There is no known instance of any white person's conviction for this crime in a slave's death in Missouri's history. Malone was tried for murder, and had he been convicted, his only available punishment in 1826 was death by hanging. The prosecutor could not obtain a guilty verdict within the county of the crime, nor could the defense obtain his acquittal. This stalemate spoke as loudly as the white male citizens of any Missouri locale dared speak during slave times when voicing their disapproval of a white man's murder of his bondgirl.

There are other known cases in Missouri in which white males seriously injured or killed female slaves. Several coroners' inquests made findings regarding the massive violence that these pitiless men inflicted on their owned or leased female property. Preserved among the papers of one member of a coroner's jury in Washington County, southwest of St. Louis, are his "Notes on the Death of Patience":

> I was summoned in the jury of inquest to take up the body of Patience, a black woman slave of Jacob Fisher and found her to have one bone broke[n] in her left arm and both in her right arm and [a] cut above her right eye, apparently done with the stroke of a stick and her left ear mashed, the hinder part off and the back of her neck broke[n] and a large bruise on her right hip, and I concluded that she was killed by her master.

It is signed William Woods and dated January 6, 1829.[37]

A former Missouri slave, William Wells Brown, recalled an incident from the late 1820s or the early 1830s that involved Daniel D. Page (1790–1869) as a bondwoman-batterer. Brown incorrectly identified him as a deacon in the Baptist Church; he was a member of the First Presbyterian Church of St. Louis. Page tied his slave, Delphia, and "whipped her nearly to death." Brown later wrote of visiting her, "Poor Delphia. I ... called to see her while [she] was upon her sick bed, and I shall never forget her appearance. She was a member of the same church with her master." Following his savage beating of her, Page did not lose the respect of his fellow churchgoers. As his obituary mentioned, he was the first mayor of St. Louis.[38]

This town was the scene of another well-publicized slavebeating in 1834. Its perpetrator, William S. Harney (1800–89), then a major in the United States Army, was posted to Jefferson Barracks. In October 1833 he had married Mary Mullanphy, a daughter of the wealthy and recently deceased St. Louis pioneer merchant John Mullanphy; she brought a large dowry to her husband.[39] Approximately eight months later at the newlyweds' St. Louis home, and over a period of three successive days, the major beat his slave woman, Hannah. He believed that she had hidden misplaced keys and that if he whipped her with sufficient severity, she would reveal their location.[40] She never did; she died. The coroner's jury viewed her body, heard the testimony of several physicians and other witnesses, and on June 28, 1834, concluded that Hannah "came to her death by wounds inflicted by William S. Harney."[41]

In 1806 the Ninth Congress adopted 101 Articles of War for the governance of the armies of the United States. Until their modification during the Civil War, which, in time of war, subjected persons in the military service to a court-martial for crimes such as murder, the army's 1806 military code remained in effect until its revision in 1873. It required that "when any soldier shall be accused of a capital crime," his commanding officer was required "upon application duly made ... to deliver over such accused person ... to the civil magistrate."[42] Surviving letters and a diary entry of St. Louis residents suggest that his commanding officer turned Harney's case over to the St. Louis County prosecutor.

The soldier nearly lost his life at the hands of a mob shortly after the public became aware that he had beaten his slave woman to death. In early July 1834 the mob's fury was aroused by the major's acknowledgment that he had killed Hannah. It attempted to flush him out of what it thought was his St. Louis hideaway, the home of Mrs. Ann Biddle, widow of his former fellow officer, Major Thomas Biddle.

Instead, and known to his wife, her sisters, their husbands, and her attorney brother, Brian Mullanphy, later mayor of St. Louis, Major Harney had left town. Four letters, dated July 4 through August 13, 1834, to him from St. Louis concerning his legal difficulties survive. He received them while on the run, and they help chart his escape route. The earliest was sent to him in Wheeling, Virginia. The writer advised the major that "a mob had assembled to pull down Mrs. Biddle's house & it required great exertion to prevent it." The writer also informed him that the circuit court would be in session in August and a grand jury, apprised of the results of the coroner's jury, "must find a bill against you. You cannot therefore return here until the excitement goes off, say two or three years." In Wheeling the major received at least one other piece of mail; it was written by James Clemens Jr., his wife's sister's husband. This family member advised him, "I was confidentially informed the grand jury brought in murder. Do not go to New Orleans or on the Ohio River. If within reach, I fear they will get the governor to demand you." A second letter from Clemens to Harney indicates that the fugitive left Wheeling, visited Baltimore, Maryland, and was in Washington, D.C., when Clemens once more emphatically cautioned him: "I repeat Again do not think of returning to this place unless I advise you to do so." A third Clemens letter advised the major that a bond, presumably a recognizance bond, would be forwarded to him, "and in order that there be no doubt concerning it, the whole of the heirs of John Mullanphy have signed as your securities."[43]

None of these extant letters concerning Harney's beating death of Hannah refer, other than euphemistically, to his crime. The word *affair* denominates it several times, but most indicative of attitudes toward the deaths of slaves at the hands of their Missouri owners is James Clemens's casual remark to the major in his last extant letter: "I am told that accidents, similar to yours, have happened to others here, of which no notice was taken by the people or any of the courts." Harney's replies to his correspondents concerning his legal difficulties of 1834 have not survived.

However, this is known: he left his eastern Missouri duty post in late June to escape a mob. Because there were no great roads west of the Ohio River prior to the Civil War, most likely he boarded a steamboat in St. Louis for its downriver trip on the Mississippi to what later became Cairo, Illinois; there he probably transferred to another steamer up the Ohio River, past Cincinnati, Ohio, to Wheeling, Virginia, then the western terminus of the National Road and the largest town in northwestern Virginia, now West Virginia.[44] Next, he likely traveled by stagecoach east from Wheeling on National Road. From 1818 on, this road connected this northwestern Virginia town with Cumberland, Maryland, a place from which one might go 134 miles east to Baltimore or 132 miles southeast to Washington, D.C. It was then the logical route from Wheeling to both Baltimore and Washington, D.C.[45] The letters Harney received from St. Louis indicate that he lingered in Wheeling, Baltimore, and Washington, conveniently for him, all then cities within slave jurisdictions.

Meanwhile, the press described his crime and flight. In July 1834 this indignant account of Harney ran in the *Cincinnati Journal*; Garrison's *Liberator* reprinted it verbatim in September 1834:

> A MONSTER! A fellow by the name of HARNEY, a few days since, MURDERED a Negro woman, by whipping her to death in St. Louis! It has been stated by gentlemen who were on the coroner's inquest that from circumstantial evidence, and the testimony of individuals to Harney's own confessions to them, that this horrible act was committed under circumstances of peculiar barbarity.. and for successive days, and that the corpse of the poor creature exhibited a most shocking sight. It is said the monster fled from the city, and that the citizens are peculiarly excited, — having formed the resolution to take him into the bushes, and leave him in precisely the same fix as he left the woman, and that measures

are in train to offer a heavy reward for him. Harney is represented
as an officer connected with the army, and has fled to Washington
city. It is hoped and believed there is virtue and firmness enough
in the army to declare non-intercourse with SUCH A MUR-
DERER.[46]

In March 1835 another St. Louis resident, James Kennerly, recorded
in his diary, "Hear that Maj. Harney is acquitted."[47] His comment suggests
that the accused returned to St. Louis from his eastern hideouts for his
trial in St. Louis County Circuit Court after any danger to his person at
the hands of a fickle mob had passed, and he, like other known men who
murdered female slaves in Missouri, escaped without punishment.

Despite the newspaper editors' heartfelt wish that Harney's crime
would impede his military career, it had no such effect. From the beginnings of his escape, his commanding officer surely knew about and
approved of his travel. Otherwise, this soldier would have been charged
with desertion, and its punishment under the 1806 Articles of War was
death by firing squad. Though the major was court-martialed four times
between 1824 and 1847, there is no mention in his military record of his
murder of Slave Hannah or any event surrounding it.[48] Even though her
death at the hands of her master was well known in the town of St. Louis,
and Missouri papers as far west as Columbia reported it,[49] less than two
years after he killed her and while his duty station remained St. Louis's
Jefferson Barracks, he was promoted to lieutenant colonel. By the time
William Wells Brown described the incident, he wrote of St. Louis as the
place where "Col. Harney, a United States officer, whipped a slave woman
to death."[50]

When the Mexican War began, Colonel Harney was transferred from
St. Louis to Texas, where he organized expeditions against hostile Indians, and in April 1847 he stormed an important mountain pass, Cerro
Gordo, on the road between Veracruz and Jalapa, Mexico. As a result of
his heroism and with the advice and consent of the Senate, President James
Polk chose him as one of three men whom the Twenty-ninth Congress
authorized the president to promote to brigadier general.[51] Because of his
suspected southern sympathies, Harney held no important command during the Civil War. Nonetheless, at the end of his active military career in
1863 and with the advice and consent of the Senate, President Lincoln
chose him as one of up to 40 men whom the Thirty-seventh Congress
authorized the president to promote to major general.[52] Because his military file contains no mention of Hannah, it is unlikely that either Polk or
Lincoln ever knew that their promoted general beat a slave woman to
death.

The standard reference works that record William Selby Harney's life and times, including his four promotions in the United States Army *after* his murder of Hannah, make no mention of his June 1834 slaying of her in St. Louis, when he was just shy of his thirty-fourth birthday.[53] Then he was in his prime, and those who knew him described him as "a magnificent specimen of manhood, tall, straight, lithe of limb, handsome, strong, cheerful, considerate, affable. He was 6'3", and every inch a soldier."[54] Equally silent about Hannah are his obituaries, which heaped praise on him and described him at his death as the oldest soldier in the U.S. Army.[55] He outlived the slave woman whom he killed by almost 55 years.

Circuit court records from Saline County, north of the Missouri River in the central section of the state, concern the death of Rachael, a slave of Thomas B. Finley, whom he whipped to death on Tuesday, April 12, 1842, in Black Water Township. His anger toward her began on Sunday evening, April 10, when, in the process of clearing the supper table, she swiped a piece of bread through a butter dish rather than taking a knife, cutting some butter, and properly spreading it on the bread. Her master observed her breach of etiquette, told her he thought what she had done was "a dirty trick," and he would whip her because of it the next day. Old marks on her dead body confirmed that someone had previously whipped her.

Instead of pleading with him to flog her only lightly, if at all, she left her master's residence early the next morning and went to the farm home of one of his neighbors, James R. Davis. There, she ate both breakfast and dinner, the noon meal, and as his evidence at the coroner's inquest clarified, she ate heartily and appeared to be well. She left the Davis residence about 1:00 P.M. on Monday. She ate no supper on Monday, April 10, and spent that night outside. Likewise, she ate neither breakfast nor the noon meal the next day, Tuesday, April 12. However, she appeared at the residence of another of Finley's neighbors, James Metchen, about 2:00 P.M. on Tuesday, the day of her death. Metchen asked her if her master had sent her for anything; she answered that he had not. He told her that she should go home to her master, and if she came to his home again during the week that he would give her a beating. About this same time, another of Finley's slaves, Emily, arrived to retrieve Rachael at their master's request, and as Metchen testified at the inquest, when Rachael and Emily left for Finley's home together, Rachael appeared to be in good health. He said that he would have fed her, but no food was prepared when she departed. Rachael had not eaten in more than 24 hours at the time she left Metchen's residence, and hunger seems to have been a motivating factor in her return to the Finley residence. There was no safe haven for battered slaves in rural Missouri, no place to run other than away, and no place to hide.

When she returned to her master's home in the late afternoon, Finley took her some distance from the house to a hollow, made her remove her clothes, and tied her before he began flaying her. She differed from other slave women, as one of the coroner's witnesses testified, in that, "She was a singular negro, … [and] she would not cry or beg." William Wells Brown observed that when slave women were whipped they usually cried, "'Oh pray — Oh pray — Oh pray' … when imploring mercy at the hands of their oppressors."[56] Rachael's unwillingness to ask her master for leniency no doubt increased the severity of her beating.

When he had finished flogging her, he asked her to put her clothes on and come to him. Though she said that she was coming, she did not. Finally, as she came walking up the hill, she threw her hands upon her head, walked 10 steps, and fell on her left side. Finley mistook her impending death for her additional defiance of him, and when he commanded her to get up, and she did not, he hit her six additional licks with a two-foot hickory stick. He told her that if she did not get up he would tie her with some rope and "leave her all night & let the wolves eat her."

After this exchange he leashed his dying slave to a shrub, went to the house, located Emily, and sent her for Rachael. Either Emily carried the whipped victim, or with her help the beaten slave woman walked to the house. Later, Clark Finley, perhaps a brother of Rachael's owner, checked on her, and thought that she was asleep. That same evening, the family discovered that Rachael "was dead, her extremities were cold, her body was getting cold."

With the help of other Finleys, almost certainly his relatives, and some of his neighbors, Thomas B. Finley built a coffin and buried Rachael in it on his property on Wednesday, April 13. However, he made no attempt to keep her death a secret. He sent for his neighbors, and by Monday, April 18, Rachael's body was both disinterred and autopsied. On Tuesday, April 19, a coroner's jury made findings regarding the cause of her death. One of the coroner's jurors testified that on Rachael's body there were both fresh and old marks of switches, some on the right side, blood under the skin on the right side, and a small bruise on her abdomen. When the physician opened her head, there was almost a teacup of clotted blood on the brain; the jury concluded that the blood clot caused her death. Dr. George Rothwell, one of the physicians who performed her autopsy, an unusual event in rural Missouri in the 1840s, testified on May 13 at Finley's preliminary hearing about "the wound on [Rachael's] head just behind the left ear," another behind the shoulder underneath the arm, and a third on the side of her lower body. In Rothwell's opinion the immediate cause of her death was "the suffusion of blood on the brain by rupture of a blood vessel," an event brought on by Thomas B. Finley's severe beating of her.

On May 13 Finley and three other men posted a $2,000 recognizance bond that he would personally appear before the circuit court of Saline County in Marshall on the first day of its next term, July 18, 1842, to "then and there answer a charge of whipping and beating to death a certain negro girl." He was charged with second-degree murder or manslaughter, both of which were bailable offenses, and there the court record ended.[57] No extant Saline County newspaper remains from this period, and expectedly, and like his fellow slave-women-batterers, the Register of Inmates, Missouri State Penitentiary, does not record Thomas B. Finley's arrival on a charge of either murder or any of the four different degrees of manslaughter then a part of Missouri law. However, and as with Obadiah Malone's beating death of his slave woman, Louese, in Cape Girardeau County in 1826 and Major Harney's murder of Hannah in St. Louis in 1834, the fact that Finley was indicted for homicide in the death of Rachael indicated community disapproval of the man who destroyed his slave because of her poor table manners, running away from him out of fear of him, and refusing to beg him for mercy as he beat her to death.

On July 28, 1842, and shortly after Finley's trial may have begun in Saline County, Conrad Carpenter and three other men posted a $2,000 recognizance bond that he would appear at the next term of the circuit court of Montgomery County to answer a charge of second-degree murder or manslaughter in his beating death of his slave woman, Minerva, four days earlier. Though the grand jury indicted Carpenter in Montgomery County in October 1842, he did not appear for trial, and his three cosureties forfeited their $2,000 bond, a forfeiture the Supreme Court of Missouri upheld on appeal.[58] From the little that is known of the proceedings against Carpenter, once more, there was widespread community disapproval of his beating death of Slave Minerva. The disapproval cost his friends approximately $40,000 in today's money because he skipped his trial on homicide charges.

Another coroner's report exists from the city of St. Louis. An inquest was held at the residence of Judge James Dunnica, and at the coroner's request six men viewed the body of a slave child named Sarah, aged eight years and two months. Her owner was Mrs. Leona Cordell, and at the time of Sarah's death, her young bondgirl was in the employment of Edwin Tanner. Six lawful male householders of the township of St. Louis swore on their oaths that she "came to her death by violence inflicted on her person." Contemporary newspaper coverage diverged on this bondchild's death. The paper, which did not report its horrifying facts, gave the coroner's verdict that Sarah "came to her death by violence inflicted on her person while in the employment of Edwin Tanner."[59] Another paper reported the following:

> Death by Cruelty…. The body exhibited evidence of the most cruel whipping and beating we have ever heard of. The flesh on the back and limbs were beaten to a jelly — one shoulder bone was laid bare — there were several cuts from a club, on the head and around the neck was the indentation of a cord, by which it was supposed she had been confined to a tree. She had been hired by a man name of Tanner, residing in the neighborhood, and was sent home in this condition. After coming home, her constant request until her death was for bread, by which it would seem that she had been starved as well as unmercifully whipped.

The paper that printed these graphic details softened the coroner's report when it stated that the victim "came to her death by blows inflicted by *some person unknown* while in the employ of Mr. Tanner."[60] The coroner wrote "the above named Sarah was evidently whipped to death probably and almost certainly by Edwin Tanner or some of his family or by himself and family." He then added this highly personal note, "Of all the inquests that I have held, numbering 317, and having seen, as I thought, the work of death in almost all its horrors, the above crime far surpasses anything I have ever seen of human depravity and cruelty." It is signed Esrom Owens and dated August 13, 1847.[61] If any crime against a slave cried out for conviction, that of beating and starving Slave Sarah, aged eight years and two months, now seems ideal for a court-imposed punishment. As in other cases wherein white men murdered slaves in Missouri, the perpetrator was neither hanged nor sent to the penitentiary.

An additional criminal record survives from 1860 in Boone County. The grand jury indicted a slaveholder, James Henderson, for the misdemeanor of cruelly beating, abusing, and whipping a certain slave named Eliza then and there under his charge and control. The case progressed as far as a trial, where the charges against the defendant slaveholder were dropped.[62]

Just as crimes against male slaves at the hands of whites are known through civil cases that the Supreme Court of Missouri decided, likewise, the mistreatment of women slaves at the hands of white men is also preserved in this same court's civil case law. The earliest appellate decision pertaining to a brutalized slave female arose in Pike County in 1827 when Slave Fanny died as a result, as the Supreme Court of Missouri noted, "of cruel and unusual treatment on the part of the defendant," who had leased her from her owner. That the lessee had earlier been criminally tried and acquitted for Slave Fanny's homicide was no bar to the civil suit, and her owner's jury award and court costs were upheld on appeal.[63] In 1833, in Clay County, Slave Dinah's former owner sold her and warranted her to be "sound in body and mind." When she died, the new owner, Soper, sued Breckenridge, the former owner, for breach of contract. On appeal the court reversed the trial court's award in favor of Soper because it refused to instruct the jury that "if they found from the evidence, that the slave was only slightly diseased, if at all, and that she came to her death by negligence or cruel treatment of the plaintiff [Soper], the defendant is not liable for the whole value of the slave, but only to the extent of the injury occasioned by the disease."[64] In 1844, in Clark County, a locale in northeast Missouri that bordered both Iowa Territory and the state of Illinois, an unnamed female slave died when Adams leased her for that year. On appeal the court upheld the jury's award to the administrator of an estate on grounds that there was an implied contract to take reasonable care of the slave, and since Adams's "ill treatment and inhumanity caused the death of the girl," he breached his contract to the estate's administrator.[65]

Yet another case arose in Buchanan County in the mid–1850s, probably in the city of St. Joseph. It also concerned a male lessee of a female slave severely beating her with a cowhide. The bondwoman ran from her abuser and up the steps to a room where she threw her arms around her mistress, Alvira B. West, who some seven or eight days earlier had given birth to a child. Mrs. West attempted to save her servant from Mr. Forrest, the slave batterer. Nevertheless, so intent was he to complete his beating of the unnamed slave woman that he began whacking her owner, Mrs. West. The result was a civil suit that Alvira B. and her husband, Francis A. West, brought against Forrest for the assault, battery, mental anguish, and wounded feelings of Mrs. West. The jury returned a verdict against Forrest of $400, and the Supreme Court of Missouri upheld the award on appeal.[66]

Did these battered slave women or their families ever bring a suit against the men who tormented, assaulted, and murdered them? Never. Unless a statute expressly allowed a slave a cause of action, she could not be a party in a civil suit. As early as 1807 Missouri's legislative authority granted slaves the right to sue their declared owners for their freedom. Throughout slavery in Missouri and elsewhere, the ability to come into court and attempt to obtain her freedom by court order remained the only reason a slave could bring a court action against anyone throughout Missouri's entire slavery period.

In 1866, the year after the Civil War ended, the Thirty-ninth Congress conferred on former slaves, among other civil rights, the power to enforce contracts, sue, give evidence, inherit, purchase, lease, sell, hold, and convey real and personal property.[67] That same year, the new federal law was used to prosecute white persons who burglarized the dwelling of a black woman in Kentucky. On appeal, a Supreme Court justice, Noah Haynes Swayne, an appointee of President Lincoln, sat as a circuit justice and reviewed the federal prosecution of the defendants for their criminal acts against the black female victim. He upheld her right to testify against these white men and declared the federal law, known as the Civil Rights Bill, constitutional in all its provisions.[68] In 1868 the Fortieth Congress insured that the 1866 civil rights statute could not be overturned by a simple majority of federal lawmakers. It proposed, passed, and the states adopted the Fourteenth Amendment to the U.S. Constitution, which mandates that no state "deny to any person within its jurisdiction the equal protection of the laws."

Until former slaves obtained rights that the federal government gave them, they had no personal legal recourse against any whites who committed monstrous crimes against them. The best any bondperson who remained in bondage could realize was a kind owner who lived a long life, did not lease her to brutish men, and at death was not in debt. Slaves either freed in last wills and testaments or willed to the owner's heirs could be sold to pay off the deceased's financial obligations. Any slave hoped that her master was solvent and either freed her or willed her and her family members to his compassionate widow and/or his tender-hearted children. Persons held in bondage almost never selected their owners; surely some slave women were lucky, but as this chapter has demonstrated, many were not.

The framers of the Missouri Constitution intended that the law extend to slave victims of white sadism the same protection its white victims received. This high-minded ideal was doomed at an early date. From the deliberations of white male juries came one acquittal after another when whites were prosecuted for crimes against persons of color. There was a different result when a white owner sued a white lessee for the damage or destruction of his human property. Then the plaintiff-owner won his lawsuit against the destroyer of his material possession. Had that property been livestock or any other personal property, the law penalized those who destroyed the material possessions of others. However, the beneficiary of the civil suit was the owner, not his cruelly treated slaves. Bondpersons, especially girls and women, were doubly victimized as both females and as blacks or mulattoes. This can never be shown by citing only the 1820 Missouri constitution and the resulting statutory law; one must, as this chapter has, also examine coroners' inquests, circuit court records, Supreme Court of Missouri case law, old correspondence, diary and journal entries, and contemporary newspaper accounts, which, taken together, blazon the awful truth of the unequal treatment in Missouri's law courts of slaves as victims of brutal white men.

The next chapter puts the shoe on the other foot. The victims, in so far as the crimes had victims, were white persons, the perpetrators were slaves and whites who illegally associated with those in bondage.

Chapter 9

Noncapital Statehood Crime, White and Black

This chapter includes a representative sample of offenses that slaves and whites who frequently interacted with them were commonly convicted of, principally during statehood years. It excludes capital cases and cases involving rape; these subjects are discussed in subsequent chapters. It covers illegal commercial transactions, offensive language, and crimes against property, the habitation, animals, and persons, such as assault and attempted murder.

Chapter 4 clarified that as early as 1806, the territorial legislature prohibited the sale of rum, brandy, whiskey, beer, and other spirits to slaves without the prior permission of their masters. Throughout slavery under American rule the law restricted the sale of alcoholic beverages to bondpersons. Nonetheless, a good supply of liquor was always manufactured within the territory. By 1811, there were no fewer than 12 distilleries and 7 breweries within St. Louis District.[1] The St. Louis merchant Christian Wilt operated a distillery near the town of St. Louis and offered its products for sale in ads such as this: "On Monday next, will be sold, without reserve, for ready money, at the Warehouse of Mr. Christian Wilt, 20 Barrels good Whiskey."[2] The St. Louis Brewery sold beer for $11 a barrel and $6 a half barrel. It refunded $1 for the redelivery of the empty barrel "in good condition and bearing the stamp of the BREWERY."[3] In 1835 the City Brewery opened in St. Louis, and it sold beer and porter by the barrel, half barrel, quarter barrel, and in bottles by the dozen.[4] By the late 1830s, 81 miles west of St. Louis, the German settlers of Hermann (Gasconade County) were extensively cultivating grapes and manufacturing wine.[5] It is unlikely that only legally authorized persons swilled the plentiful products of these liquor-making establishments. Besides, slaves as a group probably had more reason than white persons to love strong drink. The altered state brought on by bouts with the bottle surely eased, if only temporarily, the misery of living and dying as someone else's human property.

The master was equally eager to control, among most other aspects of his slaves' existence, their alcoholic intake, if any. Liquor was a contributing factor in much of the fighting that occurred among bondmen. They were both injured and killed in these encounters, and their owners lost the labor of their wounded bondmen and, in the most deadly encounters, their slaves' lives. In addition, both the quality and the amount of work an intoxicated bondperson produced would almost certainly be inferior to the labor of a sober slave. Owners and their overseers detected easily enough the drinking slave by smelling liquor on him, observing his inebriated condition, or by one bondperson's informing on another. American efforts to curb slave drinking and intoxication began during the territorial period.

Trexler examined early St. Louis ordinances, among them one enacted in 1811, the same year the distilleries in St. Louis District numbered 12 and the breweries 7. It fined any vendor of "spiritous or ardent liquor" $10 who sold a slave his products without the consent of the master. Under this same ordinance any person who came across a drunken slave within the town of St. Louis was allowed to give him or her 10 lashes, and the slave's owner was fined $5 for neglecting to punish his or her drunken property.[6]

The liquor laws pertaining to slaves changed when the territorial legislature required their owners to pay court costs for their bondpersons' noncapital offenses. Beginning in 1816, whenever the slave was convicted of most crimes, his owner paid all court costs involving his slave. Once the master was saddled with these fees, the slave's public drunkenness and purchase of alcoholic beverages without his master's permission ceased to be violations of the law. Probably, the owner, his overseer, or a hiree whipped the drinking and/or drunken slave in-house, or his owner threatened to sell him, or he actually sold him if he continued to drink. By such controls the master was spared the inevitable expenses that attached whenever the bondperson was convicted of any noncapital public wrong. During Missouri's statehood slavery years, the *seller* of "wine or spiritous liquors" broke the law when he sold his products to slaves without their owners' permission. Equally important, the law required that the merchant-seller, not the owner of the slave-buyer, pay court costs when convicted of these and similar offenses. At present, Missouri and other jurisdictions principally forbid the vending of alcoholic beverages to minors. Such sales are criminal conduct on the part of the seller, but minors also break the law when they misrepresent their age to purchase or otherwise obtain liquor or when they possess it.[7] Further, today's law does not permit underage persons to purchase alcohol for adults. In contrast, errand-running slaves always legally bought alcoholic beverages for their masters.

Missouri's antebellum liquor laws prohibited free blacks and mulattoes from obtaining licenses to sell liquor.[8] This exclusion was one more reason for them to leave Missouri; it also limited their influence with slaves, and theoretically it rigorously controlled the marketing of alcoholic beverages. In 1835 the law required that the innkeeper pay to the master or mistress between $10 and $50 for every sale the vendor made to the owner's bondperson without written permission of the master or mistress. It also fined slaveholders $300 who allowed their property to sell or deliver liquor to the slaves of other masters without permission of the latters' owners.[9] By 1845 the law punished any owner convicted of permitting his slaves "directly or indirectly" to sell intoxicating liquors. The master was fined not less than $20 or more than $100, and his offending bondpersons received 39 lashes. The owner paid court costs for both his and his alcohol-peddling slaves' prosecution and punishment.[10] These laws also made dram-shop keepers (sellers of liquor by the dram or the drink to be consumed on the premises) liable for the resulting harm when the slave customer drank without his owner's permission.

The attention lawmakers gave human chattel as buyers, consumers, delivery persons, and sellers of alcoholic beverages suggests that a lively trade in liquor involving them existed throughout slavery under American rule. Trexler underestimated both the appeal of strong drink for those in bondage and its availability when he wrote, "Despite the number of statutes on this subject, the press does not reflect a serious condition of drunkenness among slaves. Lack of money on the part of the negro as well as fear on the side of the merchant prevented the problem from assuming alarming proportions."[11] Without another accompanying harm, the fact of most anyone, especially a slave, being drunk in public was not newsworthy. As for the bondman's want of cash, that was not an obstacle in his quest for liquor. He could steal money to purchase it, or trade stolen property for it, or barter his labor for it; besides, sellers of alcohol were not always licensed. They bootlegged their products, and in any situation where the sale of a commodity was forbidden to *all* purchasers, Missouri's moonshiners may have counted those in bondage among their best customers. Their testimonial incompetence against whites surely increased their desirability as patrons of illegal-liquor makers.

However, the cases that arose under Missouri's multiple statutes concerning slaves and alcohol suggest that some prosecutors bent the rules regarding black and mulatto testimony. Unless the State used hearsay evidence against whites who sold slaves liquor without their owners' permission, it faced daunting odds in obtaining convictions. In 1841 the Supreme Court of Missouri upheld a white woman's life prison sentence for murdering her husband by poisoning him in Jackson County. It rejected her contention that the state committed reversible error in admitting her slave woman's testimony against her. The court wrote, "That negroes cannot testify against white persons is clear; but this rule cannot be carried so far as to exclude the conversation of a negro with a white person, when the conversation on the part of the negro is merely given in evidence as an inducement and in illustration of what was said by the white person."[12] It was an easy leap from this reasoning to its twin, testimony about what acts any whites engaged in with a slave, such as the illegal sale of alcohol.

The Supreme Court of Missouri decided four criminal cases involving the sale of liquor to a slave without his owner's permission. Probably the State used the owner or his white overseer as a witness, and one of them testified to the out-of-court statements of the slave customer about the defendant selling him "whiskey in Ste. Genevieve County,"[13] "a pint of whiskey" in Greene County,[14] "spiritous liquors" in Moniteau County,[15] and "one gill [1¾ pint] of whiskey" in Marion County.[16] These locales are many miles apart, and Missouri's known prosecutions of liquor violations involving slaves in each of these places suggests the prevalence of this essentially victimless wrongdoing.

A newspaper article about Cole County's February 1859 docket listed 41 upcoming criminal cases. Of this number, 39 percent involved liquor, including seven for selling it to slaves.[17] Because this county contains Jefferson City, Missouri's state capital, this lawlessness involving alcohol took place under the noses of this state's lawmakers. Further, the docketed cases concerned only those persons who were caught breaking the law, not undetected sellers of strong drink to slaves. Most likely, white persons often sold it to those in bondage without their owners' permission. Otherwise, seven separate cases involving this activity would not have crowded the docket in a single term of court in one county, especially not one with only a modest slave population. The 1856 Missouri census listed 31 other counties that contained more bondpersons than Cole with 853 slaves.[18]

Fragments of three liquor cases involving slaves survive from Cape Girardeau County; the resolutions of all are unknown. The state obtained the following indictments: John Elliott in 1852 for permitting his slave, Jim, "to directly sell intoxicating liquors, commonly called whiskey ... to Nicholas Kennell for the amount of 10 cents";[19] Frederick Wiedmann in 1856 for selling the slave of Lucy Walker liquor without the permission of his owner;[20] and Kasper Ludwig in 1861 for his sale of liquor to Slave Bill, then in the employ of John Heman, without written permission of the slave's owner or overseer.[21]

The Supreme Court of Missouri affirmed a western Missouri County's, Platte's, civil suit involving alcohol against the proprietors of a mill and a store. It concerned the actions of their clerk, who frequently sold whiskey to slaves without written permission from their owners. Mrs. Hughes's Willis, valued at $900, went to this mill with his owner's grain to be ground. While attending to his mistress's business, he also purchased a quart of whiskey, drank it, and became very drunk after consuming it. He started home near sundown and was found speechless with his jaws locked and nearly frozen to death the next day. Despite immediate medical attention, the slave only lived eight or nine days. Following the death of her valuable property, Willis, Mrs. Hughes sued the owners of the mill. The jury awarded her $900, approximately $13,500 today, and Missouri's high court upheld this sizable judgment against the proprietors, who, though not present when their clerk sold Willis liquor, were aware of other sales he had made to slaves without their owners' permission.[22] Probably, most of these transactions did not cause untimely deaths, and this unlawful commerce lasted throughout slavery.

Other Missouri laws prohibited slaves from associating with persons other than their owners and overseers. In 1836 a Saline County grand jury indicted Solomon Odle for dealing with Elick without the consent of his master. It charged that in February of that year, Odle failed to obtain the prior written permission of Nathaniel B. Tucker, Elick's owner, and Odle's act was illegal. In July Odle posted a $50 recognizance bond, and two other men the same sum that the defendant would appear for trial. In a jury trial in November 1836 he was found not guilty.[23]

Cape Girardeau County was the scene of at least three similar prosecutions. In 1841 Isaac Little was charged with harboring and entertaining a slave belonging to John Wilkinson; his trial was set for August 1, 1841, in circuit court,[24] and nothing further is known. In 1856 Samuel Lockhart was indicted for permitting his slave, John, to hire his own time. Lockhart posted a $100 recognizance bond that he would appear for trial. The jury found him guilty and fined him $20.[25] In 1861 Benjamin Taylor was indicted for permitting his Negro man, Pros, to hire his own time. His trial was set for December, and there the record ends.[26]

At least four similar cases are known because the Missouri Supreme Court decided them. In 1846, in Pike County, the grand jury indicted John S. Markley for dealing with Charles without having first obtained the written permission of his owner, Fountain Edwards. The defendant was found guilty and fined $20. On appeal his conviction was reversed because the indictment did not allege that the three persons—the owner, the master or lessee, or the overseer—who could give permission had not.[27] In 1852, in Franklin County, the defendants were indicted for dealing with Anderson, owned by Samuel Wilkinson, without the consent in writing of the master, owner, or overseer. They had hired the slave to maul rails and paid him $1.80. The circuit court judge quashed the indictment, and his action was upheld on appeal because, as the court wrote, this crime "does not include the manual labor of the slave, however wrong it may be to hire or to induce a slave to work or labor for a person without the master's or owner's knowledge and permission."[28] An 1857 civil suit from Cooper County concerned an unpaid bill for goods supplied to a slave that his owner refused to make good on grounds that the supplier dealt with his human property without obtaining prior permission. The defendant had allowed his slave to set up a shoemaker's shop and work as a free man. At the first trial the jury's instructions were in error, and it found for the slave owner. On appeal the court reversed. It held that prior permission was unnecessary because the slave was his owner's agent and doing business with the bondman was no different from doing business with the owner. Hence the bill of the plaintiff-supplier of goods to the slave shoemaker was to be paid.[29] In Moniteau County, by the middle of the Civil War, slavery had become such a topsy-turvy institution that Henry Rohlfing, who was neither the lender's owner, lessee, nor overseer, was indicted, tried, and convicted of dealing with a slave by borrowing money from him and giving the bondman notes for his cash. On appeal Rohlfing's conviction was upheld.[30]

Laws adopted in 1804 from eighteenth-century Virginia statutes provided the legal bases for all later Missouri prosecutions concerning forbidden business dealings with slaves. Among other provisions, the legislation decreed that "no white person, free negro, or mulatto ... shall harbour or entertain any slave without the consent of his or her owner"; no person shall "deal with any slave" without permission of the owner; and no master shall allow his slave either "to go at large and trade as a free man, or to hire him or herself out."[31] Today, a primary meaning of the word *entertain* is to *amuse*, but an eighteenth-century meaning of it was *to hire*.[32]

Harbouring was a civil wrong committed when one employed another knowing that he was in breach of contract with a former employer.[33] The purpose of these 1804 laws and their progeny was the same. From the start of American rule until the demise of slavery in Missouri, the legislature thought it desirable that all slaves remain impoverished. If they could earn money through their dealings with persons other than their masters, or through being hired by persons who paid them, or through their owners allowing them to hire their own time, bondpersons would have money. With it they could buy their freedom, and Missouri would experience an increase in ex-slaves. Most white Missourians believed that free blacks and mulattoes were at best a nuisance and at worst downright dangerous.

It was always important that slaves know their proper place and be kept in it. Though offensive language was not a part of the 1804 legislative package concerning slaves, in 1845 the General Assembly added a new crime: when a slave used "insolent and insulting language … to white persons," such wrongdoing was to be punished with "stripes at the discretion of a justice of the peace." Further, it was lawful for "any person, without further warrant, to apprehend slaves so offending, and carry them before the justice."[34] An 1849 Cape Girardeau County court record documents that the State prosecuted Wash, belonging to Irvin Anderson of Jackson, when the slave "did use insolent & insulting language to him, the said John McDaniel." An arrest warrant was issued for Wash, and the State subpoenaed five witnesses. The Constable of Byrd Township arrested the slave and brought him before a justice of the peace. Wash's lawyer demanded a jury trial, and the J.P. summoned six jurors; they heard the evidence and found Wash guilty. The judge ordered that the defendant receive 20 stripes on his bare back and be detained until his owner paid court costs, figured in the extant court records as $11.45 in 1849 and over $200 today. Wash appealed this judgment to the circuit court, and his owner posted a $100 recognizance bond that his slave would appear for trial in circuit court on May 28, 1849.[35] There the record ends. Probably a quarrel between the slave's owner and the victim of insulting and insolent slave language prompted the ensuing court battle and its accompanying costs. The legislature made the slave's insolent language when used on whites a crime and at least one court wasted its judicial energy on such trivia because it was important that slaves always be subordinate to whites, at least in word and deed.

An 1857 newspaper story concerned an incident from north central Missouri, Livingston County, in which insolent slave language preceded assaultive slave action. It began when Mortimer Butler hired a slave, and the bondman did not begin work on time. Mr. Butler, a plasterer, reprimanded the unnamed slave, who responded in "very insulting language." The white man then "very properly attempted to chastise [whip] him." The Negro resisted, struck his assailant "four or five times with a hoe, knocked him down, bruised his arms, and inflicted a severe wound upon his head." Upon the slave's capture he was tried and sentenced to 39 lashes, the maximum the law allowed. Under his owner's direction, a Dr. McDowell, the slave received 200 more lashes, and he was shipped for sale to the "sunny south." Butler was not seriously injured in the encounter that the newspaper headlined "Outrage by a Negro."[36]

Other public wrongs were illegal for all persons, including bondpersons. Chapter 3 detailed just how frequently slave men and women were charged with taking a variety of items that did not belong to them during territorial days. In all likelihood theft was the most prevalent offense they committed; today it remains the general population's most common crime. It was then called larceny, and under current law it is classified as stealing.

Duffner examined the criminal records of Boone County, and among them he found the following slave larceny cases. In 1823 Nancy and Jacob were convicted of stealing and received 20 lashes. She took five pieces of silver valued at five dollars and he a two-dollar water pitcher. In 1829 Billy and Barnett were convicted of stealing "five pieces of upper leather" valued at five dollars and "five pieces of sole leather" valued at five dollars. Billy was sentenced to 15 lashes, Barnett to 39, and their master was fined $8.75. Another 1829 larceny case involved three slaves who belonged to two different masters. Dr. William Jewell (name-giver of William Jewell College in Liberty, Clay County, Missouri) owned Henry and Manly, and Dr. Daniel P. Wilcox owned Charles. Henry, Manly, and Charles were jointly charged with stealing clothing from James Laughlin valued at $14.50. Charles was convicted and sentenced to 39 lashes, and Jewell's slaves were acquitted.[37] LeMond located an additional Boone County prosecution of slaves for larceny in 1829. Nathan and Ben, slaves owned by Charles Hardin and William Hitt respectively, were indicted for the theft of three hats from the shop of Tom Hadden. The prosecuting attorney dropped charges against Hardin's Ben; however, Hitt's Nathan was found guilty and sentenced to 25 lashes.[38]

Howard County Circuit Court records contain similar slave prosecutions for larceny. In 1825 Dennis was found guilty of stealing property valued at $3.75 and sentenced to 50 lashes and remained in jail until his owner paid court costs; Jerry pled guilty to larceny, returned the stolen property, and was sentenced to 20 lashes; and Vine, a woman of color, was found guilty of larceny and sentenced to 10 lashes.[39] These early Howard

County stealing cases survive in abbreviated form in docket books, which do not contain the specifics of the stolen property. However, judging from an assessed value of $3.75 in one case and punishments of 20 and 10 lashes respectively in the others, the purloined property was not of great value.

Cape Girardeau County Circuit Court records include several prosecutions of slaves for larceny. In 1828 Aaron, a black male slave, the property of Isaac Baker, pled guilty to stealing a pair of boots, among other items; the victim of the theft, Walter O'Bannon, testified that all the stolen property had been returned to him. The judge ordered that Aaron "immediately, openly, and publicly" receive 15 stripes on his bare back; further, he was to be sold at a public auction unless his owner, Isaac Baker, paid the costs and charges of the prosecution.[40] The next year, 1829, Isaac, a slave of Samuel Lockhart, was indicted for larceny of unspecified items. Following his plea of not guilty, a jury found him guilty, but his motion for a new trial was granted. After one continuance in January 1830, Isaac did not appear for trial in April of that year, and his owner, Samuel Lockhart, forfeited his recognizance bond, which he had earlier pledged to assure Isaac's court appearance for his second trial.[41] In this same county, more than 26 years later, a Samuel Lockhart was indicted for permitting his slave to hire his own time. The 1829 and 1856 criminal record may involve the same slaveholder.

A newspaper story concerns a Cooper County theft of property worth $30 in 1859. An unnamed slave, owned by Mrs. Thomas Jones and hired to Mr. Lewis Edgar, was arraigned for stealing bacon, approximately 14 pieces or slabs. He admitted taking the meat, but in mitigation he stated that a white man had promised him five dollars for his theft and had not paid him. From the string that tied the bacon, it could be traced to a particular grocer, Mr. Heim, who stated that he bought the meat from George Zickgraf, a tailor and keeper of a boarding house. Zickgraf eventually admitted that he bought the bacon from a Negro; as a result, the slave's owner, Mrs. Jones, swore out a writ against Zickgraf for "buying stolen meat from a negro, knowing it to be stolen."[42] Presumably, she bothered to come forward as a prosecution witness on new charges against Zickgraf to spare herself court costs or in an effort to reduce her payment of fees for her slave's larceny.

This Cooper County case lacks the grandeur of the St. Louis prosecution of Slave George in 1820 for the theft of beaver furs valued at $1,500, that is, $150,000 today; however, despite the ineptitude of the criminals in the 1859 case, it demonstrates that slaves who stole property in larger amounts than they could personally use were probably in league with a white fencer of the stolen items, perhaps a bootlegger. There appears never to have been a network of bondpersons who could merchandise large quantities of stolen property without assistance from whites who, while buying and selling what slaves stole, were secure in their knowledge that their black partners in crime could not testify against them.

The Missouri Supreme Court decided three cases involving slaves convicted of larceny. It upheld the owner's forfeiture of his slave's recognizance bond in Washington County Circuit Court when his slave failed to appear to answer an indictment for larceny.[43] It also affirmed the acquittal of a slave charged with stealing a bottle of cologne valued at one dollar from the shop of a free black barber in the city of St. Louis.[44] It dismissed without explanation an appeal from Marion County concerning Slave Joe's theft of a fiddle worth one dollar, a whip worth one dollar, some clothing, and other unnamed articles. He had been tried and convicted before a justice of the peace and sentenced to be whipped.[45]

Perhaps the law itself, upheld on appeal in Joe's theft of a fiddle, is the best evidence of the frequency with which slaves were convicted of larceny. In 1831 the legislature simplified the trial of bondpersons charged with stealing property whose value did not exceed $20; in 1835 it lowered the amount to less than $10, and the latter sum continued to separate petty from grand larceny throughout slavery in Missouri. The cases of bondpersons charged with petty larceny could be heard before a justice of the peace within the township wherein the theft occurred; on finding them guilty, this minor official could sentence them to up to 39 lashes. The owner of the convicted slave paid court costs and either returned the stolen property to the victim or compensated him or her for its dollar value. In keeping with the 1820 Missouri constitution, the accused could request a jury trial.[46] However, slaves charged with petty larceny were usually tried and punished without jury trials; thereby, their owners avoided higher court costs than had their bondpersons been afforded full due process in circuit court.

Closely related to the slave's larceny were crimes against the habitation such as housebreaking and burglary. The perpetrator slave's purpose in breaking and entering the dwelling of another at night was typically the theft of personal property. A Cape Girardeau County housebreaking case from 1845 involved four slave defendants: Steph, owned by Ralph Guild; Sol, owned by Nathan Van Horn; and John and Ben, owned by Franklin Carunon. All were found guilty of breaking and entering the dwelling of Johnson Rainey, ordered whipped 39 lashes, and their owners required to pay court costs. The stolen property included $60 worth of specified items: one gold chain, $30; one gold seal, $20; and three pieces of gold coin, $10.32.[47]

A newspaper account of a Columbia, Boone County, burglary early on a Sunday morning in 1845 involved Slave Bill, owned by Mr. Jefferson Garth. Bill entered the dwelling and shop of Mr. Joseph Willis, rifling a desk drawer of all its change, four or five dollars, and when caught as he was leaving, bit the hands and fingers of those attempting to detain him. However, someone hit him with a rock, and the careless thief left his hat behind. When apprehended the next day, he confessed, produced a part or all of the stolen money, and named Tom, owned by John T. Henry, as his accomplice. Tom was arrested, tried, convicted, and punished with 36 lashes. The news story concluded by mentioning three or four successful thefts from Mr. Willis's same desk over the past 18 months, "and no doubt by these same rascals."[48]

The Missouri Supreme Court reversed the only criminal case concerning a slave's burglary that it decided. In St. Louis County in 1829, certain persons caught and flogged Hector until he confessed to a burglary involving stolen money. The court sent his case back for a new trial, which excluded the slave's confession because he gave it "to gain a respite from pain." Moreover, no money was found where the beaten bondman confessed that it would be located.[49] In a civil judgment against the owners of three slaves who together committed larceny when they stole from a store in Cole County, the court held that if three unite to steal property of the value of $100, each of them has stolen $100, and the owner of any one of the slaves was liable for all the damages.[50]

Crimes such as larceny and burglary, when the latter's purpose was stealing, are easily understood. The motive of most persons who take what belongs to others is the same: personal gain. Given the slaves' property-less condition, it is only surprising that bondpersons stole as little and as infrequently as they did. Slaves took what they did not own, could not buy, and, despite years of backbreaking work, could not hope to buy. They did so because they exchanged the stolen property, slabs of bacon, for example, for money, or they stole money because they wished to make a purchase. They also fancied items they took such as water pitchers, fiddles, and bottles of cologne. Though slaves were annually given one pair of shoes for Missouri's winter, they may have needed boots or shoe leather for making extra pairs. For the most part, slaves took what they did because they wanted or needed it, and stealing was usually their only means of obtaining any valued object.

Other crimes that slaves committed were not motivated by personal gain. Among these was the mutilation and death of farm animals; all known cases concerned horses and mules. These animals were suitable for work, transportation, and sport, and most important, they were their owners' valued possessions. In the 1835 statutes the crime of abusing farm animals immediately preceded that of the inhumane treatment of slaves. The animal statute provided: "Every person who shall maliciously and cruelly maim, beat or torture any horse, ox or other cattle, whether belonging to himself or another, shall upon conviction, be adjudged guilty of a misdemeanor and fined not exceeding fifty dollars."[51] Slaves who mistreated livestock were whipped, not imprisoned or fined.

In Polk County, in southwest Missouri, an 1857 prosecution concerned Gilbert. He was indicted, as the court noted, "for wilfully and maliciously cutting the throat of a mare, the property of Charles Crane, whereby she was killed." On appeal Gilbert's indictment was judged defective.[52] Most likely he escaped public punishment, and his master was spared court costs. This case does not specify whether the mare's owner was also Gilbert's owner, but probably Charles Crane did not own the animal-abusing slave. Otherwise, his crime would have been punished in-house, and there would be neither a public record of it nor any court fees. A second animal cruelty case wherein the perpetrator was a slave survives from 1861 in Boone County. Tony, owned by James Shannon, president of the University of Missouri, was a janitor at his master's school. When another Columbia resident, R. P. Reid, rightly or wrongly accused him of stealing one of Reid's hogs, Tony took sulphuric acid from the chemistry laboratory at the university and poured it on a pair of Reid's mules, valued at $400, or almost $6,000 today. The animals were rendered practically worthless by their panicked efforts to escape the acid. Since no one had purchased such a compound from any of the town's drugstores, the university's chemistry lab was its logical source. When Tony was arrested, he confessed, pled guilty, and was punished with 39 lashes. Later his master freed him, and Tony settled in Iowa.[53]

Most likely, slaves were involved in these animal abuse cases far more frequently than extant public records indicate. The horses, mules, and oxen that slaves most readily had access to were their owners'. Among many other slave responsibilities was the care, including cleaning the stables, of their masters' prized animals. When a slave maliciously harmed his owner's livestock, his motive was revenge. The odds are that the perpetrators were males, as in the two known cases; slave women were not required to care for large farm animals when bondmen were available for such tasks.

Arson, or the intentional burning of the dwelling or other structures of another, was a slave crime whose perpetrators were both male and female. At times, in the course of their fire setting, they incidentally destroyed valued farm animals. Unlike larceny or the burglaries discussed in this chapter, arson was a felony inherently dangerous to human life. In the earliest days of American rule of Missouri, slaves convicted of it went to their deaths on public gallows. Beginning in 1836, it was an offense that might subject the slave convicted of it to a dual punishment. In addition to a public whipping, the judge could require that the convicted slave-arsonist be sold and transported out of state for 20 years. As chapter 7 clarified, the owner was required to post a $500 bond to insure that he or she complied with its terms.

In a slight majority of known cases, the accused slaves were women. They were house servants, and though likely denied access to matches after their American invention in the 1830s, bondwomen cooked and tended the wood-burning stoves of their owners. They could easily carry burning pieces of wood on small shovels from the kitchen stove to any nearby locale where they wished to place a smoldering ember or two. If they were cunning about both the timing and the placement of their kindling—for example, set it to ignite slowly, perhaps by using candles as fuses prior to electrical storms—they could be back at their duty stations in kitchens long before their blazes started. Male slaves also set these fires, and some set by both sexes were probably believed to be accidental. These there are no traces of; only those in which slave arsonists were suspected are preserved in court records and newspapers.

In an 1839 slave arson case in Howard County, the Supreme Court of Missouri ruled that if a slave committed a crime, his owner, not the lessee or temporary owner, was required to pay court costs. In the Howard County case we know only that a slave of unspecified sex was leased to Patrick Woods for a year at the time he or she committed the arson. In addition to the owner, Mr. Reed, being required to post a $500 bond to insure that he sold his convicted firebug, the circuit court ordered that Reed, the owner, not Woods, the lessee, pay all the slave-arsonist's court costs, and on appeal, the court upheld the trial judge's order.[54]

In November 1845 Slave Jane, the property of Joseph Baker, was arrested in Cape Girardeau County for deliberately setting the fire that consumed Milton Anderson's "dwelling house and kitchen" and most of their contents. At the time of the crime Anderson was leasing the bondwoman, and he and his wife were gone from their home. When he initially interrogated the slave, she blamed the fire on two unknown men, who, according to Jane, came to the Andersons' smokehouse for meat when the owners were gone. She told them that she had no authority to allow them any liberties on the Anderson property. Nonetheless, according to her first story, they walked through the house, looked under the beds and in some boxes, and threatened to kill her. They also went to the kitchen and came out of it with pieces of burnt wood, which they placed on quilt pieces under one of the beds. Despite a search for these strangers, their tracks could not be found in the direction in which Jane said they left the Anderson home.

She abandoned this account only when Milton Anderson showed her a rope strong enough to hold a man's weight and told her that her life could depend upon her telling the truth about the fire. Under these circumstances she admitted that she burned the home by using a shovel to carry a chunk from the ashes of a kitchen fireplace to some quilt pieces under a bed. Having placed the smoldering coal on easily ignited material in a backroom, she carried the shovel back to the kitchen. When he asked her if either he or his wife had ever mistreated her, she answered, "No you have always treated me well, ever since I have lived with you." To his question, "Why did you set the fire," she replied, "I done it because you and your wife both went off and left me there alone, and I did not want to stay by myself." Jane set her mark to this account before a justice of the peace, who set her recognizance bond at $1,000, a sum her owner did not pledge, and she was confined in the county jail.

A grand jury indicted her for "feloniously, wilfully, and maliciously" setting fire to and burning the Andersons' dwelling. She pled not guilty; earlier she had explained to the justice of the peace that if she had set the fire, she would have removed her clothes. Further, she would not have told Mrs. Anderson about the fire. Instead, she would have run off. On December 26 the court ordered a jury trial for her. At it, she probably spoke well of the Andersons in open court as she initially praised them before the justice of the peace when she told him that her lessee and his wife "were the best white people I ever lived with. Mr. Anderson made me acknowledge that I had burnt his houses, but it did not come from my heart because I was not guilty." Expectedly the jury found her guilty, and the judge assessed her punishment at 39 lashes and held her owner responsible for court costs.[55]

Three other slave arson cases are known between 1856 and 1861 because the Missouri Supreme Court reversed civil suits in which juries found in favor of the owners of the burned structures against the owners of the slave-arsonists. In Lewis County, in northeastern Missouri, the unnamed female bondwoman of a now deceased defendant allegedly burned the stable of the plaintiff and confided her deed to her master. In the civil case the jury heard "the girl has burned [Phillips's] stable and confessed it," and it found for Phillips. On appeal the court held that the slave woman's confession was improperly admitted into evidence because "the person from whom the information came was a slave, one forbidden by law to appear as a witness for or against a white person."[56] By excluding the slave's confession in the civil suit, her arson could not be proven, and her owner's estate avoided financial responsibility for any of her actions.

In Cooper County John, the slave of William Harriman, as the Court noted, "did wilfully set fire to and burn in the night time a barn and stable of Thomas Licklider." A bay stallion worth $300 died in the fire, and his owner sought to recover his value against the slave-arsonist's owner. The jury ruled in favor of the owner of the stallion. On appeal the court held that the slave's crime was burning the stable, not its contents, and John's master was not liable for the criminal acts of his slave, "especially when the slave is not at the time in the performance of his master's business."[57] In Lafayette County, Green, owned by the defendant, deliberately set fire to and burned a barn and stable; hemp, hay, oats, and corn in these structures were destroyed in the fire. The plaintiff sued the defendant for Green's destruction of his harvested crops, prevailed at trial, and, as in the other civil suits concerning the master's liability for his slave's arson, on appeal the court ruled that the slaves' owner was not liable for the plaintiff's loss of property, which at the time of the fire, happened to be stored in the barn, the structure the slave burned.[58]

A newspaper described another arson fire set in Lincoln County, in east central Missouri, in which the burned property consisted of two barns filled with tobacco, sheds attached to the barns, and farming utensils in the sheds. The story listed as the victim of the arson, Mr. Isaac Ellis, the unnamed slave's lessee, and Mr. Wells as the slave's owner. The account concluded that the slave of Wells, hired to Ellis, "was accordingly arrested and committed to jail. There is hardly a doubt of his committing the deed."[59]

A more detailed record of slave arson survives from Saline County. It arose on August 15, 1862: Martha, a slave of Aaron D. Lawton, was charged with feloniously setting fire and burning her master's barn and its contents, including a mare and a mule. She was arrested September 1, her bond set at $500, and the next day she was committed to the county jail in Marshall because her master did not make bail for her. The justice of the peace before whom Martha initially appeared heard all eight witnesses concerning the barn burning and Martha's alleged role in it. Four of these witnesses, including Martha, were slaves, and four were white members of the family. Her owner, Aaron Lawton, testified that he was lying in bed about 3:00 P.M. when he first heard the alarm of fire. He jumped from his bed, went to the road, and saw Martha and the three male slaves near the barn. She was a house servant, and her owner had last seen her at the kitchen door prior to his afternoon nap. Lawton further testified that his slaves were not allowed access to matches, and he had seen none in their possession. However, there was one fire in the house, the stove in one of the kitchens. Among Martha's chores was keeping it lit so meals could be cooked. Unlike the male slaves who had no means to set a fire without matches, Martha, as a house slave, had access to smoldering and burning wood in the kitchen stove and, as such, the opportunity to set her master's barn and its contents on fire. According to Aaron Lawton and members of his family, Martha made no threat of any kind. Nonetheless, as he testified before the justice of the peace, because a band of white men that same morning had threatened to burn his barn, he had earlier removed his saddle, harness, and other articles from the barn to the cornfield. By fall 1862 Lawton may have been a Saline County Unionist sympathizer or a friend of the secessionists, and whichever side he was on, or believed to be on, made him a potential enemy of the other side in war-torn central Missouri. Nonetheless, Martha, not a gang of bushwhackers, was the accused arsonist.

In addition to her owner, his daughter, wife, and son also appeared to testify against Martha before Justice of the Peace Hood in September 1862. Caroline Jeffries, a married daughter, whose husband was probably either a casualty of war or fighting on the Union or the Confederate side, was at her parents' home when the barn burned. She stated that when she first heard the alarm of fire, she was standing at the south kitchen door. Caroline saw Martha under the peach trees, coming toward the northeast corner of the house, crying fire as the bondwoman came through the kitchen to the cistern to get water. The daughter had just taken her mother, who was in the cellar, some water to clean up spilt molasses. Caroline also testified that their slaves had no matches and the only fire on the premises was in a kitchen stove.

Eunice Lawton, wife and mother of the household, testified that she was in the cellar when she heard the alarm of fire. She ran to the north kitchen, and from it she saw Martha under the peach trees coming from the north side of the barn. To Mrs. Lawton the fire "looked [as if] it had been put on the north side of the barn" and "appeared as if it had just been set on fire, the burning was principally among the hay." Like other members of the family, Eunice Lawton never heard Martha make any threats. Charles Lawton, the adult son of the household, testified that he, like his father, was lying in bed on the second floor when he heard the first cry of fire. He ran to the north window of the front upstairs room and saw smoke pouring out of the top of the barn. He raced downstairs, out the front door, and to the barn. He saw the family's three slave men all running toward the burning barn. When he reached it, young Lawton attempted to lead the mare and the mule out of the fire, but its severity prevented him from getting the animals to safety. He too saw Martha going toward the house when he returned to it; the son also stated that the fire started in the loft. This elevated place was the logical area for any arsonist to set a fire; by September it would be filled with easily ignited food for livestock, such as hay.

In addition to members of the Lawton family, three slave witnesses appeared against Martha before Justice Hood. Henry testified that when he first saw the barn on fire, he was riding on a load of hay that Harrison was driving as oxen pulled it. Henry saw Martha at the corner of the stockyard in the road as she was "running slowly" from the barn to the house. She hollered fire and threw her hand up. Harrison, the driver of the hay load, stated that he heard Henry yell that the barn was on fire, and as Harrison looked toward the barn, he saw smoke and the slave woman 80 yards north of where he stood. She was traveling toward the house in a southwest direction; Harrison heard her shouting fire. He swore that after supper, the night of the arson, she asked him not to tell he had seen her in the road because she had been accused of burning the barn and did not do it. The third slave witness, Hiram, was riding with Henry on the load of hay, and he disclosed that he saw Martha north of him in the road, as she was going toward the house "in a quick walk." The justice of the peace also examined the bondwoman; she stated in evidence that she went "off for herself" north of the house, and while she was there she heard one of "the boys," she thought Henry, holler fire. Once she heard the alarm, she jumped over in the road and began to holler fire.

From the testimony of all eight witnesses, the taking of whose statements took several days, the justice of the peace concluded that there was probable cause to believe that the accused ignited and burned Aaron D. Lawton's barn and its contents. He ordered that she be held to stand trial; the file contains her arrest warrant and the order committing her to the county jail to await her trial, which was scheduled for May 1863. In addition, on September 2, 1862, the justice of the peace accepted the $50 recognizance pledge that the four white members of the Aaron D. Lawton household would appear at the next term of Saline County's Circuit Court "to give evidence in behalf of the State, against a certain Martha, a Slave on a certain charge of arson." An undated document in the file records another recognizance pledge of Aaron Lawton that his slaves Harrison, Henry, and Hiram would appear and give their evidence on behalf of the State against Martha.

On November 29, 1862, Aaron Lawton pledged $100 and Benjamin

Chase the same sum that Martha would appear for her trial at the circuit court in Marshall at the next term of court to be held on May 4, 1863. One puzzling note in this file, dated September 2, 1862, reads, "State Pays the costs," but precisely what portion of the entire case the state paid the costs for was not clarified. Most likely the ruined Lawtons, victims of both arson and a Civil War, could not afford to pay for their slave woman's jailing between her arrest in September 1862 and her trial eight months later. Otherwise, Lawton and another man would never have posted a $200 recognizance bond that she would appear at her trial. One final document survives in this case, dated June 11, 1863, and all it contains of *State of Mo. v. Martha, a Slave* is "Commitment."[60] The likelihood is great that if there was sufficient peace in Saline County by May 1863 to hold court and have a trial, Martha was found guilty of arson in setting the fire that burned her master's barn. What happened to her at this late stage of slavery in Missouri was not clarified in these records.

In all, at least eight cases of suspected and/or proven slave arson survive in some form or another from Missouri's antebellum period. Why did slaves set fire to houses, stables, sheds, and barns? Today the primary motive for this crime is the collection of the proceeds of an insurance policy on the burned structure. During slavery, most likely no fire policies were written on the buildings that slaves burned, and if they were, their beneficiaries were never bondpersons. Therefore, financial gain did not motivate slaves to set the property of others on fire. Missouri's bondpersons evened scores when they committed arson. Women had more access to the means of starting fires and appear to have burned more structures than did bondmen, but their motives were the same, revenge for their wholly uncompensated or inadequately compensated labor. When two tobacco barns burned in Lincoln County in January 1861, the leased slave accused of setting the fire had surely worked for months from sunup to sundown to raise and harvest the tobacco that filled his lessee's barns. His intent was probably the destruction of the valuable commodity the barns contained.

Unlike wheat, which the free farmers of Kansas grew, tobacco was an especially labor-intensive crop. It required planting in beds, transplanting in fields, removing the center stalk to prevent seed formation, worming and reworming the green plants to rid them of green tobacco worms, hoeing near the plants to remove weeds, cutting both the tobacco stalk and the sturdy sticks the stalks were placed on, lifting these sticks laden with tobacco stalks to dizzying heights in barns for curing this crop, and perhaps risking a broken leg, back, or neck in an accidental fall from these heights. When all this endless work was completed, grading, bunching, and stacking the now golden and brown crop for shipment to market remained. Bondpersons had no legal right to the financial rewards of their repetitive, unpleasant, and exhausting tasks of raising tobacco or any other crop, such as hemp, hay, oats, and corn. Slave men, women, and children were all members of the work force that produced the crops that filled their masters' barns. Burning such structures when they were brimming full after the harvest seems a logical way for the powerless to give their owners and lessees their comeuppance. Whether a house or a barn was the object of the arson was not especially important to the fire-setting slave. Doubtless, both slave men and women burned whatever was handy, and insofar as they succeeded, at least partially, they reduced their owners and lessees to their own propertyless condition.

Other slave crimes discussed in this chapter ranged from simple assault and battery to attempted murder. In Cape Girardeau County in December 1837, Slave Dick, alias Slave Richard, was convicted in a jury trial of assault and battery on the body of Miss Fanny Hanley. His punishment was assessed at 10 lashes, and his owner, John Horrell, was required, by February 1838, to satisfy the costs of the prosecution or Dick was to be sold at a public auction. From the small number of lashes he was sentenced to receive, Dick's offense was a slight one; almost certainly, it was not sexual. Perhaps he bumped into her, or maybe he did not give her the right of way on a town street or a county road. The surviving records clarify neither how nor why Slave Dick unlawfully touched Fanny Hanley.[61]

What slave owners and lessees feared far more than an unwanted physical encounter with a slave or slaves was bondpersons' murder of them or their family members. Insofar as those in bondage took a substantial step toward the commission of this crime, but the victim did not die, the accused was guilty of attempted murder or some variation of it. When the slave used an obvious method in his or her failed effort to destroy another's life, little about the crime was mysterious; what had taken place was immediately known. An 1853 newspaper account concerns a slave's attempted murder of his master in Lafayette County; the unnamed slave struck his owner, James Hicklin, two blows on the head with an ax. The story mentioned that the victim's "skull was badly fractured and several large pieces of bone had to be removed."[62] Most likely, the perpetrator of this brutal deed was quickly tried for attempted murder, convicted, whipped, and transported out of state for 20 years. In cases such as an unsuccessful attack with an ax, knife, club, and the like, the victim knew there was an attempt to harm him or her.

However, as in the arson cases, the surviving records indicate that slave women were more frequently charged with attempted murder than were slave men. At times the record does not contain the manner of her crime. In Jackson County in 1829, Slave Hanna was found guilty in a jury trial of the attempted murder of her master, Asa Say. The judge sentenced Hanna to receive 39 lashes.[63] At other times the method of the attempted murder was known, and it was far more subtle than any attack with an ax, club, or knife. Poison was and remains primarily a woman's weapon, and so it was with slave women who worked in kitchens and pantries where they had access to products stored in them such as arsenic and bluestone or copper sulphate, which, among other medicinal or household uses, could be employed to poison the unsuspecting ingestors of these drugs. One newspaper account blamed the 1860 poisoning of the entire Andrew Briscoe family in Tipton (Moniteau County) on a 17-year-old bondboy. The wife and mother in the family died.[64] However, no death sentence arose in this case, and most likely the young male slave was merely one of the usual suspects. Another newspaper account published five days after the earlier story blamed the crime on "some unknown hand."[65] Someone placed some poisonous substance in ground coffee, and most likely the perpetrator remained unknown and the crime unsolved.

Insofar as either court records or a newspaper account identify the suspected perpetrator with any particularity in these poisoning cases, the accused were females. In Cape Girardeau County, Esther was indicted for administering poison with intent to murder on January 11, 1835. The indictment charged that "Esther, otherwise called Easter, a black negress slave ... being a person of wicked mind and disposition and maliciously intending to poison one Carolina Davis, an infant child, aged about two months." The victim was the daughter of P. H. Davis, then leasing Esther from her owner, Simeon English. The father of the young child testified before a justice of the peace that his wife, the mother of Carolina, had gone to her father's and that Esther accompanied her, carrying the child, who was in good health. That same evening Esther got supper for the parents, and when they seated themselves at the table, Mrs. Davis gave her daughter to Esther to nurse her. Soon thereafter, the child became fretful, and at the point Mr. Davis asked for milk, Esther, required to fetch it, gave Mr. Davis his daughter. The father noticed that her gums and mouth had a bluish cast to them, and she appeared to be gagging. He stuck his finger down the child's throat and assisted her in "puking." Several times, she threw up a considerable quantity of a bluish fluid. The father then administered an emetic, that is, a substance that caused more vomiting, and it gave the child relief. The poison that Esther admitted before the justice of the peace that she administered to the child was bluestone, or copper sulphate, a substance of a greenish-blue cast, then used as a preservative for green pickles, peas, and other vegetables,[66] but when consumed by humans, a deadly poison. She testified that "Tom," probably another slave, a day or two earlier identified the contents of a particular jar or bottle in the shop as "bluestone" and told her it was poison. Esther explained that she took a piece the size of a pea, broke it with a shovel, and gave a small piece, about the size of the head of a pin to the baby when the family was at supper. In response to the justice of the peace's asking her why she gave the infant poison, Esther replied, "I had no object in giving it to the child." On January 13 Mr. English posted a $300 recognizance bond that she would appear at the next term of the circuit court on the first Monday in February. On February 3, 1835, Esther pled guilty, the judge assessed her punishment at 30 lashes, and her owner was required to pay the costs of her prosecution.[67]

In two other known cases of slave women using poison on white persons, the substance was arsenic, a poison certainly equal in lethality to bluestone and one without its telltale blue color. In August 1848 in Boone County, Patsy was convicted of trying to poison and kill James and Mary Howlett, the couple who leased her from her owner, Montgomery P. Leintz. Patsy mixed arsenic in milk; Mrs. Howlett noticed this white liquid did not look right. The two physicians who examined the milk concluded that there was enough arsenic in it to kill the entire family. Mrs. Howlett also testified that Patsy had threatened to kill some of the family. The judge sentenced her to 39 lashes,[68] and her owner was probably required to transport her out of state for 20 years. In 1850 in Clay County, a newspaper reported that an unidentified slave woman scraped some arsenic, which a member of the family of Wade Moseby intentionally spread beneath the kitchen floor to kill vermin. After she obtained this poison, she mixed it with the coffee the family drank at breakfast. They all became very ill, but, as the story noted, "prompt and efficient antidotes have succeeded in counteracting its most violent effects, and hopes are entertained of their recovery."[69]

Two other accounts do not identify the poison, but in both cases the perpetrators were slave women. In Boone County in 1855, Ann, owned by George Lytekliter, was indicted for attempting to poison her owner's daughter. She gave the child a spoonful of some poison, and the victim became ill, but she did not die. Ann was found guilty, sentenced to 39 lashes,[70] and most likely transportation out of state for 20 years. A newspaper account of a Monroe County poisoning in 1860 concerned an unidentified female slave who belonged to Mr. Vandeventer. She put the deadly poison in coffee, which the family drank, but all the victims were expected to recover.[71] In the five known accounts described herein of slave women administering poison to whites, the victims recovered. Whether the perpetrators were unskilled in their use of poison or they never intended to kill their victims, only to make them very ill, is not known. Once more, the motive of these perpetrators was not personal gain; it was revenge.

Did all slave women who poisoned whites bungle their crimes? Likely not. Surely, some undetected women successfully poisoned their lessees and their owners. Of the many capital cases discussed in the next chapters, not one involved the use of poison. The records of these white deaths by slave poisonings could always be lost. However, the subtlety of this crime is considerable, and unless the victim suspects the killer, then and now, this crime is the reverse of obvious. The conclusion seems inescapable that some slaves got away with murder. Probably, they were women who administered to their owners and/or white family members arsenic in small doses and patiently held the hands of the dying as they writhed in agony from unsuspected and never detected arsenic poisoning. The deaths of such victims of slave stealth were mistakenly attributed to cholera or some other dreaded disease, never to the criminal designs of their seemingly faithful bondwomen.

This chapter has described a wide array of crimes that Missouri's slaves committed; court records clarify how infrequent their public wrongs were against those who owned them. In case after case the victims of these noncapital offenses were the slaves' lessees. As such, the owners of slaves, not the harmed persons, paid the costs of the prosecution. Excluding Ann's case in 1855 and Martha's in 1862, wherein the victims were the owners, most noncapital slave offenses against their owners were handled in-house. The slave was sold, and there is not now and never was a public record. In Martha's case perhaps no purchaser could be found for her in war-ravaged Missouri. The material worth of slaves had risen throughout the antebellum period until the Civil War; then it dropped precipitously.[72] In May 1862 a 30-year-old woman and her two children sold for $200; two years earlier they were worth $2,500.[73] Any woman either charged with or convicted of a major felony was not a valuable property by the fall of 1862. Martha's crime involved no particular physical strength, nor did the crimes of most slave women. Instead, advanced planning and considerable cunning were its features; these qualities characterized the mental states of the perpetrators of larceny, arson, and attempted murder, the crimes of the bondwomen described in this chapter.

The next chapters concern death penalty offenses involving bondpersons. Most of their victims were whites, and they often owned the slaves who murdered them or their white family members. Because female slaves were executed out of all proportion to women criminals in Missouri's general population, their stories are especially worth relating.

Chapter 10

Capital Cases:
Girls and Women

Excluding Slave Jane's case, this chapter discusses all known death penalty cases involving female slave defendants. The Supreme Court of Missouri reversed Jane's death sentence in 1831; it is discussed in chapter 7. The odds favor that she was not executed, because the great majority of slave women who killed their own children were not capitally punished, as far as we know. It includes four confirmed and two probable executions and two acquittals on capital charges. However, because the beginnings of capital punishment under American rule of Missouri are shrouded in mystery, there is much uncertainty about these numbers. John Long's execution in St. Louis in 1809 is assumed to be the first under the authority of the United States. The newspaper that covered his gallows death did not identify it as the first American hanging, and the odds are that it was not.

The absence of early territorial court records and newspapers makes clarification of exactly what happened in any case, including potentially capital cases, difficult to track. This much we know. Arson carried a mandatory death sentence in Missouri in 1805. The law required that any accused perpetrator of it be tried in the General Court before three federal judges, all of whom the president appointed. In 1805 this crime was the subject of a letter that the prominent St. Louis resident Pierre Chouteau wrote Henry Dearborn, President Jefferson's secretary of war. In it Chouteau stated that one of his slaves, an unnamed female, had "lighted the fire with her own hands which devoured my property and that of the

United States which I had." He assured Secretary Dearborn that he had not mistreated the accused slave, but because of her vengeance, the major part of his wealth was destroyed. The Frenchman continued his letter with this ominous comment, "She is now in prison and the first general court will decide her fate."[1] In 1805 the next session of this highest court in territorial Missouri was scheduled for May 7.

Though matches were not yet invented, we know from the court records of statehood years that slave women tended the cooking stoves of their owners, and from their duty stations in kitchens they had a greater opportunity willfully and maliciously to burn their masters' property than did slave men. Perhaps Chouteau's slave took advantage of a well-chosen moment and ignited her master's holdings. Most probably, she was put on trial for her life in St. Louis's General Court in 1805. Example setting was necessary when the victim was not only a white male but also a prominent member of the most eminent French family in Missouri Territory, the Chouteaus. Pierre was the brother of August Chouteau and President Jefferson appointed Pierre's son, August Chouteau, Jr., to the newly organized army military academy, West Point, in July 1804.[2] This appointment and others of the sons of eminent French citizens was but one way the Jefferson administration accommodated French interests in Missouri. The courts were probably another means the American government used to oblige these favored territorial residents. The odds are that the female slave of Pierre Chouteau was found guilty of willfully and maliciously burning her owner's dwelling, barn, or stable. If she was found guilty, the judges could only sentence her to death by hanging. This anonymous slave woman probably died on a public scaffold in St. Louis in 1805 as did 29 convicted arsonists in England and Wales between 1805 and 1832.[3] In Virginia between 1706 and 1865, 149 slaves were convicted of arson (a capital offense), and a significant number of these were women.[4] However, with neither court records nor a newspaper within Missouri Territory at this time, more cannot be urged regarding Pierre Chouteau's bondwoman accused of arson.

The first slave execution in Missouri that can be confirmed was of a male; it is mentioned in the next chapter and listed in appendix 4. The second that we know about was almost certainly not the second, probably not the third or the fourth. It occurred in Clay County, a locale nearly 250 miles west of St. Louis. It involved a woman named Annice. On July 27, 1828, the grand jury indicted her for the drowning death of five slave youngsters, all the property of her owner, Jeremiah Prior. Neither the parentage nor the ages of Ann, Phebe, and Nancy are specified; Bill, aged five years, and Nelly, aged two years, are identified as the perpetrator's children. Annice was found guilty of "the several counts" of murder in that on each count, probably in June 1828, she did push "one Ann a negro child slave ... into a certain collection of water of the depth of five feet and there choaked, suffocated, and drowned of which ... the said Ann [Phebe, Nancy, Bill, and Nelly] instantly died."

Because there was no jail in Clay County at this early date, Annice was incarcerated in the Jackson County jail in Independence. Since there was then no bridge across the Missouri River between the county to the north of the river, Clay, and that to its south, Jackson, a ferry conveyed her across the river when she was moved from the courthouse to the jail or vice versa. The records show that she was "quartered" in the Jackson County jail five days.

The Clay County Court more generously reimbursed various persons in this early death penalty case than did at least one other Missouri county during this same time period. As discussed in chapter 6, Sheriff Ford sued Howard County because the $10 fee it allowed him per execution, one white man's in 1830 and Slave Hampton's in 1832, was inadequate to cover all of his expenses. These included constructing a gallows, building a coffin, obtaining nails for the burial box, furnishing the hangman's rope, and digging and covering the grave. In Annice's case the extant records clarified that Sheriff Shubael Allen received $4 for attending Annice's trial and $10 for hanging her. In addition, the circuit court disbursed $6 to a Mr. Henry for nails for her coffin; $7 to Enos Vaughan for erecting her gallows, digging and covering her grave, and "handing" the criminal to the gallows; and $5 to Joel Turnham for the rope used to "hang the criminal." In all, the costs of her trial and execution, which, among other expenses, included guards, room and board at the Jackson County jail, and river ferry service, exceeded $55[5] or the better part of $5,000 today.

Was she the only slave woman put to death in Missouri for the murder of her own children, or is she the only one whose hanging for this crime can be documented? There is no satisfactory answer to this question. Contemporary newspapers from Cooper and Boone Counties contain stories about a Callaway County slave woman who in 1845 poisoned five children, four of them her own and the fifth a white child. She confessed her crimes, and almost certainly, had she lived, she would have been tried, found guilty, and hanged, but she committed suicide while in jail by taking the same arsenic she had earlier used to kill these five children. These numbers are a record of known homicide victims of any slave, male or female, throughout Missouri's entire antebellum period. Since Annice did not end her own life, she went on trial. Because the records contain no statement from her, her motivation can only be surmised. Most likely, it was the same as Missouri's many slave mothers discussed in chapter 7, who either attempted or accomplished the murder of their offspring. Without "the curse of involuntary servitude" as Garrison explained the phenomenon of slave mothers killing their children, almost certainly, Annice would never have systematically drowned one child after another, thereby depriving her owner of no fewer than five potentially valuable properties.

Her case is mentioned in two county histories. From them we know that she had a jury trial and that a defense attorney represented her at trial. Both state that she was discovered after she had drowned two or three of her children and while attempting to drown her oldest.[6] They are not accurate. Court records make clear that she was not discovered until she had murdered five slave children, two of them her own. Another Clay County Slave, also named Annice, committed a crime in the town of Liberty in 1850. She may have been an older daughter of the Annice whom Shubael Allen hanged in 1828. The second Annice's case is discussed in chapter 14.

One other remembrance of the first Slave Annice case came into existence in the mid–1970s. The Clay County Bicentennial Committee erected a plaque, approximately six miles east of Interstate 35, Exit 26 (Kearney, Missouri), just off Highway 92 in a Clay County park, Tryst Falls. In part it read, "Water falls into basin where a Negro slave drowned her children in 1828 and was hung for the deed." This sign was put up in 1976 and remained there until at least 1994. It has since been replaced by another marker, which states only, "Clay County Historical Society Historic Landmark." This obscure tablet marks the spot where more than 160 years earlier Annice sent five slave children to a watery grave. Her execution on a public gallows was almost certainly not the second instance of slave capital punishment in Missouri, but hers is the earliest confirmed in court records.

In 1837 Slave Mary's capital case arose in Crawford County, southwest of St. Louis. Unlike Annice's, for which there was neither an appeal nor any means of determining the perpetrator's age, in Mary's case both exist, as well as extant court records, census material, and at least four contemporary news stories about her. Two out-of-state newspapers reprinted a St. Louis paper's story that gave her age as "about 13" at the time of her crime. Another in-state paper described her as being "about 14." When I first wrote about her,[7] I had not located any of the news stories about her that I subsequently discovered. The county history, published in 1888, which I then relied on, listed her age as 16 at the time of her crime.

This history also stated that John Brinker owned Mary and that she drowned one of his children because she expected her master to sell her.[8] A more recent account repeated the tale that Mary committed her crime because she believed that her master, John Brinker, intended to sell her. It embellished her story with detail such as:

> She ... drowned a first child ... while the parents were away....On their next trip to town, Mr. Brinker returned to the house and hid himself to see if the Negro maid would attempt to harm their other children. Within a few minutes the Negro maid was seen to grab the Brinker child and run toward the family spring. Before reaching the spring with the youngster, she was confronted by Mr. Brinker.[9]

In their many particulars, these accounts, written 50 or more years after the events they fancifully describe, are unfounded.

All contemporary documents pertaining to her are consistent with her being 13 or 14 years old when she committed her crime. The known facts of Mary's young life include Abraham Brinker's ownership of her. The 1830 census listed him as the head of a Washington County household of 13 persons. Among its members were one free white male between the ages of 20 and 30 (probably Abraham's son, John B. Brinker) and one female slave under 10 years of age (probably Mary), who, if 13 or 14 in 1837, was aged six or seven years in 1830. In the spring of 1833 the senior Brinker, a prosperous Indian trader and resident of Potosi, was murdered by the Indians southwest of Potosi.[10] On May 16, 1833, his widow, Fanny, and his son John B. posted an $8,000 bond in order to serve as administrators of his estate. The deceased died without a will, and his estate was not probated until 1850.[11] As a result, Mary was an asset of it from the time she was 9 or 10 years old until she was hanged by the neck until dead on a public scaffold in Steelville, Crawford County's seat, when she was aged 14 or 15 years.

Court records regarding Mary's ownership rarely mention John B. Brinker. In fact, among the defendant's points for the arrest of judgment and a new trial was this argument: "said indictment does not set forth and show to whom said slave belongs." The prosecutor's omission is explained by an 1828 statute concerning bondpersons. It required the hiring of "all slaves belonging to the estate of any deceased person ... to the highest bidder"; it specifically forbade the private hiring of any slave by "any administrator" (i.e., John B. Brinker) and subjected the private hirer to a fine of up to $500. Likewise, subsequent Missouri law of 1835 and 1845 continued to require that slaves of unprobated estates "be hired to the highest bidder at the courthouse door."[12]

John B. Brinker violated the law by removing Mary from Washington to Crawford County and privately hiring her as his slave. Nonetheless, she became a member of his household sometime after her owner's death. By spring 1837, when she was 13 or 14, her responsibilities included looking after John Brinker's daughter, Vienna Jane Brinker, a child just shy of her second birthday. Court records, both circuit and Supreme Court of Missouri, in Mary's case are extensive; they never mention any contemplated sale of her, but they tell the story of what Mary did to Vienna Jane on May 14, 1837.

Two men were deposed by a justice of the peace on May 15, 1837. One, William Blackwell, stated that he was at the Brinkers' on the previous day loading a wagon when the child's absence was first noticed. At this time, Mary had been sent after wood and had taken the toddler with her. John Brinker queried Mary, who denied any knowledge of the youngster's whereabouts, but she also ran toward "the branch," a small stream of water. The men searched it, and shortly, deponent Thomas Shirley found the drowned child in it. They noticed that the baby had received a blow on the right temple. Blackwell believed from the start of her disappearance that Mary had drowned her. After Vienna Jane's body was discovered in the branch, the two men ran with her to the house. Her father attempted to revive his daughter by bleeding her in the arm, but to no avail. Next, William Blackwell took Mary

> out to a log and tied her fast. I then commenced pulling up her coat as if I were going to whip her. She then said if I would not whip her she would tell the truth. I told her "then out with it." She then told me she had thrown It in that hole of water. I then accused her of striking It with a stick before she threw the child in the water. She then said she did not strike the child before she threw It in, she threw It in the branch and It rose, and she then struck It with a Stick.

On May 16, 1837, Mary was examined before a Crawford County justice of the peace and admitted to him that "she picked up the child at the kitchen door and took It down to the branch and threw It in the branch with the intention to drowned It but It rose. She then took a stick and struck It on the head." On this same day she was charged with Vienna Jane Brinker's murder. By May 22 she was a prisoner in the nearest jail, Potosi, Washington County, 36 miles east of Steelville, a town that built its first jail in 1838.[13] Mary remained in the Potosi jail almost four months awaiting her trial on capital charges in a log building in Steelville.

At a special term of court, which convened on August 16, the preliminaries of her trial for murder began. Because she was a slave and unable to employ counsel, the law automatically entitled her to an attorney. The judge who presided, James Evans, assigned three to represent her. They were Philip Cole, John S. Brickey, and Mason Frizzell. (Frizzell was later the judge who presided at the last known capital trial of a slave in Missouri's history.) The first day of proceedings, the grand jury indicted Mary, and the second, the trial jury was selected and heard the evidence against her. The prosecution witnesses included Thomas Shirley, William Blackwell, and John B. Brinker. The prosecutor offered Mary's confession into evidence, and Judge Evans ruled that it was admissible. The defense, according to the summarizing court records, offered no evidence. Since these records contain Mary's mark, *X*, not her signature, as expected, she was illiterate.

The court instructed the jury of 12 white men that her admission of guilt could only be received by the jury as legal evidence against her if it was made "of her own free will and not under the influence of hope or fear, torture or pain." He also gave this instruction:

> If the Jury shall find from the evidence that Mary, the accused person was under the age of fourteen years when she committed the offense alleged in the indictment, then, unless they shall also find from the evidence that at the time when said offense was committed the said Mary had sufficient mind to know what act would be a crime or otherwise, they shall find for the defendant.

Despite her young age, the jury returned a verdict of first-degree murder on August 18, two days after her trial began. On August 19 Judge Evans overruled a motion for a new trial and sentenced Mary to be hanged September 30.[14] Her lawyers filed an appeal with the Supreme Court of Missouri, and it accepted her case, the third slave death case this court decided.

It may now seem surprising that Mary's age at the time of her crime was not an issue in her appeal. This was so because the law permitted the execution of young persons. Blackstone wrote of his country's death penalty for children, "a girl of thirteen has been [executed] for killing her mistress: and one boy of ten, and another of nine years old, who had killed their companions, have been sentenced to death, and he of ten years actually hanged."[15] American law, including Missouri's, adopted British precedents, and as such, there is no mention of Mary's age in the Supreme Court of Missouri's decision about her case.

However, it reversed her conviction during its September 1837 term and granted her a new trial on two grounds: inconsistent modes of death were charged in the indictment, beating the child to death with a stick and drowning her; and the prosecution continued to examine witnesses after agreeing with defendant's lawyers that the evidence be closed.[16] Mary's second trial was delayed by arguments about a change of venue from Crawford to

Gasconade and back to Crawford County. Her case was continued until 1838. At her second trial she was again found guilty; no appeal was taken from it, and the sheriff of Crawford County hanged her on August 11, 1838. She was buried in an unmarked grave on the bluff on the north side of Steelville.[17]

Community and individual efforts keep the memory of this case alive. On April 18 and 19, 1990, and in the 100-year-old courthouse of Crawford County, Willard Rand's play *The Trial of Mary, a Slave*, was presented in two acts. I attended its first performance. Act 1 takes place in the Washington County jail in Potosi, where Mary was imprisoned prior to her trial in the summer of 1837, and act 2 in the Crawford County Courtroom where she was for the second time put on trial for her life in July 1838. The play's other characters include two attorneys for the defense; the trial judge, James Evans; the murdered victim's father, John Brinker; the bailiff; the prosecuting attorney; and a jury of white males, composed in several instances of the descendants of the original jurors who found Mary guilty of first-degree murder in both her 1837 and her 1838 trials.[18]

In addition, recently discovered news stories, including a St. Louis newspaper, described the crime in these terms:

> a shocking and an unaccountable murder was committed upon the person of a child of Mr. J. B. Brinker.... This act was committed ... by a slave belonging to Mr. Brinker, about 13 years old.... No reason was assigned for ... the act, except that she said she did not like Mr. Brinker. She is described as a shrewd girl, remarkably fond of children, and exhibited no fear or compunction at the moment of apprehension. The girl is in jail at Potosi, Washington County, awaiting her trial.[19]

Slave Mary's execution when she was 14 or 15 years old for a crime she committed when she was aged 13 or 14 years makes her the youngest known person ever put to death under the authority of Missouri. The Register of Inmates, Missouri State Penitentiary, makes clear that white children of these same young ages who committed murder during the antebellum period were not executed; they were imprisoned. Prior to the Civil War the prison received at least four young white murderers: Amos Bird, a 15-year-old, from Cape Girardeau County, in 1843; Susan Seabaugh, a 14-year-old from Bolinger County, in 1855; Nicholas Trauturne, a 15-year-old; and his codefendant, Anthony Leite, a 17-year-old, from St. Louis in 1859. Because Mary was a slave, the law prohibited her being sent to prison as punishment for her crime; as a result, she was hanged.

The case against the next known slave woman sentenced to death in

The complete inscription reads, "Sacred to the Memory of Vienna Jane Brinker Born May the 26th, 1835/ Died/ May the 14th, 1837/ Aged 1 Year 11 Months/ and 19 Days./ Suffer little children/ to come unto me and forbid them not, /for such is the kingdom of God." Inscription on the tombstone of Slave Mary's victim. In 1989 members of the St. James Historical Preservation Society discovered and refurbished this gravestone in the yard of the Brinker cabin when restoring the building, a structure erected by Levi Snelson in 1834 and thereafter sold to the Brinkers. The property is on Highway 8. Photograph by Willard Rand.

Missouri concerned Fanny. It arose in Lincoln County on September 1, 1838, a Saturday, when William Florence, the owner of a mill, returned home and discovered that his wife had given their sons, William and Thomas, aged approximately 8 and 10 years, permission to go pick peaches in the orchard of a neighbor, William C. Prewitt. Their father had repeatedly refused his sons' requests to go to this grove because as he testified, Prewitt's "negroes had threatened to kill them; and if they did go I would whale them." The father also admitted under oath that his only information that Fanny had ever made any threats against her sons came from the boys themselves. William Florence Sr. went to the Prewitt orchard that same Saturday afternoon, did not see his sons, questioned Fanny and her son, Ellick, and they both said that they had not seen the children. As a part of their father's testimony at Fanny's trial, Florence Sr. stated of querying Fanny and Ellick on the same day the children were first missing, "I then discovered from their deportment that my children had been murdered by them." Two white women testified that Fanny told them that Mr. Florence had accused the slave mother's children of killing his on that same day, September 1, or three days before their murder was confirmed.

From late Saturday afternoon, September 1, through Tuesday, September 4, when their bodies were found, more than 100 men searched for the children or any trace of them. Their remains were finally located in Mill Creek. Members of the search party were directed to this locale by circling and perched buzzards. The bodies of the boys had been weighed down with stones when the water in the creek was high. As it receded, these birds of prey were attracted by the exposed dead flesh, and they had already eaten some of the face and arms of the younger child, Thomas, before their father was certain that a crime against his sons had taken place.

Once the bodies of the murdered children were located, the sheriff arrested four slaves of Mr. Prewitt: Fanny; her husband, Ben; their son Ellick; and a brother of either Fanny or Ben, Green. The sheriff and his men separated Ellick, seemingly a teenager, from his mother, father, and uncle. They interrogated him in isolation, and according to the Missouri Supreme Court decision, told their prisoner that his father, on a judge's orders, had been hanged in an adjacent county, his uncle had also been hanged, his mother was about to be hanged, and if Ellick did not confess, "Judge Hunt [Lincoln County's circuit court judge] would be there directly and hang him; that if he told the truth they would let him off." His interrogators then put a rope around Ellick's neck, and finally, under these terror-inspiring circumstances, Fanny's son, like many other persistently questioned persons, confessed. He told the sheriff and his deputies what they wanted to hear, that he had helped his mother murder the Florence children and the two of them carried their dead bodies into the woods. Once his confession was secured, as the appellate decision noted, "he says he also told the same story before the grand jury after he had been sworn on the book; that the reason why he told the grand jury so was, that he had once said it, and he thought he was bound to stick to it."

On the basis of her son's confession, which implicated his mother, Ellick's father and uncle were released, and the grand jury indicted Fanny and Ellick for the first-degree murder of William Florence, the older of the dead brothers. William Prewitt, their owner, did not sit idly by and watch the proceedings against his slaves. He was in Philadelphia (Marion County) during the week the murders occurred; as a result, he could not be called as an alibi witness for them. Instead, he hired the best legal talent he could find. One of their lawyers, Carty Wells, a resident of Troy, the seat of Lincoln County, was later both a state senator and a circuit court judge.

Prewitt also employed Edward Bates, an eminent lawyer who, among much else, had practiced law in territorial St. Louis with Joshua Barton, brother of David Barton. Bates also served with David Barton as one of the most important members of the convention that wrote Missouri's constitution during the summer of 1820; as the state of Missouri's first attorney general in 1820–21; as a member of the Missouri House of Representatives in 1822 and 1834, and as a state senator in 1830. He represented Missouri in the lower house in the Twentieth Congress, 1827–29. Later, Abraham Lincoln chose him as his attorney general; he was the first cabinet officer from a place west of the Mississippi River. The *Dictionary of American Biography* closes its entry on this distinguished Missourian with this observation: "He was modest and unpretending, but a courageous fighter for law and justice."[20] Wells, the local attorney, had as his co-counsel a nearby superstar. Bates was then a resident of St. Charles, the county adjacent to Lincoln, and he lived in the town of St. Charles. Fanny's and Ellick's owner, William Prewitt, retained the most capable lawyers he could locate, one assumes, at least in part because he believed in his bondpersons' complete innocence of the monstrous crime with which they were charged.

On Prewitt's application Fanny obtained a change of venue from Lincoln to Warren County. She was tried at the April 1839 term of its circuit court, found guilty of first-degree murder, and sentenced to death. After her motion for a new trial was overruled, she appealed through her attorneys, Wells and Bates, to the Supreme Court of Missouri, and it accepted her case. The prosecution's theory of the killings was that Fanny murdered the children in Prewitt's orchard by clubbing them to death. Her son Ellick's confession so stated, but the search party could not find the club or any other murder weapon, and none was introduced into evidence. The court issued a more lengthy and detailed statement of the facts in this case, in all 21 pages, than in any other slave criminal case it decided. Its decision contains a summary of the testimony of both prosecution and defense witnesses, and when any reviewing court bothers to recite the evidence that both sides presented at trial, it is troubled by and does not agree with the jury's guilty verdict.

In crimes of violence, blood is often a major component of the state's evidence against the accused. The sheriff of Lincoln County testified for the prosecution that in the Prewitt orchard he found a drop of blood the size of a pinhead on a blade of grass under a peach tree, "took it up, wetted it, and found it was blood." Other men, according to the sheriff's testimony, went about the orchard crying out, "'Here is blood … here is blood.…' The men were formed in a column, and were frequently crying out blood in different places. I saw what others took to be blood, but I did not think it was blood; I took it to be spots on the leaves; these were briar leaves and red on both sides." When the sheriff testified that he took it up, wetted it, and found it was blood, most likely he relied either on his own sense of taste or sight, or both, and nothing more.

The defense countered the testimony of the prosecution witnesses who saw blood everywhere with its own. One, a member of the search party, stated that he was in the orchard and in the woods near where the children's bodies were discovered on Monday, September 3, the day before their remains were located, and his nose bled profusely. He testified, "My saddle and blanket and horse's neck were covered with blood which came from my nose." Another, Robert Prewitt, uncle of William Prewitt, told the jury that, a few days before the children were missing, he had castrated 20 or 30 pigs in a pasture near the orchard and the fence between the pasture and orchard was open. A third defense witness testified that "the urine of hogs fed on red oak mast looks red.... The gentlemen in every direction in the woods were crying blood. I did not deem it blood." Whether what the various witnesses saw or thought they saw was the blood of the murdered children, or that of a nose-bleeding member of the group looking for the children, or castrated pig blood, or pig urine, or spots on leaves, or the patterns that sunlight forms on grass, trees, and rocks was never clarified by any expert testimony.

The determination for forensic purposes that any matter was, in fact, blood, that it came from a human, not an animal, and its correct identification by type were all in the distant future when Slave Fanny was put on trial for her life in 1839. Nonetheless, the Supreme Court of Missouri brought the requisite skepticism to the presentation of blood evidence in this case. More than 125 years later, the United States Supreme Court reversed and remanded a wrongful murder conviction that was in large part based on faulty blood evidence. The High Court accepted the later scientific findings that the reddish brown material on a pair of men's undershorts found near the body of the murdered child, a substance the prosecution claimed was the victim's blood and a key component of its case against the accused, was paint, red paint.[21]

The Missouri Supreme Court presented a detailed account of various witnesses' testimony regarding the blood evidence. The case also contains the statements of witnesses regarding a fresh break in a fence of the orchard; the prosecution argued that Fanny and Ellick took the children's bodies through it, and the defense argued that hogs had rooted in the area and knocked the fence down. The reviewing court's reversal, however, was not based on these factual considerations. Rather, it chose Ellick's confession, which thoroughly implicated his mother in the children's murders.

Today, such admissions are usually inadmissible against another party in any court in the United States, either state or federal; generally, they cannot be used, even if uncoerced, against anyone other than the person making the confession.

When Ellick testified before the grand jury, his owner had not then retained the distinguished lawyers who later represented Fanny at trial. Prior to the state's presentation of evidence in Warren County, Ellick did not have the advice of any attorney or any understanding that he was at liberty to repudiate his confession at trial. Once Fanny's son conferred with Wells and Bates, he knew what he was allowed to tell the jury. Her son took the stand at his mother's trial and told it that he knew neither how the children came to their death nor who killed them. Moreover, he stated that his mother never told him she killed the children. He also testified about the circumstances of the sheriff's obtaining his confession. He swore that every statement he had made against his mother and himself was false. He also told the jury that he told such lies because his interrogators coerced him. Nonetheless, the trial judge admitted Ellick's confession; the appellate court's reversal of Fanny's case is based in significant part on its ruling that Ellick's confession should not have gone to the jury.

This court had earlier shown its aversion to the prosecution's using a confession obtained from a slave by brutal interrogation techniques. In 1829 it reversed Slave Hector's conviction for burglary because he had been beaten until he made certain admissions "to gain a respite from pain." Further, the stolen money was not where his confession stated that it could be located. The manner of obtaining a statement from him violated the Missouri Constitution's provision "that the accused cannot be compelled to give evidence against himself."[22] Fanny's attorney, Edward Bates, understood what was meant by this provision because he helped write Missouri's first constitution. Obviously, in Fanny's case he convinced the Supreme Court of Missouri that compelling a confession from one slave in order to use it against another was equally improper. The decision of the judge who wrote for the court stated, "Abstracting from the evidence on the record the declarations extorted from the boy Ellick, there does not in my opinion remain any evidence to justify a jury finding the prisoner guilty."

Other evidence mentioned in the appellate decision argues against Fanny's guilt. As a starter, the children's bodies were found completely naked weighted down with stones in a creek two and one-half miles from Prewitt's orchard, the locale the prosecution presented as the crime scene. The authorities required two culprits to make a plausible case because it would never be credible to any jury that one woman, acting alone, could carry two dead children, the combined weight of which would be at least 150 pounds, the enormous distance of 4,400 yards from the orchard to the creek. Further, after she had completed the tasks of stripping her victims naked and weighing their corpses down with stones in high water, she had to dispose of their clothing because it was never located. Then she had to travel 4,400 yards back to her master's residence. Though the case contains no time frame, it does state that she was at home when the father of the children came inquiring after his sons. Nowhere in the decision is there any mention of a wheelbarrow, wagon, or other conveyance she might have used for her many labors in connection with this strenuous crime. Neither is there any mention of drag marks on either the children's bodies or the ground en route to the creek from the orchard. One would expect both if two people were transporting one dead child each.

Besides the absence of a murder weapon, the summary includes no explanation of the children's missing clothing. It mentions that the boys left home without hats, and since it was September 1, they were probably also shoeless. However, with more than 100 men searching for them over a period of three days, one or more should have found a bloodstained shirt, a pair of trousers, or some underclothing of the young victims. Since the examining physician, Dr. McClure, testified that the cause of the children's death was the crushing of their skulls, one would expect that the alleged perpetrators, Fanny and her son Ellick, accidentally smeared their own clothing with the children's blood in the process of delivering these mortal blows. No clothing of either Fanny or Ellick was introduced into evidence.

The children's murders seem best explained as the act of a stranger. The case mentions that the bodies were found 100 yards from the Jefferson Road, which probably was a public highway that led from Lincoln County to the state capitol in Jefferson City. The opinion does not indicate whether the boys were sexually violated. Dr. McClure concluded that their mortal injuries were consistent with "a weapon having a smooth surface as the skin was not broken; a rough surface would have cut the skin." This manner of death could not be produced by a club. Rather, a stone, loosely contained in a rag or a piece of leather, which the perpetrator used as a blackjack and afterward carried away with him, could account for the children's injuries and the absence of any murder weapon. Equally important, a man who lured inquisitive, unsuspecting, and adventuresome children into a perilous situation, murdered them, pocketed his weapon, and kept their clothing as trophies makes more sense than a slave woman perpetrator of such a vicious and motiveless crime. The killer was white because black men on public roads were routinely stopped and questioned. He could efficiently hide bodies in water 100 yards off a road, and once he had weighed down his victims, he could make his getaway with his weapon on his person and their clothing, either in his saddlebags as he departed on horseback or covered in his wagon as he drove off. He could do so unnoticed because unsuspected. Besides, he had three days of lead time before anyone found his victims.

Of the 28 cases listed in appendix 2 that involve slave females as perpetrators, only Fanny's supposed victims were a neighbor's children. In the other 27, wherein slave females allegedly committed violent crimes, the harmed persons were members of the slave's household, either her master, her mistress, her lessee, their children, or the slave woman's own children. As far as we know, none of these other victims were found completely naked. Likewise, there was not between the killing field and the place of the body's discovery a distance of 44 end-to-end football fields for the perpetrator to carry her freshly killed victims.

The Missouri Supreme Court did not speculate about the true killer. Appeals courts are not in the business of making findings of innocence. Instead, this court reversed Fanny's case because the prisoner did not petition for a change of venue; her owner did, and that was improper. In addition to this minor point, the reviewing court decided that the trial court in Warren County should have granted a new trial. It remanded her case to the Lincoln County Circuit Court with the expressed provision that on her retrial her son's confession was inadmissible and could not be used against her.[23] According to the county history, on her retrial, Fanny was acquitted. However, it noted of her second trial that "the people were indignant that the technicalities of law should defeat justice."[24] This was and is a typical reaction of some members of any community in which a wrongful conviction is eventually righted.

Because no newspapers survive from either Lincoln or Warren County from this early period and the Lincoln County history is not specific about Ellick's trial, whether he was tried with his mother is not clear. The Supreme Court of Missouri's decision in her case identified her son as a witness, not as a co-defendant. A St. Louis newspaper reprinted a story from the newspaper at Edward Bates's then residence, the *St. Charles Clarion*:

> In Warren Circuit Court, the case of the State against Fanny and Ellick, Slaves of Mr. C. Prewitt, indicted for the murder of Thomas and William Florence, were remanded to Lincoln Circuit Court, in consequence of a decision of the Supreme Court, that the venue had originally been illegally changed from Lincoln to Warren County. Both causes will be tried in Lincoln County.[25]

Perhaps Ellick had not yet been tried in Warren County when the appellate court reversed his mother's death sentence. Once she was retried and acquitted in Lincoln County, most likely the prosecutor dropped the charges against her son. It did so because it could not use his confession against him, and it had no other evidence to connect him with the murder of the Florence children.

After it reversed Fanny's death sentence in 1839, the Supreme Court of Missouri issued no other decision in any slave capital case. At least 17 bondpersons' deaths on county gallows in Missouri took place after this court reviewed Fanny's case. Because an appellate record exists in only four death penalty cases involving slave defendants, proofs of the legal hanging of most, insofar as authenticating documents can be located, are found in circuit court records, contemporary newspapers, and county histories.

Three other women between 1843 and 1855 almost certainly died on a public scaffold — one in Boone County and two in Callaway, counties adjacent to each other, south of the Missouri River in central Missouri. Today Boone County is best known as the home of the University of Missouri–Columbia, the oldest state university west of the Mississippi River and the oldest in the Louisiana Purchase. Missouri's Tenth General Assembly created it in 1839, and its first president took office in 1841.[26] This institution was already in existence when some of the slave criminal cases, including the one discussed in this chapter, took place.

On March 20, 1843, in Boone County, five bondpersons, three men and two women, took their owner, Hiram Beasley, by surprise and murdered him with an ax about sunset in a clearing three-quarters of a mile from home. By the next day all five were arrested, confessed their guilt before a justice of the peace, and were committed for further trial.[27] One of the women, Mary, was not publicly punished. One newspaper account stated that the grand jury discharged her, that is, it did not indict her; the county history mentioned that she was tried and acquitted. All accounts indicate that she participated in the murder of Beasley. According to one of her co-arrestees, Mary took up the ax and struck her master two licks in the head and afterward threw keys into a fire, presumably some piece of evidence connected with the crime. The full reasons that the system spared this woman are unknown. However, throughout slavery during statehood years, in no capital case were more than two slaves hanged for the same crime. Neither the U.S. government nor the state of Missouri paid slaveholders when their slaves were executed. In contrast, the Spanish compensated owners when their slaves were capitally punished. The 1795 hanging of at least 23 slaves for the Pointe Coupée, Louisiana, abortive sedition conspiracy was surely, in part, the consequence of reimbursing slave owners. Mary's light treatment reflected the absence of such cozy financial arrangements in Missouri once Spanish colonial rule ended there. Although the four other slaves were penalized, two of them, David and Simon, two males, were found guilty of second-degree murder and sentenced to 39 lashes and transportation out of state for 20 years.

The full rigor of the law in Hiram Beasley's homicide fell on a husband and wife, Henry and America. A news story stated that a female slave, presumably America, delivered the first stroke of the ax. By May 8 they had been arraigned, tried, found guilty of first-degree murder, and sentenced to hang. According to the newspaper, "Henry & America, husband and wife, were condemned to death without a word of defence." This news story dwelt on her demeanor:

> The woman, America, came forward to receive the sentence of death, with a careless smile on her countenance, and seemed as regardless of that solemn and impressing scene, as if she were passing the rounds of ordinary employment.... [She] cast a malignant and contemptuous scowl upon the crowd around....This is the woman, whom most of the accomplices charge with striking the first blow which felled her master; ... truly she appears a fit subject for the bloodiest deed.[28]

This story concluded that June 20, 1843, was the day set for her and her husband's hanging, and on that date they were publicly executed in Columbia, Boone's county seat, about 2:00 P.M., in the presence of nearly 2,000 spectators.[29]

According to the county history, after America's body was taken down from the scaffold, a dispute arose among the physicians regarding whether or not she was pregnant. Several of them examined her prior to her execution; one, Dr. William B. Lenoir, made a postmortem examination and determined "that she was pretty far gone in pregnancy."[30] Centuries of English law prohibited the execution of pregnant women.[31] Likewise, Missouri law required, whenever the sheriff suspected pregnancy in a condemned prisoner, that he summon a jury of six persons, three of whom were physicians. If the panel determined that she was with child, the sheriff suspended the execution and transmitted the necessary paperwork to the governor, who in turn either set a new execution date or commuted her punishment to life imprisonment.[32] With a condemned and pregnant slave, imprisonment was never an option. No account of America's motivation for killing her owner survives. Her husband, Henry, gave a confession that is discussed in chapter 11. However, it did not assign a reason for America's participation in Beasley's murder. This much is certain. In the county's haste to punish her it hanged a pregnant woman. When Callaway County's jail housed a pregnant death-sentenced slave, she had her baby before she was hanged.

Today, Fulton, the county seat of Callaway County, is best known as the place where Winston Churchill gave his famous Iron Curtain speech in 1946 at Westminster College regarding the expansionist aims of the Soviet Union. In 1965 a twelfth-century church, rebuilt by Christopher Wren in 1677 and damaged by bombs during World War II, was moved from London to Fulton as a Westminster College chapel and memorial to Winston Churchill. When the Berlin Wall was torn down in 1989, a portion of it was transported to Fulton and redesigned as a sculpture in 1990. In 1992, 46 years after Churchill's speech, the Russian leader, Mikhail Gorbachev, spoke at Westminster College. This town has a darker past.

The details that survive from its first known slave woman's death sentence are insufficient to illuminate that darkness. On a Sunday, July 7, 1844, while her mistress, Rosa Ann King, was napping, Susan struck her in the neck with an ax a mortal wound four inches in length and three in depth.[33] According to a news story, Susan confessed her guilt and stated that her only motive was a desire to return to her former owner, "the family of Mrs. King's father-in-law, and she thought by murdering her mistress she could effect her wish. This murder has created great excitement among the citizens of Callaway, many of whom were in favor of burning the murderer alive."[34] No such conflagration took place. Instead, Susan was committed to the county jail in Fulton, where she remained before and during her trial.[35] In October 1844 the grand jury indicted her for her mistress's ax murder. On the twenty-second of that same month, her trial jury found her guilty of first-degree murder, and the judge sentenced her to be hanged by the sheriff on November 23 between the hours of noon and 2:00 P.M. and to be closely confined in the county jail until the time of her execution.[36] She was not executed on that date, however; a jail fee showed that she was boarded from July 8 to November 30, 1844, or 145 days at 25 cents per day.[37] There the records pertaining to her break off. No mention of her is made in the Callaway County history, and no extant newspaper confirms her execution. The odds favor that she, like other slaves who murdered their owners, died on a public scaffold. However, two later death-sentenced slave inmates escaped from the Callaway County jail in Fulton, and one of them was never recaptured. There is a remote possibility that Susan was an earlier successful escapee.

The remaining known death penalty case involving a slave woman also arose in Callaway County. It is the subject of a book-length study and a case of special infamy. It concerns Celia, a slave girl whom Robert Newsom, then a widower aged more than 60 years, purchased at an auction in Audrain County, when she was 13 or 14 years old. His reason for buying her was sexual. We know from the 1850 Slave Schedule that he acquired her some time after August 1, 1850, because the census taker enumerated Newsom's slaves on that day; then he owned only males, five of them. However, sometime after this date this elderly slaveholder purchased Celia; perhaps he raped her on their journey back to Callaway County the same day he bought her. Court records suggest that this occurred. Thus began his lengthy sexual relationship with his slave girl, who was at least 50 years younger than her master.

How many other slave owners conducted similar liaisons with their bondgirls and bondwomen is anyone's guess. A county history mentioned another slave woman's unconsented sexual relationship with her master; it is discussed in the next chapter. Some "For Sale" and "Wanted" newspaper ads from territorial days suggest lecherous placers of them. For example, "For Sale, a Negro girl about 15 years old, strong and healthy, free from vice"; or "For Exchange. Will be exchanged on equitable terms, a Negro Woman and her infant child, for a young negress without an encumberance"; or "Wanted to hire, a coloured girl of 10 or 12 years of age."[38] Because the master-slave relationship was inherently coercive, the likelihood is great that other Missouri masters sexually exploited their slaves. However, without accompanying incidents that became matters of public record, more cannot be urged because more is not known. It is impossible that Robert Newsom was Missouri's only slaveholder or slave lessee who raped his human property, but he is the only one for whom located judicial records confirm his repulsive conduct with his young slave girl.

Did Celia have the legal right to defend herself? Blackstone stated that "English law justifies a woman killing one who attempts to ravish [rape] her."[39] Likewise, a Missouri statute of the 1850s permitted the use of deadly force to prevent rape.[40] It considered homicide justifiable "when committed by any person ... resisting any attempt to ... commit any felony upon him or her." It also specified that "Every person who shall take any woman, unlawfully against her will, with intent to compel her by force ... to be defiled" was punishable with up to five years in the penitentiary.[41] Only convicted felons were sent there; convicted misdemeanants served their lesser sentences in county jails. The question concerning Celia was whether a killing to prevent rape was justified under Missouri law when the sexual aggressor was a white man and his death-dealing victim his slave woman.

We pick up her story during the summer of 1855, when she had lived on Newsom's farm four or more years. By then she was the mother of at least two children. Court records contain her statement that her "second child" was fathered by her elderly owner. Also members of Robert Newsom's household were his 19-year-old daughter, Mary Newsom, and his 36-year-old daughter, Virginia Wainscott, who, with her three children, lived with their father. According to the older sister, Virginia, Celia had not been well enough to work since February. Complicating if not causing the young slave's ill health was yet another pregnancy. Because blood-type matching and the far more certain DNA testing are both twentieth-century methods of determining paternity, whether Robert Newsom, or George, a fellow slave who had begun spending nights with her, was the father of the baby she was carrying in June 1855 cannot be known.

Trial testimony clarifies that she had earlier asked for help from other white members of the household in avoiding sexual encounters with her owner. She got none. On a Saturday evening, June 23, during a weekend when various relations were visiting him, Celia asked her master to stay away from her cabin and warned him that if he tried to force her, she would hurt him. Nonetheless this septuagenarian arrived at Celia's cabin after 10:00 P.M. The next morning, a Sunday, June 24, his daughters, grandsons, and various visiting relatives eventually noticed that he was missing. Neighbors, including William F. Powell, were summoned to search for him, and one of the first persons they interrogated was George. This slave, now Celia's lover, was refusing to have anything more to do with her unless she "quit the old man." When he was questioned about his missing master, he denied any involvement in his disappearance and suggested that Celia's cabin be looked to for some trace of their owner. When William Powell first examined Celia, she denied any knowledge of Newsom's whereabouts; soon he told her she would have her children taken away from her; further he had a rope "provided for her if she did not tell." Under these circumstances she admitted that she killed Robert Newsom the previous night.

Her confession never varied. She struck her owner with a board to avoid unwelcome and unwanted sexual intercourse, and she did so after she asked him to leave, and he refused. She struck him a second time because she feared that his hand would catch her. Once she ascertained that he was dead, her next thought was disposing of the body. She was afraid that if her role in his death became known to his family, she would be hanged. She spent what remained of Saturday evening, June 23, and most of the predawn hours of June 24 burning his corpse in a fireplace in her cabin. She enlisted the help of 11-year-old James Coffee Wainscott,

Robert Newsom's grandson, to carry out the old man's ashes in the belief that they were "ordinary wood ashes." Newsom's remains were spread on the right-hand side of the path between Celia's cabin and the stable. Not surprisingly, her fire was insufficient to consume all 206 of his bones, and once she confessed her role in his death, several of her interrogators and searchers found various pieces of what was almost certainly his skeletal remains. These prosecution witnesses testified at the inquest regarding Newsom's death held on Monday, June 25. Later these same pieces of what were probably the old man's bones were introduced into evidence at her trial.

Because the Fulton newspaper from this period is not extant, out-of-town papers must be relied on for press coverage of Newsom's sensational death. One incorrectly placed the crime scene in the old man's kitchen. A cook room was a respectable place for an "old citizen, ... active and energetic in his business, ... possess[ing] a valuable farm ... and a very handsome estate" to die and be "entirely consumed by fire in the kitchen fireplace."[42] In this story, Celia's age is given as 22 or 23 years of age. She was "about nineteen years old" when she was put on trial on charges of first-degree murder in October 1855.

Some time before her trial began, probably after the grand jury indicted her for first-degree murder in August, her judge, William A. Hall, appointed three attorneys as members of her defense team. Slave Mary's trial judge had also appointed the same number for the defense in her capital case. Those assigned in Celia's were an experienced trial attorney, John Jameson, and two younger lawyers to assist him, 22-year-old Nathan Chapman Kouns and 26-year-old Isaac M. Boulware. Kouns was the son of Dr. Nathan Kouns, Fulton's most esteemed physician, and Boulware's father was Theodorick Boulware, a respected minister who founded Fulton's first Baptist church.[43]

By far the most important member of Celia's defense team was John Jameson. He had earlier represented Callaway County for three terms in the Missouri House of Representatives, 1830–36, and during the latter two, 1834 and 1836, he served as Speaker of the House. In 1835 the Missouri General Assembly passed its most significant antebellum revision of the criminal code. One assumes that Jameson, as speaker, was an influential voice in the passage of this major legislation. Among much else, the 1835 law established two degrees of murder, and only first degree, or a premeditated killing, carried a death sentence.

Jameson also served three nonconsecutive terms in the United States House of Representatives. He was first elected to the Twenty-sixth Congress following the death of another Missouri member and served from

December 1839 to March 1841; elected to the Twenty-eighth Congress (1843–45); and elected to the Thirtieth Congress (1847–49). During the intervening years and in 1848, he chose not to stand for renomination to Congress.[44] Instead, he practiced law in Fulton, beginning in 1826 when he was 24 years old, and continuing intermittently until his death at age 56 in 1857. Sometime after 1849, when he completed his last term as U.S. representative, he became an ordained minister in the Christian Church.

He and his wife had four children, three daughters and one son. The 1850 Slave Schedule listed him as owning four slaves, a 48-year-old male, a 36-year-old female, a 22-year-old male, and a 16-year-old female. Assuming that Jameson continued to own the same bondpersons in 1855 that he had five years earlier, there were 6 females in his 10-member household when he became Celia's lawyer. One was his wife, three were his daughters, and two others were slaves, one in her early forties and the other about 21 years, or a young woman slightly older than Celia. For whatever private or public reasons, as court records make clear, his representation of his client was not perfunctory; it was zealous.

His task of defending Celia was not easy. The trial of any slave accused of killing his or her master who confessed to the deed, as Celia had, had a foregone conclusion. Such a confessing bondperson was charged with murder, or after 1835, first-degree murder; the jury found him or her guilty; the judge sentenced the convicted slave to death, and the sheriff executed the death warrant in the county of the conviction of the crime, usually the county in which the crime occurred. The only exception to the first-degree murder rule took place, as in Hiram Beasley's death, when the hanging of all the perpetrators, five in his ax murder, would deplete assets of the deceased's estate. Then the prosecution settled for an acquittal and two second-degree murder convictions, and the owner-victim's estate reaped the rewards of the sale of the slaves who were not put to death, perhaps between $1,000 and $1,500, or $15,000 to $23,000 today.

Because Celia acted alone, the multiple–defendant rule did not apply in her case. Further, her attorneys were not yet appointed, let alone present, when she gave her confession. It and the accompanying inquest regarding her master's death were all vital parts of the dress rehearsal for her trial, at which there could be only one outcome. She was charged with killing him by burning him to death, that is by "casting, throwing, pushing and holding of him, the said Robert Newsom in the fire." Her confession stated that she put a dead body in the fire.[45] The variance between the facts and the charge was tolerated because she was a slave and her victim was her white master. By definition such a killing was willful, deliberate, premeditated, and of the slayer's malice aforethought, or first-degree murder. A finding of guilty carried an automatic death sentence unless the Supreme Court of Missouri reversed the conviction or the governor pardoned the condemned. The governor did not pardon Celia.

The jury heard the evidence on Monday and Tuesday, October 8 and 9, and it returned its verdict on Wednesday, the tenth. Regrettably, there is no precise record of her trial; for example, we do not know what either the prosecution or the defense said in opening or closing arguments. However, the order of the prosecution's most important witnesses and a summary of their testimony are available.

Its first witness was Jefferson Jones, a lawyer who studied under John Jameson, married his mentor's niece, and was subsequently elected to represent Callaway County in the Missouri General Assembly in 1856 and again in 1874.[46] Jones told that jury that he visited Celia 8 to 10 days after she was incarcerated in the Callaway County jail and did so at the request of several citizens. He asked her if she had had any accomplices in the crime. She denied that she had anyone else's help. She acknowledged she thought that she would be hanged, and when admonished by her visitor to tell the whole truth, she stated that the old man "had been having sexual intercourse with her." She specifically denied that Slave George had any role in Newsom's death. The prosecutor used Jones to quell any rumors that one or more other slaves helped her kill her master; Celia incriminated no one but herself.

The prosecutor's next three witnesses were Newsom's adult son, Harvey Newsom; his older daughter, Virginia Wainscott; and his grandson, Coffee Wainscott. They were used to prove the corpus delicti or body of the crime. The independent proof of death as a result of criminal agency was and is necessary before a confession to any homicide can be admitted into evidence. Usually, a dead body with visible marks of violence on it is the best evidence that a homicide was committed. In this case there was no body. However, and as in other cases lacking such criminal evidence, the prosecutor proved that the deceased disappeared under suspicious circumstances and a homicide as opposed to a natural death explained the victim's disappearance. This crucial proof was put on through the dramatic testimony of the victim's family members. The prosecutor also established the chain of custody of the physical evidence in the case, pieces of Robert Newsom's bones.

Harvey Newsom testified to his father's absence on Sunday, June 24. He told the jury that he

> examined [Celia's] cabin in and about, & in the yard. Some bones
> were found a short distance from the cabin along a path in some

ashes.... The company picked bones out of the ashes, about a handful, and placed them in my hands.... I wrapped them in paper &
put them into a box.... This is the box. I left them with Mr. Bart-
ley, the circuit court clerk. Since August the county clerk has had
them. My sister put the bones she found in the same box. These
are some of the pieces I put into the box.

The first handling of the dead man's remains and the exhibition of them
came from his son picking bones out of a box and showing them to those
assembled in the courtroom and to the jury. The state's next witness was
Virginia Wainscott. She testified that she was the daughter of the deceased,
lived with him, and last saw her father the evening of June 23, a Saturday,
at bedtime. She hunted for him the next day

> in all the paths & walks, every place ... looked in caves & along
> creeks ... found no trace of him. That evening, I learned where
> the bones were put. I found bones under the hearth in [Celia's]
> cabin. I found a gallous [suspender] buckle in the ashes ... found
> the bones in the house where Celia lived.... I gave them to my
> brother after the inquest.... These are the bones, and these are the
> buttons my sister sewed on my father's breeches.

The victim's daughter then exhibited pieces of what the state contended
were her father's bones and minute pieces of his clothing. The prosecutor's third and final witness-relative of the deceased was his 11-year-old
grandson, Coffee Wainscott. He testified that he assisted Celia in removing and scattering ashes from her cabin. When she offered him two dozen
walnuts in exchange for his help, he said "good lick. I put them out along
side of the path.... I saw people picking up bones. I got the ashes out of
the house she [Celia] lived in."

Once Newsom's Saturday evening disappearance was established and
his purported collected remains gotten into evidence, the prosecutor introduced Celia's confession through Newsom's neighbor, William Powell, the
man who initially interrogated and obtained her admission that she killed
her master. The summary of Powell's testimony reiterated that Celia's
killing of Newsom was not premeditated:

> She said she had made threats. Said she threatened him that she
> would hurt him on condition that he would not let her alone.
> Threatened to hurt him, not to kill him.... She said she threatened
> that she would hurt him if he did not quit forcing her while she
> was sick.... She said she did not intend to kill him.

The state put on two additional witnesses, Dr. Smith and Dr. Young;

both were experts, of sorts. Dr. Smith testified that the bones "appear to be the bones of an adult human. I suppose they are bones of an adult beyond a doubt." The words *appear to be* are crossed out and in their place *are* is written; *I suppose* is also struck. Dr. Young also testified, "I can speak with certainty & say these are human bones." Prior to a more precise analysis of remains, which DNA afforded, in similar cases during the twentieth century, a forensic anthropologist not only generally testified that bones were human, but he or she also identified them by sex, race, and age.[47] The prosecutor had no such expertise available; he put on the most knowledgeable persons about the human skeleton then available, physicians.

The defense presentation of evidence was brief. The judge disallowed the answer another physician, Dr. James W. Martin, would have given in answer to Celia's attorneys' questions regarding the length of time necessary to destroy or consume the body of a man in an ordinary wood fire. Its second witness was Thomas Shoatman, and he was present with Jefferson Jones at the jail when Celia told them about killing her master. Through Shoatman, the defense emphasized that Celia "said that she did not intend to kill him when she struck him, but only to hurt him.... After she struck the second blow, she examined [him] to see whether he were dead; he was dead. Waited a long time & did not know what to do.... She thought she would try to burn him." Obviously, Celia had no other means of disposing of a dead body other than to destroy it with fire.

As in most criminal proceedings, the defendant did not take the stand and testify. However, she was surely present in the courtroom throughout her trial. She may have been ill, and if she had not given birth before her trial began, she was hugely pregnant. The jury and the courtroom spectators knew that Celia believed that her master was the father of her "second child." They surely wondered as they observed her during her trial who was the father of the baby she had recently delivered or was then carrying.

Once the state and the defense rested, Judge Hall instructed the jury in writing on the facts and the law in Celia's case. The instructions he gave the jury and those he refused to give it are preserved. When present-day convictions are overturned on appeal, 80 percent to 85 percent of the reversals result from an appellate court's ruling that the jury instructions in the lower court were faulty. Perhaps the defense requested a second-degree murder or a manslaughter instruction in a killing, and the trial judge gave only the prosecutor's requested first-degree murder instruction. On appeal, if the higher court agrees with the defense, the case is reversed, and on retrial, the trial judge is required to instruct the jury as the appeals court dictates before it begins deliberations. In most homicides jurors have choices other than first-degree murder when deciding whether the accused is guilty or not guilty of the killing. Second-degree murder and some degree or another of manslaughter are other likely verdicts the jury is allowed to consider when deliberating the accused's culpability in taking a human life. Likewise, whenever the jury returns with a guilty verdict and a death sentence, there is an automatic appeal to the Supreme Court of Missouri.

This is now; Celia's case was then. The refused instructions, at least 9 of the 13 offered by the defense, all concern her right to use force "to protect herself against forced sexual intercourse." The jury never received this instruction: "An attempt to compel a woman to be defiled by using force, menace, or duress is a felony within the meaning of the [law]." Likewise refused was this defense-proffered instruction: "The words *any woman's* [right to use deadly force to resist defilement] ... embraces slave women, as well as free white women." Judge Hall's unwillingness to so advise Celia's jury meant that his interpretation of "any woman" excluded slave women when their rapists were their owners. As a result, her jury was never allowed to consider whether she was guilty of a lesser degree of homicide, such as second-degree murder or some form of manslaughter, or not guilty because she had the right to use deadly force to resist rape. Her attorneys strove mightily to put before the jury that decided her fate the law that applied to any free woman's right to act as Celia had under her circumstances. Her jurors never received that law. As a result, they found her guilty of the only crime they were allowed to deliberate, first-degree murder.

On October 11, shortly after her trial concluded, her lawyers requested that the judge set aside the jury's verdict and grant their client a new trial: "Because the court refused to allow each, all, and every of the instructions as prayed for by the defendant" and "Because the verdict of the jury is against the weight of the evidence, and contrary to the law and evidence." Most motions for a new trial before the judge who presided at the one recently concluded do not succeed. Celia's attorneys who joined in filing a motion to set aside the verdict of her jury, Jameson, Kouns, and Boulware, were expectedly unsuccessful.

On October 13 Judge Hall sentenced Celia to be hanged by the neck until dead on November 16, 1855. A bill from a physician appears in the court costs that were allowed in this case. It was for Dr. Cotten's visits to Celia in the county jail. He saw "the prisoner" because of "sickness" and because he delivered her "dead child." His services are undated, and as a result, we do not know precisely when Celia's pregnancy began, its length, or when it ended. She may have given birth almost any time after she was jailed on June 25. Perhaps she had her baby after October 13 but before

November 16. During this same period, her attorneys appealed her case to the Supreme Court of Missouri, and it accepted her appeal. However, it issued no order staying her execution until her case could be heard at its next scheduled session in January 1856 in Jefferson City. Automatically, the execution of the defendant cancels any decision an appeals court might issue; its decision is mooted by death.

In the midst of all this legal maneuvering, Celia and her cellmate, death-sentenced Slave Mat, whose case is discussed in chapter 12, escaped from jail on Sunday, November 11. Whether their attorneys played any part in their getaway cannot be confirmed; probably at least one gave them extralegal assistance. Precisely how long Celia was at liberty is also not known, but the time of her freedom included her date with death on November 16, a Friday. A news story confirms that by November 25, a Sunday, Harvey Newsom, her master's son, had returned her to the jail in Fulton. She had gone to his home to see her children, now assets of Robert Newsom's estate, and probably, in the case of one of them, a half-brother or sister of her dead owner's adult children. The 1860 Slave Schedule listed Harvey Newsom as owning only two slaves, a 37-year-old mulatto male and a 9-year-old black girl. The latter's age and color are consistent with her being Celia's first child by a Negro as opposed to her "second child" by Robert Newsom. If indeed the unnamed girl was Celia's daughter, she was about four years old when her mother endured great hardship to see her for the last time. As the newspaper wrote of Celia's escape from jail, "She lived on raw corn which she gathered from the fields.... Being thinly clad and without shoes and the nights very cool, she must have suffered considerably during the time of her absence."[48]

Soon after her return to custody, Judge Hall set a new execution date for her of Friday, December 21.[49] On December 14, one week before her scheduled hanging, the Missouri Supreme Court refused to stay her execution. In its order the court noted that it had examined the record and proceedings in her case, and "it is thought proper to refuse the prayer of the petitioner; there being seen upon inspection of the record aforesaid no probable cause for such appeal."[50] Accordingly, one week later and at 2:30 P.M. on Friday, December 21, 1855, the sheriff of Callaway County hanged Celia by the neck until she was dead. The *Fulton Telegraph* ended its January 4, 1856, coverage of her hanging: "Thus has closed one of the most horrible tragedies ever enacted in our county." Though this paper has not survived, its story about Celia was reprinted by at least two out-of-state newspapers, the *New York Times* and the *Baltimore Sun*.[51] The *History of Callaway County, Missouri*, published in 1884, or less than 30 years after Celia's crime and punishment, makes no mention of either her case or of

Mat's, her cellmate. One assumes that at least one-third of the county's population, old enough to remember her ordeal, was still alive when its county history was written. Because many court records in her case survive and several out-of-county and out-of-state newspapers carried her story, we know what happened to her outside and inside the courtroom. Her life and death are among slavocracy's most haunting. Justice failed her and not because she was represented by inadequate defense attorneys. Insofar as any Missouri lawyers legally saved any known slave client from the county gallows, they did so either because the slave had accomplices or the highest court in the territory and/or the state accepted the slave's appeal and reversed the conviction. Missouri's Supreme Court issued its most recent decision in a slave death penalty case in 1839, or when Celia was approximately three years old.

The known annals of slave girls and women being put to death in Missouri may appear relatively benign. Four can be confirmed and only two others seem probable. This may seem a slender record of hanged slave girls and women, but since slavery perished, not one African American girl or woman has been executed in this state as of this writing. Without slavery these girls and women have no owners, and they never commit crimes against them, their wives, or their children.

The next two chapters concern Missouri's death penalty for slave boys and men. There are many more cases, some briefly discussed and some at length. The capital cases involving male slaves are more various than those of the girls and women.

Chapter 11

Capital Crimes by Coerced Boys and Men

The record of male slaves put to death in Missouri is large compared to that of condemned female slaves, but when we examine slavocracy's big capital punishment picture, this state's death penalty for bondpersons makes up a small portion of the total canvas. From the start of American rule here, the absence of any statutes compensating owners for executed slaves moderated the capital punishment of bondpersons. According to Espy's research, eight states executed in excess of 50 slaves between 1800 and 1860, and all reimbursed their owners. They were Alabama, Georgia, Kentucky, Louisiana, Mississippi, North Carolina, South Carolina, and Virginia. The Commonwealth of Virginia was in a substantial lead when it came to the colonies', and later the states', killing of enslaved persons. With an early-seventeenth-century settlement and importation of slaves, 73 different capital offenses for them, and almost six times more persons in bondage in Virginia than in Missouri, this eastern seaboard state was the premier place of slave capital punishment. According to the early-twentieth-century research of Phillips, Virginia put to death at least 800 slaves in the seventeenth and eighteenth centuries and more than 500 between 1800 and 1860.[1] In Espy's more recent and detailed investigation of Virginia's executed bondpersons, he counts at least 1,500.[2] Schwarz lists 236 slaves in Virginia hanged or transported for the crimes of conspiracy and insurrection between 1785 and 1831.[3] As far as we know, only Slave Elijah was tried for conspiracy when he put arsenic in his mistress's sausage in St. Louis in 1818, and thanks to the skill and dedication of his lead lawyer, David Barton, the Superior Court reversed his conviction, and the circuit attorney elected not to retry him. As for insurrection or rebellion, there are no known Missouri cases. All in all, compared with other jurisdictions, wherein the owners were compensated when the state put to death their human property, Missouri was a minor league player. Appendix 4 lists the 37 known male bondpersons chargeable or charged with capital murder under the authority of the state of Missouri and one unnamed slave whom a Union army firing squad shot to death for attempted murder and attempted rape. In all but two cases at least one victim was white, and in one of these exceptions the slain Negro was an overseer. As chapter 7 clarified, in most cases wherein slaves killed other slaves or free blacks, there is no record of a death sentence. Murdered blacks were usually not considered of sufficient worth to end their killers' lives on a county gallows.

It was otherwise when the deceased victim was white. The most frequent slave killing that resulted in a death sentence was the perpetrator's murder of his master. Some account survives, much of it brief, of 12 cases wherein a slave was executed for killing his owner. The records indicate that he often acted alone, and usually he did so in an interior county within the state. Though some records were probably lost, excluding two masters' deaths at the hands of slaves, one in Lincoln County, which resulted in a lynching, and another in Pike, there are no other known slave cases of an owner's murder in Missouri's easternmost counties, which the Mississippi River separated from Illinois. Similarly, there are no known slave murders of their masters in this state's 12 westernmost counties. To the north, the Missouri River divided Missouri from Nebraska Territory; next, this river separated this state from Kansas Territory, and when this watercourse flowed east and ceased to form the natural boundary between them, a straight-line border laid out as early as 1820 separated Missouri from Kansas.

In 1856, and on a county-by-county basis, the state of Missouri census enumerated slaves and whites. On average, 10 percent of the population of the counties that bordered places of freedom were bondpersons, or 32,223 slaves and 312,385 whites. One should not conclude that the blacks of these many locales were good slaves who harbored no ill will toward their equally good masters. It is impossible that only easygoing bondpersons lived in counties adjacent to Missouri's free borders or that missing records account for the absence of known slaves murdering their owners in all but two of these border counties. The areas of Missouri adjacent to Iowa Territory and, after 1846, the state of Iowa are not included. They contained only trace percentages of slaves, few or no criminal cases involving bondpersons, and the route to freedom from this state was not due north to Iowa. After 1854 the slave runaway in western Missouri went west to eastern Kansas, north in Kansas to Nebraska Territory, and then east through Iowa to places of freedom such as Ohio, Michigan, Canada, New York, and Massachusetts.

The alternative to violence, which the opportunity to leave their masters afforded, best explains slaves not killing them in this state's counties adjacent to Illinois, Nebraska, and Kansas. Most likely, by 1856 the average slave population of these counties was as small as 10 percent because thousands were successful runaways. Surely the prospect of freedom provided a safety valve for the slave's rage, which would otherwise have manifested itself in many more owners dead at the hands of their bondsmen.

Excluding the Lincoln and Pike County cases, all slaves that we know about who killed their masters did so in the middle of the state. In Boone, Callaway, Cooper, Franklin, Howard, Moniteau, Montgomery, Randolph, and Warren Counties, at least one slave killed his owner. All but one of these, Randolph, bordered the Missouri River. Unlike Missouri's locales that were close to places of freedom, the areas in which owners died at the hands of their slaves had a high percentage of their population in bondage. Excluding Cooper County, for which no slave figures were included in the 1856 state census, the other eight averaged an enslaved population of 29 percent, or 29,354 slaves and 71,386 whites.[4] To be sure, large numbers of bondpersons were transported to these hinterland counties, where rich soils provided plentiful agricultural opportunities for their owners. However, many men, women, and children remained in bondage in central Missouri because running away from the middle of the state was a hard journey in a way that leaving from its eastern, northwestern, and western borders was not.

Contemporary newspapers and county histories tell the stories of seven slaves who were either charged as the sole slayers of their owners or acted alone when they killed their masters. The first one arose in Franklin County during the territorial period. Because it had not yet built its own jail when Slave Frank, aged approximately 18 years, killed his master, John Hyde, in 1819, Frank was held in the St. Louis jail on murder charges. He escaped from this facility, and there is no record of his recapture.[5] Slave Luke stabbed and killed his owner, Hezekiah Harris, to avoid a whipping, and he was tried, convicted, and hanged in Cooper County in 1826.[6]

More details are known about Slave Moses who shot and killed his owner, John Tanner, in Montgomery County in 1828. According to the county history, Moses did so after Tanner "acted disgracefully towards

Moses' wife, who was herself a slave, and ... told her husband of the fact."
As with Celia, had the wronged husband been white, at worst his crime
would have been manslaughter and probably, if even tried, he would have
been acquitted. However, he was a slave, and as the county history noted,
despite general sympathy, "there were a few who thought he richly deserved
death, because a slave, they held, ought not to have sympathies, affections,
or sensibilities, which could not be interfered with by his master in any
way, and to any extent." Obviously, those few swayed the other jurors, and
they unanimously convicted him of murder. When Moses' corpse was
taken down from the gallows in Lewiston (a village that no longer exists),
it was given to Dr. John Jones of Marthasville, then in Montgomery
County, now a town in Warren County. This physician, a graduate of
Transylvania Medical School in Lexington, Kentucky, dissected the hanged
slave's cadaver for the benefit of his students.[7]

In Boone County, about 1835, Slave Archie was charged with the murder of his master, a wealthy unnamed bachelor, notorious for cruelty to
his slaves. The circuit court judge, David Todd, appointed Sinclair Kirtley, one of the county's best lawyers, to represent the accused. Kirtley served
three terms as a representative in the General Assembly, 1828, 1834, and
1844; the 1834–35 years he served with John Jameson, Celia's lawyer. In
1840 Kirtley was elected to one term as a state senator. He argued for
Archie's acquittal by citing the dangers of a conviction based solely on circumstantial evidence. He was sufficiently skilled in his defense of his slave
client that threats were made on his life. After Archie was convicted and
executed, belief lingered that he was innocent and that other slaves of this
cruel master had murdered him.[8]

An undated account from Warren County concerns a wounded master who took the law into his own hands. When one of Mr. Bevins's slaves
deliberately shot him and the master's neighbors captured the culprit, the
dying victim persuaded one of the slave's captors, Mr. Kountze, to take
the killer to New Orleans. There he sold him for $1,000 and gave the money
to the murdered master's family. The sold slave was never indicted, and
Mr. Bevins was buried before any law enforcement officers knew a crime
had occurred.[9] Owner compensation was possible in this case because there
was no execution.

Another slave murdered his master in Pike County in 1841. His case
resembles Slave Susan's murder of her mistress, Rosa Ann King, in Callaway
County in 1844. Her motive was the hope that she might return to the family of Mrs. King's father-in-law. Similarly, on April 28, 1841, Slave Lewis killed
his owner, Resin MacKay, aged 19 years and a husband of several weeks. After
the bondman clubbed his young master to death in a field as they worked,

he ran to his mistress with a blood-stained knife in his hand and told her that someone had killed her husband; Lewis confessed the next day.

It appears likely that both Susan and Lewis were deadly wedding gifts, that their lives were uneventful until they were suddenly and without their permission transplanted from one home to another. One newspaper related of Resin MacKay that he "got the negro by his wife [from Marion County]. The negro being unwilling to live in that part of the country conceived the idea that if he killed his master, his mistress would return to her father's, and thus he would be enabled to live where he desired." As in Susan's case, the proposition to lynch Lewis by burning him to death lost by a few votes.[10] The slave was committed to the Pike County jail in Bowling Green on first-degree murder charges. His trial took place in late June–early July and lasted two days; he was convicted and sentenced to die on August 7, 1841.[11] His gallows death in the courtyard on the appointed date, a Saturday, drew a crowd estimated at 3,000 spectators, many of whom were slaves. The local newspaper reported that Lewis's "death struggles were by no means violent, though it was at least thirty minutes after the rope was severed before life was entirely extinct. He died as if he had lived destitute of feeling and hardened by crime."[12] Almost by definition, any slave who killed his owner was a depraved criminal.

The last known case of a slave who acted alone in the murder of his master arose in Moniteau County on July 9, 1863, when, to avoid a whipping, Henry shot and killed his owner, 63-year-old Alfred N. Norman. He was tried for his crime on July 27, found guilty, and hanged August 28, 1863. A contemporary newspaper gave Henry's age as "about 16 years."[13] The 1860 Slave Schedule listed Alfred N. Norman as owning 10 bondpersons; one of them, a 14-year-old black male, was probably Henry. In Slave Mary's case, the Crawford County history made her two or more years older than her actual age at the time of her crime; instead of her being age 13 or 14, she became 16 years old. Though a nineteenth-century history of Moniteau County included only, "Henry, a slave, was tried for murder in July 1863 and sentenced to be hanged August 28, 1863,"[14] another county history, first published in 1936, added approximately four years to Henry's age: "In the summer or early fall of 1863, [Alfred N. Norman] was killed by a Negro boy named Henry, whom he owned — Henry was about twenty years old and was what his race then and now call 'a mean nigger.'"[15] If this ill-tempered 16-year-old was not the last slave executed in this country, he was one of the last. Nearly eight months after Lincoln freed most bondpersons,[16] Henry died on a gallows in California, Moniteau's county seat, because he murdered his wealthy master. By the date of his hanging, in most areas of American slavocracy, there were neither masters nor slaves.

Five bondmen's murders of their masters involved two or more culprits. The first of these dual slave killings of an owner took place in Cooper County in 1830. The wife and grown stepson of John Gabriel, an old man, hired two slaves to murder him because his relatives wanted his money, including a nail keg full of silver dollars. The owner of one slave, Jack, was John B. Harris, and the other, Edmund, belonged to their victim. After Jack lured John Gabriel outside on a pretense that he wished to purchase whiskey, the slaves killed him with an ax and dragged his body to his stable in the hope that it would be believed that a horse kicked him to death. The next day, and about the time Gabriel's body was discovered, Jack was seen in Boonville with a large sum of money. Almost immediately, both slaves were arrested. Edmund, who testified against Jack, was transported out of state and sold; Jack was tried and executed in 1830. Most probably, because a slave could not testify against white persons, Mrs. Gabriel and her son were not charged. They left Cooper County and moved to what is now Texas soon after Jack's trial. In this case the dead victim's estate reaped the financial benefits of the sale of Slave Edmund.[17]

Two other slaves killed the master of one of them in Howard County in 1832. One of the perpetrators, Hampton, belonged to William B. Johnson, the victim; the other was Slave Jim, and his owner, David Todd, the judge who presided at Slave Archie's trial in Columbia in 1835, also sat as a Howard County judge. Despite two Supreme Court of Missouri decisions, one civil and the other criminal, which resulted from Johnson's murder, little is known about the crime. In a case already discussed in Chapter 6, the sheriff of Howard County sued the circuit court because the $10 it paid him to execute Hampton did not cover all of his expenses. The other was the only appellate criminal decision involving a male slave charged with a capital offense in Missouri's history. Hampton and Jim were tried together in February 1832, and both were found guilty. Although Hampton was hanged March 23, 1832,[18] his co-defendant, Jim, appealed his death sentence on grounds that his requested change of venue should have been granted because his owner was the judge. The Supreme Court of Missouri agreed and reversed his conviction:

> The statute … commands the circuit court to change the venue in a criminal case when an interest, such as is shewn in this cause, is shown to exist.… The judgement passing sentence of death on [Jim] is … reversed; and the circuit court is directed to remove the cause to some county where the same objection does not exist.[19]

Jim's fate is unknown. However, Judge Todd did not lose a valuable property by having his slave executed at the same time that Sheriff Ford hanged Hampton.

Other slave partners murdered a master of one in Callaway County. The victim, Israel B. Grant, owned Jake and he was leasing the other assailant, Conway, from Francis K. Cowherd, at the time these bondmen murdered him on December 29, 1835. The deceased represented his county in the General Assembly for two terms, 1824–28, and at the time of his violent death he was a Callaway County judge. His killers lay in wait for him as he returned home from Fulton, where he had gone to collect money from the sale of livestock. They pulled him from his horse, stabbed him to death, and dragged his body into the woods, where they concealed it. Grant's body was soon discovered and the slaves' role in his death quickly known; both were speedily arrested. Conway, who obtained a change of venue, was tried in Boone County. His judge appointed Austin A. King to represent Conway. King, afterward governor of Missouri, 1848–52, was then a resident of Callaway County. Despite a capable defense lawyer, Conway was found guilty in Columbia and executed in Fulton on April 8, 1836. Jake, tried and convicted in May in Callaway County, was hanged in Fulton on June 20, 1836.[20]

The largest known number of slaves who killed their owner, those of Hiram Beasley, did so in Boone County; their crime is discussed in chapter 10. This case has in common with other murders of the master a plot conceived by two slaves, David and Henry, who ran away during the winter of 1842 to avoid being whipped.[21] In all, five slaves axed Beasley to death in Boone County in March 1843. At trial Mary was acquitted; David and Simon found guilty of second-degree murder, whipped, and sold; and Henry and America hanged on June 10, 1843, in Columbia.

The last alleged joint killing of a master took place in Randolph County, when Benjamin Bruce died at the hands of Slave George and another bondman initially believed to be his accomplice, Simon Anderson. One or both of them attacked their master with a shovel and a poker after the victim had gone to bed for the night. Bruce had only a life estate in George because this slave was to be free after his master's death. The first news story after the murder noted of the victim's relationship with George, "Mr. Bruce had for a long time anticipated a difficulty with this negro and always went to bed armed."[22] Their master was in the habit of placing a butcher knife under his pillow, and he fought his assailant(s) with it the night he died. At George's trial he was found guilty of first-degree murder on December 3, 1858, and he was put to death on January 7, 1859, in Huntsville. Its newspaper discouraged the lynching of George. It noted, "A day being fixed for ... execution will enable masters throughout the county [to] bring their slaves to witness the punishment inflicted for such crimes and produce a wholesome effect on them." Slave owners agreed, and as the paper described it, despite cold weather, George's gallows death "drew together a large crowd, a large proportion of whom were negroes."[23]

Slave Simon Anderson fared better than his co-defendant. In all he was tried three times. The first two attempts to convict him were in Randolph County's seat, Huntsville, and both appear to have resulted in hung juries. After his second trial he obtained a change of venue to Howard County. There, despite the objection of the prosecution, the defense got Slave George's deposition, made before he was hanged, into evidence. In it George was asked whether Anderson had any part in the slaying of Benjamin Bruce. George repeatedly affirmed Anderson's innocence. The third jury agreed, and Slave Simon was acquitted of any part in Bruce's murder in Howard's county seat, Fayette, in early December 1859.[24]

Records exist of 12 murders of slave owners by one or more of their bondmen. Some had accomplices, but juries believed that most acted alone. What seems probable is that other now unknown slaves murdered one or more now unknown owners, and these victims or their families acted as did Mr. Bevins of Warren County. Instead of summoning the sheriff or a constable, the killer slave(s) were taken south and sold, and the victim's family pocketed the cash value of the slave, whose buyer never knew that he was sold for the grievous fault of murdering his master. The record of male slaves acting together in a criminal enterprise is common, so common that it seems unlikely that only Hiram Beasley's slaves joined in their owner's murder. The master's almost total power over his human properties surely increased the risk of his death at their hands.

Given the authority that lessees had over the slaves they rented, one would expect that more than two leased bondmen, one of Judge Israel B. Grant's slayers in 1835 and one other in 1857, murdered their temporary masters. The extant records confirm that Slave Joe, aged approximately 18 years and owned by William Robinson, alone killed his lessee, James T. Points, in Boone County. The dispute between them concerned the number of rails Joe actually split as opposed to the greater number the slave told Points about on a Friday, September 25. When Points discovered Joe's inflated numbers on Saturday, the boss man informed his rented slave that he intended to whip him. Rather than submit to a lashing, Joe struck Points in the head with an ax several times, placed his dead body on the lessee's horse, took it one-half mile distant into the woods, and threw the body under brush to conceal it. The dead man was missed, and neighbors suspected Joe. He confessed his crime the next day and told his interrogators where he had hidden the body. Joe was indicted August 2, tried October 10, and executed November 13, 1857, in Columbia.[25] Perhaps more lessees survived the tenure of their rented human property's time with them because the slave knew that the terms of his hire were finite, usually a year. Unlike his master, he was not the lessee's slave for life, and his short-term master had no power to sell him.

Another status relationship with the slave that placed his victim at risk of murder was that of slave trader. That there were not multiple slave killers of such persons is best explained by remembering that the purchaser was heavily armed, on guard, the slaves chained, perhaps in a coffle, and their buyer often had vigilant assistants. One bondman, Green, aged either 18 or 19 years, shot and killed the man who bought him, Francis Marion Wright, in Andrew, an interior county immediately north of Buchanan, on July 11, 1859. Under current Missouri law the defendant in any criminal case has a right to a public trial in the county in which the offense is committed.[26] Under a statute then operable, however, it was unnecessary that the prosecution try the accused in the county of the crime. The state could indict the defendant in any county, and the case "shall be tried in the same manner as if it had been alleged to have occurred in the same county where such plea is tendered."[27] As a result, Green's trial did not take place where he committed his crime. Rather, he was tried in Buchanan, and its county seat, St. Joseph, was the city wherein the victim had resided and his widow, Mrs. Wright, continued to live.

The perpetrator was born in Clay County and lived most of his life in Gentry, an interior county in northwest Missouri with, according to the 1856 state of Missouri census, 69 slaves and 8,721 whites. The young slave lived uneventfully with his owner, E. C. Whitton, 10 or 12 years. Green stated of the circumstances of his crime the same week in which he was put to death, "My master and his family always treated me kindly, and they appeared to be well-satisfied with me until they heard I was advised to run off by men in our neighborhood. Negroes were scarce …, and I had frequent conversations with men living close to my master." Green's statement about his owner's motivation for selling him is suspect. Whitton may have needed or wanted the money. For whatever reason, he sold Green to a stranger, and the entire transaction was completed before the slave knew that he was no longer a member of the Whitton family. Instead, he had a new owner. The buyer attempted to win his new property's favor by giving him a dime to curry his horse. Soon, Wright handcuffed Green, but he removed these restraints after Green promised to behave. The slave surreptitiously put a loaded pistol, which he had access to, in his pocket before his purchaser drove off with him in a buggy. They made various stops en route from Green's home to their ultimate destination, St. Joseph. At Gentryville in Gentry County, Green related in his jailhouse confession, other Negroes told him "that Mr. Wright was a negro buyer and went through the country buying negroes and taking them South." Again, his explanation of how he learned Wright's profession may or may not have been accurate. Nonetheless, Green decided to kill his captor in order to make his escape from him, and in a moment of Wright's inattention he shot him at close range in the head with the pistol he brought with him, and did so near Rochester, Andrew County. Green took no money or anything else of value from Wright's body other than some papers, including his bill of sale. Since the young slave's ignorance was so profound that he could not count to 100, he probably seized all of Wright's papers because he could not distinguish a document that transferred him from his master to his victim from any other writing. In his haste to make his getaway he took the wrong road. Within a day or so after the horse attached to Wright's buggy went several hundred yards to a farm whose owner discovered the dead man in it, Green was arrested and brought to St. Joseph.[28] His first trial, at which his jury was deadlocked, probably occurred during his first three months as a Buchanan County jail resident. In October 1859 he escaped from this facility, but instead of making his way across the Missouri River to freedom in Kansas, Green attempted to return to his home in Gentry County. He was rearrested in Andrew and returned to the jail in St. Joseph.

Though there is no extant St. Joseph newspaper from the time of Wright's murder, at least two Missouri newspapers reprinted a story about the crime from the *St. Joseph Gazette* of July 13, 1859. Its headline was "A Horrible Murder," and its story began "Yesterday morning our citizens were shocked by the announcement that Mr. F. M. Wright, for ten years a prominent citizen of St. Joseph, had been murdered." It neither identified the victim as a slave trader nor included the locale of the crime. It stated only that the victim "had bought a negro, probably in Gentry county, was bringing him to this city in a buggy." Its story concluded, "A special messenger has been dispatched to St. Louis for Mrs. Wright, who is at present in that city, and until her arrival, the remains will probably be preserved." This story also mentioned that a $500 reward was offered by two men, presumably residents of Buchanan County and slaveholders.[29]

Had young Green been free, either white or black, his defense in killing Wright would have resembled Celia's. Just as free persons had a right to kill to prevent their rape, they also had a right to kill to prevent their kidnapping. In 1839 free-born Africans were captured in Africa, transported to Cuba, and after a brief time there put on a vessel, the *Amistad*. On it they killed the white captain and cook, wounded another white man, took possession of the ship, and, unable to navigate and sail it back to Africa, they drifted in the North Atlantic until members of the U.S. Navy brought them into the port of New London, Connecticut. There all 53 Africans were jailed in a celebrated case that eventually reached the United States Supreme Court. Before it, in 1841 former president and then congressman John Quincy Adams, among others, argued in behalf of the Amistads, as they were called, that these free-born Africans should not be returned to Cuba, as the Spanish government asked, there "to be put on trial for their lives to appease the public vengeance of the ... slave-traders in Cuba."[30] In 1841 the High Court upheld the right of free men to kill to prevent enslavement. It glossed over what would have been crimes had they been born slaves; for the majority Justice Story of Massachusetts wrote, "We may lament the dreadful acts, by which they asserted their liberty, and took possession of the *Amistad*, and endeavoured to regain their country, but they cannot be deemed pirates or robbers."[31] Despite requests from Spain, the American government never sent them back to Cuba. Eventually, all 53 men, women, and children returned to Africa. None of this triumph of judging persons on a basis other than race established any legal precedent applicable to Green's case. The Africans on the *Amistad* were born free, and Green's mother, herself a slave, gave birth to a slave son, not a free infant.

Though court records are not available from Green's trials, we know that at the state's first attempt to convict the young slave, his jury could not agree. However, at the second trial it returned on November 5 with a unanimous verdict of guilty on first-degree murder charges. His judge, Elijah Hise Norton, sentenced him to hang on a Friday, December 2, 1859.[32] For the appointed day the gallows was erected just below the town of St. Joseph. One local editor hoped that Green's hanging would be his town's last public execution. At 1:00 P.M. and in the presence of approximately 2,000 persons, including men, women, and children, Green mounted the county gallows. As the trap was sprung, and because the sheriff and his deputies had failed to tie his hands correctly, their prisoner was able to grasp the rope with one hand and draw himself up on the scaffold. Green's hands were retied, the trap resprung, and he was rehanged. According to one Buchanan County history, while Green was a death-sentenced prisoner in the jail in St. Joseph, and in exchange for liquor and various fancy foods, he sold his body to several physicians. After his death they went to the county cemetery north of the city to claim it.[33] Despite some sympathy among his first jurors for this young, ignorant, and illiterate slave who killed his captor, a slave trader, because he wished to return to his home in Gentry County, his second jury understood that Green's victim was not only a white man; technically, Wright was Green's master. Its unanimous vote was the same as in the case of every other slave in Missouri who was tried without any co-defendants for murdering a white.

Other persons at risk of being the homicide victims of bondmen were their overseers. Prior to 1853 none can be documented, but between this date and the winter of 1858, four died at the hands of slaves whom they supervised. Three of the perpetrators acted alone, and two together killed their straw boss. Little is known about one slave who killed his black overseer in a tobacco factory in Glasgow, Howard County, in 1857; the slave perpetrator, Jack, escaped. His crime is listed in appendix 1. Given the potential for antagonism between the man with power and the men he supervised, it seems likely that one or more bondmen killed one or more overseers in Missouri prior to 1853. Perhaps all the earlier records of such homicides were lost, or the slave(s) who murdered their overseers were quietly sold, not prosecuted. An alternate explanation for the slave's infrequent murder of the overseer is the scarcity of such victims. Since most slaveholders in Missouri owned small numbers of slaves, the typical owner had no overseer; rather, he personally supervised his bondpersons.

The records confirm that in Platte County Abe knifed Dan to death in the spring of 1853. According to the 1850 Slave Schedule, their master, Nathan Newby, owned eight slaves: three men, one woman, and four children. Assuming that he did not significantly increase his slave holdings in the next several years, this master did not need an overseer, but he apparently enjoyed designating one of his three men, Dan, the overseer of the other two, including Abe. When Newby ordered Dan to whip Abe, rather than submit to a lashing, Abe attacked his black overseer with a knife. The wound proved mortal; Abe was tried for first-degree murder, found guilty, and hanged on June 24, 1853, from the limb of a tree near Platte City in the presence of an immense crowd of spectators.[34]

Two other overseers died at the hands of slaves in Lafayette County, one in 1856 and the other in 1858. This county bordered the Missouri River and, according to the 1856 state census, had 6,107 slaves and 10,958 whites. As such, Lafayette had more persons in bondage than any other Missouri county at this time; only in Howard County was a greater percentage of the population slave, 60 percent as opposed to Lafayette's 56 percent. The first of these headmen's deaths occurred on December 18, 1855, when Henry, owned by John Yaeger, struck the overseer, John Winslow, on the side of the head with a heavy object.[35] What the victim might have done to provoke the slave's murderous rage is not known.

Henry was tried and found guilty of first-degree murder in the spring of 1856, and the sheriff put him to death in Lexington on July 11, 1856. Unlike the enthusiastic editor of the Huntsville paper, who considered bondpersons' viewing such spectacles edifying experiences for them, the Lexington editor shared the sentiments of the St. Joseph editor whose paper covered Green's botched hanging. The Lafayette County newspaper expressed the vain wish,

> That this may be the last public execution that will ever take place in the State.... We do hope that all parents and masters will ... exercise their authority and prevent their minor children and slaves from coming to town to witness a scene so revolting. It is not our intention to give any notice of the time when the execution was to take place, and only mention it now to caution the public against permitting minors and slaves to go to places so demoralizing in their tendencies.[36]

Just how large the crowd was that attended Slave Henry's hanging has not been preserved.

On November 29, 1858, Larrell and John, owned by Robert H. Early, murdered their overseer, Peter Nance. On Early's orders Nance had whipped these men the previous afternoon, as the newspaper noted, "for absenting themselves during the day and on the general charge of night-walking." On his employer's orders and early the next morning, Nance went to the slaves' quarters to check on them; they beat him to death with clubs. Once they had finished their retaliatory battering, they went to their master and informed him they supposed that they had killed their overseer or at least that was their intention. Next, they led their owner to Nance's body.

Their crime was not the subject of a coroner's inquest; coincidentally, the county grand jury was in session when this killing occurred, and it immediately indicted John and Larrell on charges of first-degree murder.[37] They were tried December 1 and died in Lexington on December 31, 1858. One Lafayette County newspaper observed of their forthcoming execution, "It speaks well for our community that these dark-skinned, midnight assassins, should be protected by the strong arm of law, and their bodies saved from mob violence."[38] Shortly before they were put to death, the slaves acknowledged, as a newspaper recorded, "that whiskey in connection with revenge at being flogged by a man who was 'not worth a quarter' were the incentives." This paper noted, "The execution was attended by a large crowd of people, from far and near, principally blacks."[39] Another newspaper gave this event extensive coverage. It mentioned that at 1:00 P.M. the condemned men were brought from the jail to the scaffold on a hill north of Main Street. Larrell and John warned the crowd to avoid whiskey; they prayed that they would meet their fellow slaves in heaven, and once the rope was cut, they died, Farrell without a struggle, and John within a few minutes. An estimated crowd of between 4,000 and 5,000, a large proportion of which were blacks, watched the hanging of Robert Early's slaves.[40] Obviously, slaveholders encouraged, if they did not require, that their bondpersons attend.

The hanging of Larrell and John for their skull-crushing murder of Peter Nance is one of only two known in which bondpersons of the same owner were executed for the same crime in this state. America's and Henry's nearly 15 years earlier in Boone County was the other. Another case discussed in the next chapter involved the simultaneous execution of four blacks, only one of whom was a slave; the other three were free. Larrell's and John's case has one other distinction, a shorter time lapse between their crime and punishment than in any other known slave capital case in Missouri's history, 32 days. During the 1850s, insofar as information is available, the average interval between the slave's capital crime and his or her punishment was 89 days.

Another group of at-risk white victims of slave homicide were wives of owners. Unlike female slaves, there is no known record of any male slave killing or even harming his owner's children, grand children, blood relatives, or in-laws. Of the three murders of the slave's mistress that are documented, little is known of the first two. One arose in Dade County, in southwestern Missouri, in the spring of 1848, when Slave Peter Douglas killed his mistress and three of his own children and nearly beat his owner to death with a gun barrel. He was arrested and taken to the Dade County jail in Greenfield.[41] No newspaper from Dade County survives prior to the Civil War. One early Dade County history mistakenly recorded that the slave killed his own wife, and this error was repeated in the verbatim account of Peter Douglas's crime in a later Dade County history. No account of the circumstances of the slave's attempted murder of his owner and successful killing of his other victims survives. The county histories state only that the slave attempted to kill himself, was tried for his crime, found guilty, and died on the gallows in Greenfield.[42]

A second murder of a slave mistress occurred on May 23, 1851, when 18-year-old Isaac of Warren County choked Mrs. Callahan, wife of his owner, Beston Callahan, to death. According to one contemporary newspaper, "The Negro assigned no cause for the act."[43] Another stated that Mr. Callahan was not home when the crime occurred.[44] The Warren County history misdated the murder as taking place on September 22, 1851; most likely this was the date of Isaac's trial. This history also assigned a sexual motive: "Mrs. Callahan was quite old and infirm, and in her struggles to prevent the wretch from carrying out a fiendish purpose, made an outcry, when the brutal desperado choked her to death." According to this same history, Isaac was tried with Judge Carty Wells presiding, and on September 24 Wells sentenced Isaac to die on November 14, 1851. His execution, carried out on that date in Warrenton, the county seat, was Warren County's first legal hanging.[45] Earlier, this judge was co-counsel with Edward Bates at trial and before the Supreme Court of Missouri in Fanny's case, the slave woman accused, but ultimately acquitted, of the murder of the Florence children.

The last known male slave murder of his owner's wife took place in Lincoln County in July 1857 when Slave George killed his mistress, Mrs. Davis, after she threatened to sell him because he refused to whip a fellow slave at her request. He killed her while her husband, his owner, was in St. Louis. Had George not committed suicide, either a lynch mob or a sheriff armed with a death warrant would have ended his life. His case is covered in chapter 7.

All slaves mentioned in this chapter killed one or more persons primarily because of the inherently coercive nature of the slave-master relationship. Insofar as we know what motivated these killings, in most cases, either the threat or the actuality of a whipping, or the threat or the actuality of a gift or a sale that uprooted him, preceded the slave's murder of his victim. Without slavery, there would never have been masters, mistresses, overseers, slave lessees, and slave traders, and none would have died at the hands of bondmen. Whippings to make slaves mind, the standard form of plantation and farm discipline, may have produced the hoped-for results with some enslaved men, but this conduct did not achieve the desired changes in its application to the boys and men who murdered persons with power over them.

Chapter 12

Capital Crimes by Wandering Boys and Men

Other male slaves were accused of homicides that cannot be directly linked to their involuntary servitude. For example, in the 1850s Slave Edmund escaped from the Clay County jail after he was indicted on first-degree murder charges.[1] Because nothing else is known about his case, it cannot now be classified as incidental to slavery, arising from mixed causes, or a suspected killing that involved a male who was, coincidentally, a slave. Unlike every known death-sentenced slave woman, whose crimes were against members of her household, that is her own children, her master's slave and white children, her mistress, or her master, approximately one-third of the capitally indicted male slaves were charged with committing crimes against persons who were neither related to them nor in positions of power over them. Appendix 1 lists 28 slave men who assaulted and/or murdered other blacks. With the exception of one case, that of Slave Hart indicted for poisoning slave girls in Audrain County and found not guilty in September 1854,[2] all known black victims of male slaves were other males. Only two executions of black males who killed other blacks can be documented: Abe for the murder of his overseer in Platte County in 1853 and Nathan for the murder of Tom in Cape Girardeau County in 1847.

The distinctive feature of Nathan's case is not that he killed Tom; rather, its unusual aspect is its outcome, the hanging of the perpetrator. As has been shown, the death penalty was overwhelmingly reserved for slaves who killed white persons. The extant court records contain neither Nathan's nor Tom's owner's names. However, the odds favor that different masters owned these men. The economic loss to a single owner of both would have been the expense of two valuable properties, perhaps $1500 in 1840s prices (about $25,000 today). Probably, the victim-slave's owner was a wealthy and influential person and Tom one of his prized possessions. Unlike Mrs. Chouteau, whom the Spanish government compensated when soldiers accidentally shot her slave, Batiste, Tom died at the hands of another slave. In 1837 the Supreme Court of Missouri decreed, and would again in 1850, that the owner of the killer was not civilly liable to the owner of the murdered man. As a result, Tom's owner may have used the criminal law to punish Nathan's owner in his purse and, as a result, Nathan in his person.

The court records confirm that on November 28, 1846, Nathan struck Tom a mortal wound with an ax in the head, three inches in length and two in depth. He died as a result of his injuries on December 6. Two days later, and after hearing the subpoenaed testimony of three male slaves, each with a different owner, the grand jury indicted Nathan on a charge of first-degree murder. At his trial in mid–December 36 men were summoned as potential jurors, and two attorneys represented the accused. The state subpoenaed four white men and five slaves (one woman and four men), and the defense four white men, two white women, and six slaves (four men and two women). The bondpersons of five different living owners and an asset of the estate of another came into court and gave their evidence. In all, in excess of 60 persons played one part or another in Nathan's trial. In most slave-on-slave homicides the accused pled guilty to second-degree murder, was whipped, sold, and transported out of state. The judicial machinery avoided the time and expense of summoning the many witnesses, both slave and free, who testified at Nathan's trial. However, in his case the jury found him guilty of first-degree murder. After his motions for an arrest of judgment and a new trial were overruled in late December, the judge sentenced him to hang on Saturday, February 20, 1847.[3] A county history states of the case only that one slave who killed another with an ax was executed.[4] Despite the case's many subpoenas and other documents, the circumstances of the crime are not contained in the surviving portion of the file, and there is no known newspaper coverage of it. However, the state of Missouri's execution of Nathan for murdering a slave, one of only three, including Annice's in 1828 and Abe's in 1853, was an unusual event. The odds favor that more bondmen in Missouri died when struck by lightning than the gallows ever claimed when the hanged slave's victim was another black, either slave or free.

The proceedings against Mat continued the familiar story of a black sentenced to death for the murder of a white. The case arose in Callaway County on July 9, 1855, when this slave child, an asset of the estate of Peter H. Holland, but then working for the Steels, was sent to a neighbor, Allan Wommack, to borrow a singletree, a wooden bar with metal ends, which swung at the center from a hitch on a plow to the traces of a horse's or mule's harness. Wommack told Mat to go to the stable and take the requested piece of equipment from the plow under the shed. At the same time, he sent his older son, Sam, to the stable to let the horses out so they could get water. As the older children left the house for the stable, three-year-old Virgil tagged along. The older brother, Sam, testified that Mat held Virgil's hand and asked him to come home with him. Sam cautioned the child that their father would whip him if he did, and Mat said that he would not. As Sam turned his attention to watering the horses, he saw Mat and Virgil leaving the stable together, with Mat carrying the single-tree.

Later that same afternoon, the father, Allan Wommack, missed his young son. Among others, the father questioned Mat at the Steel residence regarding the child's whereabouts. At first, the slave child stated that he put Virgil through Wommack's gate; after the father searched his house, stable, and orchard, he returned to the Steels and asked Mat where he had left Virgil. He replied that he left the little boy in the vicinity of a white oak tree near Wommack's gate. Following this exchange the senior Wommack again searched the area near his gate and found drag marks on the ground along the road. Shortly, he found his young son some 200 yards from their house, lying in the corner of a fence. The father later testified that the child's "head and face was cut and mangled in a desperate manner." Someone had dragged the child about 10 yards from a tobacco patch; marks on his back and on the road itself confirmed that his body had been moved. The victim's facial and head injuries resulted from someone striking the boy with one or more heavy objects.

Almost immediately, Mat became the chief suspect in the assault on the still-living but badly injured child. The next day, July 10, Allan Wommack and several of his neighbors examined Mat's clothing for telltale signs of his having beaten young Wommack. They found a drop and some specks of what they believed was blood on his shirt, and Mat admitted that it came from Virgil. Next, these men interrogated him concerning his knowledge of the three-year-old. At first Mat said Virgil had fallen from a fence; next, that when he threw a rock at a bird's nest, it accidentally hit him. The men then stepped up their questioning of Mat. As the record makes clear, Mat "was threatened to be severely punished unless he would tell the whole truth." Wommack and his neighbors tied a rope around the young slave's neck, tightened it, and drew him up four or five times while holding his hands. Under these conditions Mat admitted that he struck the child three blows on the head with the singletree and dragged him by his heels to where his body was found. When the child groaned, Mat said he struck him three times with a rock; he admitted that he intended to kill the young boy and he did so for "devilment." Warming to the task of continuing their questioning of Mat and believing that additional punishment of him would elicit more information, Mr. Wommack and his neighbors, including James Craighead, took him to Wommack's tobacco barn, tied him, stripped him naked, and James Craighead gave him "300 lashes." The flaying of Mat caused his blood to ooze in several places; Craighead's whipping of Mat stopped because it was not prompting him to recall more detail of his injuring Virgil Wommack. Soon after his interrogation was completed, the slave boy was committed to the jail in Fulton, where he shared a cell with Celia.

On August 11 Virgil Wommack died from his face and head injuries, which on July 10, Mat confessed that he had inflicted on the young victim the previous day. At the August term of the Callaway County Circuit Court he was indicted on first-degree murder charges; two months later he went on trial for his life. His judge, prosecutor, at least one physician called as a witness for the state, and one of his defense attorneys were involved in another death penalty case that same term, Celia's. Just as John Jameson was her lead defense attorney, Judge Hall appointed him and another lawyer, Thomas R. Ansell, to represent Mat, a defendant whom the state described as "about 11 years of age" and the defense as "under 11 years old."

His trial began on October 14, 1855, before the usual 12-member all-white-male jury. The principal evidence against him came from the statements he had made to Allan Wommack, James Craighead, and other of the men who tortured a confession from him as they repeatedly hanged and later whipped him on July 10. Jameson and his co-counsel, Ansell, vigorously objected to the admission into evidence of their client's confession. Missouri law prohibited the prosecution's use of any confession that was obtained as Mat's had been. The Missouri Constitution of 1820 provided that no person can be compelled to be a witness against himself, and Missouri's high court had earlier applied this provision to two cases involving slave defendants. In 1829 it reversed Slave Hector's St. Louis County conviction for burglary and in 1839 Fanny's conviction for murdering the Florence children in Lincoln County because the confessions of Hector's and Fanny's son, Ellick's were obtained by brutal interrogation. Nonetheless, the trial judge in Mat's case ignored the law and admitted Mat's confession. Besides all the detail of Mat's confession, gotten into evidence through the testimony of Alan Wommack and his neighbors, the jury probably saw Mat's principal murder weapon, Wommack's singletree, perhaps a sizable rock, and Mat's shirt with its drop and specks of a reddish substance on it, material that the accused had, on July 10, admitted was his victim's blood. The jury also heard on behalf of the defense from Mrs. Steel that in raising Mat he had been kind to her and her child and though "wild in little frivolous pranks" she saw no violence in him. The record contains neither any additional defense evidence nor the opening and closing arguments of either side.

The jury instructions, both those that the judge gave and those he refused to give, are preserved in this case. The prosecution's are straightforward: "If the jury believed from the evidence that Mat wilfully, deliberately and premeditatedly killed Virgil Wommack …, they will find him guilty of murder in the first degree." Mat's age of "about 11 years" was no obstacle to finding him guilty of first-degree murder "if … he had the mental capacity to know right from wrong and [killed] knowing it was wrong." The prosecution stated in its instructions that deliberation and premeditation need only "exist but for a moment, before the killing … and they together with the capacity to commit crime may be inferred from the circumstances." Despite the objection of Mat's lawyers, Judge Hall gave the jury all of the prosecution-requested instructions.

Some of the defense-requested instructions that the judge refused to give concerned the manner of obtaining Mat's confession. The jury was never required to disregard Mat's admission if "the jury believe the prisoner was induced by fear, or terrified by threats of punishment, or that the confession was extracted by *ACTUAL TORTURE*."[5] Other defense-requested instructions concerned Mat's age. The judge gave some, such as the need on the part of the prosecution to prove malice by proof beyond a reasonable doubt, if the defendant was under the age of 14 years when he committed the act with which he was charged. However, he refused to instruct the jury that if Mat "was under the age of sixteen years, when he committed the offense, they cannot assess and declare in their verdict that he shall suffer the penalty of death." In 1988 the United States Supreme Court finally limited the death penalty to persons who were aged at least 16 years at the time of their crimes.[6] Until more than 125 years after Mat's case, the states determined the minimum age, if any, for the imposition of a death sentence.

In a decade in Missouri's history, the 1850s, in which mobs lynched more slaves than the state's sheriffs put to death under the authority of a court's death warrant, it comes as no surprise that once the jury received

Mat's case and retired to deliberate its verdict, it found him guilty of murder in the first degree. The judge overruled Jameson's and Ansell's motions for the arrest of judgment and a new trial. Unlike Celia's case, Mat's surviving record contains no judge-set execution date for Mat. However, one newspaper reported that Judge Hall sentenced Mat to hang on November 16;[7] this was also the date he selected for Celia's death. Shortly after their slave-child client was returned to his jail cell, which he continued to share with Celia, Jameson and Ansell filed an appeal on Mat's behalf with the Supreme Court of Missouri, and it agreed to review his case. The issues it probably would have decided had it heard his attorneys argue before it were two: the admissibility of his confession and the legality of executing someone who was either aged 10 or 11 years at the time of his crime.

What might have happened if the child perpetrator were white and his victim a slave cannot be determined with any reference to Missouri because there are no known cases involving these demographics. Such a death probably occurred because children then and now, both white and black, kill other children. One out-of-state instance of the punishment meted out to a white child who killed a slave child is preserved. Eleanor Roosevelt's great-uncle, her grandmother's brother, Daniel Stewart Elliott, killed his bondchild in a fit of pique on a Georgia plantation in the 1850s. Elliott was approximately the same age as Slave Mat, and his victim was known as his little black shadow. This white upper-class perpetrator was sent to Europe for a year.[8] In 1882 the Missouri Supreme Court reversed and remanded the death sentence of a 12-year-old, Tom Adams, because of his young age. The condemned child, an illiterate black male, killed a 17-year-old white male with a pitchfork in Morgan County. After his case was remanded to the Morgan County Circuit Court, at age 12 or 13 years, Adams pled guilty to manslaughter in the third degree, and the judge sentenced him to pay the costs of the prosecution and to serve 12 months in the Morgan County jail.[9] By age 14 years at the oldest, this youthful offender had already come and gone from Missouri's criminal justice system.

We know what happened to a white child who killed a slave child in Georgia at the time of Mat's offense. We also know that 27 years after the Missouri Supreme Court accepted Mat's appeal it reversed the death sentence of a young black child who killed a white teenager. What we do not know, and never will, is whether the Supreme Court of Missouri would have reversed Mat's death sentence. It could have done so by either following its own precedents and ruling his confession should not have gone to the jury or by deciding that his age, either 10 or 11 years at the time of his crime, made him too young for the state to put him to death.

However, in 1851 a change occurred in the selection process for membership on the Supreme Court of Missouri. The governor no longer appointed its judges with the advice and consent of the senate. Instead, and by a two-thirds vote of both houses, the General Assembly amended the state's 1820 constitution and decreed that, beginning in August 1851, the three members of this court should be elected by the qualified voters to a term of six years.[10] To what extent this change affected the decisions of Missouri's only appellate court is always open to debate. However, in 1853, and by a two-to-one vote, it overruled many years of its own legal precedents in deciding that Dred Scott, a Missouri slave who had resided in free territory with his U.S. Army officer master, was not entitled to freedom. Though the better known and far more notorious opinion about this famous slave is the U.S. Supreme Court's decision in 1857, the Missouri Supreme Court case concerning him reads as follows:

> The consequences of slavery ... are much more hurtful to the master than the slave. There is no comparison between the slave in the United States and the cruel, uncivilized negro in Africa.... We are almost persuaded that the introduction of slavery among us was, in the providences of God ... a means of placing that unhappy race within the pale of civilized nations.[11]

Perhaps Jameson and Ansell reasoned that if the Supreme Court of Missouri could overrule its own case law, such as one from 1836, dealing with Slave Rachael, whose U.S. Army officer master took her with him when he was posted to free territory and thereby entitled her to freedom,[12] nothing prevented this court from overruling its own precedents concerning coerced confessions. It might easily have distinguished Hector's and Fanny's cases from Mat's by finding that, unlike the earlier slave confessions that it rejected, evidence of Mat's guilt existed independent of his confession.

Likewise, nothing in either English law, the statutes of other states, or those of Missouri prohibited the execution of convicted persons who were under the age of 14 years at the time of their crime. The British authority, Gatrell, mentions that 103 Old Bailey death sentences were passed on children under 14 for theft between 1801 and 1836; however, none were executed.[13] The research of Espy confirms that Alabama, Connecticut, Louisiana, New Jersey, and Virginia all executed children who were aged between 10 and 12 years when they committed capital offenses. Though three of these states carried out their executions of preteenagers in the late eighteenth and early nineteenth centuries, Louisiana executed a 10-year-old in 1855 and Alabama a 12-year-old in 1858.[14] Missouri's own precedent for putting to death young slave children convicted of the murder of still younger white children was Slave Mary, hanged for a murder she committed when she was slightly older than Mat. His attorneys could not have had high hopes for saving their young client's life as a result of a favorable decision by the Supreme Court of Missouri.

On November 15, 1855, Celia and Mat escaped from the Callaway County jail in Fulton. On their first try for freedom Mat went only a short distance from town, and the newspaper specified that he was brought back by an unnamed gentleman at whose house he stayed. The paper speculated that "they were most likely assisted in their effort to escape from the outside."[15] The pair escaped a second time, and Celia, who went to visit her children at Harvey Newsom's, was captured, returned to jail, and put to death on December 21, 1855. Her cellmate, Mat, was never taken into custody a second time. Despite the telegraph, which was then in use, there is no account of him as late as four years later. The winter of 1855–56 was especially severe. One Missouri newspaper reported that in Brunswick, Chariton County, on January 9 the temperature was 24 degrees below zero and on February 3, 1856, it dropped to a record 28 below zero.[16] If Mat had been found frozen to death, eaten by wolves, or dead as a result of any other mishap, one or more extant newspapers from counties adjacent or near Callaway County would have carried stories about him. There are none in any of the papers that covered accounts of his crime, trial, death sentence, and first escape. It is not credible that an 11- or 12-year-old boy managed to reach safe haven without considerable assistance. Mat's lawyers were the most likely persons to help him make his getaway.

These men were in the best position to assess their client's chances before the Supreme Court of Missouri. Jameson knew the treatment Celia received at the hands of this elected judicial body, and he surely feared the worst regarding any decision it might reach about his other death-sentenced slave client. Though now a minister in the Christian Church, he was formerly both Speaker of the Missouri House and three times a member of the U.S. Congress. During his first terms, the Twenty-sixth and the Twenty-eighth Congresses, he served with a former U.S. president, John Quincy Adams of Quincy, Massachusetts. During his last term, the Thirtieth Congress, he served with Adams until the latter's death in 1848 and with a future president, Abraham Lincoln of Springfield, Illinois.[17] The chances are good that Jameson, an affable man, made and maintained friendships with some members of these congresses from all over the United States, including the upper Midwest and New England. His co-counsel, Thomas R. Ansell, was not a slave owner. He was born in London in 1796, educated in England, and performed on the English stage with the British actor Edmund Kean. Mat's English lawyer came to America in 1828 at age 32, and he toured the large cities with prominent actors of his day including the elder Booth, Junius Brutus. After Ansell left the stage, he taught school, first in Lexington, Kentucky, and beginning in 1833, in Fulton, Missouri. Soon, his interests turned to law, and he was admitted to practice in 1839 and continued this profession until his death in 1866.[18]

Neither John Jameson nor Thomas Ansell was a country bumpkin; both knew considerable of the world outside Callaway County, and between them, most likely, they had friends and acquaintances who detested slavery and knew that no white child of Mat's age would be put to death for his crime. This much seems clear — someone helped this slave child permanently leave Missouri. In July 1858 the Supreme Court of Missouri discontinued Mat's appeal because "he is not in the custody of the law, but has escaped therefrom."[19] In 1859, and because Mat fled before he was executed, the General Assembly passed an appropriation that refunded to the clerk of the Circuit Court of Callaway County $188.75, the sum this county spent on Mat's trial.[20] Beginning in 1843, in death penalty cases the state, not the county, paid such fees. Nothing more is known of the slave who might have been the youngest person put to death in this state's history but for the active intervention of certain persons, most likely his lawyers and some of their out-of-state or out-of-country friends.

The remaining slave death penalty cases all involve persons chargeable with two or more felonies. At least in part, two murders of slave masters already discussed, John Gabriel's in Cooper County in 1830 and Israel Grant's in Callaway in 1855, were motivated by the perpetrator-slaves' desire for personal gain. Gabriel's killers were hired, and a search of one of Grant's uncovered two bank bills on him that belonged to his victim. Nonetheless, because these white men owned or leased one or both of the slaves who murdered them, the victims' relationship with the perpetrators is classified as coerced, that of owner and owned.

An involuntary association did not exist between the victim and alleged perpetrator in any of the remaining slave death penalty cases. Burglary or attempted or completed robbery appears to have been the dominant, if not the exclusive, motive in at least three cases. The first of these arose in Howard County in the spring of 1837 when two slaves, Washington Hill, the property of Judge C. C. P. Hill, and David Gates, property of Daniel Gates, robbed three blind brothers at their house a few miles from Fayette. Their victims primarily earned their living by making neat and durable chairs. The day before the crime, the victims had sold some land, and the slaves went to the residence of these disabled men for the purpose of obtaining the money they received from this sale and killed one of them in the course of robbing them. They were arrested, tried at the June term of the Howard County Circuit Court, found guilty, and sentenced to die. They were hanged from the limb of a large oak tree in a pasture north of Fayette, probably during the summer of 1837.[21]

In 1841 the city of St. Louis was the scene of the only known crime in St. Louis City or County that resulted in a slave death sentence. This county was probably the place of one or more slave executions during early American rule; most likely Pierre Chouteau's unnamed female was convicted of arson and hanged in 1805, but no bondperson's death on a county gallows can be documented in St. Louis until 1841. On April 17 of that year and at night, four burglars broke into a bank for purposes of taking sizable sums of money from it. In the course of their attempted robbery, they were interrupted by the return of two white male clerks, both aged 22 years, Jesse Baker and Jacob Weaver. The perpetrators killed both, set fire to the bank building to cover their murders, and fled the scene without the anticipated cash proceeds of their crime.

The next day, the mayor of a horrified city offered a $5,000 reward for information leading to the criminals' arrest and conviction. In today's money that sum is worth approximately $100,000, and no other slave crime in Missouri's history approaches this remuneration for its solution. Money soon talked; within a week a free black barber, Edward Ennis, who eventually received $1200 of the reward, with its remainder going to others, told a friend that he knew the identities of those responsible. His friend went to the authorities, and they arrested Ennis on April 25. In exchange for immunity he gave the police both the names of the four suspects and their intended destinations. In keeping with the ever-diminishing percentage of the population that was slave within the city of St. Louis, it is not surprising that only one was a slave, 34- or 35-year-old Madison Henderson. His owner, Samuel G. Blanchard, resided in New Orleans, some 800 river miles south of the crime scene. Blanchard had left Madison in St. Louis to hire his own time while he attended to business elsewhere. When the slave arrived in New Orleans, Madison's owner arranged for his bondman's transportation back to St. Louis; there the slave was arrested while sleeping on a steamboat's deck. The other three were free blacks, all in their late twenties: Charles Brown, James W. Seward, and Amos Alfred Warrick. Brown only remained in St. Louis for a few days after the failed robbery; he left the city on a steamboat for Cincinnati, his hometown, a place at least 500 river miles from St. Louis. Passengers reached this Ohio city by traveling down the Mississippi to Cairo, Illinois, and up the Ohio River. St. Louis law enforcement officers arrested Brown in Cincinnati.

Seward left St. Louis with Brown, and at Cairo he took a steamboat for New Orleans; a St. Louis police officer arrested Seward on the boat, and instead of this suspect continuing south on his river journey, he was returned to St. Louis in police custody. Warrick, a St. Louis barber, remained in the city for almost a week after the crime. When his fellow perpetrators left town, he secured work on a steamboat that traveled west on the Missouri River. He was arrested when St. Louis law enforcement officers boarded his boat at the central Missouri town of Arrow Rock, Saline County.

By May 11 all four suspects were returned to St. Louis and incarcerated in its jail. Shortly, they were arraigned and assigned able counsel: a future governor of Missouri, Hamilton Gamble; a former mayor of St. Louis, John Darby; a former state legislator, Wilson Primm; and a former city of St. Louis alderman and school board member, Josiah Spalding, were each appointed to represent one of these four defendants. Their trial began May 24 before the usual all-white-male jury. Since each man had made damaging admissions regarding either his own or his co-defendants' role in the crime, there was little doubt of the four's guilt in the minds of the jury. It quickly found all guilty of first-degree murder, and on June 1 the judge sentenced them to hang on July 9. The simultaneous execution of the four condemned prisoners is a record number under Missouri statutes; it still stands more than 160 years later.

Crowd estimates of those eager to glimpse some or all of the public spectacle of their gallows deaths range as high as 20,000 persons, half of whom were women, in a city whose population was then less than 30,000. On the appointed date, July 9, 1841, all four were hanged on Duncan's Island, an area approximately a mile south of the St. Louis Courthouse. After their execution the severed heads of the four hanged blacks were displayed in the showcase window of a St. Louis drugstore, and its proprietor made plastic casts of their heads for the then budding pseudoscience of phrenology,[22] the study of character by examining the bumps on the head. This case, with its massive press coverage, geographically diffuse capture of the suspects, closely watched trial, and swarms of witnesses to the guilty men's punishment, did not touch the purse of even one Missouri slaveholder. The only slave hanged for the crime was owned many miles away in the state of Louisiana.

The case against Charles, a slave of Benjamin Horrell, arose in Cape Girardeau County in a public place, the Old Bloomfield Road, when, between 6:00 and 7:00 A.M. on a Sunday, March 28, 1863, an unnamed Negro man of William Cross alerted his owner that the body of Julian Deblanc, apparently the victim of a homicide, was lying in the road. After

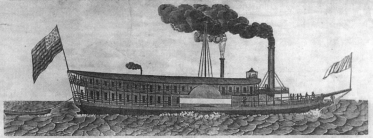

Handbill for the steamboat *Eagle,* advertising a round trip from Alton, Illinois, to Duncan's Island, St. Louis, Missouri, for passenger viewing of the hanging of the free blacks Charles Brown, James W. Seward, and Amos Alfred Warrick, and Slave Madison Henderson. Broadside Collection, Missouri Historical Society, St. Louis.

briefly examining the corpse and noticing a stick or club near it, Cross went to the home of his neighbor, William Alford, awakened him, and together they inspected the crime scene. Cross went to the town of Jackson for the coroner, and he also reported Deblanc's death to A. B. Dorman, justice of the peace.

About 11:00 that same morning, the coroner, W. R. Wilson, M.D., made a postmortem examination of the deceased. Two days later, he testified before Dorman that the victim came to his death by blows on his head made by a blunt implement, probably a club. Wilson stated, "The whole back of his head was so beaten, you could see no distinct marks of the weapon with which he was struck. The skull was beaten into a jelly." Several persons, including Dr. Wilson, identified a stick or club found near the dead man's body as the murder weapon.

Additional witnesses testified before Justice of the Peace Dorman regarding this homicide. One, R. Nathan, stated that he last saw the victim alive on Saturday, March 28, between 2:00 and 4:00 P.M. At that time Nathan paid Deblanc a "$20 bill greenback" and a "$3 city of St. Louis Treasury bill." The last testifying person to see the deceased alive and on the Bloomfield Road on March 28 was William Beaudeau, a passenger in Deblanc's unloaded wagon drawn by two yoked oxen. He stated that when he left Deblanc it was "after sundown and not quite dark." Another witness, David W. Smith, also testified that he had examined the deceased at the scene, and when he turned over his body, he noticed that the dead man's left hand and wrist appeared to have been struck because they were badly swollen. The implication regarding these injuries was that the victim was attempting to defend valuables on his person when his killer struck his hand and wrist with a club or stick in order to rob him. Smith also noticed that one of the victim's pockets was turned out. When John St. David, a law enforcement officer, searched all of Deblanc's pockets between 11:00 and noon on that same Sunday, March 29, he found neither money, a "pocketbook" (i.e., a billfold), nor the city of St. Louis Treasury bill in them. The motive for Deblanc's murder was well established; it was robbery.

Who did it was not so easily confirmed. On March 30 Cross and Alford, the first witnesses to arrive at the murder scene, saw, or thought they saw, two distinct sets of human foot tracks on the road. One appeared to be made by a person wearing shoes, believed to be those of the victim, and the other by someone in socks. Cross saw tracks made by another pair of shoes a considerable distance from Deblanc's body, 300 yards away. After Charles was arrested, Cross and other men took the shoes the prisoner was then wearing, and according to Cross's statement, Charles's shoes "did fit" the distant shoe tracks. The stocking feet tracks began where the distant shoe tracks stopped. The inference was that the perpetrator lay in wait, and, without shoes on, he greatly surprised his victim.

Cross and Alford also testified that there were signs of a struggle near Deblanc's body. The soil was yellow clay; they noticed that the ground was wet in some places and not in others. When Alford inspected the stocking feet tracks, he noticed that "the big toe and the second one seem to have been bare, protruding from the socks, and made their mark very plain." Alford believed that two persons were in a scuffle on the road and the one in stocking feet had the advantage from the way he braced himself. The man with shoes on, he continued, broke and ran from his attacker, and the victim soon fell on his face. Drawing on his extensive knowledge of Charles, based on knowing him since the slave's childhood and having leased him once for a year, Alford testified that, to the best of his knowledge, the sock-feet tracks were made by Charles. His former lessee stated of various impressions on the ground at the murder scene, "I think I know his track." On the testimony of Cross and Alford, and specifically because Cross stated his belief in a March 30 deposition that Charles murdered Julian Deblanc on March 28, 1863, Justice of the Peace Dorman issued an arrest warrant for the slave on March 30. The next day, Dorman signed another warrant for a daytime entry to Charles's cabin for "a diligent search" for the $20 bill, the $3 city of St. Louis Treasury bill, and other money believed to have been taken from the murdered man.

Despite Cross's and Alford's sleuthing regarding the sock and shoe tracks at the crime scene, their imaginative analysis did not provide sufficient information for any court officer to issue warrants for Charles's arrest or a search of his cabin. From the start of American rule of Missouri in 1804, the Fourth Amendment to the U.S. Constitution required that no search or arrest warrants shall issue but upon probable cause. Federal law governed Missouri Territory between 1804 and 1820; afterward, the Missouri Constitution of 1820 required that no search or arrest warrants can issue without probable cause.[23] In 1981 the U.S. Supreme Court upheld an investigative stop of suspected illegal alien smugglers on the basis of distinctive shoe prints. The High Court characterized the Border Patrol's matching of shoe print patterns at the Mexican-American border with the known prints of the suspects as a "reasonable surmise,"[24] in other words, an educated guess. The proof necessary for such a stop is not probable cause, that is, the requisite amount of trustworthy information that allows a person of reasonable caution to believe that a person has committed a crime. Rather, law enforcement officers often begin and end inspectional stops within minutes, and the briefly detained person is soon at liberty. A formally arrested person may spend many months in pretrial detention. For example, on the basis of Cross's and Alford's notarized speculations regarding shoe and sock prints that placed the slave at the crime scene, and this alone, as far as the record reveals it, he was arrested on charges of first-degree murder on March 31. When Alford was cross-examined on March 30 (and by whom is unclear), he admitted that he could not distinguish boot from shoe tracks, and he also stated, "I don't know, of my own knowledge, that the track made by stocking feet is the track of [Charles]. It was my opinion when I first saw the track made by sock-feet, that track was made by him."

When the authorities searched Charles incident to his arrest, they found a revolver on him, a small pocketknife, and a pocketbook but no money or any other property of the victim. Since the murder weapon was a heavy object, such as a club or a stick, the arrestee's weapons did not tie him to the murder of Julian Deblanc. Likewise, during a diligent search at Charles's cabin for bills and notes belonging to Julian Deblanc, nothing mentioned in the warrant was found. This writ should also have specified that the search was for any other evidence that might connect the slave to Deblanc's murder, but it did not. However, when Allen Bruner and Sergeant Walker searched Charles's cabin, his wife brought a sack out from under a bed that contained a pair of socks and pants. The trousers had one muddy knee; the stockings were very wet. The big toe of the left foot protruded, and they were caked in yellow clay mud one-fourth of an inch thick. Best of all from the prosecution's point of view, Charles readily admitted that the under-the-bed clothing was his. Though his recovered hose appeared to tie him to the crime scene, when a practicing physician of 16 years, August Bierworth, examined them on March 31, he found no blood. Another physician, W. R. Wilson, the postmortem examiner of the deceased, also inspected them; he would go no further than to testify, "I find what I think may be one spot of blood." The record contains no additional mention of the pants recovered from Charles's cabin.

If Charles were wearing the seized footwear when he beat his victim's skull into a jelly, there would have been massive amounts of blood on the socks he was then wearing, especially if he committed this brutal crime in his stocking feet. Surely, any examiner would find more than what he thought might be one spot of blood on the suspect's socks. Moreover, if Charles or his wife had later washed the hosiery he wore the night he murdered Deblanc, its laundering would remove more than the victim's splattered blood; it would also remove the yellow clay mud, a substance caked one-fourth of an inch thick when law enforcement officers found Charles's dirty footwear in his cabin two days after the crime.

As for the mud on Charles's socks, just as soil is present at most outdoor places of crime, it is also present at most outdoor places of innocent activity. Since the crime scene was a public road, Charles might have been on it for any number of noncriminal reasons. It also is probable that the earth of many locales within Cape Girardeau County contained yellow clay mud in the early spring of the year. Perhaps of greatest significance, despite the many advances in forensic evidence in criminal cases during the twentieth century, Moenssens, Inbau, and Starrs note:

> The accurate, scientific analysis and comparison of soil is very difficult because of the presence of extremely small particles not capable of accurate analysis…. There are undoubtedly cases where two soil samples might be positively identified as having come from a common source, but these cases would be rather rare. In most instances, the opinion would be couched in terms of probable, possible, or consistent with.[25]

Fairly obviously, the authorities failed to develop any solid evidence against Charles concerning Deblanc's murder. Despite a weak and wholly circumstantial case against the accused slave, he was committed to the jail in Jackson without eligibility for bail. As far as the record indicates, he remained an inmate from April 1, 1863, until June 1864. In 1860 the Missouri General Assembly decreed that the Cape Girardeau County Circuit Court was to be in session on the first Monday in both June and December.[26] Though the county history stated that the courts were suspended in 1861 and 1862,[27] presumably because of the Civil War, there is no indication that they were not in session during 1863. Perhaps the prosecution hoped that if Charles's trial were delayed a sufficient length of time it might develop more substantial evidence against him.

Justice Dorman initially ordered Charles to stand trial for Deblanc's murder at the regular June 1863 session of court; in the meanwhile he committed the prisoner to the county jail. On August 1, 13-year-old Slave Mary's former defense lawyer, Mason Frissell, now a circuit court judge of the tenth judicial circuit, which included Cape Girardeau County, ordered that a special term of court be held for purposes of trying six cases, all felonies, including Charles's capital crime. However, the grand jurors did not indict him until December 10, 1863, or more than 10 months after his arrest. They did so after they heard the testimony of Cross and Alford, the sock-print detectives; Beaudeau, the last known person to see the victim alive; and Bruner, one of the men who searched Charles's cabin.

In an undated but post-indictment motion, the defendant requested that a deposition be taken from Jim, alias James, a Negro inmate in the county jail, because Jim was about "to be enlisted as a soldier in the federal army." As such, Charles believed that this material witness would soon be removed from the state and unavailable to testify at his trial. As a result, on December 15, 1863, one of Charles's appointed attorneys deposed Jim alias James. His asked and answered questions concerning Charles included: Q. Are you acquainted with Charles? A. Yes, Q. What kind of boots or shoes did Charles wear the week of the killing of Julian Deblanc? Describe them. A. An old pair of cavalry boots, "one of the boots had been mended at the toes & the patch had worn off again & it was open." The relevance of Jim's testimony is unclear. To be sure, William Alford had testified that shoe tracks more than one-half mile from the murdered man's body were Charles's, but the prosecution's theory was that the accused committed the crime in his stocking feet. At the time of Alford's testimony before Justice Dorman, he admitted that he could not distinguish shoe prints from boot prints. Nonetheless, and for whatever purposes, the court ordered that Jim's sworn testimony be read into evidence at Charles's trial. The defendant's witness list is dated December 14, 1863. From it, we know that "Joe, a colored man living with Mr. John Cross and Nelly and Nancy, colored women living on the farm of Benjamin Horrell," were named as material witnesses for the accused. Though the extant record contains no subpoenas, most likely Joe, Nelly, and Nancy all came into open court and testified as alibi witnesses on Charles's behalf.

The only remaining documents in this file are jury instructions. From their date of June 1864, we know that a longer time elapsed between Charles's arrest and trial than in any other extant slave death penalty case in Missouri's history. Doubtless much of the delay was caused by the dislocations of the Civil War. However, unlike Slave Henry, who murdered his Moniteau County master, Alfred Norman, on July 9, was tried July 27, and hanged August 28, 1863, a time lapse between crime and punishment of 50 days, the pace of proceedings against Charles was extraordinarily slow. Perhaps the prosecution always hoped that he would confess; he never did.

The prosecutor may have asked for a number of jury instructions, but the record contains only one: "If the jury believe from the testimony that the defendant Charles ... wilfully, deliberately, maliciously and feloniously beat ... Julian Deblanc with a club or stick of wood on the back part of his head and that his death ensued in consequence of said striking or beating, they will find the defendant guilty of murder in the first-degree." At the request of the defense, the court gave one unnumbered and five numbered jury instructions. From these we know that the state could produce no direct evidence of Charles's guilt; its case was entirely circumstantial. One instruction pinpoints Charles's defense: "If the jury from the evidence believe that at the very time the murder was committed, the defendant, Charles, was in another place, they are bound to acquit." Presumably Joe, Nancy, Nelly, and perhaps Charles himself all took the stand and testified that he was with one or more of them and not near the scene of the crime the night of March 28 and the early morning of March 29, 1863. Other defense instructions suggest just how many holes the defense poked in the prosecution's case: "The evidence against the accused must be such as to exclude, to a moral certainty, every hypothesis, but that of his guilt of the offence imputed to him," and "If the jury have a *reasonable doubt* as to the guilt of the defendant, Charles, they are bound to acquit."[28]

One of Charles's appointed lawyers, Greer W. Davis (1799–1878), was born in Mercer County, Kentucky, moved to Missouri in 1818, located in Jackson, and practiced law there from his arrival until his death.[29] This capable, experienced, and prominent lawyer had surely argued numerous cases before juries, and many of its members were probably farmers who had spent a lifetime occasionally slaughtering cattle, hogs, and sheep. These men knew well the amount of blood that any person who bludgeoned such creatures to death in his stocking feet collected on his socks. Given the flimsy evidence against Charles in this case, the odds favor that the jury acquitted the last known slave whom the state of Missouri put on trial for his life. The county history was quite explicit; as of 1883 Cape Girardeau County's last execution was Slave Nathan's in 1847.[30] There is a remote possibility that, after the jury found him guilty, Charles either escaped from the county jail or died of natural causes prior to his scheduled hanging. The likelihood is great, however, that the jury found him not guilty and he was released from the Cape Girardeau County jail a freed slave. Six months later he was once more a freedman because slavery in Missouri was abolished.

The length of time between Charles's arrest and trial in 1863 and 1864 in a southeastern Missouri county, Cape Girardeau County, is in stark contrast to that of an unnamed slave in 1862 in Ray County, an interior western county immediately north of the Missouri River. The slave accused in 1862, and the remaining defendants whose cases are discussed in this chapter, probably committed sexual offenses and one other felony. The evidence concerning the case is brief, only newspaper coverage. According to it, on Thursday night, September 4, 1862, a Negro man owned by Arnold Windsor of Lafayette County was living at John S. Porter's in Ray County. The slave stopped at 10:00 or 11:00 P.M. at Porter's neighbors, the Bowmans. He called to Mr. Bowman, and as the husband and father approached him, the slave fired a pistol at him. Next, the unnamed culprit, as the newspaper described it, "attempted to seize Mrs. B. and commit violence upon her, but in this, he was foiled. He then caught a little girl about 12 years of age, and attempted to gratify his diabolical desire upon her, but the screaming and halloing of the ... girl, finally caused him to abandon his designs and leave." Two days later, a Saturday, Mr. Bowman came to Richmond, the seat of Ray County, and at this time a Union Army headquarters. Bowman related the events of 36 or so hours earlier to a military official, an unnamed provost marshal. He in turn had the slave arrested that same day. According to the news story, on Saturday, "The witnesses were brought forward, and the guilt of the negro established beyond doubt, not only by the negro's own voluntary admissions, but by independent testimony." Accordingly, this commanding officer sentenced the unnamed slave that same "evening," meaning the last part of the day, and on September 6, 1862, he was shot to death,[31] presumably by a Union Army firing squad.

The authority of the provost marshal to act as prosecutor, judge, and jury was martial law. It arises, as Fairman noted, when "an insurrection has ripened into war.... The inhabitants of the hostile territory become public enemies, beyond the pale of constitutional protection." Under martial law, as Fairman described the matter, "Individuals deemed troublesome will be seized and held without judicial process, and in some instances may be tried and sentenced even to death.... Soldiers may be ordered to take life to prevent the commission of a felony, or to punish, or perhaps to produce a moral effect."[32] Some documentation confirms that Union Army firing squads shot to death no fewer than 37 white men between August 7 and October 18, 1862, in Adair, Linn, Macon, Marion, and Randolph, all counties, like Ray, north of the Missouri River.[33] Most likely, the Union Army put to death one or more other slaves in outlying areas of Missouri during these years. Unlike St. Louis, a solidly Union stronghold, which remained under civilian control throughout the Civil War, the only rule in various war-torn sections of this state was martial law. Its punishment was, at times, not only severe, but breathlessly swift.

In the same county as the Union Army punishment of Arnold Windsor's slave in 1862, another dual crime involving slaves took place in 1837. It resembles a case discussed in the last chapter: Slave Isaac's Warren County murder in 1851 of his owner's wife, Mrs. Beston Callahan, a crime that may also have involved an attempted rape. The perpetrators in the 1837 Ray County case were Ish, owned by Richard Cleavenger, a man who lived near the victim and was her father-in-law, and Henry, owned by Abraham Froman. On a Sunday evening, May 28, 1837, as an 1881 history of the county recorded, "a nameless crime and the most atrocious murder ever committed in Ray County" took place. Since the victim, Mrs. Dorcas Cleavenger, was a married woman, the mother of two children, aged three and five years, and she was murdered in her bedroom while her husband was gone fishing, most likely she was also sexually assaulted. The word *nameless* carried meanings such as "left unnamed in order to avoid giving offense" and "unfit for mention." Like most indictments in death penalty cases, the defendants were not charged with any underlying felony such as burglary or rape.

When the coroner's jury was first empaneled the day after the crime, it assessed the deceased's cause of death as "an attack of apoplexy." Then a physician examined the dead woman, and he was convinced that this malady had not ended her life. Soon the community believed that she was murdered. Armed men went to the home of her father-in-law, Richard Cleavenger, and they demanded that they be allowed to talk to Ish. The slave soon implicated Froman's Henry. However, Ish admitted that he had helped Henry put Dorcas Cleavenger to bed, and that is how he happened to get "Miss Dorky's" blood on his coat sleeve. Both slaves were arrested; the evidence against them was heard before two justices of the peace on June 1. They were committed to the Ray County jail in Richmond. On July 10 the grand jury indicted them for murdering their victim by violently squeezing and pressing her throat and jumping and pitching their knees "in and upon the belly of the said Dorcas Cleavenger, giving to her ... one mortal bruise." Ish was also charged with aiding and abetting Henry in this killing. The judge appointed three attorneys to represent them: Alexander W. Doniphan, William T. Wood, and Eldridge Benner. Their lead attorney, Doniphan (1808–87) was a member of the state legislature at the time of their trial and, later, among other accomplishments, a hero in the Mexican War.[34] In 1840 Wood represented Clay County in the General Assembly. The trial began and probably ended on July 11, and the jury found them guilty as charged. They were hanged on a gallows erected near Richmond between 10:00 A.M. and 3:00 P.M. on Friday, August 11, 1837.[35]

Both extensive newspaper coverage and circuit court records are extant for the remaining slave death penalty case. The crime took place in Union Township, Marion County, on October 30, 1849. On that day two children of Maria and Michael Bright, 12-year-old Susannah and 10-year-old Thomas, left their home on "a very gentle nag," as their father later testified, for the purpose of gathering walnuts. He was certain that the children did not have a barlow knife with them because the family did not own such an instrument, a penknife with a single blade, named for the original maker of it, Barlow.[36] The children were expected to be home an hour before sundown, and their parents became uneasy when they failed to arrive at the designated time. Soon a search was underway, the party conducting it throughout that night and the next morning. It was composed of Mr. Bright and a number of his neighbors. The father knew that his missing children had gone toward Brower's Branch. A more diligent search was undertaken of this branch from Mr. Brower's to where it emptied into the Fabius, a larger body of water.

A neighbor of the Brights, Joseph Sallee, on Tuesday, October 31, had hunted all night for them with others until about sunrise and mainly near Brower's Branch. They located the mare first; she was hitched to a sapling approximately 15 feet from where someone spied clothes. Sallee then saw the body of Susan. She was lying on her back; her body was naked 10 or 12 inches above her hips, and her stockings were turned down over her shoes. About 70 yards further up the branch, he found the body of 10-year-old Thomas. He was lying in the branch, and his skull was crushed. There were the marks of visible blows to the forehead, crown, and left side. A large rock the size of a man's fist was found near the head of the boy, and one of the testifying physicians reasonably inferred that, from its position, this rock was the weapon used to murder the boy.

Sallee observed, among other conditions of the children's bodies, that their hands were stained from the multiple walnuts which they had hulled after gathering them. He saw that Susan's face was scratched and bruised, and he found a club nearby, five feet long with a section of it 12 to 18 inches long broken off. The smaller piece had hair on it, and he saw what he thought was blood on the larger piece. Someone in the group now summoned by the party on the scene's "hallooing" saw a barlow knife lying a foot or two from the girl's left foot. Sallee immediately recognized its importance and said, "Let no one touch the knife, let it lay." He described the instrument as having a handle part horn and part iron with a gap near the middle of the blade and what he thought were several small spots of blood where the knife joined the handle.

Sallee remained with the children's bodies between 20 and 30 minutes. His testimony and that of the two physicians, Dr. John L. Taylor and Dr. Daniel Johnson, who made postmortem examinations of the victims at the scene, present a chilling account of the violence done the person of Susannah Bright and the mutilation and desecration of her dead body. Though there was no attempt to ascertain the particular order of events, probably the killer first grabbed the girl and subdued her by hitting her in the face with the club found near her body. Then he raped her and murdered her by making a six-inch-long cut across her throat. As often happens at death, the girl had a bowel movement. The perpetrator then smeared his victim's thighs and abdomen with her own excrement; gave her several small cuts under her chin, partially or entirely cut off her ears, almost cut off her nose, and pulled big clumps of her hair out. Dr. Johnson gave as his opinion that the victims' ears were cut with a dull instrument. Both physicians testified to their belief that the children had been murdered to cover up the girl's rape.

Two male slaves were soon suspected as perpetrators because both had been hauling rock with separate teams and wagons at Mr. Brower's quarry on the day of the crime, an area near where the children's bodies were found. One was Isaac, and his owner was William Callaghan. Though Isaac was placed in the Marion County jail at Palmyra, he was soon released. His owner came with friends who swore to his good character, and more important, he had been on time as he hauled a full load of rock on the day of the crime.[37] The other suspected slave was Ben, owned by Thomas W. Glascock of nearby Shelby County. He was not on time with a full load on the day of the crime. Chancellor Brower, who hired Ben for this work, testified that from the place where this slave got fieldstone to where the girl lay was between 50 and 100 yards. Ben left about 12:30 P.M. and did not return until about 3:00 P.M.; Brower stated that it took him about an hour and one-half to bring back a full load. Ben was an hour late, and he did not have with him the rock he had been sent for; rather, those he obtained he had not carried across the branch.

Ben was arrested at about 10:00, the same morning the bodies were found. The two physicians went with the arresting party, and they testified that the suspect's clothes gave the appearance of having been recently washed. They further noted a small amount of blood on his pantaloon, and his explanation of how it was obtained, a splinter in his leg, was not supported with any physical evidence. On the front of Ben's shirt was a smeared spot; it might have been walnut stains made by the hand of the dead girl or fecal matter that had been transferred from her body to Ben's clothing. On his knuckle was an old wound that had recently been reinjured. When Dr. Taylor first spoke to Ben, he told him either that they had found evidence or a knife; the witness could not later recall his precise words. What was certain is that Ben responded that he had lost his knife on Monday, October 29, or the day before the crime. He said it was a barlow, broken in the middle, and he misdescribed its handle as being entirely horn. He volunteered that he had obtained it by trading it with one of his owner's sons, John M. Glascock.

The men who detained Ben also took him to the crime scene and forced him to look at the body of Susan Bright. According to Dr. Taylor, the slave did not exhibit any such awe or feeling as might be expected on such an occasion. However, the shock of seeing the girl's severely mutilated body might explain the suspect's emotional blankness. By November 1, after Justice of the Peace William R. Markley heard the testimony of the two physicians and one other witness, he issued an arrest warrant for Ben, and he was confined in the Marion County jail in Palmyra. At this same time the barlow knife found at the crime scene was deposited in the clerk of the circuit court's office. Later it was identified by a number of witnesses at Ben's trial. At the November 1859 term of court, the grand jury indicted him for inflicting a "mortal wound of the depth of three inches & the length of six" on Susan M. Bright "with a certain knife ... in & upon the neck & throat" which caused her instant death.

On November 24 at least 48 men were summoned for potential jury duty for Ben's trial on the charge of the first-degree murder of Susan Bright, a trial that began on Monday, November 26. His judge was Carty Wells, formerly Edward Bates's co-counsel in Fanny's case and afterward Slave Isaac's judge in a Pike County capital case. Wells appointed two lawyers to represent Ben, Samuel T. Glover and Richard F. Richmond; the latter had represented Marion County in 1844 in the General Assembly. Colonel Richmond, as the newspaper referred to him, cautioned the jury that the horror of the crime should not prejudice it against his client.

In addition to Michael Bright, the father of the children, Joseph Sallee, the man who found their bodies and some shoe tracks, perhaps Ben's, and the two doctors, the state put on two other important witnesses, children of Ben's owner, 19-or 20-year-old Mary Glascock and her brother, 9- or 10-year-old John Glascock. Mary testified that about a month before the murder she had purchased a barlow knife in Palmyra for 10 cents. She could not recall where she bought it, and she had no receipt for it. She described its handle as part horn and part steel or iron with a sharp, rather than a square, point. When she was shown the knife found at the crime scene, she stated that to the best of her knowledge it looked very much like the one she bought and later gave to her younger brother. John testified that he had traded his barlow knife, which had a gap in the middle of its edge, for one Ben owned, which had four blades, on the Saturday before the children were murdered on Tuesday. When young Glascock was shown the knife in court found at Susan Bright's feet, he stated, "I believe this is the knife I traded to Ben. I broke this gap on a piece of oak wood."

The defense put on several persons who testified about shoe tracks at the crime scene. One, Guerrant Moseley, stated that a track that the prosecution ascribed to Ben was "made by a finer shoe than blacks usually wear." Another, Josephus Terrill, a member of the Bright children's search party, testified that the track did not correspond with the defendant's foot: "he could not wear the shoe that made it." Other defense witnesses included three slaves whom Ben stayed with the night of the children's murder: Fanny, David, and John, bondpersons of Mr. French Flurrie. They took the stand and said that they noticed nothing unusual about the demeanor of the accused. No one observed his clothes, believed his clothes were wet, or saw him washing them. He arrived October 30 after dark, went to bed about 10:00 P.M., and left before daylight.

The jury then heard closing arguments. Neither court records nor newspaper coverage contain any summary of them. A. W. Lamb opened for the prosecution; Richmond and Glover stated the defense's case, and Thomas L. Anderson closed for the prosecution. Judge Wells gave all the jury instructions contained in the extant portion of the file. Some concerned circumstantial evidence; the jury was allowed to convict on its basis, but it was required to prove the guilt of the prisoner beyond all rational doubt. The jurors were permitted to decide if they found Ben guilty of murder, and if so, the degree of murder, whether first or second. They received his case at about 1:00 P.M. on Saturday, December 1, 1849, and concluded their deliberations in about 15 minutes. Their decision is contained in the surviving court record; "We the jurors find a verdict of guilty of murder in the first degree against the prisoner." It is signed Owen T. Barber, foreman. On December 4, 1849, Judge Wells sentenced Ben to hang on January 11, 1850, between noon and 2:00 P.M. The sheriff of Marion County, Barney B. King, attested on the reverse of the death warrant that he took Slave Ben from the jail of Marion County at 12:00 noon and conveyed him to the place of execution and did hang him by the neck until he was dead before the hour of 2:00 P.M. on the eleventh day of January 1850.[38] Ben's hanging was Marion County's first, and its occurrence on a warm and pleasant day on a gallows erected north of Palmyra drew a crowd estimated at 5,000 spectators. Local residents believe that he was buried in a potter's field near Palmyra that is now farmland, and no trace of his remains survives.[39]

On his way to his hanging Ben admitted his guilt. In the idiom of earlier indictments and confessions of his time and place, he said, "The devil tempted me." He went on to explain, "I saw the children and the girl looked so pretty." He acknowledged that he killed the boy first by luring him to look at "some nice fish I had caught in the branch." He hit 10-year-old Thomas Bright in the head with a rock; he approached Susan and told her when she inquired about her brother's whereabouts that he was fishing. He then caught the girl, threw her down, and "for fear she would tell, I took out my knife and cut her throat. Somehow I dropped my knife, and I was so excited I could not find it, and I ran away without it."[40]

Unlike several death-sentenced Missouri slaves, whose confessions have survived, there is no known copy of Ben's. Condemned bondmen gave their county jail statements to one or more eager hearers who transformed

Inscription on the tombstone of Slave Ben's victims, Bethany Baptist Church Cemetery, near Philadelphia, a town 12 miles west of Palmyra, Marion County, Missouri. Its inscription, "Lovely and pleasant in their lives, in death they were not divided," takes its text from the death of Saul and Jonathan in II Samuel 1:23. The Bright children are now interred in the churchyard. Over time their original burial place became a pig pen; in the early 1930s a highway district engineer, Frank Cooper, and several of his workers, disinterred their remains and moved them and their marker to its current resting place. Photograph by Helen Hollowell.

their plain-speaking words into a pseudoformal English of the previous century. In their much-doctored form they were often printed in a local newspaper soon after the slave's hanging. The genre was sufficiently popular in the antebellum period to attract enterprising publishers and avid readers. To be sure, illiterate persons needed assistance with the pompous wording for their tell-all accounts of their misdeeds. Slave Henry, hanged with his wife, America, for the murder of their master, Hiram Beasley, in 1841, began his confession, "Knowing that I have in a few days to appear in the presence of my God; I feel it to be my indispensable duty to give a correct history of the unfortunate transaction for which I am condemned to be hung."[41] This is not the language of illiteracy; however, the particulars of the crimes confessed to were probably accurately enough described. The slave confession is best described as "told to" an exploitive eager listener and writer of sensational information. The most lengthy extant confessions are those of the 1841 St. Louis crime and punishment of Slave Madison Henderson and his three free black confreres. It is 76 closely printed pages and contains an estimated 45,000 to 50,000 words. Despite the fact that all four men could read and write, they too probably had help with their highflown rhetoric. For example, Amos Alfred Warrick "confessed in contrition and deep humiliation to the Supreme Omniscience ... the most high and heinous offence known to law."[42]

Joseph Ament, editor and publisher of the *Hannibal Missouri Courier,* gave Ben's crime and trial extensive coverage. He also published his confession. His newspaper ran advertisements for it in at least three issues. One ad promised that the work would include "Ben's own confession of the manner in which he did the atrocious deed and his villainous transactions and adventures through life. The respectability of the gentleman who heard the confession is a guaranty that it is no humbug."[43] By late February 1850, "Confessions of Ben" was available at Ament's Hannibal office. Single copies were 25 cents; five copies were $1; and 20 copies were $4.[44] One or more copies were probably still in existence when the Marion County history was written in the early 1880s and they may have survived as late as the 1940s because mention is made in a book published in this decade that Ben believed he was worth $1,000.[45] He did not testify at his trial, and neither the court record nor the newspaper accounts contain any statement from him other than his insistence that he was innocent of the crime.

One reader of all Joseph Ament published regarding Slave Ben is especially interesting: Mark Twain. He was 14 years old when Slave Ben raped Susan Bright and killed her and her younger brother, Thomas. Because his father, John Clemens, died in March 1847, the family of Samuel Clemens was in difficult financial circumstances. Sam, or young Mark Twain, was required to go to work, and he found employment with Joseph Ament as a "printer's devil," that is as an apprentice in his printing shop in January 1850.[46] Sam's duties probably included setting the type for Ben's confession. What he read regarding this ghastly crime haunted him in his old age. Though he misremembered it as occurring earlier than it did, he wrote of Ben's case at least 47 years later in 1897: "The Hanged Nigger. He raped and murdered a girl of 13 in the woods. He confessed to forcing 3 young women in Virginia, and was brought away in a feather bed to save his life — which was a valuable property."[47]

Ben's exploits in Virginia were almost certainly included in his confession. The Thomas W. Glascock family, who owned him, came from this eastern seaboard state. The 1850 census stated that only the youngest of the seven children, three-year-old Nimrod, was born in Missouri. The parents and their six other children were born in Virginia, including Mary and John, who testified at Ben's trial. Ben may have fetched a higher price on the auction block than his owner would have received in compensation had he been hanged for any one of his rapes in Virginia. Most likely, he was purchased at an attractive price and brought to Missouri when the family moved to Being Township, Shelby County, in approximately 1847. Ben's new owner, Glascock, had no idea of the evil that lurked within his seemingly valuable young bondman when he bought him in Virginia, transported him to Missouri, and allowed him considerable freedom of movement away from the family's Shelby County residence and farm. The perpetrator of this horrendous crime against the Bright children was a despicable criminal who also happened to be a slave. The peculiar institution did not make him a serial rapist who preyed on innocent children, but his cash value probably motivated the authorities in Virginia to look the other way when Ben's former owner sold him to Thomas Glascock. He in turn unknowingly brought a vicious man into northeast Missouri when he and his family moved there. Slave Ben should never have been permitted to wander.

The next chapter concerns the crime of rape when it was the only felony with which the bondman was charged. In punishment of this crime, Missouri differed from every other slave state. The 1820 Missouri Constitution required that no slave suffer death for a crime that was not a capital offense for a white person. Missouri law first made rape a death penalty crime after the Civil War, and this state executed its first black rapist in the late nineteenth century and its first white one in the twentieth.

Chapter 13

Rape: The Crime, Its Punishment, and Its Pardons

With one exception, in 15 states and the District of Columbia, places where slavery existed throughout much of the Civil War, the law capitally punished any slave convicted of raping a white female. Missouri did not. Neither the District of Louisiana (1804–05), renamed Louisiana Territory (1805–12), renamed Missouri Territory (1812–21), nor the antebellum and Civil War state of Missouri (1821–65) ever executed convicted rapists. Missouri's death penalty was reserved for murderers until late in the nineteenth century. It was 1879 before death became a punishment option in this state's rape convictions,[1] and not until 1891 did this state legally hang its first rapist. The Saline County sheriff dispatched William Price at Marshall on May 8, 1891, for a rape he committed November 18, 1890. At least three newspapers describe this unappealed case as Missouri's first legal instance of an execution for rape. Predictably, Price was black and his victim white.[2]

The area that later became the state of Missouri enacted its earliest American law concerning rape in 1808. The statute both defined the crime and decreed the particulars of the punishment: "Any person or persons, who shall have carnal knowledge of any woman, forcibly and against her will, shall be deemed guilty of rape, and upon conviction thereof, shall be sentenced to castration, to be performed by the most skillful physician."[3] Its source was Virginia, a jurisdiction in which a 1792 statute distinguished between the slave's rape of a white woman (punishable by death) and the

237

slave's attempted rape of a white woman (punishable by castration). Though Virginia legislation of 1819 continued these distinctions, in 1823 it enacted a death penalty for any African American's *attempted* rape of a white woman, and it retained a death penalty for any male person of color who either raped or attempted to rape a white female throughout slavery.[4]

Likewise, and without regard to race, federal law punished rape with death as early as 1825 and retained a death penalty as late as 1984. George Washington first signed the punishment option of the additional sentence of dissection into federal law in 1790, and as late as 1948 the federal statute retained this judge-ordered choice for convicted rapists.[5] However, in 1977 the U.S. Supreme Court struck the final blow against death sentences for convicted rapists of adult women; it declared that "a death sentence is a disproportionate punishment for rape"; it violates the cruel and unusual punishment provisions of the Eighth and the Fourteenth Amendments to the U.S. Constitution.[6]

In keeping with the racial neutrality of the federal law, Missouri's earliest statutes not only made no provision for attempt crimes, but its earliest rape statute failed to distinguish between slave and free, black and white, young and old. In 1818 the Missouri Territorial Legislature continued the rape statute of 1808 without alteration.[7] However, in 1825 Missouri's General Assembly dropped the "most skillful physician" requirement of the 1808 law and substituted for it, "some skillful person under the direction of the sheriff." In rural Missouri, farmers proficient in the gelding of livestock were surely far more plentiful than physicians. Then and now doctors may have wished to disassociate their profession from punishment for crime. Sheriffs might still employ physicians to castrate convicted rapists, but doing so was no longer mandatory. The 1825 Missouri law, which remained unaltered for the next 10 years, added a jail term not to exceed seven years and a fine not to exceed $3,000 for assault with intent to commit rape. It also classified rape as carnal knowledge and abuse of any female child under the age of 10 years.[8] Though this statute was racially neutral, its imprisonment and fine provisions did not apply to Missouri's slave perpetrators. They never had liberty or property to lose.

In 1835 Missouri's legislature passed comprehensive sexual offense statutes that endured until slavery perished. Because the legislators anticipated the completion of the state penitentiary in Jefferson City, for the first time in this state's history the law provided a penitentiary term for rape, and on April 25, 1837, the recently built prison received its first rapist. He was 25 years old, convicted in Randolph County, an Irishman named Brian Johnston, and he served nearly three years.[9] The early imprisoned rapists were white, and their victims were also white. If any colored male, slave or free, attempted to rape or actually raped a white female, his punishment remained castration, to be performed under the direction of the sheriff, by some skillful person.[10]

For the most part, the preserved records of slaves as victims or perpetrators of sexual offenses are sketchy. Counting all sources of information, that is, circuit court records, county histories, newspaper accounts, appellate court decisions, and governors' pardon papers, there are approximately 25 cases. Of these, 10 are discussed in the next chapter. A history of Hickory County, in south central Missouri, related that "Among the early trials on the criminal side was that of a slave indicted for criminal assault upon a white woman. He was convicted and punished."[11] Equally euphemistic was an 1843 newspaper account about an unnamed slave who attempted to rape a German girl in St. Charles County. He has been "sentenced to the severest penalties known to our law in such a case."[12] An 1860 news story described the arrest of a Randolph County slave, Jordan, belonging to Henry Austin, for the attempted rape of Miss Lydia Blair, daughter of Dr. Blair.[13] As in other arrests of slaves for sex crimes, its outcome is unknown. Five years earlier, in 1855, two in-state papers and Garrison's *Liberator* carried the story of the attempted rape of the granddaughter of General Rogers, owner of the accused slave, in a Platte County case.[14] The unnamed slave was captured; he confessed and was committed to await his trial. There was no follow-up in either of the Missouri newspapers that initially reported the incident, and an 1864 courthouse fire destroyed all earlier Platte County court records. However, it seems reasonable to infer that there was no court action; otherwise, there would be newspaper coverage of it. Most likely, the case was handled in-house, and the slave was sold. He would be far more valuable intact than mutilated.

The odds are that when a slave sexually attacked a member of his owner's family but did not murder her, his crime was not referred to a court. Instead, his owner sold him, probably through an agent, to a southern buyer who did not know that his new property had raped or attempted to rape a white Missouri woman or girl. This was so for two reasons. His owner was required to pay all court costs in any rape or attempted rape conviction, and the court-ordered punishment severely reduced the value of the castrated slave. Likewise, when male slaves sexually attacked slave girls and women, the evidence suggests that their cases were never referred to the courts. In addition to the factors that discouraged the prosecution of bondmen who attacked white members of the owner's family, the owner of any raped female whose slave had attained pubescence enjoyed this advantage. He became the owner of any child born of the assault. The owner decided the attacker's punishment, if any, and it was surely limited to a whipping, a sale, or both. Finally, it is no surprise that whenever males of any race or condition of servitude sexually assaulted free women of color, there are no known antebellum records. However, free African Americans, as a percentage of the total of Missouri's black population, hovered between two and three percent in all five federal censuses between 1820 and 1860.[15] There were few free women of color in this state; especially in rural areas, the overwhelming majority were slaves.

The race of the victim in the earliest of Missouri's known court records concerning slavery and sexual assault is a surprise. The case arose in the town of Cape Girardeau, Cape Girardeau County, in 1834. On November 30 of that year, Reuben Sherwood, a resident of Scott County, was committed to the common jail in Jackson for committing a rape on Nancy Ellis, a Negro girl. It is not credible that the accused was a black or a mulatto because this state's court records of the time invariably identified the race of any African American mentioned in them. Four witnesses, three men and a boy, appeared before Justice of the Peace Levi L. Lightner to testify against Sherwood. Their evidence placed him in the town of Cape Girardeau on November 26, a Wednesday. One witness, John Jacobs, a boy, testified that he was at the mouth of the branch that empties into the Mississippi River when he heard Nancy's "hallooing." At first he thought that it was children playing, but as he ascended the branch's bank, he saw the prisoner and "asked him what he was doing there, and was answered by the prisoner's saying 'go to hell.'" Jacobs then saw that Sherwood had the bondchild on the ground. She was "hallooing" and telling her assailant that he hurt her; Sherwood was on top of her, and there was blood on the girl's garments. The next day, the boy asked the prisoner what he was doing the previous night: "the prisoner answered that 'he would kill this deponent if he told on him' and further this deponent saith not." James Boon testified that he had seen Sherwood on November 26 at a grocery store in which the proprietor told him that "he, Sherwood, had drank enough." Later, Boon was returning from across the branch about 8:00 P.M. when he heard some person say at least three times, "Let me alone or [I] will tell master." Boon saw a boy there whom he afterward learned was the witness, John Jacobs. A third person, John Cree, stated that he was one of the men who followed the accused to Commerce, a town on the Mississippi River in Scott County. There, Cree observed blood on Sherwood's shirt-tail and said, "This is a bad deed you have done. He answered it was. He said he knew he had done the deed, but he was intoxicated with liquor." Another witness, A. P. Ellis, probably the victim's owner, stated that he knew nothing of the circumstances charged against the prisoner, but the girl Nancy "is between 7 and 8 years of age."

The file also clarified that John Cree appeared before a Scott County justice of the peace, T. S. Smith, to state that Sherwood "did violently and feloniously make an assault in and upon the said Nancy Ellis ... forcibly and against the will of her the said Nancy ... did ravish and carnally know" her. As a result, Justice of the Peace Smith authorized Sherwood's arrest and delivery to a Cape Girardeau County constable. Court costs in the case included guarding the prisoner in Commerce and hiring two guards for transporting him from there to the town of Cape Girardeau, the scene of the crime.[16] Because there were sufficient white witnesses against Sherwood, Missouri law, which barred persons of color from testifying against Caucasians, was no obstacle. The prosecutor did not need the testimony of the black victim against the white perpetrator in order to make his case against the accused. If he had, it is unlikely that any charges would have been filed. Regrettably, this case's outcome is unknown.

These brief documents clarified that Missouri filed criminal charges against a white male for the rape of a bondchild, aged seven or eight years. It is unlikely that the prosecution persuaded an all-white-male jury to convict him because castration was the state's only available punishment for rape in 1834. However, Missouri law allowed charges to be brought for rape when the victim was a slave, and the odds are that most slave states did not. For example, the Supreme Court of Mississippi dismissed an indictment brought against a male slave for the rape of a female slave. It held that "the crime of rape does not exist in this state between African slaves."[17] Schwarz summarizes the law of Virginia as one that "simply did not criminalize the rape of slave women."[18] In North Carolina the rape of a slave was not a crime against the slave; it was a trespass upon her master's property. Yellin cites several North Carolina statutes to document that Harriet Jacobs, a former slave from this eastern state, had no legal remedy against the sexual advances of her owner.[19] Jacobs well described these advances in her 1861 narrative, *Incidents in the Life of a Slave Girl*, which Yellin edited in this century. To be sure, the Callaway County prosecution of Slave Celia in 1855 cast a lengthy shadow over any imagined protection that Missouri law actually afforded slave victims of their owners' rape. Nonetheless, 21 years earlier and in Cape Girardeau County, a white man, Reuben Sherwood, was charged with the rape of Nancy Ellis, a slave child. Though this rape case was the only discovered one involving a white perpetrator and an African American victim, its existence is important. Such a court record creates one exception to the all-pervasive racism associated with the slave states' prosecutions of sex offenses. However, in all other known sex crimes in Missouri involving slaves, the victims were white, and the alleged perpetrators were bondboys and -men.

In October 1843 the grand jurors of Callaway County indicted William for the rape on August 27, 1843, of Malcena Threekeld, a white female. William pled guilty, and the circuit court ordered the slave prisoner's owner, John B. Leaper, to pay court costs and the sheriff to see that his prisoner was castrated. There are no records of whether William's court-ordered punishment was either appealed or carried out.[20] The same is true of an 1854 Cooper County case wherein a 23-year-old unnamed slave attempted to rape his mistress, herself the daughter of one of the county's best-known and wealthiest citizens. The newspaper account closed with mention of the defendant's conviction.[21] All other extant records of sexual offenses concerning slaves either specify that one man owned the slave charged with a sexual offense and the victim was not a member of the owner's family, or the sketchy record is silent regarding the slave's ownership.

Fragments of a case involving a sex crime that was filed against a slave survive from southeastern Missouri. It arose August 12, 1854, in Mississippi County, which bordered the state of Kentucky and the Mississippi River, when Simon allegedly assaulted, with the intent to rape, Mary Weekly, a white female over the age of 10 years. After Simon's indictment for an attempt to commit rape, he sought and secured a change of venue on grounds that "the minds of the inhabitants of [Mississippi County] are so prejudiced against him that he cannot have a fair trial." Elish Keen, presumably Simon's owner, posted a $1,000 recognizance bond, to be levied of his goods and chattels, lands and tenements, to guarantee the court appearance of Simon in Cape Girardeau County Circuit Court on November 28, 1854. The file also contains a subpoena for Elizabeth Weekly, most likely a relative of the victim, to testify on the part of the defendant on May 28, 1855. On that same date and for now unknown reasons, the prosecutor filed a nolle prosequi, that is a dismissal of charges against Simon,[22] the only located change of venue in a slave rape case.

Fragments of two slave sex crime cases survive from Saline County. The first arose on July 31, 1844, when Henry, who belonged to John A. Trigg and was living with Mr. Smith, probably the slave's lessee, assaulted with an attempt to rape Mrs. Margaret Bright, a white female over 18 years of age. Her testimony before a justice of the peace the next day detailed the perpetrator's lies, criminal acts, and evidence of his presence at the crime scene. According to her testimony, Henry was at her house the previous day. When she questioned him regarding the reason for his presence on her and her husband's property, he told her that he was "hunting horses," belonged to "old man Faber," and was living with a "Roberts" or "Robison," she could not recall the exact name. She stated that as she sat weaving in her home, Henry looked at her through cracks in the boards. He invited her to join him in the cornfield; she declined and threatened him with a shovel if he did not leave. Her testimony continued,

> He then came in at the door with the ax and drew it over me and said he would kill me. I said no you won't. He said yes I will, and raised the ax to strike me. I then took hold of the ax, and he let it go and caught hold of me and tried to choke me, and I let go [of] the ax and got loose from him, and I then got the ax again, and I saw no more of him.

Her statement concluded that in all the commotion, Henry's "hat got knocked off ... [and] he left it together with his coat, blanket, and shirt." On the basis of her statement before the justice of the peace, the slave was committed to the Saline County jail.

In September 1844 the grand jury indicted him for striking at "the head, neck, shoulders, arms, and body of Margaret Bright with intent thereby to commit a rape," that is with an attempt to "defile" her. On September 27 John A. Trigg, as principal, and Abner Trigg, as surety, pledged $500 that Henry "shall be taken or sent out of the state of Missouri within sixty days ... and *shall not return* into the state for twenty years" because he "has been convicted of a felony, ... [and in] the opinion of the ... circuit court ... it is not safe that ... Slave Henry should remain in the state." The file contains one additional document, a motion for a new trial.[23] Significantly, the record does not disclose Henry's precise felony conviction. Probably it was assault, a crime punished with a whipping, not castration. As such, Henry remained a valuable property and his sale at a southern market routine.

Another Saline County sex crime case arose on July 17, 1854, when Lee, a Negro man, leased by William Parks but owned by David Todd, beat, bruised, wounded, and ill treated a white female over 10 years of age, Laura Neil, with an intent "to forcibly ravish and carnally know" her. The slave was arrested and confined in the county jail in Marshall, and bail set at $1,000, at least $15,000 today. At its November 1854 term the grand jury voted a true bill against Lee for "attempting to commit a rape," and the trial jury found the prisoner guilty "as charged in the second and third counts of the written indictment." Since the indictment is missing, the offense(s) that formed the basis of Lee's conviction is unknown. Because the bill of costs did not include any postconviction services rendered by the sheriff, most likely the jury did not find him guilty of any crime punishable with castration. Rather, the usual fees for subpoenas, recognizance bonds, transporting, safekeeping, and maintaining the prisoner made up the charges of $14.80 in this case. Another bill totaling $14.30 was issued to David Todd on February 5, 1855,[24] and it does not appear to be a rewrite of the other. Most likely, Lee's owner was also Jim's owner. A Howard County jury sentenced Jim to death in 1832. When the Supreme Court of Missouri issued its only decision in a male slave death penalty case, Todd's Jim obtained a change of venue. The Honorable David Todd died in Columbia, Boone County, in his seventy-third year in June 1859,[25] or four and one-half years after David Todd's Slave Lee was convicted in Saline County. Any slave owned in Boone County was easily leased in Saline, two counties west of Boone.

The remaining files concerning slavery and rape consist of either appeals court records, governors' pardon papers, or both. From territorial days only one known appellate decision survives, and because there are no references in it to either the defendant's or the victim's race, both are presumed to have been white. It took place at an unspecified time in what is now the state of Arkansas, but what was then either still a part of Missouri Territory or recently created Arkansas Territory. In a territorial court, the jury found Thomas Dickinson guilty of the rape of Sally Hall. The judge pronounced judgment of castration to be performed on Dickinson, the convicted rapist, by a skillful physician under the direction of the sheriff of Arkansas County. An appeal was taken from this decision to the Superior Court of Arkansas Territory. This court came into existence when the Fifteenth U.S. Congress in March 1819 established Arkansas Territory from the southern part of Missouri Territory. Though this newly created appellate court upheld the trial court's judgment, the defendant was not mutilated. A note followed the case: "This sentence was not executed, the prisoner having been pardoned by ... the governor of Arkansas Territory."[26]

In 1844 the Supreme Court of Missouri decided its first of two cases concerning slaves convicted of sex crimes against white women. It affirmed a conviction for Slave Nathan's attempted rape of an unnamed white woman in Macon County,[27] in north central Missouri. A county history mentioned that Rebecca Matthews owned Slave Nathan, who was charged with a "nameless crime" in August 1842, a date that is probably earlier than the actual event. This history concluded of this case, "It is presumed that the order of the court was carried out."[28] When Williams visited the Macon County Courthouse in Macon, she attempted to ascertain whether any extant court documents affirm Nathan's punishment. She could locate none.[29]

Another sex crime case arose in Howard County in December 1847 when Bill was indicted for attempting to rape a white woman. His trial was set for June 1848, and on June 7 of that year his owner, David H. Witt, posted a recognizance bond in the amount of $500 that Bill would be present on December 4 for trial, and he was found guilty on December 11, 1848.[30] Pardon papers in his case explained its outcome. The initial request for executive clemency for him was made to Governor John Edwards. The earliest letter about his case was signed by 50 male citizens of Howard County, one of whom identified himself as one of Bill's jurors. The petition assured the governor that no attempt could be made to help a prisoner "believed to be guilty of a crime so outrageous, inhuman, and revolting." However, in closing, the petitioners emphasized that if the sentence was carried out, the many signers would "forever be impressed with the opinion that a humble but innocent human being, has suffered wrongfully." Another letter to Edwards repeatedly insisted that Bill was innocent, and it requested that the governor take action. On December 25, 1848, Edwards, who would soon leave office, granted Slave Bill a three-week respite.

Other letters in the file are addressed to Edwards's successor, Governor A. A. King. A number of men, at least 45, signed a petition to him requesting a pardon for Bill. In the petition one signer identified himself as a juror in the case and another as a witness for the state. In a letter from the appointed prosecutor, these details emerged. Lucy Wilkerson, the 75-to-80-year-old widowed victim, was the one witness to prove that it was Bill who assaulted her, and she recognized him only by his voice in the daytime on a public road. The vagaries of victim testimony become especially suspect when she, never described as blind, can only identify her attacker by his voice when the crime against her took place in broad daylight. One suspects that the elderly victim was impaired both physically and mentally, but Bill's attorney feared effective cross-examination of any white woman who charged a black male with a sex crime. The prosecutor wrote Governor King that "the evidence was very unsatisfactory, and I thought the jury should, and believed they would, acquit Bill. I have understood that executive clemency will be invoked in Bill's behalf and believing that he is innocent do not hesitate to recommend him." In closing, the prosecutor assured the governor that "Mr. Witt will dispose of Bill out of this state if he should be pardoned by your Excellency." The profit motive, which allowed the owner to sell a nongelded and hence more valuable slave, lurked in the background of several of these cases, including Bill's. However, for reasons that surely included the righting of a wrongful conviction, on January 4, 1849, Governor King pardoned Slave Bill.[31]

The remaining case concerning a slave's rape of a white woman contained the most detailed documentation. Nine years after the Supreme Court of Missouri affirmed Slave Nathan's conviction, it upheld another slave castration case from St. Louis Criminal Court, that of John Anderson for the attempted rape of Rebecca Ann Hewett, a white female. The defense team of more than three lawyers argued, among other points of law, that the punishment was unconstitutional, being "cruel and unusual."[32] Though the 1820 Missouri Constitution prohibited the infliction of "cruel and unusual punishments,"[33] the court affirmed without addressing the constitutionality of the statute. However, the sheriff of St. Louis County did not carry out the mutilation of John Anderson.

A detailed packet of documents has survived in his case. Among much else that it made known is the identity of the convicted slave's lessee. He was a grandson of General Daniel Bissell, an early St. Louis pioneer. At Bissell's death in 1833 he owned a large farm nine miles north of the city of St. Louis on the road to Cantonment Bellefontaine. One of General Bissell's daughters, Mary, married Risdon H. Price, and his slave, Elijah, is discussed in chapter 4. Elijah is probably the same slave whom David Barton defended in 1818 on charges of conspiring to murder his mistress, Mrs. John Smith. Certain it is that Mary and Risdon H. Price were the parents of Frederick Price and Risdon H. Price. Their son Frederick was living on his grandfather's estate in the 1850s.[34] Among the slaves in residence at the Negro quarters on this farm in the 1850s was Slave John Anderson. One or both of Bissell's grandsons, Frederick and Risdon H. Price, rented John Anderson from Miss Mildred Reardon, described in the pardon papers as "an old maid" who inherited her Negro man from her father. She leased him to Mr. Price on a yearly basis, and her slave's labor was her sole means of support as well as her ability to provide charity for her widowed sister and sister's child. "The sentence if carried into effect would render him of little or no value," read a part of a petition to the governor signed by more than 30 men. The Price brothers were the first to sign this document requesting executive clemency for John Anderson, sentenced to be castrated.

James R. Lackland, judge of the St. Louis Criminal Court, and formerly one of the defendant's attorneys before the Supreme Court of Missouri, wrote to Governor Sterling Price the most detailed explanation of Anderson's case, a 13-page letter. In it Judge Lackland explained that some time prior to the encounter between the 18-year-old white woman, Rebecca Ann Hewett, and the convicted slave, "Mr. Price, the gentleman for whom defendant was working, had ordered her off his place." On an unspecified date, Lackland's letter continued, Anderson was coming to the city with a load of hay for Mr. Price when he met Hewett, who asked him for money.

He knew that she had been in the habit of "visiting his master's or hirer's negro quarters and would sell her favor to men." Anderson told her that he had no money, "but he would give her some in the evening as he came home, if she would let him have connection with her," a common nineteenth-century euphemism for sexual intercourse. Miss Hewett agreed, and on his return trip, Anderson alighted from the wagon and sent it on with another man, probably another owned or leased slave of Mr. Price.

Once Anderson paid Hewett 50 cents for her future services, she refused to have connection with him. He walked beside her and demanded either the return of his money or the bargained-for sex. When they happened to meet two men on the road, she cried, "Rape!" Her story before "the committing magistrate" involved a tale of violence, that Anderson threw her down on the plank road, dragged her 40 or 50 yards from it, tossed her down in the leaves, and "accomplished his purpose.... She resisted by struggling and hallooing with all her might." After his rape of her, according to Hewitt's initial story, "they both came out to the plank road and walked down the road together toward St. Louis until they met Edgington and Shordon," later witnesses in the case.

At trial neither of these men corroborated her story. They testified that they saw no marks of violence on either her or her clothing. Further, when they inspected the place on the road from which she claimed Anderson had dragged her to a particular stump, they saw no disturbance in the leaves, which were four inches thick in the location. Edgington stated that he scrutinized the area a second time because "he could easily see the tracks made by himself the first time he was there.... He examined the leaves ... and could see no sign whatever of any such struggling or violence as described by Hewett." These men also denied that Anderson "attempted to molest her in their view and denied that she called upon them for help and denied that they rescued her."

Later the complaining witness changed her story. Instead of being the victim of rape, as she had previously sworn before the committing magistrate, she testified at trial that Anderson had attempted to rape her: "defendant did not effect his purpose ... [and] there was no penetration of her body because he was too large for her." Afterwards, according to Hewett, Anderson "choked and smothered her until her face and throat were black and blue." To make him cease his violence toward her, she gave him 50 cents, and once they were strolling down the road together, "he gave it back to her." When Edgington and Shordon met the alleged rapist and his victim, she was carrying "a shoulder of bacon, some cakes, quilt pieces, and a half-dollar in money.... She had her bonnet on, had her hair done up close and nice," and they saw "no signs of external violence about her person or dress or the person or dress of the defendant." Lackland noted the contradiction between Hewett's words and deeds when he wrote, "It [is] absurd to say that she would calmly walk, in the middle of one of the most thronged thoroughfares leading out of the City, with a man who had robbed her ... of her virtue,.... and under such circumstances, she should take such care of her little things." The judge reemphasized that Hewett's "meat, quilt pieces, cakes, and money and all her clothes [were] in perfect order. Does this look like the flight of an honest virtuous virgin from one who had been and was endeavoring to ruin her?"

At his trial the defendant proved, as Lackland wrote, "that Hewett was a worthless degraded creature without any visible means of support.... She associated with and visited negroes, bond and free, and no person else." Further, after her alleged rape/attempted rape, "she took up her abode in a bawdy house ... and has been reportedly seen in company with notorious prostitutes, visiting birds of a like feather confined in our county jail." A letter to Governor Price from James Carteld, the St. Louis County jailer, supported Lackland's opinion of Miss Hewett: "She frequently visited the jail to see prisoners and prostitutes, and a more slovenly, filthy looking, creature of her sex cannot be seen in the streets of the city." The petition signed by more than 30 men also described her as "a base and abandoned woman of bad character for virtue."

These same documents spoke highly of Anderson's reputation. The jailer began his pardon-requesting letter, "The slave, Anderson, who is under sentence for rape I have known for nearly 20 years. No slave in our vicinity bears a better character." Another petitioner, Frederick Hyatt, of Florissant, St. Louis County, wrote the governor, "I have known the said Anderson from a boy and never before heard any complaint of him." Lackland also advised Price that at his trial, Anderson put on evidence to prove that he had a good character. Under such circumstances, how could any jury believe Hewitt and convict Anderson of attempted rape? The judge clarified that the defendant took the stand in his own behalf and admitted that he offered her 50 cents for sex. The jury was prejudiced by what "they believed to be audacious conduct in a negro to solicit a white woman to commit fornication with him." There could be no other "grounds upon which we can account for the extraordinary verdict of guilty rendered against him."

Among the documents in the packet concerning Slave John Anderson is Governor Price's unconditional pardon of him, dated January 27, 1854.[35] That there were monetary considerations at stake in the petitioners' request for justice does not render the pardon unworthy. These letters, including one from the clerk of the circuit court and another from a marshal, speak well of the enlightened St. Louisans who signed a petition on the slave's behalf. They also bear witness that capable attorneys represented him, carried his case to the Supreme Court of Missouri, and when unable to obtain relief for their client from the judiciary, then, especially Judge James Lackland, sought, vigorously pursued, and obtained it from the governor.

Given the immense variety in these cases, generalizations about slavery and rape in Missouri are not easy to make. However, we know that the framers of Missouri's 1820 constitution, men such as David Barton and Edward Bates, put in this document several important provisions for the equal protection of slaves. Among them was the requirement that "a slave convicted of a capital offense shall suffer the same degree of punishment and no other that would be inflicted on a free white person for a like offence." In 1836 Arkansas's first constitution contained an almost identical provision. However, when Slave Charles was sentenced to death in 1850 for an attempted rape of a white woman and his attorney argued that his client's death violated the Arkansas Constitution because no white could be sentenced to death for the same offense, the Supreme Court of Arkansas dismissed the constitutional provision as nothing more than a "feeling of humanity toward the unfortunate African race."[36] Though it reversed Charles's death sentence on other grounds, there are no Supreme Court of Missouri decisions in any slave criminal cases, including any sex crimes, that casually dismissed Missouri's constitutional protections regarding bondpersons, either those accused or convicted of crimes. Likewise, the introduction of a bill in 1855 in the Missouri General Assembly dealing with slave sex crimes and white females did not become law. Had it passed, this bill would have made it a capital offense for a Negro to rape or attempt to rape a white woman. The legislators who argued against it cited the provisions of the Missouri Constitution that prohibited any distinction in capital cases in either offense or method of executing slave and free white.[37]

All other American slave jurisdictions punished the slave's rape of a white woman much more harshly than did Missouri. For example, Schwarz reports that between 1785 and 1865 Virginia executed at least 58 slaves for raping white women.[38] No court-ordered hanging of slaves for this crime ever took place in Missouri. After castration, barring death through infection, life was not extinct as it was after punishment by death. Though there is no known surviving documentation regarding the actual punishment of castration, probably it occurred but not with any frequency. One expects county histories, not court records, to gloss over delicate subjects such as rape and its punishment. Insofar as there are details concerning slave rape convictions, the details are in the pardon papers. Both Slave Bill's and Slave John Anderson's exonerations are welcome discoveries.

As long as Missouri was a slave state, castration remained the only legal punishment of a slave convicted of the rape or attempted rape of a white woman. Once slavery ended in Missouri, the legislature soon repealed the castration statutes. Between 1866 and 1891 all convicted rapists, both black and white, lucky enough to escape mob violence were punished with a term of years in the penitentiary in Jefferson City. Missouri law protected slaves convicted of rape from the most extreme legal consequences of racism, namely execution by the county sheriff pursuant to court order. However, the extralegal deaths of slaves, many of whom were suspected of sexual offenses against white women, were never controlled by constitutional provision or state statute.

The next chapter discusses what historians who generalize about the punishment of slaves tell us did not take place, that is their lynching. Contrary to such assertions, Missouri slaves were the victims of mob violence.

Chapter 14

Antebellum Lynchings of Blacks, Slave and Free

Missouri's black victims of mobocracy during its antebellum and Civil War eras are listed in appendix 5. Before discussing any particulars, it is necessary to clarify what a lynching is and what it is not. As used in this book, it is the work of a mob that, without any legal authority, fatally harms another human. No court authorizes the action against the killed, and no sheriff or other law enforcement officer carries out the destroyed person's punishment pursuant to a warrant, which specifies the method, date, time, and place of death. The nature of the torment is not its essence; hanging, burning, shooting, stoning, or any other manner of causing intentional death(s) of the mob's victim(s) are all possible means. Equally important, a death always results, and it is directly caused by mob action. Among the listed but unqualified as victims of lynchings in Missouri were those who, though wounded, no matter how seriously, survived their injuries; were murdered by fewer than four persons; committed suicide rather than risk capture by a mob; died of a heart attack while sitting in a chair at home; and the crowd threatened but law enforcement officers protected from vigilantes. Likewise, excluded from Missouri lynchings were any deaths that, though reported in in-state newspapers and otherwise meeting all tests, occurred in another state. At least 25 incidents that the *Chicago Tribune* (the foremost and most complete collector of such atrocities nationwide between 1881 and 1918) listed as this state's lynchings did not fulfill all criteria for one or more of these reasons. Yet another factor that is always a vital component of this peculiar form of lawlessness, as McGovern explains, is "community approval, either ..., in the ... general participation by the local citizens, or ... in the ... acquittal of the killers with or without a trial. Approbation by the community [is] also usually confirmed by such public activities of the lynch mob as a manhunt and chase and display of the victim's body in a conspicuous place."[1]

Probably because the great flowering of rabble violence in America occurred after the Civil War, the belief exists that slavery protected blacks from mob rage. In an otherwise extremely perceptive study of Missouri, Michael Fellman writes, "Lynching of blacks commenced in Missouri at the end of the War."[2] Lawrence M. Friedman notes that "Lynching was hardly necessary as an instrument of terror and domination during slavery. But after the war lynching became a 'crucial extramural prop' of white supremacy."[3] Edward L. Ayers describes a new threat, "the crime that haunted so many ... white Southerners in the late 1880's and early 1890's; the rape of white women by black men."[4] Clearly, the black man's imagined sexual assault of white women disturbed white Missourians far earlier.

In jurisdictions wherein the law authorized the compensation of the slaveholder when a court condemned his human property to death and a sheriff carried out the sentence, the murder of slaves at the hands of a crowd was probably uncommon. After all, the lawful execution of bondpersons was fortuitous for the owner. Any mob that ended a slave's life wrongfully interfered with the master's right to the state's (or the District of Columbia's) compensation of the slaveholder for his property loss. Equally important, the slavery of states that reimbursed owners when their human properties were executed has been much more intensively studied than that of states that did not. When reading antebellum Missouri newspapers, I found no pre–Civil War stories about vigilante action against African Americans in Delaware, the District of Columbia, Florida, Georgia, Louisiana, Maryland, North Carolina, or Virginia. I located Missouri news stories about mob acts against slaves in South Carolina, Alabama, Kentucky, Arkansas, Mississippi, Tennessee, and Texas. Most of these acts took place in jurisdictions that either provided no compensation to owners when slaves were legally executed (Arkansas and Tennessee), or restricted it to one-half of the slave's value (Mississippi), or hemmed it in with other restrictions (Texas).

Some occurred in states that compensated owners of executed slaves; one in South Carolina is especially memorable. It took place, as did most of these mob deaths of slaves, in the 1850s. A man who killed his master there fled to Georgia, where he was arrested and returned to the Abbeville,

South Carolina, jail. Near this town, reported one Missouri newspaper, "Slave Mose ... was burned ... in the presence of a large concourse of people.... It was determined without a dissenting voice, to inflict summary punishment upon the criminal, instead of leaving the matter to take the ordinary legal course."[5] The mob numbered more than 4,000 persons, and it, as another Missouri newspaper reported, "heaped fat pine-wood, so as to make a pile six-feet in diameter and four feet high. Fire was then applied, and the poor wretch was burned to ashes."[6] This was the same South Carolina county where, as late as 1830, a slave convicted of the attempted murder of his mistress was burned to death pursuant to court order. In contrast was Missouri, a place with a territorial history. From the inception of American rule, its judges could not impose a more harsh death sentence than the hanging permitted by federal law. On the other hand, as late as 1840 the South Carolina legislature left to the discretion of its judges "the kind of death to be inflicted" when capitally sentencing bondpersons.[7] Under such circumstances the Abbeville, South Carolina, mob used fire to lynch a slave; a generation earlier and in the same locale, burning had not only been legal, but the state had executed a condemned slave by igniting him.

The earliest located stories that the rural Missouri press carried concerned the citizens of Vicksburg, Mississippi, finding "the laws of the State insufficient for their protection against the swarms of professional Gamblers and sowers of sedition among the Negroes." The newspaper reported that in addition to various gambling white men, 13 blacks had been hanged for "attempting to excite a rebellion among the negroes." An account of another incident, headlined "Insurrection of Slaves in Mississippi," explained that in Madison County "an insurrection has ... been on hand among the negroes, for the last six months, headed by white men.... About ten negroes and five or six white men have been hung, without any form of law or trial, except an examination before the examining committee. They are still going on trying and hanging."[8]

Other Mississippi lynchings of slaves include three separate incidents that resulted in the death of the captured slave by burning him to death, one in Hinds County[9] and the other two in Washington County.[10] After one bondman in the latter locale killed a slave woman, local vigilantes set him on fire in the presence of the Negroes on adjacent plantations. As the paper reported "all [the slaves] seemed terrified out of their wits on viewing so awful a scene.... The spirit of the negro was unsubdued. He died cursing his judges—his last words being that he would 'take vengeance on them when they met each other in h—l.'"[11]

The sheriff of Hot Spring County, Arkansas, brought a chained Negro through Memphis, Tennessee. He had murdered his master, another white man, and three Negroes and had burned their homes. The paper referred to the culprit slave as "the infuriated demon," and its story concluded, "The wretch will most assuredly expiate his diabolical infamy in the flame. We raise our protest against such punishment, notwithstanding the monstrous crime."[12] Another Arkansas lynching took place near Old Town, after two slaves brutally murdered their master while he was "gunning" on his plantation. As the newspaper described it, "The body was found the next day, and the guilt of the negroes being ... established, they were taken out, tied to a tree, and burnt to death."[13]

Almost certainly, a more systematic examination of the extant antebellum newspapers would uncover still more lynchings in the same states about which Missouri's press reported, but not in states such as Virginia, which potentially subjected its human chattel to execution for any of its 73 capital offenses for those in bondage. Schwarz concludes of the infrequency of bondpersons' lynchings in Virginia that "Before 1865, white leaders' insistence that major slave crimes be tried in courts of law ensured at least some protection for slave defendants and convicts."[14] In Missouri white leaders did not have the same pecuniary interests as those of Virginia. On the contrary, due process for accused persons, including slaves, never enriched Missouri's slaveholders. Richard Maxwell Brown notes that although ordinary men formed the rank and file of any vigilante movement, "usually, its direction was firmly in the hands of the local elite. The local vigilante leaders often paid the highest taxes. They had the customary desire to whittle down the tax rate and keep local expenses in check."[15] When lynch law was used prior to any judicial proceedings, it avoided the multiple fees in criminal cases, described principally in chapter 6. In addition to its cost effectiveness, mob law was swift and its results usually certain.

Just as county sheriffs legally executed slave women and girls in Missouri, two known bondwomen were lynched. The first incident that resulted in fatal mob violence against a slave woman took place in Clay County. The most intriguing aspect of the case is the victim's possible relationship to the subject of the first execution of any Missouri slave that extant court records document. In the summer of 1828 Sheriff Shubael Allen hanged Annice in Clay County, following her conviction for the drowning murder of five of her master's, Jeremiah Pryor's, slave children, two of whom, Bill, aged five years, and Nelly, aged two years, were the murderer's own children. However, no records specify that Slave Annice was the mother of only two children.

The year after his hanging execution of Slave Annice I, Shubael Allen placed a runaway ad in several Missouri newspapers, the *Galena (Illinois) Intelligencer,* and the *Vandalia (Illinois) Advertiser.* He offered a $60 reward for the apprehension and delivery of two Negro men and one girl, described as "about 17 years old, common size, of a yellow complexion, down look, well grown, and likely: her clothing is not recollected."[16] Allen's runaway girl was also named Annice, and she was of an appropriate age to have been an older daughter of Annice I, hanged for murder when Annice II was about 16 years old. Though no known bill of sale survives that documents Jeremiah Pryor's transfer of Annice II to Sheriff Allen, the conveyance of bondpersons from one owner to another was a common occurrence. Moreover, no bill of sale concerning any slave was located in the course of researching this book. Therefore, her consignment to the man who may have been her mother's hangman remains a possibility.

Sheriff Allen's runaway ad bore fruit, at least in the case of the "likely girl" who ran away; Annice II was returned to him. When her owner, one of Clay County's most prominent early citizens, died in 1842, at age 48, his widow, Dinah Allen, became the administratrix of his estate. In April of that year she petitioned the probate court that she be permitted to retain his goods and chattels and to pay all debts of the estate from the sale of various lands her late husband had owned. In the court order granting her petition the document specifically mentioned "Annice" as one of four slaves who were not to be sold.[17]

Eight years later, in 1850, Annice II remained a bondwoman of Dinah Allen. In the first newspaper article about her owner, headlined "Daring Attempted Murder," her mistress was described as "universally esteemed and beloved, … a universal favorite among all who know her." The news story explained that on April 1 about 3:00 A.M., she was awakened by "what she supposed [was] the bite of a rat." The victim went into the bedroom where her sons were sleeping and exclaimed that she was bleeding to death. She had been struck in the face with an ax or a large knife. Two physicians were immediately sent for, and she survived the attack by a person or persons then unknown.[18] Four weeks later the local newspaper linked the attempted arsenic poisoning of four members of a Clay County family, Wade Moseby's, by their "negro woman" with the attempted murder of Dinah Allen. The paper stated of the crime against Mrs. Allen: "the general impression [is] that the author of this brutal and unheard of outrage is a negro woman and servant to the unfortunate sufferer." The story requested for both these suspected slave women offenders "exemplary and condign [suitable] punishment. If the law which takes cognizance of such offences is not sufficiently rigid to prevent their commission, then it is time that some signal measures should be taken…. This thing should be looked into."[19]

On the basis of the Allen sons' suspicions that Annice II had some knowledge of the attempt on their mother's life, the slave woman was incarcerated in the Clay County jail in Liberty. Just as the authorities sent a minister to the St. Louis jail in 1818 to obtain Slave Elijah's admission that he attempted to poison his mistress, so too did an unnamed Clay County minister visit Annice "at different times" and gradually obtain her confession, as the newspaper phrased it, "voluntarily and without any description of compulsion" that she had attempted to kill her owner.

She told the minister that "a white man by the name of McClintock" suggested to her that they murder Mrs. Allen so they could get all the money she had, and afterward, "he would take her to California and make her his wife," and she would be "free." Annice agreed to McClintock's plan, and according to her statement, he brought the murder weapon, an ax, with him when he came into the Allen kitchen where she was sleeping; together they left the cook room, a separate building. Next, her fellow assailant opened Mrs. Allen's bedroom window, and both these early morning burglars went to the sleeping place of their victim. According to Annice, McClintock related to her Dinah Allen's position in bed, told her where to strike, and directed her blow to her mistress' face. When the axed woman struggled rather than died, her assailants left the crime scene. The white man scurried away over the yard fence, and the slave woman returned to her pallet in the kitchen.

The presentation of this story and evidence corroborative of it to a jury in a court of law had an immense difficulty: the Missouri statute that, from 1804 until the end of slavery, barred a black or mulatto from testifying against a white person. Further, because their intended victim survived their attack on her, neither Annice nor McClintock were death-eligible under the law. They had not committed murder. Had they been tried and found guilty of attempted murder, Annice could only have been sentenced to a whipping, sale, and transportation out of state and McClintock to a maximum of 10 years in the penitentiary.

As the newspaper saw it, "The statute laws of the state afford no adequate remedy ... to protect [the people] against the villainous machinations of negroes and their white abettors." As a result, the county's white male citizenry, comprising "farmers, mechanics, merchants, lawyers, physicians, and others," met at the Clay County Courthouse to decide on an appropriate extralegal remedy. In the presence of the assembled, Annice appeared, as did McClintock, and she accused him of being a willing partner in the plot to murder Dinah Allen. After those present made "a full and deliberate investigation of all the facts and circumstances," by acclamation the "ablest and most respectable citizens" decided that both Annice and McClintock "should be publicly executed, and there was not a voice against it." Some present opposed the lynching, "but they remained silent when the vote was taken." Accordingly, on Thursday, May 9, 1850, and "in broad open daylight, by men of as much respectability as can be found in the United States," Annice and, afterward, McClintock "were taken half a mile from town and hung." The paper stated of the men who lynched the black woman and her white male accomplice: "The term 'mob' cannot with any degree of justice be applied in this case. No people on the face of the earth are more law-abiding and more respectable than the people of Clay County, but they will no longer witness the butchery ... of their best citizens, by their own household, instigated ... by those devils in human shape, called abolitionists."[20]

Though a Clay County history, published in 1885, and an out-of-county newspaper of the time[21] termed the hanging of Annice II and McClintock a *lynching,* in all local and contemporary newspaper coverage their deaths at the hands of the county's most respectable citizens were termed *executions.* The motion made at the courthouse meeting was that the offenders should be "publicly executed." According to the county history, "McClintock denied to the last that he was guilty, but the negro woman asserted that her confession was true."[22] Neither newspapers nor the county history used a Christian or first name of McClintock. He seemed to be a pariah in his own county. As for Annice II, any person about 17 years old in 1829 was about 38 years old in 1850. She was unsuccessful in her one known runaway attempt as a teenager, but her desire to be free was never extinguished. Her love of liberty left her open to the blandishments of the mysterious McClintock, whom the best but unnamed citizens who put him to death termed an abolitionist, the standard term for any white person with heterodox ideas regarding slavery. However, he was lynched because a slave accused him of assisting her in the attempted murder of her mistress, not because, standing alone, he attempted to entice Annice II to leave Missouri, journey to California with him, and become his wife. Whether Annice II, lynched in Clay County in 1850, was an older daughter of Annice I, executed in this same county 22 years earlier, remains speculation.

Less is known about the other slave woman whom a mob hanged a decade later. The incident took place in Callaway County, a locale with considerable expertise in trying slaves on capital charges. In its county seat, Fulton, Slaves Jane, Conway, Jake, Susan, Celia, and Mat were sentenced to death for murder; and probably Susan and certainly Conway, Jake, and Celia were hanged. Likewise, Slave William was sentenced to castration for the rape of a white woman. Precisely why this place did not afford Slave

Teney a trial when she was accused of the murder of her mistress was not, as in Annice's and McClintock's case, a matter of the incompetence of a slave to testify against a white person. Teney acted alone.

Her crime against her mistress and the slave woman's resulting lynching cannot be precisely dated. Probably, both events took place on a weekend in late October. The year, 1860, is not in question. On a Saturday when all the white members of the household, except one, had gone to church, someone bludgeoned Miss Susan Jemima Barnes to death. She was first attacked in the east room as she sat knitting, and she fled from this section of her home to the kitchen, then back to the east room, and from there to the west room where, as the newspaper described her death, "she was completely overpowered, her head beaten into atoms, not a bone remaining whole save the right cheek bone. Her brains lay scattered over the floor.... Marks of bloody hands were on the wall, blood was on everything about the house." The coroner's jury surmised that the murder weapons included a shovel and fire tongs. The handle of the shovel was straight in the morning and later "very much bent." Gashes on Miss Barnes's hands and elsewhere on her body suggested that her attacker also used a knife, but it was not located.

Suspicion fell on Teney, a leased bondwoman, who in the absence of the man of the house, Miss Barnes's brother, "was very impudent.... She had had several difficulties with her young mistress." On the morning of the crime, Teney was sent to a field to shuck corn, and she resumed her work that same afternoon. She initially wore a copper-colored garment, the tuck, or pleat, of which was ripped about five or six inches. When she returned to the cornfield, a neighbor, Mrs. Miller, observed that Teney had on a different dress. On Sunday the coroner resumed his investigation of Miss Barnes's murder. Meanwhile, two men, William Booth and Solomon Thomas, searched for Teney's copper-colored dress; they found it splattered with what appeared to be blood, concealed in a corn sheaf near where she had worked the previous day. Mrs. Miller identified the recovered garment as one Teney had worn to her house about 1:00 P.M. the day of the murder. When confronted with all the available evidence against her, she admitted that she killed her young mistress. She was immediately arrested, and a deputy constable, Henry Willing, obtained a horse for her journey to the Callaway County jail in Fulton. However, he never brought in his prisoner.

Despite Willing's "entreaties, threats, and persistent efforts," a "large and excited crowd" took Teney from him "some distance from the road and hung her to a tree." One newspaper ended its story, headlined "Horrible Murder. A Negro Girl Hung By a Mob ... Under the excitement of the occasion, some of our best and most responsible citizens engaged in the mob. It seems to have met the approbation of the owners of the negro."[23] Other newspaper coverage of Teney's crime and lynching mention that after "the officers had proceeded about two miles, the incensed community wrestled her from the officers and hung her to the first tree until she was dead." One story from the *Missouri Republican*, reprinted in several rural newspapers, concluded, "The remains of the young lady were conveyed to Loutre Island [Loutre Township, Montgomery County], and there neatly interred. The bereaved brother and mother have the entire sympathy of the whole community."[24] A Callaway County history quoted from a local newspaper, which estimated the strength of the mob at "some forty or fifty exasperated men." This history reported that Teney's body was taken down and buried the same evening.[25] In the community's solution to the murder of Miss Susan Jemima Barnes, the perpetrator was not hanged on a government rope, as Celia had been almost five years earlier. In Teney's case all the expenses associated with legal niceties, such as a trial, were avoided.

Just as no African American women were executed in Missouri once slavery ended, likewise, none were lynched. *The Chicago Tribune* reported that Paralee Collins was a West Plains, Missouri, victim of a lynch mob because of an "unnamed cause" on June 17, 1914.[26] However, a contemporary West Plains newspaper clarified that a mob burned the home of Paralee and Isaac Collins, shot her in the leg and him in the head, and these events occurred in adjacent Douglas County, in southwestern Missouri. Ten days later she appeared for medical treatment, and he continued to suffer from his wounds. The local coverage did not state the couple's race(s), only that "the mob burned the cabin in which they had been living as a warning that such undesirable citizens are not wanted in the community."[27] Presumably, either Paralee Collins, Isaac Collins, or both were African American. In his collection of news stories about lynchings, Ralph Ginzburg included their names in a section entitled " A Partial Listing of Approximately 5,000 Negroes Lynched in [the] United States Since 1859."[28] More important, excluding Paralee Collins, no known source lists any woman whom a Missouri mob lynched from the close of the Civil War to the present day.

Annice II committed a serious crime against an owner, and Teney against a member of her lessee's family. Once slavery ended, no one owned or leased another human being in America. In post–Civil War Missouri and elsewhere, the fury of the mob took male lives, not female, and many of its victims were black.

As Chapters 11 and 12 clarified, the legal hangings of slave boys and men greatly outnumbered those of girls and women. Though pre–Civil War acts of community violence against black males were not common, neither were they rare. Working from court records and some current research, but largely from newspaper and county histories, at least 36 known lynchings in Missouri can be documented before the close of the Civil War. Of them, at least 20 were black or mulatto; at least 17 males and 2 already discussed females were slaves. One Negro whom a mob hanged was not identified as a slave; he was probably a free black. The other person of color on whom infuriated St. Louisans spent their rage was a free mulatto.

The incident, about which little is known, occurred in Jefferson County, adjacent to southwestern St. Louis County. A county history stated only, "About the year 1842 a Mr. Jeude, living near the present village of Pevely, was murdered by a negro, who killed him for the purpose of getting his money. The negro was not annoyed with a trial as citizens caught him and hung him until he was dead."[29]

The other lynching of a free black was unusually well documented. It took place in the city of St. Louis on April 28, 1836. It occurred in the same decade in which an enraged mob drove Major Harney out of town. When the mob's victim of that time and place was a free African American, the results were especially stomachturning.

His name was Francis McIntosh, a mulatto from Pittsburgh, and his life ended in St. Louis. He arrived in this city because he was an employee on the steamboat *Flora*. Almost certainly, his journey from western Pennsylvania to eastern Missouri was, like those of other pre–Civil War voyagers, almost entirely by water. Probably he traveled in a southwestern direction on the Ohio River from Pittsburgh to Wheeling, Virginia; to Cincinnati, Ohio; to Cairo, Illinois; and from this last named place, where the Ohio flows into the Mississippi River, either south to New Orleans or north to various stops in Missouri, including St. Louis.

On the last day of his life McIntosh had earlier interfered when St. Louis law enforcement officers arrested a couple of sailors for disturbing the peace. Thanks to him, the river men escaped. Very likely, he was drunk or, at the least, had had too much to drink. When Deputy Sheriff George Hammond and Deputy Constable William Mull took him into custody for interfering with the arrest of the sailors, en route to jail and on the courthouse square he broke loose from these officers and drew a knife with which he wounded Mull and cut the large arteries in Hammond's neck, thereby causing the deputy sheriff's immediate death. Shortly, he was captured and placed in the county jail, but his stay was brief. A mob took him from it, carried him to the edge of town, and surrounded him with fire.

A contemporary physician's eye-witness account of this *auto-da-fé* mentioned that, as McIntosh sang and prayed, he was chained to a tree where the crowd "built a slow fire around him. The lower part of his legs were burnt partly off and when the flames had burnt him so as to let out his bowels, some asked him if he felt any pain, he said yes, great pain. It was 18 minutes after the fire was kindled before he died."

The sheer horror of this lynching gave St. Louis one black eye. The Honorable Luke E. Lawless, the circuit court judge who presided at the May 1836 grand jury investigation of McIntosh's death, blackened the city's other eye. Lawless's charge to the grand jury required it to decide whether the killing of the free mulatto was "the act of the few" or "the act of many." If the latter, then "it is beyond the reach of human law. The attempt to punish ... would ... be fruitless.... How are we to indict ... two or three thousand offenders? ... If the thousands congregated round the fire were the actors ..., it would be impossible to punish and absurd to attempt it." Lawless laid the blame for McIntosh's crime of wounding one law enforcement officer and killing another on the attempts of outsiders to end slavery. He discovered "the abolitionist influence ... [in] the peculiar character of [McIntosh's] language and demeanor. His rabid denunciations of the white man ... his hymns and prayers" as he slowly burned to death. The judge also discussed the dangers of Indians and Negroes uniting against whites. As one would expect, when a grand jury composed entirely of white men was so charged, its foreman's report, of May 24, 1836, concluded of McIntosh's murder, "It was the act of the populace, an assemblage of several thousand persons, for which five or ten individuals could not be made responsible."

The burning of McIntosh was widely denounced. Garrison wrote several articles about it; one lengthy one concluded, "What was his offence! What in a white man under the same circumstances would have been called only manslaughter."[30] When Abraham Lincoln deplored mob rule in a Springfield, Illinois, speech in 1838, he emphasized the lynchings of gamblers and slaves in Mississippi mentioned in this chapter and McIntosh's fire death.[31] The English novelist and economist, Harriet Martineau (1802–76), journeying in Missouri and Illinois at the time of this lynching, wrote, "No one would have dreamed of treating any white man as this mulatto was treated." She also observed that "the charge of Judge Lawless (his real name) to the Grand Jury is a sufficient commentary upon the state of St. Louis society."[32] In April 1842 English novelist Charles Dickens, who had earlier read Martineau's book about her western American travel, visited St. Louis, and on a steamboat from it to Cincinnati wrote a friend about "the mob ... (among whom were men of mark, wealth and influence) [who] *burned [McIntosh] alive*. This, I say, was done within six years in broad day; in a city with its courts, lawyers, tipstaffs [court criers], judges, jails, and hangman; and not a hair on the head of one of those men has been hurt to this day."[33] In early newspaper accounts of the wounding of Mull, the death of Hammond, and the incineration of McIntosh, the St. Louis *Missouri Republican* ended its coverage, "Let the veil of oblivion be drawn over the fatal affair."[34] Another St. Louis paper, the *Missouri Argus*, wrote, "Upon this awful scene we drop the curtain."[35] However, McIntosh's case was not forgotten. For many years following his death, St. Louis's white population remembered 1836 as "the year the nigger was burned."[36]

However, for all its vitriol against African Americans, especially free ones, there is neither a known court-ordered castration, a death sentence of a slave owned in Missouri, nor a slave lynching in the history of the city and county of St. Louis. The odds greatly favor that the county of St. Louis put one or more bondpersons to death in early territorial days. But apart from a letter that Pierre Chouteau wrote, suggestive of his slave woman's later hanging, no known documentation supports this speculation. In all, St. Louis city and county slaveholders lost a bare minimum of valuable properties to the vagaries of either the law or the mob.

Other places share St. Louis's absence of both documented lynchings and execution of slaves. One expects the extralegal and the legal deaths of bondpersons to go hand in hand. This is not true in Missouri. In fact, excluding Callaway, Clay, and Boone Counties, where both took place, locales that lynched slaves did not legally hang them. I have no explanation for this split. Perhaps it is attributable to lost court records and newspapers of the period; it is always possible that, in most Missouri counties, both the sheriff and the people put bondpersons to death. However, my research uncovered no such duality in capitally punishing slaves.

Documentation for most mob violence against slaves consists of newspapers and county histories, including what may be the earliest known instance. According to an 1897 newspaper retrospective, Slave Leonard, "probably the largest and most powerful slave" in Franklin County, "assaulted and nearly killed ... an old German woman [Mrs. Tiematin] a few miles from Washington, and ... so beat up ... [the] wife of a merchant near Campbellton, that she died of her injuries." The slave was arrested and put in jail in Union, the county seat. A mob broke open the jail, took Leonard out and hanged him to a tree.[37] The lynching of Slave Eli may be fused with Leonard's almost 30 years earlier. The victim's name, Mrs. Teaman; the sexual nature of the crime; and breaking into the jail in Union, Franklin County, in order to obtain and hang the indicted but not yet tried bondman — these are all incidents reminiscent of the 1818 case. An 1888 county history dated Eli's crime as March and his death as April 1847.[38]

In 1840, in Washington County, an unnamed slave demanded from his unnamed mistress what money there was in her house, raped her, and ran into the woods. A week later he assaulted another woman. After the citizens captured him, they brought him before his mistress and valued him at $300, which she was paid. According to contemporary news coverage, a crowd of approximately 60 persons "said with one voice *hang him!* which was done [April 15] at 12 o'clock at the village of Caledonia ... in the presence of some three or four hundred persons."[39] In 1844, in Herculaneum, Jefferson County, a slave who belonged to an estate killed a Dutch shoemaker and his wife. He was arrested and confined in the Jefferson County jail in Hillsboro. About 300 persons collected at the jail, broke open its doors, took the prisoner on a cart to the scene of his crime, and hanged him. The newspaper's mild disapproval appeared in these comments in its story headlined "Lynch Law — The Murderer Hung": "We cannot approve of this violation of the law, but the murder appears to have been so deliberate and cold blooded that the only wonder is that the community did not proceed more rashly."[40]

Beginning with the next known incident of the people's violence against a slave and continuing throughout the 1850s, mobs dealt more rashly with some slaves than others. Though citizens hanged the only known slave women, Annice II and Teney, whom they put to death, six known Missouri mobs burned slave men to death. All who were ignited were believed guilty of murder, and all known slave lynchings by fire took place in counties in which there were no known slave executions.

The first of these bonfire deaths of slaves took place in Pettis County, in central Missouri. It occurred after Slave Sam, aged 19 or 20 years, allegedly murdered Mrs. John Rains of Heath's Creek Township on July 3, when he was unable to rape her. In order to eliminate witnesses against him, he also attempted to, and believed that he had, killed her children. However, one child lived and was able to identify the perpetrator as the property of a neighbor. The slave was arrested, lodged in the jail in the county seat, Sedalia, and a young attorney, George G. Vest (1830–1904), later U.S. Senator Vest (1879–1903),[41] was appointed to represent him. In the middle of Sam's trial a mob removed him from jail, and General Smith, the founder of Sedalia, persuaded it to cease and desist. It dispersed, only to come together a second time about 100 men strong. On July 6, 1853, they took their prisoner from the jail approximately one-half mile from town, invited all the bondpersons in the vicinity to witness their actions, tied Sam to a walnut sapling, built a circle of wood shavings and other combustible materials around him, and burned him to death.[42]

In Carthage, Jasper County, in extreme southwestern Missouri, two slaves purchased from Cherokee Indians—Colley, whom John B. Dale owned, and Bart, owned by John J. Scott—allegedly robbed and murdered a physician, Dr. John Fisk, raped and murdered his wife, choked their infant to death, and set fire to the physician's home. Colley's motivation was Dr. Fisk's scolding him on several earlier occasions for the slowness with which this former Indian slave performed various tasks. Colley persuaded Bart, then a runaway, to help him eliminate the John Fisk family in return for Colley's assistance in helping Bart commit another murder. When these miscreant slaves were arrested, the citizens of the surrounding country took them from law enforcement officers and burned them to death on July 30, 1853. Slaves from Jasper County were rounded up as unwilling spectators, given the closest proximity to the stake, and required to light the blaze. Crowds from Arkansas, Kansas, and Indian Territory, now Oklahoma, assembled to watch the human bonfire.[43]

In Lincoln County on December 24, 1858, Slave Giles stabbed his owner, Simeon B. Thornhill, in retaliation for being "reprimanded" (i.e., whipped). The white victim survived two days, named his killer, and the slave was arrested and placed in jail at Troy. On January 1, 1859, the mob forced its way into this facility, removed Giles, and lynched him by setting him on fire.[44] The final known incineration of a slave in Missouri occurred on July 19, 1859, near Marshall, the county seat of Saline County. His name was John; he had been convicted of the first-degree murder of Benjamin Hinton at a special term of the Saline County Circuit Court. He was in jail awaiting sentencing when a mob removed him and burned him to death.

However, most lynched slaves in Missouri were not incinerated. In addition to the already discussed mob violence against bondpersons in this state, enraged citizens hanged eight other slaves between 1853 and 1862. Five were presumed guilty of sex crimes against white girls and women; one cut his victim so badly that the injured man lost the use of his arm; one killed his owner, and another his owner's wife.

In Boone County on August 12, 1853, Hiram, owned by Edward Young, allegedly attempted to rape 15-year-old Nancy Hubbard. Initially, the suspected slave was brought before several justices of the peace and discharged, but he was reexamined and held for trial. After what a newspaper described as the accused slave's "full confession," and debate among the leading citizens as to whether he should be burned or hanged, the vote to burn him was about six, and the hanging motion carried. A committee was appointed to force the jail doors, take Hiram prisoner, and obtain a rope, a cart on which to convey him to the place of his lynching, and a coffin in which to bury him. One local newspaper and a county history printed the full names of the "respectable and influential citizens," including the chairman, who were members of this lynching committee. Accordingly, and in the presence of "a large concourse of people," on Monday, August 22, 1853, Hiram was, as one newspaper described it, "deliberately hanged with nearly as much order as usually attends *legalized* executions of criminals. He was buried and thus ended the summary punishment."[45]

In Clay County on February 12, 1855, Peter gained entrance into William O. Russell's home and slashed him with a corn knife. The attacker's provocation was Russell's earlier severe beating of a slave woman he owned, Peter's wife. Approximately two weeks later, the stabbed white man died from his injuries. Peter was arrested, indicted, and committed to the jail on first-degree murder charges. His trial was scheduled to begin at the April term of the Clay County Circuit Court. When the mob first assembled to lynch Peter, his owner, Major Lightburne, persuaded it to abandon its plan, but on March 5, 1855, it reassembled, dragged Peter from his jail cell, and hanged him from a tree in the courthouse yard.[46]

When the clerk of the Clay County Circuit Court submitted bills of costs in two slave capital cases, Edmund's, mentioned in chapter 12, and Peter's, the state auditor refused to pay them on grounds that the state was not liable for them. Both the Clay County circuit clerk and Missouri's attorney general agreed that fees in both cases accrued under laws passed in 1845. One relevant statute read, "If a slave be convicted of any capital offence *and executed*, costs shall be paid by the state."[47] The Supreme Court of Missouri upheld the public auditor's refusal to reimburse the county. It wrote of Peter's lynching: "The lawless violence of a mob, in its impatience to inflict punishment, taking the life of a slave, is not the execution contemplated by this [1845] statute, even if the slave had been convicted before he was hung by the mob."[48] The court construed legislation already in existence when Peter was hanged. Nonetheless, and in obvious reaction to the Clay County claim and the potential for the claims of the clerks of other Missouri circuit courts, the General Assembly amended the law to accommodate any county's collection of fees in slave cases, including those that were capital, whether or not the sheriff officially hanged the bondperson. Under legislation approved December 5, 1855, among other changes the state paid court costs "for a conviction of a slave in capital cases."[49] The lawmakers silently omitted the earlier requirement that the sheriff officially execute the condemned bondpersons. As a result, the legislature required that either the state or the county pay court costs in some cases in which mobs lynched slaves. The amount depended on what services, if any, each county official actually performed.

In some remaining lynchings no court costs accrued. On October 10, 1855, George murdered his master, Judge Thomas Plenmons, in Carroll County, in the north central section of the state. Plenmons had acquired George several years earlier by marriage, and as in Susan's and Lewis's capital cases, the union of master and slave was a disaster. As one newspaper explained, the day before the murder, the judge had "corrected [whipped] this negro for some dereliction of duty." When George was ordered to dig potatoes 200 yards from the house, he lured his owner to the patch on the pretext that he needed to be shown where to begin his potato digging. Once the judge was in the field, George struck him in the back of the head with his hoe. Afterward, the slave repeatedly struck his speechless but still living owner with his hoe until he finally expired. That night he put his body on a horse and conveyed it one and one-half miles from the house, dragging the corpse several hundred yards to create the illusion that his owner had been thrown from his horse and dragged to death. When his family missed him the morning of October 11, George was the prime suspect in his master's disappearance. After the slave was "severely thrashed," he led his interrogators to his owner's body. Once George made a "full confession," many of the neighbors took him out and hanged him from a tree. As for the cause of this slaveholder's murder, one paper decided that Judge Plenmons "was very indulgent to his Negroes and allowed them to have their own way, till they were ruined.... If you wish your slaves to respect and honor you, they must be kept in their place. They cannot stand indulgence."[50] Garrison's *Liberator* ran a short article about the killing of Judge Thomas *Clingman* and the slave being "instantly hung by Lynch Law." Instead of the surname, *Plenmons,* the garbled name remained *Clingman* in an early-twentieth-century study of American lynchings.[51]

On July 18, 1859, in Saline County, a white girl named Lamb, aged between 11 and 12 years and the daughter of Mr. Lamb, whom one newspaper termed "one of the most worthy citizens of Arrow Rock," was raped by an unnamed slave as she and other children returned from picking blackberries. The alleged assailant was cutting grass near the patch, and the children had asked him questions regarding its locale. The attacker came naked out of the bushes, grabbed the girl, and after "the villainy had been perpetrated," returned to cutting grass. The other children ran, spread the alarm, and soon a number of Negroes were placed in a lineup. A minister and other respectable citizens investigated the crime, and they concluded that Dr. William Price's Negro man was the culprit. After a committee decided the slave's guilt, Dr. Price locked him in a stable, posted a guard over him, and planned to have him taken to the county jail in Marshall the next day. However, while the alleged assailant was under lock and key, he confessed, "corroborating the statements of the children in all particulars." That same evening, four or five men, dressed in women's clothing, came for the accused rapist, forced the key to the stable from the guard, entered, took out their prisoner, and "in the presence of a large concourse of citizens, hung him to the limb of a tree, where they left him hanging, near the town of Arrow Rock."[52]

On August 13, 1859, Martin or Mart, who belonged to the estate of Finley Danforth, allegedly raped Mrs. John Morrow in Greene County, southwest Missouri. She threw scalding water on her asailant, and a wound on his chest matched the area where she dashed the hot water. In addition, he confessed, despite the fact, noted a newspaper, that "no force or threats were used to induce him to tell." After he was indicted, but before his trial began, a crowd of 300 or 400 men surrounded the place of Mart's lockup, Temperance Hall in Springfield, the county seat, took him from this place to the edge of town, and, as the county history phrased it, "strung him up. In a few minutes he was dead. The body was cut down and given hasty burial. Afterwards, it was 'resurrected' and dissected by a Springfield physician."[53]

In November 1862, near Hackberry Ridge in Andrew County, in northwest Missouri, an unnamed slave, belonging to Edmond Gee, allegedly raped and murdered an 11-year-old girl and almost murdered her brother as the children were returning from school. After the slave confessed his crime, as a news story described it, he "was hung by the citizens at the place where he committed his crime."[54]

Apart from the Greene County lynching of Mart, it seems doubtful that any clerk of the circuit court recovered court costs in any of these lynchings. When George murdered Judge Plenmons, the new law was not in effect; the Arrow Rock and Hackberry Ridge lynchings had insufficient involvement of any law enforcement officers or court personnel for any court fees to accrue. However, three other known mob deaths of slaves took place in Saline County in July 1859. In fact, within a 24-hour period, the rabble ended the lives of four slaves. This is the largest known number of lynched bondpersons in one locale and at almost the same time in Missouri's history. No court records exist in the Arrow Rock hanging for the alleged rape of the 11-year-old girl, but they document those that took place in Marshall. The county seat lynchings all contain bills of costs, and these fees were payable because the legislature amended the law to allow them after Clay County was denied any reimbursement in Peter's 1855 lynching. Though Saline County is the place where a slave woman was beaten to death because of her poor table manners in the 1830s, in keeping with most Missouri counties where mobs put slaves to death, there are no known slave executions within this county.

Each slave whom the people put to death had a different owner. Dr. William Price owned the slave lynched in Arrow Rock on July 18, and Giles Keizer owned John, valued at $1,500; Mrs. Virginia Howard owned Holman, valued at $1,000; and James White owned James, valued at $1,000. The latter three slaves were lynched in Marshall; all committed their crimes on different dates and in different locales within the county. On May 13 John murdered Benjamin Hinton of Waverly, Lafayette County, near Miami in Saline County. Prior to his trial and for safekeeping he was detained in the Cooper County jail in Boonville. During and after his trial and conviction on first-degree murder charges, he was held in the jail in Marshall. Also inmates in this same facility were Holman and James. Holman was being detained prior to his trial for attempting to murder William S. Durrett on June 21. In the process of this assault Holman cut Durrett's arm so deeply that he crippled him for life. On July 19 James was on trial at the courthouse for an attempted rape of Mrs. Mary Habecot on July 12.

On July 19 the mob broke into the county jail in Marshall and got possession of John and Holman, and it also seized James at the courthouse. It burned the convicted murderer, John, and it hanged Holman and James; all three men died approximately 200 yards north of the public square in broad daylight. Judge Russell Hicks, later a law partner of George G. Vest, was holding a special term of court in this county for all these murdered slaves. He resigned his judgeship to protest the lawlessness of one bondman's burning and the extralegal hanging of two others. Though the county history later stated that the mob's leaders were not citizens of Saline County, it did not discount the participation of the many county residents who were members of it.[55]

Perhaps the most distinctive features of the three slave lynchings in Marshall are the circuit court records. Each contains a detailed listing of fees for personnel such as the clerk of the circuit court, the sheriff, the jailer, and justices of the peace. In John's case the record specified that the sheriff "placed him within the walls of said jail & locked the door of said jail from which place said Negro man John was by force and violence taken from said jail & publicly executed."[56] In Holman's case, the grand jury had indicted him, but "before he was brought into the courthouse and placed upon his trial, [he] was forcibly taken from the jail and by the people publicly executed."[57] In James's case, "said Negro man was placed upon his trial ... and whereas after the adjournment of said Court for dinner [the noon meal], the ... defendant was forcibly by the people seized [and] taken from the custody of the sheriff & his deputies and publicly executed."[58] At the November 1859 term of the Saline County Circuit Court, bills of costs were itemized in the cases of the three slaves lynched in Marshall on July

19. In Holman's and James's noncapital cases court costs were certified to be paid by the county. Because John's case was capital, fees in it were certified to be paid by the state.

As this chapter has demonstrated, the lynching of blacks did not begin after the Civil War. In fact, between 1865 and 1869 most persons whom Missouri mobs hanged were white. Many of these extralegal deaths occurred because of the Civil War, a conflict that continued here until 1866, many months after Lee surrendered to Grant at Appomattox on April 9, 1865. In addition, post–Civil War score-settling and the paucity of official law enforcers in many rural counties added to the lawlessness of white against white. However, commencing in 1870 and continuing into the early 1940s, African American males were victims of mob violence out of all proportion to the percentage of crimes they committed or of Missouri's population. Recovery from the disease of racism has proven an almost never-ending process, and the legacy of what the French began when they introduced human beings as their personal property in eastern Missouri in the 1720s remained a problem nearly three centuries later.

Assault and Homicide by Black Males with Black Male Victims: Tabular Summary

	Perpetrator	Date	Victim	P's Owner	V's Owner	Co.	Weapon	Result	Outcome	Source
1	Murphy	1820	U	U	U	St. L.	U	Assault	5 L	CR
2	George & Jim	1821	U	Relfe & Madden	U	Ste. G.	U	Affray	U	CR
3	Jepe	1822	Sam	Gordon	Hartshorn	St. L.	Rock	Death	U	CR
4	Cato	1824	U		U	Howard	U	Death	U	CR
5	Clifford	1834	Sandy	estate of Fugate Knight		St. L.	Knife	Death	U	CR
6	Alfred & Peter	1834	John Steele	U	none	St. L.	U	Death	U	CR
7	Sam	1836	William	Fletcher	U	St. L.	Rock	Death	U	CR
8	U	1837	U	Kavanaugh	Jennings	Cooper	U	Death	U	AR
9	Mat	1838	Haburn	Latimer	Brown	St. L	Knife	Assault	39 L & T	PP
10	Nathan	1846	Tom	Watson	Criddle	Cape G.	Ax	Death	Executed	CR
11	U	1846	U	Scott	Watts	Cape G.	Ax	C.S.	U	CR
12	U	1846	U		Thompson	Boone	Fists	Death	U	CR
13	Anderson	1848	U	Ewing	none	Clay	U	Death	39 L & T	3
14	John	1852	Free Jack	Brown	Newby	Jeff.	U	Death	39 L	CR
*15	Abe	1853	Dan	Newby	Boone	Platte	Knife	Death	Executed	CH
16	U	1856	U	Boone	Keebaugh	Monroe	Club	C.S.	U	N
17	U	1856	U	Fray	Christian	Rand.	Knife	Assault	U	N
18	U	1856	U	Williams		Rand.	Pistol	Assault	U	N
19	Pete	1856	Tom	Lenoir	Estes	Boone	Knife	Death	U	N
20	Isam	1857	Al Barnes	U	none	Calla.	Knife	Death	No Ind.	N
21	Dan	1857	George	Redmon	Currant	Jack.	Knife	Assault	U	N
22	Jack	1857	Overseer	Rollins	U	Rand.	U	Death	U	N
23	U	1859	U	Porter	Crump	Marion	Knife	C.S.	U	N
24	Jim	1859	U	U	U	Buch.	U	U	U	N
25	U	1860	U	Gordon	Ecton	Clay	Knife	Death	U	N
26	U	1862	U	Stanford	Yeager	Pike	Knife	Death	U	N
27	U	1862	U	Givens	Brown	Pike	Knife	Death	U	N
28	Martin	1862	Godfrey	Lewis	Murrell	Saline	Knife	Death	U	CR

*Watt Espy supplied initial information. Abbreviations: *P's Owner* = Perpetrator's Owner; *V's Owner* = Victim's Owner; *Co.* = County; U = Unknown; Buch. = Buchanan; Calla. = Callaway; Cape G. = Cape Girardeau; Jack. = Jackson; Jeff. = Jefferson; Rand. = Randolph; St. L. = St. Louis; Ste. G. = Ste. Genevieve; C.S. = Critical Situation; L = Lashes; T = Transportation; No Ind. = No Indictment; CR = Court Records; AR = Appellate Court Records; PP = Pardon Papers; 3= Appellate Court Record, County History, and Newspaper; CH = County History; N = Newspaper.

Appendix 2

Capital and Other Violent Crimes by Accused Female Slaves: Tabular Summary

Name	Date	County	Crime	Victim(s)	Manner	Outcome	Punishment
1 U	1805	St. L.	arson	WMAM	U	U	prob. executed
2 Annice I	1828	Clay	murder	5SC; 2P's	drowning	died	executed
3 Hanna	1829	Jack.	att. murder	WMAM	U	lived	whipped
4 Jane	1831	Calla.	murder	P's infant	pois. & suff.	died	U
5 U	1834	Marion	murder	P's 3SC	axing	died	suicide
6 Esther	1835	Cape G.	att. murder	L's WF infant	pois.	lived	whipped
*7 Mary	1837	Craw.	murder	WF2	drowning	died	executed
8 Fanny	1839	Linc.	murder	WM8 & 10	skulls crushed	died	acquitted
*9 Mary	1843	Boone	murder	WMAM	axing	died	not indicted
*10 America	1843	Boone	murder	WMAM	axing	died	executed
11 Susan	1844	Calla.	murder	WFAM	axing	died	prob. executed
12 Margaret	1845	Cole	murder	P's infant	knif.	died	U
13 U	1845	Calla.	murder	P's 4SC & 1WC	pois.	died	suicide
14 Nelly	1846	Warren	murder	P's infant	U	died	pardoned
15 Patsy	1848	Boone	att. murder	P's lessees	pois.	lived	whipped
16 U	1850	Clay	att. murder	P's M & fam.	pois.	lived	U
17 Annice II	1850	Clay	att. murder	WFAM	axing	lived	lynched
18 U	1853	Mont.	murder	P's SC	cut off head	died	U
*19 Celia	1855	Calla.	murder	WM70M	hit over head	died	executed
20 Emily	1855	Aud.	murder	P's SC	burn. & suff.	died	U
21 Ann	1855	Boone	att. murder	M's WFC	pois.	lived	whipped
22 U	1857	Rand.	murder	P's SC	hanging	died	suicide
23 U	1857	Monroe	att. murder	P's 2SC	drowning	lived	U
24 Mariah	1858	Saline	murder	P's infant	knif. & suff.	died	U
25 U	1860	Monroe	att. murder	P's M & fam.	pois.	lived	U
26 Teney	1860	Calla.	murder	WFAM	axing	died	lynched
27 U	1862	Pike	murder	Black infant	drowning	died	lynched
28 Evaline	1863	Cape G.	murder	P's infants	U	died	U

*Watt Espy supplied initial information. Abbreviations: Audr. = Audrain; Calla. = Callaway; Cape G. = Cape Girardeau; Craw. = Crawford; Jack. = Jackson; Linc. = Lincoln; Mont. = Montgomery; Rand. = Randolph; St L. = St. Louis; att. murder = Attempted Murder; WMAM = White Male Adult Master; 5SC = Five Slave Children; 2P's = two of Perpetrator's children; L's = Lessee; WF2 = White Female aged two years; WM8 & 10 = White Males aged eight and ten; WFAM = White Female Adult Mistress; 1WC = One White Child; WM70M = White Male Aged 70, Master; WFC = White Female Child; pois. = Poisoning; suff. = Suffocating; knif. = knifing prob. executed = Probably Executed.

Appendix 3

Battering of Black and Mulatto Females by White Males: Tabular Summary

	Name	Date	County	Perpetrator	Manner of Injury	Outcome	Punishment
1	Negress Sylvia	11-16-1813	St. L.	Joseph LeBlond, C.	Legs Chained	Died	2 mo. & f.
2	Julie Labaddie	11-5-1818	St. L.	William Gordon, C.	Head Beaten	Injured	U
3	Slave Fanny	1826–27	Pike	___ Mann, L.	U	Died	None
4	Slave Louese	4-24-1826	Cape G.	Obadiah Malone, O.	Whipping	Died	None
5	Slave Patience	1-6-1829	Wash.	Jacob Fisher, O.	Whipping	Died	U
6	Slave Delphia	1820s–1830s	St. L.	Daniel D. Page, O.	Whipping	Injured	U
7	Slave Dinah	1833–34	Clay	___ Soper, L.	U	Died	None
8	Slave Hannah	6-27-1834	St. L.	William S. Harney, O.	Whipping	Died	None
9	Slave Rachael	4-13-1842	Saline	Thomas B. Finley, O.	Whipping	Died	U
10	Slave Minerva	7-24-1842	Mont.	Conrad Carpenter, O.	Whipping	Died	U
11	Slave Female	1844–45	Clark	___ Adams, L.	U	Died	None
12	Slave Sarah	8-13-1847	St. L.	Edwin Tanner, L.	Whipping & Starving	Died	U
13	Slave Female	1854–56	Buch.	___ Forrest, L.	Whipping	Injured	U
14	Slave Eliza	1860	Boone	James Henderson, O.	Whipping	Injured	None

Abbreviations: Buch. = Buchanan; Cape G. = Cape Girardeau; Mont. = Montgomery; St. L. = St. Louis; Wash. = Washington; C = Companion; L. = Lessee; O = Owner; U = Unknown; 2 mo. & f. = 2 months in jail, $500 fine, and court costs.

Appendix 4

Capital and Other Murders by Accused Male Slaves: Tabular Summary

	Name	Date	County	Victim	Relationship Between P & V	Manner	Outcome
1	Frank	1819	Franklin	WMA	Owner	U	Escaped
2	Luke	1826	Cooper	WMA	Owner	Stabbing	Executed
*3	Moses	1828–29	Montgomery	WMA	Owner	U	Executed
4	Jack	1830	Cooper	WMA	Neighbor	Axed	Executed
5	Edmond	1830	Cooper	WMA	Owner	Axed	Sold
*6	Hampton	1832	Howard	WMA	Owner	U	Executed
7	Jim	1832	Howard	WMA	Neighbor	Axed	Reversed
8	Archie	1835	Boone	WMA	Owner	U	Executed
9	Conway	1835–36	Callaway	WMA	Lessee	Throat slit	Executed
10	Jake	1835–36	Callaway	WMA	Owner	Throat slit	Executed
11	David Gates	1837	Howard	WMA	Stranger	U	Executed
12	Wash. Hill	1837	Howard	WMA	Stranger	U	Executed
*13	Henry	1837	Ray	WMA	Neighbor	Choked	Executed
*14	Ish	1837	Ray	WMA	Neighbor	Choked	Executed
15	Ellick	1838	Lincoln	2 WM 8 & 10	Neighbor	Hit Head	Charges Dropped
*16	Madison	1841	St. Louis	2 WMA	Stranger	U	Executed
*17	Lewis	1841	Pike	WMA	Owner	Clubbed	Executed
*18	Henry	1843	Boone	WMA	Owner	Axed	Executed
19	Nathan	1846–47	Cape Girardeau	SMA	Neighbor	Axed	Executed
20	Peter Douglas	1848	Dade	WFA & 3SC	Owner's wife & P's 3 SC	U	Executed
21	U	Undated	Warren	WMA	Owner	Shot	Sold
*22	Ben	1849–50	Marion	2 WC 10 & 12	Strangers	Clubbed	Executed
*23	Isaac	1851	Warren	WFA	Owner's wife	Choked	Executed
*24	Abe	1853	Platte	SMA	Overseer	Knifed	Executed
25	Edmund	1854	Clay	U	U	U	Escaped
26	Hart	1854	Audrain	SF	U	Poison	Acquitted
*27	Mat	1855	Callaway	WM3	Neighbor	Hit in Head	Escaped
*28	Henry	1855–56	Lafayette	WMA	Overseer	Hit in Head	Executed
29	Joe	1857	Boone	WMA	Lessee	Axed	Executed
*30	John	1858	Lafayette	WMA	Overseer	Hit in Head	Executed

*31	Larrell	1858	Lafayette	WMA	Overseer	Hit in Head	Executed w/ rock
*32	George Bruce	1858–59	Randolph	WMA	Owner	Beaten	Executed w/ rock
33	Simon Anderson	1858–59	Randolph	WMA	Owner	Hit in Head	Acquitted
*34	Green	1859	Buchanan	WMA	Slave Buyer	Shot	Executed
35	U	1862	Ray	WMA, WFA, & WFC	Neighbor	Attempts to M & R	Prob. Acquitted
*36	Henry	1863	Moniteau	WMA		Shot	Executed
37	Charles	1863–64	Cape Girardeau	WMA	Stranger	Clubbed	Prob. Acquitted

*Watt Espy supplied initial information. Abbreviations: P & V = Perpetrator and Victim; WMA = White Male Adult; SMA = Slave Male Adult; 2WM 8 & 10 = Two White Males Aged eight and ten; WFA = White Female Adult; SC =Slave Children; 2 WC 10 & 12 = Two White Children Aged 10 and 12; WFC = White Female Child; P = Perpetrator; SF = Slave Female; Attempts to M & R = Attempts to Murder and Rape; Prob. Acquitted = Probably Acquitted.

Blacks and Mulattoes Lynched in Missouri During Slavery: Tabular Summary

	Date	Name	County	Method	Crime of Black or Mulatto	White Victim	Relationship between P & V
1	1818	Slave Leonard ?	Franklin	H	M	woman	none known
2	1836	Francis McIntosh	St. Louis	B	M	LEO	none known
3	1840	Slave U	Washington	H	R	woman	owner
4	1842	Negro man	Jefferson	H	M	stranger	none known
5	1844	Slave U	Jefferson	H	M	H & W	none known
6	1847	Slave Eli ?	Franklin	H	Att. R & Att. M	mother & son	none known
7	1850	Slave Annice II	Clay	H	Att. M	woman	owner
8	1853	Slave Sam	Pettis	B	M & Att. R	mother & son	none known
9	1853	Slave Colley	Jasper	B	A, Ro, R, & M	physician, wife, & child	none known
10	1853	Slave Bart	Jasper	B	A, Ro, R, & M	wife, & child	none known
11	1853	Slave Hiram	Boone	H	Att. R	girl 15	none known
12	1855	Slave Peter	Clay	H	M	male	wife's owner
13	1855	Slave George	Carroll	H	M	male	owner
14	1859	Slave Giles	Lincoln	B	M	male	owner
15	1859	Slave U	Saline	H	R	girl 14	none known
16	1859	Slave John	Saline	B	M	male	none known
17	1859	Slave Jim	Saline	H	Att. R	married woman	none known
18	1859	Slave Holman	Saline	H	Assault	male	none known
19	1859	Slave Mart	Greene	H	R	married woman	none known
20	1860	Slave Teney	Callaway	H	M	young woman	lessee
21	1862	Slave U	Andrew	H	Assault, R & M	girl 11 & boy	none known

Abbreviations: B = Burned; H = Hanged; M = Murder; R = Rape; Att. R = Attempted Rape; Att. M = Attempted Murder; A = Arson; Ro = Robbery; LEO = Law Enforcement Officer; Relationship between P & V = Relationship between perpetrator and victim.

Notes

Abbreviations

BDAC: *Biographical Directory of the American Congress, 1774–1996.* Alexandria, Va.: CQ Staff Directories, 1997.

DAB: *Dictionary of American Biography.* 11 vols. New York: Charles Scribner's Sons, 1964.

FHC: Family History Center, Church of Jesus Christ of Latter-Day Saints, 705 W. Walnut St., Independence, Mo.

LT: *Liberty Tribune*

MHS: Missouri Historical Society, 225 S. Skinker, St. Louis, Mo.

MORE: *Missouri Republican* (St. Louis).

MSA: Missouri State Archives, 600 W. Main, Jefferson City, Mo.

RC: *Randolph Citizen* (Huntsville).

SLCP: St. Louis Courthouse Papers, MHS.

WHMC: Western Historical Manuscript Collection, Ellis Library, University of Missouri, Columbia, Mo.

Chapter 1. Spanish Colonial Administration

1. Harrison Trexler, *Slavery in Missouri,* 13.
2. Gaillard Hunt, ed. *Journals of the Continental Congress,* 26:246–47. See also Peter Kolchin, *American Slavery, 1619–1877,* 79.
3. Louis Houck, *History of Missouri,* 1:282.
4. Eugene M. Violette, "The Black Code in Missouri," 289–91.
5. David D. March, *History of Missouri,* 1:79.
6. Edwin Adams Davis, *Louisiana, a Narrative History,* 130.
7. March, *History of Missouri,* 1:71.
8. Morris S. Arnold, *Unequal Laws unto a Savage Race,* 16.
9. Davis, *Louisiana,* 138.

10. Arnold, *Unequal Laws*, 50. Throughout, unless expressly attributed to another source, I have for the designated current American equivalencies of Spanish and French colonial moneys relied on the most recent authority, Derek N. Kerr, *Petty Felony, Slave Defiance, and Frontier Villainy*, Table V, "Money and Monetary Terms Used in Spanish Louisiana," and Table VI, "Approximate Comparison of Monetary Values" (70–71).

11. Morris S. Arnold, *Colonial Arkansas, 1686–1804*, 144.

12. Kerr, *Petty Felony*, 12.

13. *Ibid.*, 14.

14. *Ibid.*, 160.

15. Alcée Fortier, *History of Louisiana*, 2:140–41.

16. Carl J. Ekberg, *Colonial Ste. Genevieve*, 378.

17. Alejandro O'Reilly, "Ordinances and Instructions," 44–48.

18. Fortier, *History of Louisiana*, 2:7. Also cited in *Marguerite* v. *Chouteau*, 2 Mo. 71, 84 (1828).

19. Louis Houck, ed. *The Spanish Regime in Missouri*, 1:44–45.

20. *Ibid.*, 2:308–12.

21. "Indian Slaves at Ste. Genevieve," May 28, 1770, and "Indian Slaves at St. Louis," July 12, 1770, in Lawrence Kinnaird, ed. *Spain in the Mississippi Valley*, 2:167–70, 172–79.

22. "Emancipation given by Mr. Jean Louis de Noyon to an Indian Woman named Jeanette," Oct. 29, 1779, trans. Sylvie L. Richards. F19, Collection 3636, WHMC.

23. O'Reilly, "Ordinances and Instructions," 45.

24. *Marguerite* v. *Chouteau*, 3 Mo. 540 (1834).

25. William E. Foley, "Slave Freedom Suits before Dred Scott: The Case of Marie Jean Scypion's Descendants," 1–23.

26. Houck, *Spanish Regime*, 1:54.

27. *Ibid.*, 2:142.

28. "Inquest: Body of an Indian Woman," and "Inventory of Céledon's Property," March 18, 1773, trans. Sylvie L. Richards. F421, Collection 3636, WHMC; Ekberg, *Colonial Ste. Genevieve*, 109–12.

29. Kerr, *Petty Felony*, 98.

30. *Ibid.*, 34; O'Reilly, "Ordinances and Instructions," 39.

31. O'Reilly, "Ordinances and Instructions," 39.

32. Kerr, *Petty Felony*, 221, 252.

33. "Notice Concerning Six Escalins to Be Paid for Each Slave," trans. Thomas Fairclough. F426, Collection 3636, WHMC.

34. Jack D. L. Holmes, "The Abortive Slave Revolt at Pointe Coupée, Louisiana, 1795," 341–62; Kerr, *Petty Felony*, 144–45, 188, 203. Both are excellent examinations of Spanish documents of this insurrection. There is no newspaper account of it.

35. Kerr, *Petty Felony*, 76.

36. Houck, *Spanish Regime*, 1:325.

37. Holmes, "Abortive Slave Revolt," 355.

38. Kerr, *Petty Felony*, 138.

39. Ekberg, *Colonial Ste. Genevieve*, 210–11.

40. Joe Gray Taylor, *Negro Slavery in Louisiana*, 195.

41. "Inquest: Slave Belonging to Jean Baptiste Datchurut," November 16, 1783, trans. Sylvie L. Richards. F421, Collection 3636, WHMC.

42. Ekberg, *Colonial Ste. Genevieve*, 372–73.

43. *Ibid.*, 371–72.

44. Kerr, *Petty Felony*, 130.

45. Davis, *Louisiana*, 139.

46. Kerr, *Petty Felony*, 238.

47. Houck, *Spanish Regime*, 1:244–45.
48. Frederic L. Billon, *Annals of St. Louis ... 1764–1804*, 158–60.
49. *Ibid.*, 199.
50. *Ibid.*, 233.
51. *Ibid.*, 234.
52. *Ibid.*, 241–42.
53. Houck, *History of Missouri*, 3:37; March, *History of Missouri*, 1:216; Ekberg, *Colonial Ste. Genevieve*, 122–23; William E. Foley, *Genesis of Missouri*, 92–93; Jacqueline Brelsford Baker Humphrey, "The 1802 Murder of David Trotter in Missouri," 198–203.

Chapter 2. Early American Rule

1. U.S. Const., art. 4, Sec. 3, cl. 2.
2. March, *History of Missouri*, 1:184.
3. "Treaty of Cession," art. 3 (1803), *Laws of a Public and General Nature of the District of Louisiana, of the Territory of Louisiana, of the Territory of Missouri, and of the State of Missouri Up to the Year 1824*, 2. Hereafter cited as *Laws*.
4. 2 Stat. 245.
5. Amos Stoddard to W. C. C. Claiborne and James Wilkinson, March 26, 1804, Stoddard Papers.
6. 2 Stat. 245.
7. Claiborne and Wilkinson to Stoddard, Jan. 16, 1804, Stoddard Papers.
8. Stoddard to Claiborne and Wilkinson, March 16, 1804, Stoddard Papers (italics in the original).
9. William Blackstone, *Commentaries On the Laws of England*, 4:210.
10. *DAB*, s.w. William Cushing and Amos Stoddard; Kermit L. Hall, ed. *The Oxford Companion to the Supreme Court*, 213–14.
11. Helen Catterall, ed., *Judicial Cases Concerning Slavery*, 4:480–81.
12. Stoddard to William Henry Harrison, June 3, 1804, Stoddard Papers.
13. Committee of the Town of St. Louis to Stoddard, Aug. 4, 1804, Stoddard Papers.
14. Stoddard to August Chouteau, Aug. 6, 1804, Stoddard Papers.
15. 2 Stat. 283.
16. Foley, *Genesis of Missouri*, 319.
17. March, *History of Missouri*, 1:162.
18. 2 Stat. 287.
19. Clarence E. Carter, *Territorial Papers of the United States*, 13:76.
20. Violette, "Black Code in Missouri," 301.
21. *Laws* (1804), chap. 3, sec. 6, 28.
22. James Curtis Ballagh, *A History of Slavery in Virginia*, 60–61.
23. *Laws* (1804), chap. 3, sec. 15, 30.
24. *Ibid.*, secs. 18 and 19, 30–31.
25. Cited in Wyndham B. Blanton, *Medicine in Virginia in the Eighteenth Century*, 402.
26. John Duffy, *From Humors to Medical Science: A History of American Medicine*, 14.
27. *Ibid.*, 71–72.
28. John Duffy, ed. *The Rudolph Matas History of Medicine in Louisiana*, 1:186–87.
29. Davis, *Louisiana*, 147.
30. *Ibid.*, 89; E. J. Goodwin, *A History of Medicine in Missouri*, 15–21; and Howard L. Conard, ed. *Encyclopedia of the History of Missouri*, 4:296.

31. Duffy, *History of Medicine in Louisiana*, 1:174.

32. John Walton, Paul B. Beeson, and Ronald Bodley Scott, eds. "Poisoning," *The Oxford Companion to Medicine*, 2:114.

33. D. M. Jolliffe, "A History of the Use of Arsenicals in Man," 287–89; Albert S. Lyons and R. Joseph Petrucelli, *Medicine: An Illustrated History*, 524; W. F. Bynum and Roy Porter, eds. *Companion Encyclopedia of the History of Medicine*, 1:262; Madge E. Pickard and R. Carlyle Buley, *The Midwest Pioneer: His Ills, Cures, & Doctors*, 110.

34. *Treatise on the Diseases Most Prevalent in the United States with Directions for Medicine Chests*, 22.

35. Alfred Swaine Taylor, *The Principles and Practice of Clinical Jurisprudence*, 256.

36. Conversation, Robert Hudson, M.D., Professor Emeritus, Dept. of the History of Medicine, University of Kansas, Kansas City, Kans. The medical literature on the history of the autopsy stresses its milestones rather than its routine practice.

37. S. N. De, *Cholera: Its Pathology and Pathogenesis*, 9–18.

38. Ralph W. Webster, *Legal Medicine and Toxicology*, 325.

39. LeMoyne Snyder, *Homicide Investigation*, 262.

40. Taylor, *Clinical Jurisprudence*, 193.

41. Webster, *Legal Medicine and Toxicology*, 486–87.

42. Cited in Blanton, *Medicine in Virginia*, 402.

43. Duffy, *Humors to Medical Science*, 74.

44. Joseph E. Fields, comp. *"Worthy Partner": The Papers of Martha Washington*, 401.

45. Cited in James Thomas Flexner, *Washington, the Indispensable Man*, 393.

46. See Philip J. Schwarz, *Twice Condemned: Slaves and the Criminal Laws of Virginia, 1705–1865*, esp. "Poisoning in an Early American Slave Society," 92–113.

47. "A Law Respecting Crimes and Punishments," in *Laws of Northwest Territory, 1788–1800*, 322–29.

48. *Laws* (1804), chap. 13, sec. 13, 61.

49. *Laws* (1806), chap. 17, sec. 1–3, 67.

50. 2 Stat. 743–47.

51. *Laws* (1808), chap. 65, sec. 35, 217.

52. *Laws* (1816), chap. 168, sec. 11, 477.

53. 1 Stat. 119.

54. *Laws* (1808), chap. 65, sec. 41, 218.

55. Cited in Leon Radzinowicz, *A History of English Criminal Law and Its Administration from 1750*, 1:206.

56. Toby Gelfand, *Professionalizing Modern Medicine: Paris Surgeons and Medical Science and Institutions in the 18th Century*, 48–49, 102–04.

57. See Ruth Richardson, *Death, Dissection and the Destitute* for an explanation of how the 1832 Anatomy Act became British law.

58. Steven Robert Wilf, "Anatomy and Punishment in Late-Eighteenth-Century New York," 507–30.

59. *Laws of Arkansas Territory Compiled and Arranged by J. Steele and J. M'Campbell Esq's Under the Direction and Superintendance of John Pope Esq. Governor of the Territory of Arkansas* 1835), 198; and *Laws* (1808), chap. 65, sec. 2, 210.

60. Frederick C. Waite, "The Development of Anatomical Laws in the States of New England," 716–26.

61. *Ibid.*, 719.

62. See David J. Rothman, *The Discovery of the Asylum: Social Order and Disorder in the New Republic*, for an extensive analysis of northeastern and eastern public facilities for these regions' people of the abyss.

63. Mo. Rev. Stat., art. 8, secs. 11–14 (1835).

64. Pickard and Buley, *Midwest Pioneer*, 120.

65. *Encyclopedia of the History of Missouri*, 3:325, 4:256–57, 6:394.

Chapter 3. Noncapital Territorial Wrongdoing

1. *U.S.* v. *Jesse*, St. Charles County Circuit Court Records, June 23, 1818, 219–20, FHC.

2. *U.S.* v. *Bill*, St. Charles County Circuit Court Records, June 23, 1818, 220–21, FHC.

3. Houck, *History of Missouri*, 2:392.

4. Carter, *Territorial Papers*, 13:361.

5. Houck, *History of Missouri*, 2:384. *Missourian* (St. Charles) Dec. 20, 1821. Those obituaries without page and column come from death records that Lois Stanley, George F. Wilson, and Maryhelen Wilson compiled in (1) *Death Records of Missouri Men, 1808–1854*, (2) *Death Records of Pioneer Missouri Women, 1808–1853*, (3) *More Death Records from Missouri Newspapers, 1810–1857*, (4) *Death Records from Missouri Newspapers, Jan. 1854–Dec. 1860*, (5) *Death Records from Missouri Newspapers: The Civil War Years, Jan. 1861–Dec. 1865*, and (6) *Death Records from Missouri Newspapers, Jan. 1866–Dec. 1870*. Those with page and column have been independently verified as they appear in extant newspapers.

6. *U.S.* v. *Phil*, Howard County Circuit Court Records, July 13, 1819, 6, FHC.

7. J. Thomas Scharf, *History of Saint Louis City and County*, 1:313.

8. Blackstone, *Commentaries*, 2:503.

9. *Sarah Pickens* v. *Pascal Cerré*, Box 5, F 7; *Sarah Pickens* v. *Antoine Soulard*, Box 5, F 8, MSA.

10. Frederic L. Billon, *Annals of St. Louis … 1804 to 1821*, 9–11.

11. *U.S.* v. *John Pickens*, Box 5, F 6, MSA.

12. See Houck, *History of Missouri*, 2:374, and *Encyclopedia of the History of Missouri*, 3:89–90, for Gratiot's importance.

13. Carter, *Territorial Papers*, 13:251, 264.

14. *Laws* (1804), chap. 3, sec. 22, 31.

15. Houck, *History of Missouri*, 2:75.

16. *Ibid.*, 2:58. See also Carter, *Territorial Papers*, 13:630, for numerous references to Antoine (Anthony) Soulard.

17. *U.S.* v. *Connor*, Box 8, F 15, No. 57, SLCP, MHS.

18. William A. Craigie and James R. Hulbert, *A Dictionary of American English on Historical Principles*, 2:773.

19. *Laws* (1806), chap. 26, secs. 1–5, 84–85.

20. Houck, *History of Missouri*, 3:73.

21. *Laws* (1808), chap. 69, sec. 1, 224; Billon, *Annals of St. Louis … 1804 to 1821*, 12.

22. *U.S.* v. *Helene*, SLCP, Box 6, F 13 No. 21, MHS.

23. Houck, *History of Missouri*, 2:21.

24. *Ibid.*, 2:53, 205–06, and 3:193; *Encyclopedia of the History of Missouri*, 5:482–83; Billon, *Annals of St. Louis … 1804 to 1821*, 330; *MORE*, Oct. 9, 1818.

25. *U.S.* v. *Catherine*, July 17, 1811, Manuel Lisa Collection, Box 2, MHS.

26. Houck, *History of Missouri*, 2:137, 3:44; Carter, *Territorial Papers*, 13:68; Roy D. Blunt, *Historical Listing of the Missouri Legislature*, 71; *MORE*, Jan. 19, 1843.

27. Houck, *History of Missouri*, 2:55; Carter, *Territorial Papers*, 14:299, 303, 487; Billon, *Annals of St. Louis … 1804 to 1821*, 211–12; *MORE*, Feb. 3, 1840.

28. Houck, *History of Missouri*, 2:253–54; *Encyclopedia of the History of Missouri*,

4:82; see *Missouri Gazette*, July 25, 1811, 3:4 for his son Raymond's obituary; *MORE*, Aug. 16, 1820, for Lisa's; *MORE*, Aug. 10, 1826, 2:3, for his 17-year-old son's, Manuel Lisa Jr.

29. U.S. Department of Commerce, *Negro Population, 1790–1915*, 57.

30. *U.S.* v. *Don Quixote*, St. Louis Circuit Court, May 8, 12, 16 and Oct. 14, 1817, 117, 24, 47, 57, FHC.

31. See Harriet C. Frazier, *A Babble of Ancestral Voices*, esp. "Don Quixote in Eighteenth Century England," 107–26.

32. *Oxford English Dictionary*, s.v. *quixotic*.

33. *Encyclopedia of the History of Missouri*, 5:224–25; Carter, *Territorial Papers*, 15:372–73, Houck, *History of Missouri*, 3:10–11.

34. *Encyclopedia of the History of Missouri*, 3:50; Houck, *History of Missouri*, 21–22; Billon, *Annals of St. Louis ... 1804 to 1821*, 280–82; *DAB*, s.v. Geyer, Henry.

35. Carter, *Territorial Papers*, 15:85, 278.

36. *Encyclopedia of the History of Missouri*, 6:397; Houck, *History of Missouri*, 3:22; Billon, *Annals of St. Louis ... 1804 to 1821*, 241–42; see *MORE*, Dec. 3, 1856, 2:6, for Judge Wash's obituary.

37. *Marguerite* v. *Chouteau*, 3 Mo. 540, 572–73 (1834).

38. Billon, *Annals of St. Louis ... 1804 to 1821*, 134.

39. *U.S.* v. *Maria*, St. Louis Circuit Court Records, June 9, 1818, 203, FHC.

40. *U.S.* v. *Simon and Ned*, St. Louis Circuit Court Records, Aug. 8, 12, 17, 1820, 187, 196, 200–01, 205, FHC.

41. *U.S.* v. *Lilise*, Box 7, F 13:13, SLCP, MHS.

42. *U.S.* v. *Lilise*, St. Louis Circuit Court Records, Oct. 17, 21, 1817, 65, 69, 86, 105–06, FHC.

43. Scharf, *History of Saint Louis*, 1:149.

44. *U.S.* v. *George and Joe*, Box 2, F 6:34, SLCP, MHS.

45. *U.S.* v. *Joe*, Box 1, F 2:63, SLCP, MHS.

46. Houck, *History of Missouri*, 3:41; Carter, *Territorial Papers*, 13:618, 14:881–82; *MORE*, May 12, 1829.

47. *Encyclopedia of the History of Missouri*, 2:346; Houck, *History of Missouri*, 3:13; Carter, *Territorial Papers*, 13:590–91 and 14:840.

48. *U.S.* v. *George and Joe*, Box 1, F 2:63, SLCP, MHS; *U.S.* v. *Carlos, George, and Dick*, St. Louis Circuit Court Records, April 10, July 31, 1819, 350, 423, FHC.

49. Houck, *History of Missouri*, 3:60; Carter *Territorial Papers*, 13:618.

50. *U.S.* v. *Carlos, George, and Dick*, St. Louis Circuit Court Records, April 10, 1819, 350, FHC.

51. Billon, *Annals of St. Louis ... 1804 to 1821*, 174–75.

52. Carter, *Territorial Papers*, 14:474.

53. *U.S.* v. *Carlos and George*, St. Louis Circuit Court Records, April 16, 1819, 365, FHC.

54. *Laws* (1813), preamble and sec. 1, 278.

55. *Encyclopedia of the History of Missouri*, 1:586–89; Houck, *History of Missouri*, 2:8–9; Billon, *Annals of St. Louis ... 1804 to 1821*, 164–66; *MORE*, Feb. 24, 1829, 3:3; *DAB*, s.v. Chouteau, August.

56. *U.S.* v. *Carlos, George, and Dick*, St. Louis Circuit Court Records, Aug. 4, 1819, 425, FHC.

57. *Papers of the St. Louis Fur Trade*, pt. 1, *The Chouteau Collection*, reel 9, frame 898.

58. Marsha Moore, Dept. of Corrections, Jackson County, Kansas City, Mo., conversation with author.

59. Houck, *History of Missouri*, 2:68.

60. *Papers of the St. Louis Fur Trade*, pt. 1, *The Chouteau Collection*, reel 10, frames 7–14, trans. Mrs. Max Myer.

61. *U.S. v. George*, St. Louis Circuit Court Records, Aug. 10, 1820, 198, FHC.

62. William E. Foley and C. David Rice, *The First Chouteaus*, 64.

63. Kathleen Maguire and Ann L. Pastore, eds. *Sourcebook of Criminal Justice Statistics*, 406.

Chapter 4. Slave Elijah's 1818 Trial on a Charge of Conspiracy

1. *U.S. v. Negro Elijah*, Box 6, F iii:13, SLCP, MHS.

2. Ibid.

3. Ibid.

4. Billon, *Annals of St. Louis... 1804 to 1821*, 109, 112, 194–95.

5. Ibid., 85–87, 269–70; Houck, *History of Missouri*, 3:235; MORE, Dec. 23, 1845, 2:3.

6. 1 Stat. 746.

7. *Laws* (1804), chap. 3, sec. 14, 30.

8. *Oxford English Dictionary*, s.v. *Conspire*.

9. Ibid.

10. Antonia Fraser, *Mary Queen of Scots*, 557.

11. Jessica Mitford, "Conspiracy," in *The Trial of Dr. Spock*, 62.

12. Billon, *Annals of St. Louis ... 1804 to 1821*, 86.

13. *Missouri Gazette* (St. Louis), Feb. 6, 13, 1818, 1:3.

14. Ibid., Feb. 20, 1818, 3:2.

15. *U.S. v. Elijah*, Box T 11/13, MSA. All subsequent citations to any aspect of this case derive from this source.

16. *Laws* (1804), chap. 3, sec. 12, 30.

17. Billon, *Annals of St. Louis... 1804 to 1821*, 96, 382, 392.

18. Scharf, *History of Saint Louis*, 1:313.

19. *U.S. v. Elijah*, "Motion for a New Trial and in Arrest of Judgment," filed Sept. 10, 1818.

20. Houck, *History of Missouri*, 2:228. See also Foley, *Genesis of Missouri*, 274; MORE, Feb. 7, 1828, 3:2.

21. Billon, *Annals of St. Louis ... 1804 to 1821*, 79–80.

22. *U.S. v. Elijah*, "Motion for New Trial," filed Aug. 10, 1818. The filing appears to be misdated; it should be Sept. 10, 1818.

23. *Trial of Henry Garnett*, 2 Howard State Trials 217 (1606). See also *Dictionary of National Biography*, s.v. Garnett, Henry.

24. John Henry Wigmore, *Anglo-American System of Evidence*, 5:228–29.

25. Carter, *Territorial Papers*, 15:275, 373.

26. 1 Stat. 118–19.

27. Charles Alan Wright, *Federal Practice and Procedure*, 3A:38–39.

28. Billon, *Annals of St. Louis... 1804 to 1821*, 330–31. See also MORE, July 20, 1826, 3:3.

29. Billon, *Annals of St. Louis... 1804 to 1821*, 245–46.

30. Ibid., 86.

31. Houck, *History of Missouri*, 3:80; Carter, *Territorial Papers*, 15:341–42. See *Brunswicker* (Brunswick), July 12, 1849, for Dr. Farrar's obituary and MORE, April 12, 1824, 3:1, for Dr. Walker's.

32. Houck, *History of Missouri*, 3:8.

33. Edward Cleary, ed. *McCormick's Handbook of the Law of Evidence*, 141.

34. See, for example, *President and Directors of the Bank of St. Louis* v. *John B. N. Smith*, St. Louis Circuit Court Records, Nov. 2, 1818, FHC.

35. See *MORE*, Sept. 4, 1822, 3:2, for John B. N. Smith's obituary and September 11, 1822, 3:1, for his wife's, Mary Noyes Smith.

Chapter 5. The 1820 Missouri Constitution and Its Background

1. Houck, *History of Missouri*, 3:244.

2. Ibid., 3:248.

3. 1 Stat. 545.

4. 1 Stat. 546.

5. Floyd Shoemaker, *Missouri's Struggle for Statehood, 1804–1821*, 96–97, 203–04.

6. Ibid., 329–55, reprints this document in its entirety. All subsequent references to it are cited to the Mo. Const. William Draper's unpublished work on Missouri's constitutions has been an invaluable source. See also *DAB* entries on Edward Bates, Henry Dodge, and Duff Green, as well as *BDAC* entry on David Barton.

7. William F. Swindler, "Missouri Constitutions: History, Theory, and Practice Part I," 47.

8. *LT*, Jan. 26, 1849, 1:6.

9. *Missouri Gazette* (St. Louis), March 14, 1821, 3:1.

10. Richard C. Wade, *Slavery in the Cities*, 327.

11. Ibid.

12. *Jefferson Republican* (Jefferson City), Dec. 17, 1836, 1:6.

13. *LT*, Jan. 26, 1849, 1:6.

14. *California News*, Nov. 29, 1858, 2:2.

15. Wade, *Slavery in the Cities*, 329.

16. Francis Thorpe, ed. *The Federal and State Constitutions*. Thorpe's seven volumes contain the text, among much else, of all slave-state constitutions; I have examined them for the many comparisons with Missouri's 1820 constitution.

17. Shoemaker, *Missouri's Struggle for Statehood*, 218.

18. Lois Stanley, George F. Wilson, and Maryhelen Wilson, comps. *Missouri Taxpayers, 1819–1826*, 218.

19. Frederick N. Judson, *Treatise Upon the Law and Practice of Taxation in Missouri*, 20.

20. Thomas R. R. Cobb, *Law of Negro Slavery*, 268.

21. *Kansas City Journal*, May 5, 1893, 3:4.

22. *Knob Noster Gem*, Feb. 23, 1912, 2:2.

23. Schwarz, *Twice Condemned*, 17.

24. Cobb, *Law of Negro Slavery*, 269.

25. Mo. Const., art. 3, sec. 27.

26. Peter H. Wood, *Black Majority: Negroes in Colonial South Carolina from 1670 through the Stono Rebellion*, 135.

27. Schwarz, *Twice Condemned*, 92.

28. Ibid., 115.

29. Ulrich B. Phillips, "Slave Crime in Virginia," 338.

30. William H. Perrin, ed. *History of Crawford and Clark Counties, Illinois*, 38.

31. John Reynolds, *Pioneer History of Illinois*, 143.

32. Thanks to Kent C. Olson, public services librarian, University of Virginia Law Library, Charlottesville, who graciously checked the index to *The Statutes at Large; Being a Collection of All the Laws of Virginia from the First Session of the Legislature in the Year 1619*, ed. William Waller Hening. Mr. Olson could locate no references to witchcraft statutes.

33. Billon, *Annals of St. Louis ... 1804 to 1821*, 207.

34. *Southerner* (Tarboro, N.C.), Aug. 31, 1830, 1:4.

35. George M. Stroud, *A Sketch of the Laws Relating to Slavery*, ix.

36. *Missouri Gazette* (St. Louis), April 5, 1820, 1:5; *Missouri Herald* (Jackson), April 8, 1820, 1:3.

37. Blackstone, *Commentaries*, 4:18.

38. Radzinowicz, *History of English Criminal Law*, 1:4.

39. Blackstone, *Commentaries*, 4:75.

40. Ibid., 4:204.

41. Stroud, *Sketch of the Laws*, 78.

42. Mo. Const., art. 3, sec. 35.

43. Houck, *History of Missouri*, 3:244.

44. Mo. Const., art. 5, sec. 13.

45. Isidor Loeb, "Constitutions and Constitutional Conventions in Missouri," 12.

46. Marvin L. Kay and Lorin Lee Cary, "'The Planters Suffer Little or Nothing': North Carolina Compensations for Executed Slaves, 1748–1772," 290.

47. *Barron* v. *Baltimore*, 32 U.S. 243 (1833) held that the Bill of Rights did not apply to the states; *Chicago, B. & Q. R. Co.* v. *Chicago*, 166 U.S. 226 (1897) applied the Fifth Amendment's Just Compenstion Clause to the states.

48. *U.S.* v. *Amy*, 24 Fed. Cas. 792, 810 (C.C.D. Va 1859) (No. 14, 445).

49. Kay and Cary, "'Planters Suffer Little or Nothing,'" 289.

50. Ibid., 290.

51. *Jack, a Slave* v. *State* (TX), in Catterall, *Judicial Cases Concerning Slavery*, 5:310.

52. R. A. Campbell, ed. *Campbell's Gazetteer of Missouri*, 691. Neither the Missouri territorial censuses of 1814, 1817, and 1819, nor state of Missouri censuses of 1821, 1824, and every four years thereafter until 1868, nor any federal census of what is now Missouri prior to 1830 are extant. Therefore, all information in these many enumerations that are currently available derives primarily from contemporary Missouri newspapers.

53. U.S. Department of Commerce, *Negro Population*, 51.

Chapter 6. Costs in Criminal Cases

1. *Laws* (1806), chap. 20, secs. 6, 18, 71, 75.

2. Ronald Vern Jackson, ed. *Missouri 1850 Slave Schedule* and *Missouri 1860 Slave Schedule* are separate volumes of alphabetical lists by owner's name, county, and page number to multiple reels of microfilmed censuses about slaves owned in Missouri in 1850 and 1860.

3. *Laws* (1806), chap. 22, secs. 1–2, 79–81.

4. Harry D. Penner, "The Missouri Criminal Costs System Re-Examined," 2.

5. *U.S.* v. *Long*, Box 7, F 13:32, SLCP, MHS, hereafter cited as *U.S.* v. *Long*.

6. Kim William Gordon, "George Gordon, Owner of Taille de Noyer, 1804–1805," 6.

7. Billon, *Annals of St. Louis ... 1804 to 1821*, 15.

8. 2 Stat. 431; *Laws* (1822), chap. 407, sec. 1, 975.

9. *U.S.* v. *Long.*

10. *Laws* (1808), chap. 67, sec. 1, 222.

11. Billon, *Annals of St. Louis ... 1804 to 1821*, 15.

12. *Laws* (1807), chap. 38, sec. 5, 107.

13. *Louisiana Gazette* (St. Louis), March 14, 1811, 3:4.

14. Cf. *Laws* (1807), chap. 45, secs. 1–25, 162–171, with *Laws of Indiana Territory, 1801–1809*, 467–80.

15. Billon, *Annals of St. Louis ... 1804 to 1821*, 48–49.

16. *Laws* (1816), chap. 168, sec. 11, 477.

17. Mo. Rev. Stat., art. 7, sec. 44 (1835).

18. *Missouri Intelligencer* (Fayette), April 25, 1828, 3:1.

19. *Ford, Sheriff* v. *Circuit Court of Howard County*, 3 Mo. 309 (1834).

20. Mo. Rev. Stat., art. 7, sec. 41 (1835).

21. "An Act Concerning Costs in Criminal Cases," 1841 Mo. Laws at 28, sec. 4.

22. *Louisiana Journal*, April 11, 1861, 3:1.

Chapter 7. Against Themselves: Black-on-Black Crime

1. Karl Menninger, *Man against Himself*, 32, 45, 67.

2. *Missouri Gazette*, April 21, 1819, 3:2.

3. Aaron S. Fry, Notebook, Journals & Diaries, MHS.

4. *Missouri Intelligencer* (Columbia), April 25, 1835, 2:3.

5. *Boonville Weekly Observer*, April 10, 1844, 2:3.

6. *Missouri Statesman* (Columbia), June 13, 1845, 2:6.

7. *RC* (Huntsville), March 19, 1857, 2:5.

8. *Louisiana Journal*, July 12, 1860, 3:1.

9. *RC*, Feb. 6, 1858, 3:2.

10. *Palmyra Whig*, July 9, 2:2, July 16, 1857, 2:2.

11. *RC*, July 2, 3:1, July 9, 1:7, 2:7, July 16, 1857, 2:1.

12. The headlines concerning George's case included, "The Murderer of Mrs. Davis," "Atrocious Murder," "Brutal Murder," "The Murder in Monroe," and "Stop the Murderer."

13. *Brunswicker*, March 22, 1856, 1:6.

14. *U.S.* v. *Murphy*, St. Louis County Circuit Court Records, April 4, 1820, 79, FHC.

15. *State* v. *George and Jim*, Ste. Genevieve County Circuit Court Records, Book A, Feb. 16, June 12, June 15, 1821, 34, 47, 52, FHC.

16. 1836 Mo. Laws 60.

17. Pardon Papers, Box 1, F 20, MSA.

18. Trexler, *Slavery in Missouri*, 74.

19. *LT*, Aug. 25, 2:2, Oct. 13, 1848, 2:1. See also *History of Clay and Platte Counties, Missouri*, 140.

20. *Ewing* v. *Thompson*, 13 Mo. 132, 137–39 (1850); *Jennings* v. *Kavanaugh*, 5 Mo. 25 (1837).

21. *State* v. *Jepe*, Box 14, F 29:107–08, Nov. 26, 30, and Dec. 3, 1822, SLCP, MHS.

22. *State* v. *Cato, a Black Man*, Howard County Circuit Court Records, Book 3, Feb. 19, 24, 25, 1824, 17, 19, 28, 29, 36, FHC.

23. *Inquest: Sandy, a Slave*, Box 14, F 29, 109, March 23, 1834, SLCP, MHS.

24. *Inquest: John Steele*, Box 14, F 29, 117, July 23, 1834, SLCP, MHS.

25. *Inquest: William, a Slave*, Box 14, F 29, 180, April 12, 1836, SLCP, MHS.

26. *RC*, Jan. 1, 1857, 1:4.

27. *Louisiana Journal*, Sept. 18, 1862, 3:1.

28. *Missouri Statesman* (Columbia), Dec. 25, 1846, 3:3.

29. *RC*, Nov. 26, 1857, 2:3.

30. *LT,* June 1, 1860, 2:1.

31. *RC*, Oct. 29, 1857, 2:6.

32. *History of Franklin, Jefferson, Washington, Crawford and Gasconade Counties, Missouri*, 405.

33. *State* v. *Martin, a Slave,* Saline County Circuit Court Records, June 1862–May 1864.

34. George P. Rawick, ed. *The American Slave*, 11:269–71.

35. *Jane, a Slave* v. *The State*, 3 Mo. 61 (1831).

36. *Boonville Observer*, March 25, 1845, 1:2. See also *Missouri Statesman* (Columbia), March 7, 1845, 2:1.

37. See Janet Farrell Brodie, *Contraception and Abortion in Nineteenth-Century America.*

38. Pardon Papers, Box 3, F 16, MSA.

39. Lorenzo J. Greene, Gary R. Kremer, and Anthony F. Holland, *Missouri's Black Heritage*, 41.

40. *LT*, Oct. 16, 1853, 1:6.

41. *RC*, May 7, 1857, 2:1.

42. Ibid., Sept. 17, 1857, 2:1.

43. *Louisiana Journal*, April 10, 1862, 3:2.

44. *State* v. *Emily,* Audrain County Circuit Court Records, April 1856 and Nov. 1857; *History of Audrain County Missouri*, 243.

45. *State* v. *Mariah,* Saline County Circuit Court Records, Oct. 30, 1858–May 23, 1859.

46. *State* v. *Evaline*, Cape Girardeau Circuit Court Records, Aug. 1863.

47. Michael P. Johnson, "Smothered Slave Infants: Were Slave Mothers at Fault?" 493–95.

48. *Liberator* (Boston), July 24, 1834, 1:6.

49. *RC*, Feb. 14, 1856, 2:1.

Chapter 8. White Perpetrators, Black and Mulatto Victims

1. *Rennick* v. *Chloe*, 7 Mo. 197 (1841); *Scott* v. *William* (NC) and *Becton* v. *Ferguson* (AL), in Catterall, *Judicial Cases*, 2:54, 3:187; and *Randon* v. *Toby*, 52 U.S. 493, 520 (1850).

2. *Foreman* v. *Deakins,* Cape Girardeau District Court Records, Sept. 1799.

3. *Nash* v. *Primm*, 1 Mo. 178 (1822).

4. *Posey* v. *Garth*, 7 Mo. 94 (1841).

5. *Peters* v. *Clause*, 37 Mo. 337 (1866).

6. Mo. Const., art. 3, secs. 26, 28.

7. Mo. Rev. Stat., art 8, sec. 36 (1835).

8. *Grove* v. *State*, 10 Mo. 232 (1846).

9. *State* v. *Peters*, 28 Mo. 241 (1859).

10. Trexler, *Slavery in Missouri*, 69.

11. Rawick, ed. *American Slave*, 11:96.

12. *RC,* March 13, 1856, 2:3.

13. *Brunswicker,* July 14, 1855, 1:5; *RC,* July 19, 1855, 2:3.

14. *RC,* April 3, 1856, 3:2.

15. *LT,* Aug. 24, 1860, 4:1.

16. *California News,* April 28, 1860, 1:1.

17. Gordon N. Allport, *Nature of Prejudice,* 183.

18 U.S. Department of Commerce, *Negro Population,* 57.

19. *U.S.* v. *Joseph Leblond,* Nov. 16, 20, 1813, John B. C. Lucas Collection, MHS.

20. *U.S.* v. *Alex Morine,* Box 1, F 2:17, Dec. 16, 27, 1812, and March 1813, SLCP, MHS.

21. At the November 1812 term of the Court of Quarter Sessions, District of St. Louis, the grand jury refused to indict William Rupill for an assault on Mary Crosby, "spinster," whom he was charged with beating, wounding, ill-treating, ravishing, and carnally knowing. It voted him not guilty. The victim's fault in this instance appeared not to have been her race; it was her sex and marital status. The records did not specify any demographics of the alleged perpetrator of these crimes against her, Box 1, F 1, No 3, SLCP, MHS.

22. Trexler, *Slavery in Missouri,* 68–69.

23. Correspondence, Coralee Paul.

24. Billon, *Annals of St. Louis, ... 1804 to 1821,* 421–22.

25. *MORE,* Sept. 11, 1840.

26. *MORE,* Dec. 28, 1846.

27. Billon, *Annals of St. Louis, ... 1804 to 1821,* 382–83.

28. *MORE,* Jan. 3, 1821.

29. *U.S.* v. *William Gordon,* Box 1, F 1:45, Nov. 6, 9, 1818, and April 1819, SLCP, MHS.

30. Allport, *Nature of Prejudice,* 183.

31. Blackstone, *Commentaries,* 4:182–83.

32. *Independent Patriot* (Jackson), Aug. 28, 1824.

33. *State* v. *Obadiah Malone,* Cape Girardeau County Circuit Court Records, April 1826, contains the coroner's inquest of Louese's death, including the evidence of Polly Johnson, John M. Johnson, and Malinda Jenkins, and Malone's arrest warrant on charges of murdering Slave Louese, his bondwoman.

34. *Independent Patriot,* April 29, 1826, 2:2.

35. Ibid., May 13, 2:2, May 26, 2:1, 1826.

36. Ibid., June 24, 1826, 2:1.

37. *Inquest: Slave Patience,* in Woods-Holman Family Papers, F 1, 1820–29, MHS.

38. Brown, "Slave Narrative of William Wells Brown," 191; Farrison, *William Wells Brown,* 26–27; *MORE,* April 30, 1869.

39. *St. Louis Globe Democrat,* May 10, 1889, 8:2.

40. Theodore Dwight Weld, *American Slavery As It Is,* 89.

41. *MORE,* June 30, 1834, 3:3.

42. 2 Stat. 364, art. 33; 12 Stat. 736, art. 30; 18 Stat., Pt 1, 235, art. 58; see also William Winthrop, *Military Law and Precedents,* 979.

43. Robert [surname illegible] to William Selby Harney, July 4, 1834; James Clemens Jr. to WSH, Aug. 2, 4, 13, 1834, Mary C. Clemens Collection, MHS.

44. Otis K. Rice and Stephen W. Brown, *West Virginia, a History,* 76.

45. Balthasar Henry Meyer, *History of Transportation in the United States before 1860,* 18.

46. *Cincinnati Journal,* July 25, 1834, 2:3; *Liberator,* Sept. 6, 1834, 1:2.

47. Journals and Diaries, James Kennerly Collection, March 27, 1835, MHS.

48. Correspondence, William E. Lind and David H. Wallace, Old Military and Civil Records, National Archives, Washington, D.C.

49. *Missouri Intelligencer* (Columbia), July 5, 1834, 2:5.

50. Brown, *Narrative of William Wells Brown*, 186 (italics mine).

51. 9 Stat. 184.

52. 12 Stat. 506.

53. Scharf, *History of Saint Louis*, 1:518; L. U. Reavis, *Life and Times of General Harney*; and *DAB*, s.v. Harney, William Selby.

54. *Encyclopedia of the History of Missouri*, 4:184, also omits any mention of Hannah in its Harney entry.

55. *New York Times*, May 10, 1889, 5:6; *Kansas City Globe*, May 10, 1889, 1:1; *St. Louis Globe*, May 10, 1889, 8:2.

56. Brown, *Narrative of William Wells Brown*, 180.

57. *State v. Thomas B. Finley*, Saline County Circuit Court Records, April–May 1842, contains, among other material, the evidence of Dr George Rothwell, Clark Finley, James Metchen, and James R. David and the defendant's arrest warrant.

58. *Carpenter v. State*, 8 Mo. 291 (1843).

59. *Union* (St. Louis), Aug. 16, 1847, 3:1.

60. *MORE*, Aug. 16, 1847, 2:2 (italics mine.)

61. *Inquest: Slave Sarah*, Coroner's Report of Inquests, 1838–48, MHS.

62. *State v. James Henderson*, Boone County Circuit Court Records (1860), cited in Robert W. Duffner, "Slavery in Missouri River Counties, 1820–1865," unpub. Ph.D. diss. University of Missouri-Columbia, 1974, 91.

63. *Mann v. Trabue*, 1 Mo. 709 (1827).

64. *Soper v. Breckenridge*, 4 Mo. 14, 16 (1835).

65. *Adams v. Childers*, 10 Mo. 778 (1847).

66. *West and wife v. Forrest*, 22 Mo. 344 (1856).

67. 14 Stat. 27.

68. *U.S. v. Rhodes*, 27 Fed. Cas. 785 (C.C.D. Ky 1866) (No. 16, 152).

Chapter 9. Noncapital Statehood Crime, White and Black

1. *Louisiana Gazette* (St. Louis), Jan. 16, 1811, 3:2.

2. *Missouri Gazette* (St. Louis), Oct. 14, 1815, 2:2.

3. Ibid., Aug. 17, 1816, 4:3.

4. *MORE*, March 20, 1835, 1:3.

5. *Encyclopedia of the History of Missouri*, 3:232–33.

6. Trexler, *Slavery in Missouri*, 66–67.

7. Mo. Rev. Stat. 311.310–311.325 (1994).

8. Mo. Rev. Stat., sec. 9, 543 (1845) and sec. 6, 684 (1855).

9. Mo. Rev. Stat., sec. 22, 318 (1835).

10. Mo. Rev. Stat., secs. 18, 19, 25, 544–45 (1845).

11. Trexler, *Slavery in Missouri*, 68.

12. *Hawkins v. State*, 7 Mo. 190 (1841).

13. *Fraser v. State*, 6 Mo. 195 (1839).

14. *State v. Swadley*, 15 Mo. 515 (1852).

15. *State v. Leapfoot*, 19 Mo. 375 (1854).

16. *State v. Guyott*, 26 Mo. 62 (1857).

17. *California News*, Feb. 26, 1859, 3:1.

18. *Brunswicker*, Feb. 27, 1857, 1:6.

19. *State v. John Elliott*, Cape Girardeau County Circuit Court Records, 1852.

20. *State* v. *Frederick Wiedmann*, Cape Girardeau County Circuit Court Records, May 1856–April 1858.

21. *State* v. *Kasper Ludwig*, Cape Girardeau County Circuit Court Records, 1861.

22. *Skinner* v. *Hughes*, 13 Mo. 440 (1850).

23. *State* v. *Solomon Odle*, Saline County Circuit Court Records, 1836.

24. *State* v. *Isaac Little*, Cape Girardeau County Circuit Court Records, 1841.

25. *State* v. *Samuel Lockhart*, Cape Girardeau County Circuit Court Records, 1856.

26. *State* v. *Benjamin Taylor*, Cape Girardeau County Circuit Court Records, 1861.

27. *Markley* v. *State*, 10 Mo. 291 (1847).

28. *State* v. *Henke & Henke*, 19 Mo. 225 (1853).

29. *Douglass* v. *Ritchie*, 24 Mo. 177 (1857).

30. *State* v. *Henry Rohlfing*, 34 Mo. 348 (1864).

31. *Laws* (1804), chap. 3, secs. 11, 18, 19, 29–31.

32. *Oxford English Dictionary.*

33. David M. Walker, *Oxford Companion to Law,* 553.

34. Mo. Rev. Stat., chap. 167, sec. 22 (1845).

35. *State* v. *Slave Wash*, Cape Girardeau County Circuit Court Records, 1849.

36. *RC,* July 16, 1857, 1:6.

37. Duffner, "Slavery in Missouri River Counties," 54–56.

38. Don W. LeMond, "Slavery and Slave Crimes… in Boone County, Missouri, 1821–1861," unpub. M.A. thesis, Lincoln University, Jefferson City, Mo., 1972.

39. *State* v. *Slave Dennis, State* v. *Slave Jerry,* and *State* v. *Slave Vine,* Howard County Circuit Court Records, vols. 3 and 4, 1824–1833, 155–56, 219, 222–23, 237, 247, FHC.

40. *State* v. *Aaron, a Black Man Slave,* Cape Girardeau County Circuit Court Records, Aug. 11, 1828, 522–24, FHC.

41. *State* v. *Isaac, a Black Man Slave,* Cape Girardeau County Circuit Court Records, Dec. 1829–April 1830, 97, 104, 112, 119, 129, FHC.

42. *Boonville Observer,* July 23, 1859, 2:2.

43. *Todd* v. *State,* 1 Mo. 566 (1825).

44. *State* v. *Henry, a Slave,* 2 Mo. 218 (1830).

45. *State* v. *Joe, a Slave,* 19 Mo. 223 (1853).

46. 1831 Mo. 277–78; Mo. Rev. Stat., art. 9, secs. 26–28 (1835).

47. *State* v. *Steph, Sol, John, and Ben,* Nov. 1845, Cape Girardeau County Circuit Court Records, Book H, 24–26, FHC; Indictment, Cape Girardeau County Circuit Court Records, Nov. 25, 1845.

48. *Missouri Statesman* (Columbia), Aug. 22, 1845, 2:4.

49. *Hector, a Slave* v. *State,* 2 Mo. 166 (1829).

50. *Fackler* v. *Chapman,* 20 Mo. 249 (1855).

51. Rev. Mo. Stat., art. 8, sec. 35 (1835).

52. *State* v. *Gilbert, a Slave,* 24 Mo. 380 (1857).

53. LeMond, "Slavery and Slave Crimes … in Boone County," 76–77, contains the most detailed account of Tony's crime. Duffner, "Slavery in Missouri River Counties," 70–71, and Greene, Kremer, and Holland, *Missouri's Black Heritage,* 37, also mention it.

54. *Reed* v. *Circuit Court of Howard County,* 6 Mo. 44 (1839).

55. *State* v. *Jane, a Slave,* Cape Girardeau County Circuit Court Records, Nov.–Dec. 1845.

56. *Phillips* v. *Towler's Administrators,* 23 Mo. 401 (1856).

57. *Stratton* v. *Harriman,* 24 Mo. 324 (1857).

58. *Armstrong* v. *Marmaduke,* 31 Mo. 327 (1861).

59. *Louisiana Journal,* Jan. 27, 1862, 3:1.

60. *State* v. *Martha, a Slave*, Saline County Circuit Court Records, Sept. 1862–June 1863.

61. *State* v. *Dick, a Slave*, Cape Girardeau County Circuit Court Records, Book E, Dec. 11, 1837, 451–52, FHC.

62. *LT,* May 13, 1853, 1:7.

63. Correspondence, Betty Harvey Williams.

64. *California News*, Oct. 20, 1860, 3:1.

65. *Louisiana Journal*, Oct. 25, 1860, 2:2.

66. Conversation, Professor Robert Hudson.

67. *State* v. *Slave Esther*, Cape Girardeau County Circuit Court Records, Jan.–Feb. 1835.

68. Duffner, "Slavery in Missouri River Counties," 63.

69. *LT,* May 3, 1850, 2:1.

70. Duffner, "Slavery in Missouri River Counties," 63.

71. *California News*, Sept. 29, 1860, 1:5.

72. Trexler, *Slavery in Missouri*, 37–44.

73. *LT,* May 2, 1862, 2:2.

Chapter 10. Capital Cases: Girls and Women

1. Pierre Chouteau to Henry Dearborn, March 11, 1805, Pierre Chouteau Letter-book, MHS.

2. Houck, *History of Missouri*, 2:381; *Encyclopedia of the History of Missouri*, 3:90.

3. V. A. C. Gatrell, *Hanging Tree*, 618.

4. Schwarz, *Twice Condemned*, ix, 212.

5 *State* v. *Annice, a Slave*, Clay County Circuit Court Records, 1828.

6. *History of Clay … [County] Missouri*, 108; William H. Woodson, *History of Clay County*, 89.

7. Harriet C. Frazier, "The Execution of Juveniles in Missouri, Part I," 636–38.

8. *History of Franklin, Jefferson, … Counties, Missouri*, 556–58.

9. James Ira Breuer, *Crawford County and Cuba, Missouri*, 19.

10. Houck, *History of Missouri*, 3:182.

11. Abraham Brinker File (93), Probate Clerk's Office, Washington County, Potosi, Mo.

12. 1828 Mo. Law, chap. 1; sec. 1 Mo. Rev. Stat., "Administration," secs. 41, 43 (1835).

13. Correspondence, Martin Mazzei, prosecuting attorney of Crawford County in 1990.

14. *State* v. *Mary, a Slave*, Crawford County Circuit Court Records, 1837.

15. Blackstone, *Commentaries,* 4:23.

16. *Mary, a Slave* v. *State*, 5 Mo. 71 (1837). See also the Supreme Court of Missouri file on this case.

17. *Salem News*, Dec. 19, 1989, 6A:1.

18. See playbill and brochure, Rand's *The Trial of Mary, a Slave.*

19. The MORE story was reprinted in the *Sun* (Baltimore), June 15, 1837, 2:3, and the *Liberator*, June 16, 1837, 3:4. See also *Jefferson Republican* (Jefferson City), Sept. 30, 1837, 2:3, for another account of Mary's crime.

20. *DAB*, s.v. Edward Bates.

21. *Miller* v. *Pate*, 386 U.S. 1 (1967).

22. Mo. Const., art. 13, sec. 9 (1820).

23. *Fanny, a Slave v. State*, 6 Mo. 122 (1839). All quotations regarding this case, unless otherwise attributed to another source, derive from this decision.

24. *History of Lincoln County, Missouri*, 364.

25. *MORE* (St. Louis), Dec. 3, 1839, 2:4.

26. *Official Manual State of Missouri, 1997–1998*, 403.

27. *Missouri Statesman* (Columbia), March 24, 1843, 2:3.

28. Ibid., May 12, 1843, 2:1.

29. Ibid., May 19, 1843, 2:1.

30. *History of Boone County, Missouri*, 343.

31. Blackstone, *Commentaries*, 4:388.

32. Mo. Rev. Stat., art. 7, secs. 22–24 (1835).

33. Hugh P. Williamson, *Kingdom of Callaway*, 19.

34. *Boonville Observer*, July 17, 1844, 2:2.

35. *Reveille* (St. Louis), July 22, 1844, 13:4.

36. *State v. Susan*, Callaway County Circuit Court Records, Oct. 22, 1844.

37. Williamson, *Kingdom of Callaway*, 19.

38. *Missouri Gazette*, June 24, 1815, 3:4, Feb. 6, 1813, 3:4, July 5, 1817, 4:1.

39. Blackstone, *Commentaries*, 4:181.

40. Mo. Rev. Stat., art. 2, sec. 4 (1845).

41. Mo. Rev. Stat., art. 2, sec. 29 (1845).

42. *RC*, July 5, 1855, 2:5.

43. Melton A. McLaurin, *Celia, a Slave*, 74–75. For an earlier interpretation see Hugh P. Williamson, "Document: The State against Celia, a Slave," 408–20.

44. *BDAC*, John Jameson entry.

45. At least one Missouri newspaper, probably repeating the story in the *Fulton Telegraph*, reported the manner and place of Newsom's death substantially as detailed in Celia's confession, *Palmyra Whig*, July 12, 1855, 2:5.

46. Ovid Bell, *The Story of the Kingdom of Callaway*, 29.

47. See Wilton Marion Krogman, *The Human Skeleton in Forensic Medicine*.

48. *Brunswicker*, Dec. 1, 1855, 2:4.

49. *Missouri Statesman* (Columbia), Dec. 14, 1855, 3:1.

50. *State v. Celia, a Slave*, Callaway County Circuit Court Records, June–Dec. 1855. This material consists of over 60 unnumbered and handwritten pages. Unless attributed to another source, all quotations concerning Celia's case come from this file.

51. *New York Times*, Jan. 16, 1856, 2:6; the *Sun* (Baltimore), Jan. 17, 1856, 1:5.

Chapter 11. Capital Crimes by Coerced Boys and Men

1. Phillips, "Slave Crime in Virginia," 336–40.

2. Correspondence, Watt Espy.

3. Schwarz, *Twice Condemned*, 323–34.

4. *Brunswicker*, Feb. 27, 1857, 1:6.

5. *Missouri Gazette*, Oct. 20, 1819, 3:5.

6. *Missouri Intelligencer* (Fayette), Aug. 17, 3:1, Sept. 7, 1826, 2:5; *History of Howard and Cooper Counties*, 780.

7. *History of St. Charles, Montgomery and Warren Counties, Missouri*, 578. There are no extant Montgomery County court records from this period. See also Lois Stanley, George F. Wilson, and Maryhelen Wilson, comps., *Death Records of Missouri Men, 1808–1854*, 83, for mention of Dr. Jones's murder in 1842.

8. North Todd Gentry, *The Bench and Bar of Boone County, Missouri,* 114–15.

9. *History of St. Charles, Montgomery, ... Counties,* 1004.

10. *MORE,* May 7, 1841, 2:2.

11. *Salt River Journal* (Bowling Green), July 3, 1841, 3:4.

12. Ibid., Aug. 14, 1841, 3:2. For additional mention of this case see *Palmyra Whig,* May 8, 1841, 2:4; *History of Pike County, Missouri,* 203–04; Dennis Naglich, "The Slave System and the Civil War in Rural Prairieville," 259.

13. *California News,* July 18, 1863, 2:1.

14. *History of Cole, Moniteau, Morgan, Benton, Miller, Maries and Osage Counties, Missouri,* 333.

15. James E. Ford, *History of Moniteau County,* 47.

16. Stephen B. Oates, *With Malice toward None: The Life of Abraham Lincoln,* 332.

17. *History of Howard and Cooper Counties,* 780–81.

18. *Missouri Intelligencer,* March 24, 1832, 2:4.

19. *Jim, a Slave* v. *State,* 3 Mo. 84, 99 (1832).

20. *History of Callaway County, Missouri,* 283–86; Williamson, *Kingdom of Callaway,* 15.

21. *Missouri Statesman* (Columbia), June 16, 1843, 2:2.

22. *RC,* Nov. 26, 1858, 2:2.

23. Ibid., Dec. 3, 1858, 2:3; Jan. 7, 1859, 2:6.

24. Ibid., March 18, 2:2, June 10, 2:1, Dec. 9, 2:1, Dec. 16, 1859, 2:2.

25. *History of Boone County, Missouri,* 388; *RC,* Oct. 1, 2:1, Oct. 8, 3:2, Oct. 15, 2:1, Oct. 22, 1857, 2:4.

26. Mo. Rev. Stat. 541.033 (1999); *State* v. *Morrison,* 869 S.W. 2d 813 (1994).

27. Mo. Rev. Stat., chap. 27, art. 5, sec. 7 (1855).

28. *West* (St. Joseph), Dec. 3, 1859, 2:8.

29. *Louisiana Journal,* July 21, 1859, 2:4; *Boonville Observer,* July 23, 1859, 1:8.

30. John Quincy Adams, "Argument of John Quincy Adams before the Supreme Court of the United States," *The Amistad Case/The Basic Afro-American Reprint Library,* 40.

31. *U.S.* v. *The Amistad,* 40 U.S. 518, 593 (1841). See also Steven Spielberg's 1997 film, *Amistad,* and David Pesci, *Amistad, a Novel.*

32. *Free Democrat* (St. Joseph), Nov. 12, 1859, 2:3.

33. Chris L. Rutt, ed. *History of Buchanan County and St. Joseph,* 215; *West,* Dec. 3, 1859, 2:8; *Free Democrat* (St. Joseph), Dec. 3, 1859, 2:2; *Louisiana Journal,* Dec. 8, 1859, 3:2; *California News,* Dec. 10, 1859, 2:5.

34. W. M. Paxton, *Annals of Platte County, Missouri,* 170. No court records survive from this county's antebellum period.

35. *RC,* Dec. 20, 1855, 3:2.

36. *American Citizen* (Lexington), July 9, 1856, 3:1.

37. *RC,* Dec. 3, 1858, 3:3; *LT,* Dec. 3, 1858, 1:7.

38. *Saturday Morning Visitor* (Waverly and St. Thomas), Dec. 11, 1858, 2:5.

39. *RC,* Jan. 7, 1859, 2:6.

40. *Saturday Morning Visitor,* Jan. 8, 1859, 2:5.

41. *LT,* April 21, 1848, 2:1.

42. *History of Hickory, Polk, Cedar, Dade and Barton Counties, Missouri,* 454; *History of Dade County and Her People,* 259.

43. *Times* (Glasgow), May 29, 1851, 2:1.

44. *LT,* May 30, 1851, 2:1.

45. *History of St. Charles, Montgomery ... Counties,* 1003–04.

Chapter 12. Capital Crimes by Wandering Boys and Men

1. *Calhoun* v. *Buffington,* 25 Mo. 443 (1857).
2. *State* v. *Slave Hart,* Audrain County Circuit Court Records, 1848–54.
3. *State* v. *Slave Nathan,* Cape Girardeau County Circuit Court Records, Nov. 1846–Feb. 1847.
4. *History of Southeast Missouri,* 323.
5. *State* v. *Mat, a Slave,* Callaway County Circuit Court Records, July–Oct. 1855 (italics and capitalization in the original).
6. *Thompson* v. *Oklahoma,* 487 U.S. 815 (1988), holds that the cruel and unusual punishments clause of the Eighth Amendment, applicable to the states through the due process clause of the Fourteenth Amendment, prohibits the execution of any person aged less than 16 years at the time of the capital crime, and *Stanford* v. *Kentucky,* 492 U.S. 361 (1989), allows the states to impose a death sentence for any person aged 16 years or older at the time of the capital crime.
7. *RC,* Nov. 1, 1855, 2:3.
8. Blanche Wiesen Cook, *Eleanor Roosevelt,* 1:28.
9. *Adams* v. *State,* 76 Mo. 355 (1882); Docket Book, April 21, 1883 entry, Morgan County Circuit Court; *Gazette* (Versailles), April 26, 1883, 3:6.
10. 1849 Mo. 4.
11. *Scott, a Man of Color* v. *Emerson,* 15 Mo. 576, 586 (1852).
12. *Rachael, a Woman of Color* v. *Walker,* 4 Mo. 350 (1836).
13. Gatrell, *Hanging Tree,* 4.
14. Victor Streib, *Death Penalty for Juveniles,* 191–208.
15. *Missouri Statesman,* Nov. 23, 1855, 2:5.
16. *Brunswicker,* Jan. 12, 2:1, Feb. 9, 1856, 2:3.
17. *BDAC,* 119–22, 128, 136.
18. *History of Callaway County,* 273–77.
19. *State* v. *Mat, a Slave,* Callaway County Circuit Court Records, July 1858.
20. 1859 Mo. Laws 7.
21. *History of Howard and Chariton Counties, Missouri,* 254–55.
22. Excluding the mention of Josiah Spalding's elective offices found in Scharf, *History of St. Louis,* 1:663 and 837, the particulars of this case are taken from Mary E. Seematter's "Trials and Confessions: Race and Justice in Antebellum St. Louis," 36–47, an excellent piece of far-ranging and thorough scholarship.
23. Mo. Const., art. 13, sec. 13.
24. *U.S.* v. *Cortez,* 449 U.S. 411 (1981). However, Judy E. Zelin writes of barefoot evidence, "Footprints, like fingerprints, remain constant throughout life and furnish an adequate and reliable means of identification." "Admissibility of Bare Footprint Evidence," 45 *American Law Reports,* 4th Ed. 1178, 1182 (1987).
25. Andre A. Moenssens, Fred E. Inbau, and James E. Starrs, *Scientific Evidence in Criminal Cases,* 515.
26. 1860 Mo. 33–34.
27. *History of Southeast Missouri,* 323.
28. *State* v. *Slave Charles,* Cape Girardeau Circuit Court Records, March 1863–Dec. 1864 (italics in the original).
29. *History of Southeast Missouri,* 753.
30. Ibid., 390.
31 *Northwest Conservator* (Richmond), Sept. 11, 1862, 2:2; *LT,* Sept. 19, 1862, 3:2.
32. Charles Fairman, *Law of Martial Rule,* 22, 41.

33. Eugene M. Violette, *History of Adair County*, 103; *LT*, Aug. 29, 1862, 2:2; W. F. Switzler, *History of Missouri*, 420–21.

34. *DAB*, s.v. Doniphan, Alexander.

35. *History of Ray County, Missouri*, 470–73.

36. Craigie and Hulbert, *Dictionary of American English*, 1:147.

37. Harold H. Haines, *The Callaghan Mail*, 42–43.

38. *State v. Slave Ben*, Marion County Circuit Court Records, Oct. 31, 1849–Jan. 11, 1850; *Missouri Courier* (Hannibal), Dec. 6, 1849, 1:1–5.

39. Correspondence, Helen A. Beedle.

40. *History of Marion County*, 298–99.

41. *Missouri Statesman*, June 16, 1843, 2:2.

42. *Trials and Confessions of Madison Henderson, Alfred Amos Warrick, James Seward, and Charles Brown*, 37.

43. Were Slave Ben's confession in existence, the Mark Twain Project, University of California-Berkeley Library, Berkeley, California, is the place most likely to have it. It kindly supplied me a copy of Ament's Dec. 6, 1849, coverage of Ben's trial and various advertisements for his confession, including *Missouri Courier*, Feb. 21, 1850.

44. *Missouri Courier*, Feb. 28, March 14, 1850.

45. Haines, *Callaghan Mail*, 42.

46. Margaret Sanborn, *Mark Twain: The Bachelor Years*, 65, 67. See also Dixon Wecter, *Sam Clemens of Hannibal*, 214–15.

47. Mark Twain, "Villagers of 1840–43," in *Huck Finn and Tom Sawyer among the Indians*, 101.

Chapter 13. Rape: The Crime, Its Punishment, and Its Pardons

1. Rev. Mo. Stat., art. 2, sec. 1253 (1879).

2. *Kansas City Star*, May 8, 1:5; *Kansas City Journal*, May 9, 1:1; *Kansas City Times*, May 9, 1891, 1:1.

3. *Laws* (1808), chap. 65, sec. 8, 211.

4. Va. Code, chap. 158, sec. 4 (1819); chap. 226, sec. 2 (1833).

5. 1 Stat. 113; 62 Stat. 837–38; 98 Stat. 1987.

6. *Coker v. Georgia*, 433 U.S. 584, 599 (1977).

7. *Digest of the Laws of Missouri Territory*, 137 (1818).

8. 1825 Mo. Laws 283.

9. Missouri State Penitentiary, Register of Inmates, Reel 1, First Series, 4.

10. Rev. Mo. Stat., art. 2, secs. 23–28 (1835).

11. *History of Hickory, Polk ... Counties*, 235.

12. *Missouri Statesman*, Nov. 17, 1843, 2:4.

13. *California News*, Aug. 4, 1860, 1:5.

14. *RC*, Oct. 25, 1855, 2:1; *LT*, Oct. 26, 1855, 1:7; *Liberator*, Jan. 18, 1856, 2:5.

15. U.S. Department of Commerce, *Negro Population*, 57.

16. *State v. Sherwood Reuben*, Cape Girardeau County Circuit Court Records, Nov. 1834.

17. *George, a Slave v. State*, 37 Miss. 316 (1859).

18. Schwarz, *Twice Condemned*, 159.

19. Jean Fagan Yellin, ed. *Harriet Jacobs, Incidents in the Life of a Slave Girl, Written by Herself (1861)*, 265.

20. Williamson, *Kingdom of Callaway*, 17–19. The author, now deceased, was a Fulton

resident, circuit court judge for many years, and wrote several tracts on Callaway County slave cases. He apparently had available to him the Callaway County circuit court records about these cases, including Slave William's. With few exceptions these records are no longer extant.

21. *LT*, Sept. 22, 1854, 2:5.

22. *State* v. *Simon, a Slave*, Mississippi and Cape Girardeau County Circuit Court Records, Nov. 1854, May 1855.

23. *State* v. *Henry, a Colored Boy*, Saline County Circuit Court Records, Aug.–Sept. 1844 (emphasis in the original).

24. *State* v. *Lee*, Saline County Circuit Records, July 1854–Feb. 1855.

25. *RC*, June 24, 1859.

26. *U.S.* v. *Dickinson*, 25 Fed. Cas. 849, 850 (Superior Court, Terr. of Ark. 1820) (No. 14, 957).

27. *Nathan, a Slave* v. *State*, 8 Mo. 631 (1844).

28. *General History of Macon County, Missouri*, 34.

29. Correspondence, Betty Harvey Williams.

30. Howard County Circuit Court Docket Book, vols. 10–11, 68, 142, 146, 233, FHC.

31. Pardon Papers, Box 4, F 27, MSA.

32. *State* v. *Anderson*, 19 Mo. 241, 243 (1853).

33. Mo. Const., art. 13, sec. 12 (1820).

34. Billon, *Annals of St. Louis ... 1804 to 1821*, 222, 270.

35. Pardon Papers, Box 6, F 39, MSA.

36. *Charles* v. *State*, 11 Ark. 389, 405 (1850).

37. *LT*, Dec. 7, 1855, 2:2.

38. Schwarz, *Twice Condemned*, 209.

Chapter 14. Antebellum Lynchings of Blacks, Slave and Free

1. James R. McGovern, *Anatomy of a Lynching*, x.

2. Michael Fellman, *Inside War*, 70.

3. Lawrence M. Friedman, *Crime and Punishment in American History*, 190.

4. Edward L. Ayers, *Vengeance & Justice*, 237.

5. *LT*, Feb. 6, 1857, 2:5.

6. *Kansas City Enterprise*, Feb. 21, 1857, 1:7.

7. "Acts Relating to Slaves," No. 314, *The Statutes at Large of South Carolina, 1840*, 7:355.

8. *Missouri Intelligencer* (Columbia), Aug. 1, 1835, 1:3, 2:4.

9. *LT*, Nov. 29, 1859, 2:5.

10. *California News*, April 28, 1860, 2:6.

11. Ibid., April 28, 1860, 2:6.

12. *Jefferson Republican*, Jan. 7, 1837, 3:3.

13. *LT*, Dec. 14, 1849, 2:5.

14. Schwarz, *Twice Condemned*, 321.

15. Richard Maxwell Brown, *Strain of Violence*, 117.

16. *MORE*, Nov. 3, 1829, 3:5; *Missouri Intelligencer*, Oct. 30, 2:5, Nov. 6, 1829, 2:4.

17. *Estate of Shubael Allen*, Clay County Probate Court Records, April 1, 1842.

18. *LT*, April 5, 1850, 2:1.

19. Ibid., May 3, 1850, 2:2.

20. Ibid., May 10, 2:2, May 17, 1850, 1:5.

21. *Springfield Advertiser*, May 25, 1850, 2:6.

22. *History of Clay and Platte Counties*, 159.

23. *Boonville Observer*, Nov. 10, 1860, 1:8.

24. *Louisiana Journal*, Nov. 8, 1860, 2:2, and *California News*, Nov. 10, 1860, 2:2, mention Miss Barnes's interment. LT's Nov. 9, 1860, 2:5, coverage ends with Teney's lynching.

25. *History of Callaway County*, 286–87.

26. *Chicago Tribune*, Dec. 31, 1914, 22:7.

27. *Howell County Gazette* (West Plains), June 18, 1914, 1:1.

28. Ralph Ginzburg, *100 Years of Lynchings*, 265.

29. *History of Franklin, Jefferson ... Counties*, 405.

30. Janet S. Hermann, "The McIntosh Affair," 123–43, a careful and detailed discussion of this subject, is the origin of any quoted material regarding this case not attributed to another source. See also the *Pittsburgh Gazette*, May 12, 1836, 2:1, which reprints a *MORE* story about McIntosh's death; *Liberator*, May 14, 1836, 3:5, May 21, 1836, 3:3.

31. Abraham Lincoln, "Address before the Young Men's Lyceum of Springfield, Illinois," Jan. 27, 1838, in Arthur Brook, Lapsley, ed., *The Writings of Abraham Lincoln*, 1:148–50.

32. Harriet Martineau, *Retrospect of Western Travel*, 2:206–09.

33. Madeline House, Graham Storey, and Kathleen Tillotson, eds. *Letters of Charles Dickens*, 3:197 (emphasis in the original).

34. Cited in Hermann, "The McIntosh Affair," 126.

35. Reprinted in *Jefferson Republican*, May 7, 1836, 2:3.

36. William Hyde and Howard L. Conard, *Encyclopedia of the History of St. Louis*, 4:1913.

37. *Franklin County Tribune* (Union), July 16, 1897, 1:3.

38. *History of Franklin, Jefferson ... Counties*, 285.

39. *Salt River Journal*, May 2, 1840, 1:5. See also *Jefferson Republican*, May 2, 1840, 1:4.

40. *MORE*, March 8, 1844, 2:1. See also *Missouri Statesman*, March 15, 1844, 2:4.

41. Vest is best known as the attorney who, in 1870, argued the value of the dog to the jury in a case wherein one man shot another's named *Old Drum*. A fine statue of this hound is on the courthouse grounds where Vest gave his memorable speech in Warrensburg, Johnson County, Missouri. See Vest's *BDAC* entry.

42. *LT,* July 22, 1853, 1:6; *History of Pettis County*, 931–32; Michael J. Cassity, *Defending a Way of Life*, 42–43.

43. *LT,* Aug. 5, 2:6, 19, 1853, 2:6; *Sentinel* (Columbia), Aug. 4, 1853, 2:1; *Jefferson Examiner*, Aug. 9, 1853, 2:5; *Joplin Globe*, Feb. 14, 1954, 7E:1; *History of Newton, Lawrence, Barry and McDonald Counties*, 453–54.

44. *RC*, Jan 7, 1859, 3:5; *California News*, Jan. 22, 4:1, and 28, 1859, 1:7; *LT*, Jan. 18, 1859, 1:7; *History of Lincoln County*, 365–67; Trexler, *Slavery in Missouri*, 72.

45. *Sentinel*, Aug. 25, 1854, 2:1 (emphasis in the original); see also *LT*, Aug. 26, 2:5, Sept. 2, 1853, 2:5; *Jefferson Examiner*, Aug. 30, 1853, 2:4; *History of Boone County*, 371–74.

46. *LT,* Feb. 16, 2:2, 23, 2:1, March 5, 1855, 2:1; *History of Clay and Platte Counties*, 166–67.

47. Mo. Rev. Stat., "Costs," art. 2, sec. 16 (1845) (emphasis mine).

48. *Calhoun v. Buffington*, 25 Mo. 443 (1857).

49. Mo. Rev. Stat., "Fees," chap. 64, sec. 2 (1855).

50. *RC*, Oct. 18, 1855, 2:4. See also *Brunswicker,* Oct. 13, 1855, 2:1; *LT*, Oct. 26, 1855, 1:4.

51. *Liberator,* Jan. 18, 1854, 12:4; James Elbert Cutler, *Lynch-Law,* 119.

52. *Boonville Observer,* July 23, 1859, 2:1. See also *California News,* July 23, 1859, 2:2.

53. *History of Greene County,* 265–66. See also *LT,* Sept. 2, 1859, 2:4.

54. *LT,* Dec. 5, 1862, 2:3.

55. *History of Saline County,* 259–65; *Missouri Statesman,* July 29, 1859, 2:4; *Boonville Observer,* May 28, 1859, 3:2; *California News,* July 30, 1859, 2:3; *LT,* July 29, 1859, 1:2.

56. *State* v. *John,* Saline County Circuit Court Records, May–Dec. 1859.

57. *State* v. *Holman,* Saline County Circuit Court Records, June–Nov. 1859.

58. *State* v. *James,* Saline County Circuit Court Records, July–Nov. 1859.

Bibliography

Books

Adams, John Quincy. "Argument of John Quincy Adams before the Supreme Court of the United States," *The Amistad Case/The Basic Afro-American Reprint Library*. New York: Johnson Reprint, 1968.

Allport, Gordon N. *The Nature of Prejudice*. Cambridge, Mass.: Addison-Wesley, 1954.

Arnold, Morris S. *Colonial Arkansas, 1686–1804: A Social and Cultural History*. Fayetteville: Univ. of Arkansas Press, 1991.

_____. *Unequal Laws unto a Savage Race: European Legal Traditions in Arkansas*. Fayetteville: Univ. of Arkansas Press, 1985.

Ayers, Edward L. *Vengeance & Justice: Crime and Punishment in the 19th-Century American South*. New York: Oxford Univ. Press, 1984.

Ballagh, James Curtis. *A History of Slavery in Virginia*. Baltimore: Johns Hopkins Press, 1902; rpt. New York: Johnson Reprint, 1968.

Bell, Ovid. *The Story of the Kingdom of Callaway*. Fulton, Mo.: Published by the author, 1952.

Billon, Frederic L. *Annals of St. Louis in Its Early Days under the French and Spanish Dominations, 1764–1804*. St. Louis: Published by the author, 1886.

_____. *Annals of St. Louis in Its Territorial Days from 1804 to 1821*. St. Louis: Nixon-Jones, 1888.

Blackstone, William. *Commentaries on the Laws of England, A Facsimile of the First Edition of 1765–1769*. 4 vols. Chicago: Univ. of Chicago Press, 1979.

Blanton, Wyndham B. *Medicine in Virginia in the Eighteenth Century*. Richmond: Garnett & Massie, 1931.

Breuer, James Ira. *Crawford County and Cuba, Missouri*. Cape Girardeau: Ramfre Press, 1972.

Brodie, Janet Farrell. *Contraception and Abortion in Nineteenth-Century America*. Ithaca, N.Y.: Cornell Univ. Press, 1994.

Brown, Richard Maxwell. *Strain of Violence: Historical Studies of American Violence and Vigilantism*. New York: Oxford Univ. Press, 1977.

Brown, William Wells, "The Slave Narrative of William Wells Brown," in *Putting On Ole Massa*, ed. Gilbert Osofsky. New York: Harper and Row, 1969.

Bynum, W. F. and Roy Porter, eds. *Companion Encyclopedia of the History of Medicine*. 2 vols. London: Routledge, 1993.

Campbell, R. A., ed. *Campbell's Gazetteer of Missouri*, St. Louis: Published by the author, 1875.

Cassity, Michael J. *Defending a Way of Life: An American Community in the Nineteenth Century*. Albany: State Univ. of New York Press, 1989.

Catterall, Helen, ed. *Judicial Cases Concerning American Slavery and the Negro*. 5 vols. New York: Octagon Books, 1968.

Cleary, Edward, ed. *McCormick's Handbook of the Law of Evidence*. 2d ed. St. Paul: West, 1972.

Cobb, Thomas R. R. *Law of Negro Slavery*. 1858. Rpt. New York: Negro Universities Press, 1968.

Conard, Howard L., ed. *Encyclopedia of the History of Missouri*. 6 vols. St. Louis: Southern Historical Press, 1901.

Cook, Blanche Wiesen. *Eleanor Roosevelt*. Vol. 1. New York: Viking, 1992.

Craigie, William A. and James R. Hulbert, eds. *A Dictionary of American English on Historical Principles*. 4 vols. Chicago: Univ. of Chicago Press, 1940.

Cutler, James Elbert. *Lynch-Law: An Investigation into the History of Lynching in the United States*. London: Longmans, Green, 1905.

Davis, Edwin Adams. *Louisiana, a Narrative History*. Baton Rouge: Claitor's Book Store, 1965.

De, S. N. *Cholera: Its Pathology and Pathogenesis*. London: Oliver and Boyd, 1961.

Dictionary of American Biography. 11 vols. New York: Charles Scribner's Sons, 1964.

Duffy, John. *From Humors to Medical Science: A History of American Medicine*. 2d ed. Urbana: Univ. of Illinois Press, 1993.

_____, ed. *The Rudolph Matas History of Medicine in Louisiana*. Vol. 1. Baton Rouge: Lousiana State Univ. Press, 1958.

Ekberg, Carl J. *Colonial Ste. Genevieve*. Gerald, Mo.: Patrice Press, 1985.

Fairman, Charles. *The Law of Martial Rule*. Chicago: Callaghan, 1943.

Farrison, William Edward. *William Wells Brown: Author and Reformer*. Chicago: Univ. of Chicago Press, 1969.

Fellman, Michael. *Inside War: The Guerrilla Conflict in Missouri during the American Civil War*. New York: Oxford Univ. Press, 1990.

Fields, Joseph E., comp. *"Worthy Partner": The Papers of Martha Washington*. Westport, Conn.: Greenwood Press, 1994.

Flexner, James Thomas. *Washington, the Indispensable Man*. Boston: Little, Brown, 1974.

Foley, William E., *The Genesis of Missouri: From Wilderness Outpost to Statehood*. Columbia: Univ. of Missouri Press, 1989.

Foley, William E., and C. David Rice. *The First Chouteaus: River Barons of Early St. Louis*. Urbana: Univ. of Illinois Press, 1983.

Ford, James E. *History of Moniteau County, Missouri*. California, Mo.: Marvin H. Crawford, 1936.

Fortier, Alcée. *A History of Louisiana*. Vol. 1. New York: Manzi, Joyant, 1904.

Fraser, Antonia. *Mary Queen of Scots*. London: Cox & Wyman, 1970.

Frazier, Harriet C. *A Babble of Ancestral Voices: Shakespeare, Cervantes, and Theobald*. The Hague: Mouton, 1974.

Friedman, Lawrence M. *Crime and Punishment in American History*. New York: Basic Books, 1993.

Gatrell, V. A. C. *The Hanging Tree: Execution and the English People 1770–1868*. New York: Oxford Univ. Press, 1994.

Gelfand, Toby. *Professionalizing Modern Medicine: Paris Surgeons and Medical Science and Institutions in the 18th Century*. Westport, Conn.: Greenwood Press, 1980.

General History of Macon County, Missouri. Chicago: H. Taylor, 1910.

Gentry, North Todd. *The Bench and Bar of Boone County, Missouri*. Columbia: Published by the author, 1916.

Ginzburg, Ralph. *100 Years of Lynchings*. Baltimore: Black Classic Press, 1988.

Goodwin, E. J. *History of Medicine in Missouri*. St. Louis: W. L. Smith, 1905.

Greene, Lorenzo J., Gary R. Kremer, and Anthony F. Holland, *Missouri's Black Heritage*. St. Louis: Forum Press, 1980.

Haines, Harold H. *The Callaghan Mail*. Hannibal, Mo.: Published by the author, 1944.

Hall, Kermit L., ed. *The Oxford Companion to the Supreme Court of the United States*. New York: Oxford Univ. Press, 1992.

History of Audrain County, Missouri. St. Louis: National Historical Co., 1884.

History of Boone County, Missouri. St. Louis: Western Historical Co., 1882.

History of Callaway County, Missouri. St. Louis: National Historical Co., 1884.

History of Clay and Platte Counties, Missouri. St. Louis: National Historical Co., 1885.

History of Cole, Moniteau, Morgan, Benton, Miller, Maries and Osage Counties, Missouri. Chicago: Goodspeed, 1889.

History of Dade County and Her People. Greenfield, Mo.: Pioneer Historical Co., 1917.

History of Franklin, Jefferson, Washington, Crawford and Gasconade Counties, Missouri. Chicago: Goodspeed, 1888.

History of Greene County, Missouri. St. Louis: Western Historical Co., 1883.

History of Hickory, Polk, Cedar, Dade and Barton Counties, Missouri. Chicago: Goodspeed, 1889.

History of Howard and Chariton Counties, Missouri. St. Louis: National Historical Co., 1883.

History of Howard and Cooper Counties, Missouri. St. Louis: National Historical Co., 1883.

History of Lincoln County, Missouri. Chicago: Goodspeed, 1888.

History of Marion County. St. Louis: E. F. Perkins, 1884.

History of Newton, Lawrence, Barry and McDonald Counties, Missouri. Chicago: Goodspeed, 1888.

History of Pettis County, Missouri. N.p.: 1882.

History of Pike County, Missouri. Des Moines, Iowa: Mills, 1882.

History of Ray County. St. Louis: Missouri Historical Society, 1881.

History of Saline County, Missouri. St. Louis: Missouri Historical Co., 1886.

History of Southeast Missouri. Chicago: Goodspeed, 1888.

History of St. Charles, Montgomery and Warren Counties, Missouri. St. Louis: National Historical Co., 1885.

Houck, Louis. *A History of Missouri*. 3 vols. Chicago: R. R. Donnelley, 1908.

_____, ed. *The Spanish Regime in Missouri*. 2 vols. Chicago: R. R. Donnelley & Sons, 1909.

House, Madeline, Graham Storey, and Kathleen Tillotson, eds. *Letters of Charles Dickens*. Vol. 3. Oxford: Clarendon, 1974.

Hyde, William, and Howard L. Conard, eds. *Encyclopedia of the History of St. Louis*. 6 vols. St. Louis: Southern History Co., 1899.

Jackson, Ronald Vern, ed. *Missouri 1850 Slave Schedule*. North Salt Lake City, Utah: Accelerated Indexing Systems, 1988.

_____, ed. *Missouri 1860 Slave Schedule*. North Salt Lake City, Utah: Accelerated Indexing Systems, 1990.

Judson, Frederick N. *Treatise Upon the Law and Practice of Taxation in Missouri*. Columbia, Mo.: E. W. Stephens, 1900.

Kerr, Derek N. *Petty Felony, Slave Defiance, and Frontier Villainy: Crime and Criminal Justice in Spanish Louisiana, 1770–1803*. New York: Garland, 1993.

King, Wilma. *Stolen Childhood: Slave Youth in Nineteenth-Century America*. Bloomington: Indiana Univ. Press, 1995.

Kolchin, Peter. *American Slavery, 1619–1877*. New York: Hill and Wang, 1993.

Krogman, Wilton Marion. *The Human Skeleton in Forensic Medicine*. Springfield, Ill.: Charles C. Thomas, 1962.

Lapsley, Arthur Brook, ed. *The Writings of Abraham Lincoln*. Vol. 1. New York: P. F. Collier & Son, 1905.

Lyons, Albert S., and R. Joseph Petrucelli. *Medicine: An Illustrated History*. New York: Harry N. Abrams, 1979.

March, David D. *The History of Missouri*. 4 vols. New York: Lewis Historical, 1967.

Martineau, Harriet. *Retrospective of Western Travel*. 3 vols. London: Saunders and Otley, 1838. Rpt. New York: Greenwood Press, 1969.

McGovern, James R. *Anatomy of a Lynching: The Killing of Claude Neal*. Baton Rouge: Louisiana State Univ. Press, 1982.

McLaurin, Melton A. *Celia, a Slave*. Athens: Univ. of Georgia Press, 1991.

Menninger, Karl. *Man against Himself*. New York: Harcourt Brace & World, 1938. Rpt. Harcourt Brace Jovanovich, 1966.

Meyer, Balthasar Henry. *History of Transportation in the United States before 1860*. Washington, D.C: Carnegie Institution of Washington, 1948.

Mitford, Jessica. *The Trial of Dr. Spock*. New York: Alfred A. Knopf, 1969.

Moenssens, Andre A., Fred E. Inbau, and James E. Starrs. *Scientific Evidence in Criminal Cases*. Mineola, N.Y.: Foundation Press, 1986.

Morrison, Toni. *Beloved*. New York: Alfred A. Knopf, 1987.

Oates, Stephen B. *With Malice toward None: The Life of Abraham Lincoln*. New York: Harper & Row, 1977.

Oxford English Dictionary. 20 vols. Oxford: Clarendon, 1989.

Paxton, W. M. *Annals of Platte County, Missouri*. Kansas City: Hudson-Kimberly, 1897.

Perrin, William H., ed. *History of Crawford and Clark Counties, Illinois*. Chicago: O. L. Baskin, 1883.

Pesci, David. *Amistad, a Novel*. New York: Marlowe & Co., 1997.

Pickard, Madge E., and R. Carlyle Buley. *The Midwest Pioneer: His Ills, Cures & Doctors*. New York: Henry Schuman, 1946.

Radzinowicz, Leon. *A History of English Criminal Law and Its Administration from 1750*. Vol. 1. New York: Macmillan, 1948.

Rawick, George P., ed. *The American Slave: A Composite Autobiography*. Vol. 11. Westport, Conn.: Greenwood Press, 1972.

Reavis, L. U. *Life and Times of General Harney*. N.p.; N.d.

Reynolds, John. *The Pioneer History of Illinois*. Belleville, Ill.: N. A. Randall, 1852.

Rice, Otis K., and Stephen W. Brown. *West Virginia, a History*. 2d ed. Lexington: Univ. Press of Kentucky, 1993.

Richardson, Ruth. *Death, Dissection and the Destitute*. New York: Routledge & Kegan Paul, 1987.

Rothman, David J. *The Discovery of the Asylum: Social Order and Disorder in the New Republic.* Boston: Little, Brown, 1971.

Rutt, Chris L., ed. *History of Buchanan County and the City of St. Joseph.* Chicago: Biographical, 1904.

Sanborn, Margaret. *Mark Twain: The Bachelor Years.* New York: Doubleday, 1990.

Scharf, J. Thomas. *History of Saint Louis City and County.* 2 vols. Philadelphia: Louis H. Everts, 1883.

Schwarz, Philip J. *Twice Condemned: Slaves and the Criminal Laws of Virginia, 1705–1865.* Baton Rouge: Louisiana State Univ. Press, 1988.

Shoemaker, Floyd. *Missouri's Struggle for Statehood, 1804–1821.* New York: Russell & Russell, 1916, reissued 1969.

Snyder, LeMoyne. *Homicide Investigation.* 2d ed. Springfield, Ill.: Charles C. Thomas, 1972.

Stanley, Lois, George F. Wilson, Maryhelen Wilson, comps. *Death Records from Missouri Newspapers, January 1854–December 1860.* Greenville, S.C.: Southern Historical Press, 1990.

_____. *Death Records from the Missouri Newspapers: the Civil War Years, January 1861–December 1865.* Greenville, S.C.: Southern Historical Press, 1990.

_____. *Death Records for Missouri Newspapers, January 1866–December 1870.* Greenville, S.C.: Southern Historical Press, 1990.

_____. *Death Records of Missouri Men, 1808–1854.* Greenville, S.C.: Southern Historical Press, 1990.

_____. *Death Records of Pioneer Missouri Women, 1808–1853.* Greenville, S.C.: Southern Historical Press, 1990.

_____. *Missouri Taxpayers, 1819–1826.* Decorah, Iowa: Privately printed, 1979.

_____. *More Death Records from Missouri Newspapers, 1810–1857.* Greenville, S.C.: Southern Historical Press, 1990.

Stephen, Leslie, and Sidney Lee, eds. *Dictionary of National Biography.* Vol. 7. London: Oxford Univ. Press, 1921–22.

Streib, Victor L. *Death Penalty for Juveniles.* Bloomington: Indiana Univ. Press, 1987.

Stroud, George M. *A Sketch of the Laws Relating to Slavery.* 1856. Rpt. New York: Negro Universities Press, 1968.

Switzler, W. F. *History of Missouri.* St. Louis: C. R. Barnes, 1881.

Taylor, Alfred Swaine. *The Principles and Practice of Clinical Jurisprudence.* Philadelphia: Henry C. Lea's Son, 1883.

Taylor, Joe Gray. *Negro Slavery in Louisiana.* New York: Negro Universities Press, 1963.

Treatise on the Diseases Most Prevalent in the United States with Directions for Medicine Chests. St. Louis: J. Charles & Son, 1830.

Trexler, Harrison. *Slavery in Missouri, 1804–1865.* Baltimore: Johns Hopkins Press, 1914.

Trials and Confessions of Madison Henderson, ... Alfred Amos Warrick, James Seward, and Charles Brown. St. Louis: Chambers and Knapp, 1844.

Twain, Mark. *Huck Finn and Tom Sawyer among the Indians and Other Unfinished Stories.* Berkeley: Univ. of California Press, 1989.

Violette, E. M. *History of Adair County.* N.p.: Denslow History, 1911.

Wade, Richard C. *Slavery in the Cities: The South 1820–1860.* New York: Oxford Univ. Press, 1964.

Walker, David M. *Oxford Companion to Law.* Oxford: Clarendon, 1980.

Walton, John, Paul B. Beeson, and Ronald Bodley Scott, eds. *The Oxford Companion to Medicine.* 2 vols. New York: Oxford Univ. Press, 1986.

Webster, Ralph W. *Legal Medicine and Toxicology*. Philadelphia: W. B. Saunders, 1930.
Wecter, Dixon. *Sam Clemens of Hannibal*. Boston: Houghton Mifflin, 1961.
Weld, Theodore Dwight. *American Slavery As It Is: Testimony of a Thousand Witnesses.* New York: American Anti-Slavery Society, 1836. Rpt. New York: Arno Press and the New York Times, 1968.
Wigmore, John Henry. *Treatise on the Anglo-American System of Evidence in Trials at Common Law*. 5 vols. 2d ed. Boston: Little, Brown, 1923.
Williamson, Hugh P. *The Kingdom of Callaway*. N.p.: N.d.
Wood, Peter H. *Black Majority: Negroes in Colonial South Carolina from 1670 through the Stono Rebellion*. New York: Alfred A. Knopf, 1974.
Woodson, William H. *History of Clay County*. Indianapolis: Historical, 1920.
Wright, Charles Alan. *Federal Practice and Procedure*. Vol. 3A. St. Paul: West, 1982.
Yellin, Jean Fagan, ed. *Harriet Jacobs, Incidents in the Life of a Slave Girl, Written by Herself (1861)*. Cambridge: Harvard Univ. Press, 1987.

Articles

Foley, William E. "Slave Freedom Suits before Dred Scott: The Case of Marie Jean Scypion's Descendants." *Missouri Historical Review* 79 (Oct. 1984): 1–23.
Frazier, Harriet C. "The Execution of Juveniles in Missouri, Part I." *Journal of the Missouri Bar* 46 (Dec. 1990): 636–38.
Gordon, Kim William, "George Gordon, Owner of Taille de Noyer, 1804–1805." *Florissant Valley Historical Society Quarterly* 9 (Oct. 1992): 5–8.
Herman, Janet S. "The McIntosh Affair." *Bulletin of the Missouri Historical Society* 26 (July 1970): 123–43.
Holmes, Jack D. L. "The Abortive Slave Revolt at Pointe Coupée, Louisiana 1795." *Louisiana History* 11 (fall 1970): 341–62.
Humphrey, Jacqueline Brelsford Baker. "The 1802 Murder of David Trotter in Missouri." *Missouri State Genealogical Association Journal* 13 (fall 1993): 198–205.
Johnson, Michael P. "Smothered Slave Infants: Were Slave Mothers at Fault?" *Journal of Southern History* 47 (1981): 493–520.
Jolliffe, D. M. "A History of the Use of Arsenicals in Man." *Journal of the Royal Society of Medicine* 86 (May 1993): 287–89.
Kay, Marvin L., and Lorin L. Cary. "'The Planters Suffer Little or Nothing': North Carolina Compensations for Executed Slaves, 1748–1772." *Science and Society* 40 (1976): 288–306.
Loeb, Isidor. "Constitutions and Constitutional Conventions in Missouri." *Journal of Missouri Constitutional Convention of 1875 I*. Columbia: State Historical Society of Missouri, 1920.
Naglich, Dennis. "The Slave System and the Civil War in Rural Prairieville." *Missouri Historical Review* 87 (April 1993): 253–73.
Pener, Harry D. "The Missouri Criminal Costs System Re-examined." *UMKC Law Review* 46 (fall 1977): 1–68.
Phillips, Ulrich B. "Slave Crime in Virginia." *American Historical Review* 20 (1915): 336–40.
Seematter, Mary E. "Trials and Confessions: Race and Justice in Antebellum St. Louis." *Gateway Heritage* 12 (fall 1991): 36–47.
Swindler, William F. "Missouri Constitutions: History, Theory, and Practice, Part I." *Missouri Law Review* 23 (1958): 32–59.

Violette, Eugene M. "The Black Code in Missouri." *Proceedings of the Mississippi Valley Historical Association* 6 (1912–1913): 287–316.
Waite, Frederick C. "The Development of Anatomical Laws in the States of New England." *New England Journal of Medicine* 233 (1945): 716–26.
Wilf, Steven Robert. "Anatomy and Punishment in Late-Eighteenth-Century New York." *Journal of Social History* 22 (spring 1989): 507–30.
Williamson, Hugh P. "Document: The State against Celia, a Slave." *Midwest Journal* 8 (spring–fall 1956): 408–20.
Zelin, Judy E. "Admissibility of Bare Footprint Evidence." 45 *American Law Reports*, 4th ed. 1178 (1997).

Theses, Dissertations, and Unpublished Papers

Draper, William. "Missouri Constitutions." UMKC Law School, Kansas City, Mo., N.d.
Duffner, Robert W. "Slavery in Missouri River Counties, 1820–1865." Ph.D. diss., University of Missouri-Columbia, 1974.
LeMond, Don W. "Slavery and Slave Crimes ... in Boone County, Missouri, 1821–1861." M.A. thesis, Lincoln University, Jefferson City, Mo., 1972.

Newspapers

American Citizen (Lexington), *Boonville Observer, Brunswicker* (Brunswick), *California News, Chicago Tribune, Cincinnati Journal, Franklin County Tribune* (Union), *Free Democrat* (St. Joseph), *Gazette* (St. Joseph), *Gazette* (Versailles), *Hannibal Journal, Howell County Gazette* (West Plains), *Independent Patriot* (Jackson), *Jefferson Examiner* (Jefferson City), *Jefferson Republican* (Jefferson City), *Joplin Globe, Kansas City Enterprise, Kansas City Globe, Kansas City Journal, Kansas City Star, Kansas City Times, Knob Noster Gem, Liberator* (Boston), *Liberty Tribune, Louisiana Gazette* (St. Louis), *Louisiana Journal, Missourian* (St. Charles), *Missouri Courier* (Hannibal), *Missouri Democrat* (St. Louis), *Missouri Gazette* (St. Louis), *Missouri Herald* (Jackson), *Missouri Intelligencer* (Fayette & Columbia), *Missouri Republican* (St. Louis), *Missouri Statesman* (Columbia), *New York Times, Northwest Conservator* (Richmond), *Palmyra Whig, Pittsburgh Gazette, Randolph Citizen* (Huntsville), *Reveille* (St. Louis), *Salt River Journal* (Bowling Green), *Salem News, Saturday Morning Visitor* (Waverly & St. Thomas), *Sentinel* (Columbia), *Southerner* (Tarboro, N.C.), *Springfield Advertiser, St. Louis Globe, Sun* (Baltimore, Md.), *Times* (Glasgow), *Union* (St. Louis), *West* (St. Joseph).

Government Documents

Biographical Directory of the American Congress, 1774–1996. Alexandria, Va.: CQ Staff Directories, 1997.
Blunt, Roy D. *Historical Listing of the Missouri Legislature.* Jefferson City: Missouri State Archives, 1998.
Carter, Clarence E., ed. *The Territorial Papers of the United States.* Vol. 13, *Louisiana-*

Missouri, 1803–1806 (1948); Vol. 14, *Louisiana-Missouri, 1806–1814* (1949); Vol. 15, *Louisiana-Missouri, 1815–1821* (1954). Washington, D.C.: Government Printing Office, 1934–1962.

Hunt, Gaillard, ed. *Journals of the Continental Congress, 1774–1789.* Vol. 26. Washington, D.C.: Government Printing Office, 1928.

Kinnaird, Lawrence, ed. *Spain in the Mississippi Valley.* Vol. 2. Annual Report of the American Historical Association for the Year 1945. Washington, D.C.: Government Printing Office, 1949.

Maguire, Kathleen, and Ann L. Pastore, eds. *Sourcebook of Criminal Justice Statistics.* Washington, D.C.: U.S. Dept. of Justice, Bureau of Justice Statistics, 1995.

Official Manuals State of Missouri. Jefferson City: Office of Secretary of State, 1977–78 through 1999–2000.

Thorpe, Francis N., ed. *Federal and State Constitutions, Colonial Charters, and Other Organic Laws of the States, Territories, and Colonies Now or Heretofore Forming the United States of America.* 7 vols. Washington, D.C.: Government Printing Office, 1909.

U.S. Department of Commerce. *Negro Population, 1790–1915.* Washington, D.C.: Government Printing Office, 1915.

Winthrop, William. *Military Law and Precedents.* 2d ed. Washington, D.C.: Government Printing Office, 1920.

Archival Material

Family History Center, Church of Jesus Christ of Latter-Day Saints, Independence, Mo.
    Circuit Court Records, State of Missouri.
Mid-Continent Public Library, Independence, Mo.
    Papers of the St. Louis Fur Trade, Part I: The Chouteau
        Collection, 1752–1925 (microfilm). William R. Swaggerty.
    Bethesda, Md.: University Publications of America, 1991.
Missouri Historical Society, St. Louis, Mo.
    Chouteau, Pierre, Letterbook.
    Clemens, Mary C. Collection.
    Coroner's Record of Inquests, 1838–1848.
    Journals and Diaries Collection.
    Kennerly, James Collection.
    Lisa, Manuel Collection.
    Lucas, John B. C. Collection.
    Tiffany Collection.
    Stoddard, Amos, Papers.
    St. Louis Courthouse Papers.
    Woods-Holman Family Papers.
Missouri State Archives, Jefferson City, Mo.
    Missouri State Penitentiary, Register of Inmates, 1836–1865.
    Pardon Papers, 1839–1854.
    Territorial Court Records, St. Louis.
Western Missouri Manuscript Collection, Columbia, Mo.
    Ste. Genevieve District and County Court Records, Collection 3636.

Statutory Law

Laws of Arkansas Territory (1835).
Laws of Indiana Territory (1801–1809).
Laws of Kentucky (1860).
Laws of Missouri (1804–1999).
Laws of Northwest Territory (1788–1800).
Laws of Virginia (1819–1833).
South Carolina, "Acts Relating to Slaves," (1842).
[Spanish Colonial Law] O'Reilly, Don Alejandro. "Ordinances and Instructions," trans. Gustavus Schmidt. *Louisiana Law Journal 1* (Aug. 1841): 1–65.

Court Records

Handwritten Court Records: Missouri's Districts/Counties

Audrain
Emily, State v. (1856–57); *Hart, State* v. (1848–54).
Callaway
Celia, State v. (1855); *Mat, State* v. (1855); *Susan, State* v. (1844).
Cape Girardeau
Aaron, State v. (1828); *Charles, State* v. (1863–64); *Dick, State* v. (1837); *Elliott, State* v. (1852); *Esther, State* v. (1835); *Evaline, State* v. (1863); *Foreman v. Deakins* (1799); *Green, State* v. (1859–60); *Hart, State* v. (1850–51); *Isaac, State* v. (1829–30); *Jane, State* v. (1845); *Little, State* v. (1841); *Lockhart, State* v. (1856); *Ludwig, State* v. (1861); *Malone, State* v. (1826); *Nathan, State* v. (1846–47); *Reuben, State* v. (1834); *Simon, State* v. (1855); *Steph, Sol, John, and Ben, State* v. (1845); *Taylor, State* v. (1861); *Wash, State* v. (1849); *Wiedmann, State* v. (1856–58).
Clay
Allen, Shubael, In Re Estate of (1842); *Annice, State* v. (1828).
Crawford
Mary, State v. (1835).
Howard
Bill, State v. (1848); *Cato, State* v. (1824); *Dennis, State* v. (1825); *Jerry, State* v. (1825); *Phil, U.S.* v. (1819); *Vine, State* v. (1825).
Marion
Ben, State v. (1849–50).
Morgan
Adams, State v. (1883).
St. Charles
Bill, U.S. v. (1818); *Jesse, U.S.* v. (1818).
Ste. Genevieve
George and Jim, State v. (1821); Inquest: *Indian Woman* [unnamed] (1773); Inquest: *Tacouä* (1783).
St. Louis
Carlos, George, and Dick, U.S. v. (1819); *Catherine, U.S.* v (1811); *Connor, U.S.* v. (1806); *Don Quixote, U.S.* v. (1817); *Elijah, U.S.* v. (1809); *Elijah, U.S.* v. (1819); *George, U.S.* v. (1819); *George, U.S.* v. (1820); *George and Joe, U.S.* v. (1810); *Gordon,*

U.S. v. (1818–19); *Helene, U.S.* v. (1809); Inquest: *Sandy, a Slave* (1834); Inquest: *Sarah, a Slave* (1847); Inquest: *Steele, John* (1834); Inquest: *William, a Slave* (1836); *Jepe, State* v. (1822); *Joe, U.S.* v. (1809); *Leblond, U.S.* v. (1813); *Lilise, U.S.* v. (1809); *Lilise, U.S.* v. (1817); *Long, U.S.* v. (1809); *Maria, U.S.* v. (1818); *Morine, U.S.* v. (1813); *Murphy, U.S.* v. (1819–20); *Pickens* v. *Cerré* (1804); *Pickens* v. *Soulard* (1804); *Pickens, U.S.* v. (1804); *President and Directors of the Bank of St. Louis* v. *John B. N. Smith* (1818); *Rupill, U.S.* v. (1812); *Simon and Ned, U.S.* v. (1820).

Saline

Finley, State v. (1842); *Henry, State* v. (1844); *Holman, State* v. (1859); *James, State* v. (1859); *John, State* v. (1859); *Lee, State* v. (1854–55); *Mariah, State* v. (1858–59); *Martha, State* v. (1862–63); *Martin, State* v. (1864); *Odle, State* v. (1836).

Washington

Brinker, Abraham, In Re Estate of (1833–50).

Printed Court Records

STATE

Adams v. *Childers*, 10 Mo. 778 (1847); *Adams* v. *State*, 76 Mo. 355 (1882); *Anderson, State* v., 19 Mo. 241 (1853); *Armstrong* v. *Marmaduke*, 31 Mo. 327 (1861); *Calhoun* v. *Buffington*, 25 Mo. 443 (1857); *Carpenter* v. *State*, 8 Mo. 291 (1843); *Charles* v. *State*, 11 Ark. 389 (1850); *Douglass* v. *Ritchie*, 24 Mo. 177 (1857); *Ewing* v. *Thompson*, 13 Mo. 132 (1850); *Fackler* v. *Chapman*, 20 Mo. 249 (1855); *Fanny, a Slave* v. *State*, 6 Mo. 122 (1839); *Ford, Sheriff* v. *Circuit Court of Howard County*, 3 Mo. 309 (1834); *Fraser* v. *State*, 6 Mo. 195 (1839); *George, a Slave* v. *State*, 37 Miss. 316 (1859); *Gilbert, a Slave, State* v., 24 Mo. 380 (1857); *Grove* v. *State*, 10 Mo. 232 (1846); *Guyott, State* v., 26 Mo. 62 (1857); *Hawkins* v. *State*, 7 Mo. 190 (1841); *Hector, a Slave,* v. *State*, 2 Mo. 166 (1829); *Henke & Henke, State* v., 19 Mo. 225 (1853); *Henry, a Slave, State* v., 2 Mo. 218 (1830); *Jane, a Slave* v. *State*, 3 Mo. 61 (1831); *Jennings* v. *Kavanaugh*, 5 Mo. 25 (1837); *Jim, a Slave,* v. *State*, 3 Mo. 84 (1832); *Joe, a Slave,* v. *State*, 19 Mo. 223 (1853); *Leapfoot, State* v., 19 Mo. 375 (1854); *Mann* v. *Trabue*, 1 Mo. 709 (1827); *Marguerite* v. *Chouteau*, 2 Mo. 71 (1828), reargued 3 Mo. 540 (1834); *Markley* v. *State*, 10 Mo. 291 (1847); *Mary, a Slave* v. *State*, 5 Mo. 71 (1837); *Morrison, State* v. 869 SW2d 813 (1994); *Nash* v. *Primm*, 1 Mo. 178 (1822); *Nathan, a Slave* v. *State*, 8 Mo. 631 (1844); *Peters* v. *Clause*, 37 Mo. 337 (1866); *Peters, State* v., 28 Mo. 241 (1859); *Phillips* v. *Towler's Administrators*, 23 Mo. 401 (1856); *Posey* v. *Garth*, 7 Mo. 94 (1841); *Rachael, a woman of color* v. *Walker*, 4 Mo. 350 (1836); *Reed* v. *Circuit Court of Howard County*, 6 Mo. 44 (1839); *Rennick* v. *Chloe*, 7 Mo. 197 (1841); *Rohlfing, State* v. 34 Mo. 348 (1864); *Scott, a man of color* v. *Emerson*, 15 Mo. 576 (1852); *Skinner* v. *Hughes*, 13 Mo. 440 (1850); *Soper* v. *Breckenridge*, 4 Mo. 14 (1835); *Swadley, State* v., 15 Mo. 515 (1852); *Stratton* v. *Harriman*, 24 Mo. 324 (1857); *Todd* v. *State*, 1 Mo. 566 (1825); *West and wife* v. *Forrest*, 22 Mo. 344 (1856).

FEDERAL

Amistad, U.S. v., 40 U.S. 518 (1841); *Amy, U.S.* v., 24 Fed. Cas. 792 (C.C.D. Va. 1859) (No. 14, 445); *Barron* v. *Baltimore*, 32 U.S. 243 (1833); *Chicago, B. & Q. R. Co.* v. *Chicago*, 166 U.S. 226 (1897); *Coker* v. *Georgia*, 433 U.S. 584 (1977); *Cortez, U.S.* v., 449 U.S. 411 (1981); *Dickinson, U.S.* v., 25 Fed. Cas. 849 (Superior Court, Terr. of Ark. 1820) (No. 14, 957); *Miller* v. *Pate*, 386 U.S. 1 (1967); *Randon* v. *Toby*, 52 U.S.

493 (1850); *Rhodes, U.S. v.*, 27 Fed. Cas. 785 (C.C.D. Ky. 1866) (No. 16, 152); *Scott v. Sandford*, 60 U.S. 393 (1857); *Stanford v. Kentucky*, 492 U.S. 361 (1989); *Thompson v. Oklahoma*, 487 U.S. 815 (1988).

ENGLISH

Garnett, Henry, Trial of, 2 Howard State Trials 217 (1606).

Index

The name(s) or class(es) preceding the slash are the perpetrators or alleged perpetrators. The name(s) or class(es) following the slash are the victims or alleged victims. Years and county names are provided in parentheses to help the reader differentiate between slaves with the same name.

317

Lockhart, Samuel 149, 153
Long, John, Jr. 99–103, 116
Lorine 22
Louese 133
Lucas, John B. C. 10, 75–76, 100, 130
Ludwig, Kasper 149
Luke 197
lynching of slaves: defined 251–52; instate *see* Appendix 5; out of state 252–54

MacKay, Resin 198–99
Macon County: Nathan/unnamed white female 244
male, crimes against slaves by white males, Corder/unnamed 129; Deakins, William/Ned 126; Posey, Bird/unnamed 126–37; Prinne/Walter 128; Riault, Pedro/Quierry 15
Malone, Obadiah 133–35
Manly 152
Maria 57–58
Mariah 122
Marianne, Indian slave (1773) 14–15; (1779) 22
Marion County: Ben/Susannah and Thomas Bright 229–36; Joe, stealing 154; liquor violations 148; slave mother/3 sold sons 121
Markley, John S. 150
Mart 267
Martha 159–62
martial law 228
Mary (1837) 170–75; (1843), 182–84
Mat (late 1830s) 114; (1855) 212–18
Matthews, Rebecca 244
McClintock 256–57

McDaniel, John 151
McIntosh, Francis 260–62
Mississippi County: Simon/Mary 242
Mississippi River, slave suicide on 111
Missouri Compromise 82
Missouri Constitution (1820): comparison with constitutions of other slave states 83–84, 91–92, 94–96; comparison with U.S. Constitution 84; slave rights enumerated in 87–88, 90
Missouri Constitutional Convention (1820) 83–85, 88–90, 96
Missouri, Supreme Court of: creation of 92–93; decides no slave death penalty case after 1839 194; freedom of Indian slaves 13; membership of, change from appointive to elective 216; slave rape of white woman 244, 246
Missouri, territorial organization 39–41
Moniteau County: dealing with a slave without owner's permission 150; Henry/Alfred Norman 199; liquor violations 148; unknown/Briscoe, Andrew, family 164
Monroe County: black-male-on-black-male violence 113; George/murder of Mrs. John Davis and suicide 111–113; slave female/Van-

deventer, family of 165; slave mother, attempted drowning of self and children 121
Montgomery County: Carpenter, Conrad/Minerva 141; Moses/John Tanner 297–98; slave mother/unnamed child 121
Morrison, Toni 124
Morrow, Mrs. John 267
Moses 197–98
Mull, William 260
Murphy 113

Nance, Peter 207–08
Nancy (1823) 152; (1828) 168–69
Nathan (1829) 152; (1844) 244; (1846) 210–11
Ned (1799) 126; (1820) 58
Negress Sylvia 130–31
Neil, Laura 243–44
Nelly (1828) 168; (1846) 120–21
New Madrid District/County: founding of 9; Tewanaye/Trotter 24–25
New Orleans, Spanish government seat 10
Newby, Nathan 206
Newsom, Robert 184–94
Norman, Alfred 199
Northwest Ordinance 7, 26, 30, 89
nuisance law 51

O'Reilly, Alejandro: laws for Louisiana Territory 11–12, 16
Odle, Solomon 149
offensive language to white persons 151
owner compensation for executed slaves; Spanish 19; American 94–95, 195

owners of slaves, French and Spanish: Aubuchon, Widow 14–15; Caron, Louis 21; Cerre, Pascal 49–50; Chancellier, Joseph 22; Chenie, Antoine 53–54; Chouteau, August 29, 61–63; Chouteau, Marie Thérése 22–23; Chouteau, Pierre 167–68; Datchurut, Jean 19–20; De Leyba, Fernando 22; De Noyon, Louis 12; Dodier, Widow 22; Lammé, Madame 58–59; Lisa, Manuel 53–54, 61–62; Reynal, Antoine 48; Roublieu, M. and Mme. 22; Sanguinet, Charles 53; Soulard, Antonio 49–50

Page, Daniel D. 135
pardons of slaves: Anderson, John 246–49
Patience 135
Patsy 165
Patterson, Lucinda, "Slave Delicia" 119
Peebles, Thomas 57
Penrose, Clement B. 59, 61
Peter (1830s) 116; (1855) 265
Pettis County: Sam/Mrs. John Rains 263
Phebe 168
Phil 48–49
Philippe 20–21
Pickens, John 49–50
Pickens, Sarah 49
Pike County: dealing with a slave without owner's permission 150; Lewis/Resin MacKay 198–99; slave male/slave